CUBA'S COSMOPOLITAN ENCLAVES

Caribbean Crossroads: Race, Identity, and Freedom Struggles

Cuba's Cosmopolitan Enclaves

Imperialism and Internationalism in Eastern Sugar Towns

Frances Peace Sullivan

Lillian Guerra, Devyn Spence Benson, April Mayes, and Solsiree del Moral, Series Editors

UNIVERSITY OF FLORIDA PRESS

Gainesville

Cover: Cuban American Sugar Company, Chaparra Mill. Cover design by Larry Leshan.

Copyright 2025 by Frances Peace Sullivan
All rights reserved
Published in the United States of America

30 29 28 27 26 25   6 5 4 3 2 1

DOI: https://doi.org/10.5744/9781683405115

Library of Congress Cataloging-in-Publication Data
Names: Sullivan, Frances Peace, author.
Title: Cuba's cosmopolitan enclaves : imperialism and internationalism in eastern sugar towns / Frances Peace Sullivan.
Description: Gainesville : University of Florida Press, 2025. | Series: Caribbean crossroads : race, identity, and freedom struggles | Includes bibliographical references and index. | Summary: "This book explores how northeastern Cuba became a hub of international solidarity and transnational movements in the 1920s and 1930s, showing how the Oriente Province emerged as a focal point for global visions of resistance"—Provided by publisher.
Identifiers: LCCN 2024053246 (print) | LCCN 2024053247 (ebook) | ISBN 9781683405115 (hardback) | ISBN 9781683405337 (paperback) | ISBN 9781683405276 (ebook) | ISBN 9781683405177 (pdf)
Subjects: LCSH: Sugar trade—Cuba—Oriente (Province)—History—20th century. | Sugar workers—Cuba—Oriente (Province)—History—20th century. | Sugar factories—Cuba—Oriente (Province)—History—20th century. | Company towns—Cuba—Oriente (Province)—History—20th century. | Strikes and lockouts—Agricultural laborers—Cuba—Oriente (Province)—History—20th century. | Oriente (Cuba : Province)—History—20th century. | BISAC: HISTORY / Caribbean & West Indies / Cuba | SOCIAL SCIENCE / Ethnic Studies / Caribbean & Latin American Studies
Classification: LCC HD9114.C943 O757 20225 (print) | LCC HD9114.C943 (ebook) | DDC 338.1/73610972916—dc23/eng/20250130
LC record available at https://lccn.loc.gov/2024053246
LC ebook record available at https://lccn.loc.gov/2024053247

| UF PRESS
UNIVERSITY
OF FLORIDA

University of Florida Press
2046 NE Waldo Road
Suite 2100
Gainesville, FL 32609
http://upress.ufl.edu

GPSR EU Authorized Representative: Mare Nostrum Group B.V., Mauritskade 21D, 1091 GC Amsterdam, The Netherlands, gpsr@mare-nostrum.co.uk

CONTENTS

List of Abbreviations   vii
Acknowledgments   ix

Introduction: Company Towns and Cosmopolitanism in the US-Caribbean World   1
1. Constructing Oriente's Cosmopolitan Coast   14
2. Garveyism, Community Building, and Forging Diaspora in Company Towns   47
3. "The Weakest Link of Imperialism's Chain in the Caribbean": Sugar Workers, Organized Labor, and Global Communism   86
4. "Hands Off Cuba": The Sugar Insurgency of 1933 and International Responses   117
5. In Defense of the Spanish Republic: *Oriental* Antifascism at Home and Abroad   154

Conclusion   181

Notes   189
Bibliography   233
Index   255

ABBREVIATIONS

AANPE	Asociación de Auxilio al Niño del Pueblo Español
BSL	Black Star Line
CASC	Cuban American Sugar Company
CNOC	Confederación Nacional de Obreros de Cuba
Comintern/CI	Communist International
CPs	Communist Parties
CPUSA	Communist Party of the United States
CSLA	Confederación Sindical Latinoamericana
DEU	Directorio Estudiantil Universitario
DOI	Defensa Obrera Internacional
EPR	Ejército Popular de la República
FOH	Federación Obrera de la Habana
GOMA	Gremio de Obreros Metalúrgicos y Anexos
ITUCNW	International Trade Union Committee of Negro Workers
LJC	Liga Juvenil Comunista
ORCA	Organización Revolucionaria Cubana Antiimperialista
PBL	Partido Bolchevique-Leninista
PCC	Partido Comunista de Cuba
PCE	Partido Comunista de España
PIC	Partido Independiente de Color
Profitern	Red International of Labor Unions
RAI	Red Aid International
SNOIA	Sindicato Nacional de Obreros de la Industria Azucarera
SPTC	Sindicato Provincial de Trabajadores de Camagüey
UOA	Unión de Obreros Antillanos
UNIA	Universal Negro Improvement Association

ACKNOWLEDGMENTS

Since beginning this project years ago, I have accrued countless debts of gratitude. I had the privilege of completing my doctoral research under the guidance of the incomparable Ada Ferrer at New York University. Ada pushed me to ask big questions and helped me understand the broader implications of this work. She is not only a brilliant scholar and a beautiful writer, but she is also a generous and wise mentor. I am forever grateful to have studied with Ada. Michael Gomez also supported me with grace and good humor during my graduate studies, provided essential feedback, and included me in the phenomenal African Diaspora programming he runs at NYU and beyond. Greg Grandin, Sinclair Thomson, and Barbara Weinstein provided detailed comments and offered encouragement throughout my doctoral research. I am also grateful to Mark Healey, Michael Hardt, and Charles Payne who fostered my interests in history and encouraged me as an undergraduate at Duke University.

Dozens of archivists, librarians, and support staff have enabled this project. I am especially grateful to the marvelous teams at the Instituto de Historia de Cuba in Havana, the Biblioteca Provincial Elvira Cape in Santiago de Cuba, the Archivo Nacional de Cuba in Havana, and the Cuban provincial archives of Holguín, Santiago de Cuba, and Las Tunas. Belkis Quesada at the Instituto de Historia made possible my trips to Cuba. Marilú Uralde took me under her wing and made me feel at home during my visits. Stateside, Isabel Dumois kindly shared her family history, beautifully compiled by her father, Alfred Dumois, with me.

Through the course of researching and writing this book, I have been inordinately lucky to be supported by some of the most generous minds in the fields of Caribbean, Latin American, and African Diasporic history. Frank Guridy, Adam Ewing, Reena Goldthree, Robert Hill, and Barry Carr have all come to my rescue at one point or another over the years. The hilarious and wise Gillian McGillivray has thought to include me in conferences and edited collections, and I am truly honored. Lara Putnam has provided invaluable feedback, pushed me to go deeper with my research and analysis, and expanded my intellectual horizons. Jorge Giovannetti-Torres's generosity is without bounds. In addition to sharing sources and encouraging my scholarship over the years, he has provided thoughtful and detailed feedback for not one but two iterations of this book.

It has been an absolute pleasure to work with the whole team at the University of Florida Press. This book simply would not exist without Stephanye Hunter's guidance and expertise. I am especially grateful for her kind, calm demeanor and for bearing with me. Thanks are also due to the meticulous Chloe Phillips. My second peer reader defied all stereotypes about "reader #2" and offered detailed and extremely helpful feedback. Lillian Guerra, co-editor of the UFP Caribbean Crossroads Series, transformed this manuscript with her wealth of knowledge about the Cuban past and her uncanny ability to connect the dots in academic prose. Her brilliant—and humorous—comments gave me the confidence to keep going, and they firmly grounded the stories told here in Cuba's national historiography.

The long journey of writing this book was made manageable—and even joyful—thanks to several cadres of comrades-in-arms. Though it seems like another era, I still cherish my cohort of graduate students who supported one another through doctoral research at NYU. Abena Asare, Anne Eller, Kendra Field, Kiron Johnson, Rashauna Johnson, and Priya Lal all brought joy and laughter, as well as intellectual nourishment, to a process that can be arduous and intimidating. I am also indebted to my fellow Cubanists, Michelle Chase, Ariel Lamb, Daniel Rodríguez, and Justino Rodríguez who commented on chapters, shared sources, and filled in the gaps. In the Cuban archives, David LaFevor, Elena Schneider, and Matt Casey shared tips about not only research matters but also living and working in Cuba. Lauren Kaminsky, Ezer Vierba, Rebecca Kennedy, Greg Childs, Kirsten Weld, and Kerri Greenidge all provided helpful feedback, listened to talks, and commiserated or celebrated over a pint or two, as the occasion dictated. At Simmons University, Sarah Leonard, Stephen Berry, Stephen Ortega, and Laura Prieto helped protect my time and kept me accountable to my scholarly agenda. Over the years, several writing groups have sustained me, and special thanks are due to Joanna Dee Das, Arthi Devarajan, and Mariska Kappmeier on one of end on this work, and Laura Prieto, Sarah Purcell, Yunxin Li, and Marda Messy on the other end. I do not know where I would be without these "roving packs of mutually-dependent academic writers," to use a term coined by Laura Brown, who is dearly missed.

I would be utterly lost without the family and friends who sustain me though the highs and lows of academia, family, and life. Elissa Crum and Juliet Guzzetta have been my rocks for decades now. Elissa's laughter has a magical healing effect and the mere thought of her lifts my spirits. Juliet is my comrade in parenthood, academia, and life; I am grateful day in and day out for her encouragement, love, and brilliance—from the micro to the macro. Likewise, Kendra Field, who makes all things possible, has been a friend, a mentor, and a co-warrior who fills today with laughter and makes tomorrow amazing. Special thanks are also due to Rajitha Bearden, Nicole Katz, Jenni Katzman, Kate Shawver, and Lisa Zelznick for their enduring friendship. I am also grateful for all the friends—tias and tios to our children—who have buoyed me and my family in these last few years. Tal Astrachan, Alex Gourevitch, Monica Bueno, Jacob Brauer, Amanda Beatty, Chris Lopes, Alissa Coggins, Khary Jones, Anna and Mike Edwards, Kashif Hoda, Zainab Lakhani, and especially Patricia Freitas, thank you.

My husband and children put up with a lot, and that would be feat enough. But they somehow manage to do so much more. Eddie Geisinger has supported and encouraged me through workplace dramas, a terrifying political landscape, a global pandemic, and the births of our three beautiful children. He has kept the show running and done so with love and inconceivable patience. Most importantly, he is a father beyond compare to Myra, Noreen, and Orin. These kids enrich my life more than I can put in words. Their love and joy and the glorious chaos of our household keep me going day in and day out.

My mother, Peace Sullivan, has celebrated my achievements and supported me in innumerable ways along the road. I am so grateful for all that she has done over the years not only as a loving parent, but also as a fabulous and generous host, an ear to bend, and a champion of my work. My brother, Patrick Sullivan, not only tolerates but also encourages my shenanigans, and yet still keeps me grounded. Sandra Colliver, Jeff Geisinger, and Alexandra Markiewicz are cherished family supporting me, Eddie, and the kids day in and day out. This book is for my father, Robert Sullivan, who introduced me to Cuba in 1999. He has read every sentence here and brought a journalist's eye to these pages (while graciously withholding judgement about academic deadlines). For as long as I can remember, he has encouraged my interests and taken the time to indulge them. I am forever grateful. Pop, thank you.

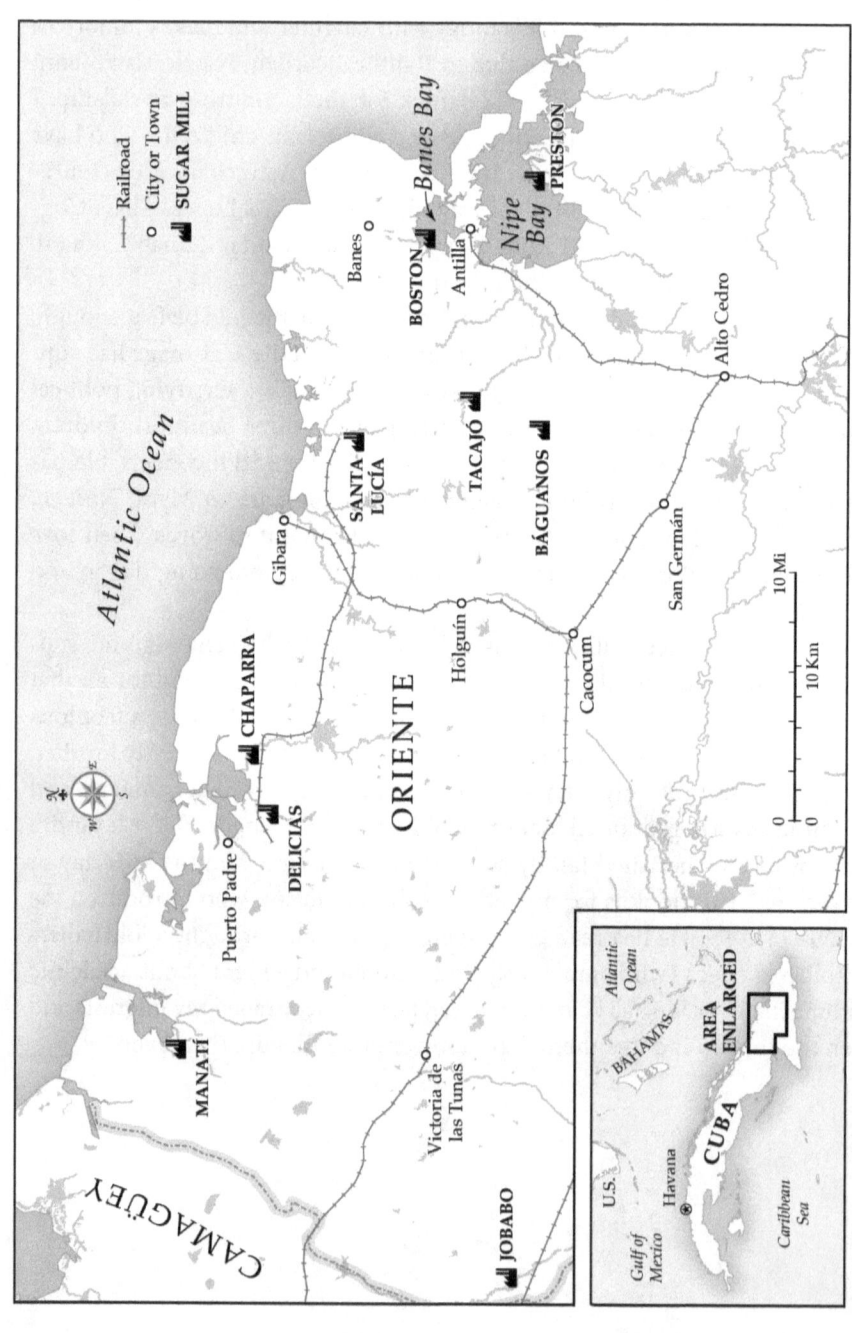

Key US-owned sugar mills of northern Oriente Province, 1925.

Introduction

Company Towns and Cosmopolitanism in the US-Caribbean World

This book tells the story of how a region in Cuba famous for labor subjugation came to be a key node in multiple networks of radical internationalism in the 1920s and 1930s. At the dawn of the twentieth century, powerful US agricultural companies set up shop exporting sugar along the northern coast of Cuba's easternmost province, Oriente.[1] In just ten years, foreign capital transformed northern Oriente from a region of multiracial independent cultivators into one of the most concentrated zones of US economic imperialism in the Americas. There, foreign corporations operated vast agricultural-export enclaves in which the company owned and controlled everything needed to grow, harvest, process, and ship sugar. They displaced local peasants and imported workers from other Caribbean islands, especially Haiti and the British West Indies. Most famous among these corporations was the United Fruit Company, nicknamed "el pulpo" (the octopus) for its tentacles reaching across the Americas. United Fruit alone owned over 250,000 acres near the Banes and Nipe Bays by 1914 and headquartered its operations in the town of Banes.[2] By the late 1910s, Banes and other US-run sugar towns had become quintessential spaces of the company power and labor subjugation wrought by foreign capital.

Yet, in the years that followed, several transnational movements for race and class solidarity took off in this very region. In the early 1920s, immigrant sugar workers in northern Oriente led the Caribbean arm of Marcus Garvey's Universal Negro Improvement Association (UNIA), the largest Black organization in history. By mid-decade, sugar workers associated with organized labor were increasingly articulating their local concerns in terms of wider anti-imperialist struggles, and communists were mobilizing laborers under the red flag by the early 1930s. Amid Moscow's newfound focus on interracial, international proletarian unity, Cuba's multinational, multiracial sugar workers figured prominently in leftist conceptualizations of the intertwined global struggles against labor exploitation and imperialism. When a massive insurgency erupted among sugar workers and rocked Cuba in 1933, the global left followed closely and heralded Cuba's proletariat as harbingers of anti-imperialist revolution. Three years later, sugar workers and their families in northern Oriente were supporting the besieged Spanish Republic during the Spanish Civil War. As they explained it, their personal experiences with land loss and labor exploitation led them to fight fascism in Spain. In short, northeastern Cuba, a space that epitomizes the potentially totalizing power of imperialist enclaves, emerged as both a hub of internationalism and as a focal point for oppositional visions of resistance during the interwar period.

Historical treatments of mass mobilization in republican Cuba tend to overlook northern Oriente's important role in internationalist politics. This makes sense. After all, both imperialists and anti-imperialists had a vested interest in emphasizing company dominance in company jurisdictions (or "fiefdoms," depending on one's perspective), as well as enclaves' relative isolation from wider political processes. For foreign businesses and their supporters, US capital was bringing (Anglo-American) efficiency and modernity to an otherwise backward space and protecting production from the social and political upheavals of (Latin American) society. For detractors, foreign-dominated sugar enclaves meant brutal labor conditions and a loss of national sovereignty because foreign capital controlled ports and other infrastructure, housing, the favor of local officials, and more. What these opposing viewpoints (and the histories that followed them) share, however, is a sense that northern Oriente in the early-to-mid-twentieth century was a space that was *acted upon*, not a center of action in its own right.

This is at odds with historical understandings of the province of Oriente at large, which is commonly considered the birthplace of Cuba's revolutionary tradition. All three of Cuba's independence wars began and were fought largely in the east. It was in Oriente near Manzanillo that a planter named Carlos Manuel de Céspedes freed his slaves in 1868 and launched the call for independence from Spain, thus sealing the ideological bond between Cuban liberation and the struggle for Black rights. When these goals fell short in the new republic, it was also in Oriente that frustrated Black veterans associated with the Partido Independiente de Color (PIC) rose up in 1912, calling for full inclusion in the Cuban polity and economic rights. And Oriente was where the worst of the racist backlash against the PIC took place, leaving thousands dead. It was also in the east that peasants facing eviction near Guantánamo in the mid-1930s refused to leave and formed a collective known as Realengo 18.

In the most famous of all the revolutionary processes that began in Oriente, Fidel Castro and his band of revolutionaries landed a yacht near Niquero in 1956 and launched their guerrilla campaign against the dictatorship of Fulgencio Batista. The war was largely waged in Oriente's Sierra Maestra, culminating with the triumph of the Cuban Revolution in 1959.

If Oriente—or at least southern Oriente—is the cradle of Cuba's revolutionary tradition, then Banes and the sugar towns on the province's northern coast are the poorly understood cradle of Cuba's internationalist tradition. For all their efforts to exert tight control in their dominions and to insulate production from labor instability and political turbulence, sugar companies still relied heavily on constant exchange with the outside world. This tension—sugar towns as closed yet open—produced two significant developments. First, the influx of foreign capital created internally diverse, cosmopolitan local societies. Across the Americas, US economic expansion resulted in the widespread movement of people to emerging sites of empire, including the Panama Canal, Central America's banana plantations, and Cuba's sugar towns. Laborers, tradespeople, engineers, professionals such as teachers and nurses, missionaries, merchants, domestic servants, and their families all moved to towns like Banes, where they built vibrant communities with rich civic lives.

The second development of this closed-yet-open tension is that residents generated outward-looking visions and international networks. Steamers sailed in and out of company towns, bringing with them merchant mariners, letters, newspapers, rumors, and political ideas. Individuals in the region understood intimately the global systems of capitalism and imperialism shaping their lives—whether they were well-traveled or had never been more than a few miles from home. Take, for example, the Cuban and Jamaican stevedores working the docks at Macabí near United Fruit's Boston sugar mill. Week after week, they loaded sacks of raw sugar aboard ships bound for refineries in the United States and unloaded processed sweets and other consumer goods bound for the elite households of company managers.[3] They rubbed shoulders with sailors from across the Americas and passed the time with other transport workers, including the Spanish railroad laborers who predominated in the nearby port of Antilla, so Spanish it was dubbed "la España Chiquita."[4] In the 1920s and 1930s, these stevedores and other working men and women of northeastern Cuba became forerunners in transnational movements for racial uplift, for class solidarity, and against imperialism. In short, the nonelite women and men of eastern Cuba harnessed avenues of capital, migration, and information opened by profit-seeking companies toward spreading some of the interwar period's most significant radical internationalist movements.

"Going Local" to See the Transnational

This book tells the transnational history of a local place. It therefore deploys multiple geographical scopes of analysis. First and foremost, *Cuba's Cosmopolitan Enclaves* is a local history of the northern coastal region of Oriente Province. By the 1920s, the stretch of land between the Nipe and Banes Bays to the east and Oriente's western border with Camagüey comprised one of the most concentrated zones of US economic power in the Americas, and the region was well established as a prototypical space of corporate imperialism. As the headquarters of United Fruit's operations in Cuba, the town of Banes in particular would come to represent all that was welcome about US-led development for some and all that was wrong with imperialism for others. As the most famous northeastern sugar town, Banes became something of an ideological crossroads where every possible avenue for Cuba's political future was initially waged.[5] Two of Cuba's most important leaders (and bitter enemies) hailed from the area. Future Cuban dictator Fulgencio Batista was born and raised in Banes and bestowed on the town honors and gifts during his tenures as President of Cuba in the 1940s and 1950s. Fidel Castro was also from the area; his father was a farmer who sold cane to the company.[6] As a young man, Castro married a woman from Banes, and he later vilified United Fruit as North American imperialism exemplified during his revolutionary campaign.[7] The opposing political visions deployed by these towering figures had deep roots in battles waged in northern Oriente during the interwar period.

The outward-facing social and political engagements of sugar workers and their families are the heart of this history, but this book also traces several ways outsiders looked in to northern Oriente. Merchant mariners, visitors, and new arrivals to the region all brought news and newspapers, political ideas and circulars, and other forms of the printed word to the region. Major political figures of all stripes visited Banes and towns like it, delivering speeches, raising funds, and mobilizing around their respective causes. These include Marcus Garvey himself, Cuban communists Julio Antonio Mella and Rubén Martínez Villena, and a host of Spanish officials drumming up support for the Republican cause. Meeting residents living and working at the heart of Cuba's sugar economy was an essential stop on many an organizing tour, and these visits contributed to the broad outlook of local residents. Moreover, when multinational groups of laborers struck and seized mills at the heart of US economic operations in Cuba, the global left paid attention, celebrating the sugar workers who had demonstrated that they were, at least for a moment, the revolutionary vanguard of anti-imperialist revolution in the Americas.

While this book is a history of northern Oriente, it also demonstrates that local spaces are—and have long been—inherently transnational. As Ada Ferrer writes, "sometimes it is 'going local' . . . and really looking that allows us to glimpse some of these transnational connections at work."[8] By focusing on one space, this book asks questions about how exactly local, national, and global processes meaningfully interact and with what consequences. Harvey Neptune writes, frameworks of "diaspora, globality, [and] transnationalism . . . ought to constitute a point of embarkation not a destination."[9] Zooming into eastern Cuba's sugar towns reveals two overarching categories of transnational connections, points of embarkation, for this history. First, hegemonic international structures, mainly imperialism and economic dependence, weighed heavily "from above" on local residents who were displaced in the service of the sugar economy and whose lives revolved around the seasonality of production. Second, sugar workers were far from passive tools of international capital; rather, "from below" they forged alliances and connections with far-flung places like Panama and Costa Rica as well as Harlem, Madrid, and Moscow. Deeply enmeshed in multiple forms of transnational solidarity, they were nothing short of cosmopolitan.

Focusing on one single setting in an account of multiple transnational social and political movements (as opposed to following one movement across multiple locations) has several advantages. First, it uncovers just how many radical solidarity movements proliferated in one place. Far from a political backwater, northern Oriente was a key nexus in the global Garvey movement, transnational communism, and antifascism. Second, holding place steady reveals the connections between these movements. Scholars typically treat Garveyite pan-Africanism and leftist radicalism separately, but a focus on northern Oriente reveals that they emerged from many of the same phenomena—namely, US economic imperialism, racialized labor subordination, and political repression—and developed in relation to one another. The popularity of the UNIA demonstrated the importance of race as an organizing category, and communists in eastern Cuba, Havana, New York, and Moscow certainly noticed. Similarly, the sugar insurgency of 1933 had a profound effect on a generation of young women and men who collected supplies for and volunteered to fight on the Spanish front. A third advantage of a local approach to transnational organizing is that it reveals the usefulness of solidarity movements. Lofty expressions of transnational Black solidarity or proletarian internationalism could get workers only so far. Men and women deployed these frameworks not only to contextualize their own grievances but also to achieve concrete goals with immediate, material relevance. Through their involvement in long-distance discussions about race and class, laboring women and men in eastern Cuba addressed issues ranging from projecting immigrant respectability to demanding land reform along the US-dominated northern coast.

Cuba's Cosmopolitan Enclaves is not alone in elucidating the multiple forms of racialism that can thrive in a single setting. Most recently, Thomas Lindner's *A City Against Empire* details Mexico City's 1920s decade as home to an "unprecedented proliferation of internationalism."[10] Much like this book, Lindner's is "not the re-telling of a story of elite cosmopolites who traveled across national boundaries without problems, but rather the story of the transnational creation of cosmopolitan thought zones characterized by severe incongruities of power and wealth."[11] Sarah McNamara's study of the working-class Ybor City neighborhood of Tampa, Florida, demonstrates that Ybor City was "an integral hub within a cross-national network of leftist activism and intellectualism that reached from the Caribbean to the Americas and across the Atlantic Ocean."[12] Similar stories can be (and in many cases, have been) told about Buenos Aires, New York, Paris, London, and Shanghai. The sugar towns of eastern Cuba, however, appear as outliers in this list, as they were not major metropolises, but rather "remote" towns thoroughly controlled by foreign capital.

The sugar zone of northern Oriente thus also constitutes a fruitful avenue for the study of "everyday encounters of empire."[13] This book explores the day-to-day experience of US imperialism in eastern Cuba and, in particular, the ways that experience affected labor struggles and other forms of activism. Much of Cuban historiography on the republican period as well as international scholars writing from a dependency-theory perspective have pointed to the tremendous power disparities characterizing the relationship between companies and workers in agricultural-export enclaves. According to Lionel Soto, sugar companies ran their territories like "colossal sugar empires [to whose] mercy the majority finds itself subjected." Cuban cane cutters were "simply precarious paupers, always on the brink of being thrown out," while Haitian and Jamaican workers lived in conditions of "semi slavery" and endured a "life of isolation."[14] Living and working conditions were indeed terrible, yet revisionist histories of foreign-dominated enclaves have revealed the complex ways subaltern subjects nevertheless maneuvered outside of the company's purview. Rather than view enclaves exclusively through the perspective of company dominance, this body of scholarship—led by Catherine LeGrand, Lara Putnam, Aviva Chomsky, and most recently Joan Flores-Villalobos—asks questions about worker subjectivity, the formation of racial, ethnic, and gender identities, legal battles, labor relations, and activism.[15]

Cuba's Cosmopolitan Enclaves continues this work, emphasizing export zones' myriad outward political and social projections.

Historians of Latin America have long understood that US militarism and economic imperialism generated nationalism.[16] In the late nineteenth century, José Martí warned of the dangers posed by US hegemony, and since that time, Cuban nationalism was (and is) inseparable from concerns about the island's northern neighbor.[17] During the first third of the twentieth century, the United States was an ascendant global power whose military, political, and economic influence rapidly transformed much of the American hemisphere. The US militarily intervened in the Caribbean and Central America no fewer than thirty times between 1900 and 1933, including full-scale occupations of the Dominican Republic, Cuba, Puerto Rico, Haiti, and Nicaragua, and shorter invasions in Mexico, Guatemala, and Honduras.[18] American banks and private firms dominated the region's economy, as some of the world's earliest multinational corporations took over local resource-extraction industries.[19] The Spanish-speaking Caribbean, Central America, and the northern coast of South America bore the brunt of expanding US power, and Latin American nationalism rose in response to US hegemony. A growing field of scholarship explores how these experiences of imperialism also generated transnational solidarity movements, such as anarchism and support for Augusto César Sandino's guerrilla insurgency against the US Marines in Nicaragua.[20] *Cuba's Cosmopolitan Enclaves* joins this field and demonstrates, on a local level, how popular classes grappling with transnational capital often developed equally transnational visions and networks.

This history is inextricably linked with the wider circum-Caribbean basin and with patterns developing across what Frank Guridy has called the "US-Caribbean World" of US hegemony and of interconnected networks of trade, cultural exchange, and migration.[21] Afro-Caribbean workers from Haiti and the British West Indies provided essential labor in the US-Caribbean world, moving throughout the region to build the Panama Canal, harvest bananas in Central American plantations, and cut cane in Cuba's sugar fields. US employers believed these "third-country laborers,"—workers from neither the host nation nor the United States—constituted an ideal workforce. Unlike native workers, Antillanos[22] were unprotected by local governments and lacked nearby kinship networks to buoy them during labor conflicts. Employers hoped linguistic and racial barriers would mitigate against labor alliances or, better yet, spur competition between native and foreign workers, leaving immigrants socially isolated and dependent on the company for even their most basic needs.[23] Consistently, however, Antillanos pushed against these boundaries and connected with wider diasporic communities, as Lara Putnam, Jorge Giovannetti-Torres, Kaysha Corinealdi, Yurisay Pérez Nakao, and others have demonstrated.[24]

Finally, the stories unfolding in this corner of the US-Caribbean world have wider, global significance. This book takes a cue from historians and anthropologists who place the Caribbean at the center of world-historical processes and thus shift common perceptions of where the "core" and "periphery" are located in global history. In 1996, Michel-Rolph Trouillot wrote, "The global village is now a cliché. But those who work on the Caribbean know that the world was global since at least 1492."[25] Similarly, on more than on occasion Sidney Mintz noted that much of what is considered unprecedented about late-twentieth-century "globalization" (migration, the view of persons as faceless numbers, and creole culture making, to name just a few processes) has been going on in the Caribbean for hundreds of years and that the Caribbean has been fundamental to the construction of the modern world.[26] In this spirit, *Cuba's Cosmopolitan Enclaves* places northeastern Cuba at the center of the history of interwar internationalism. There, women and men were deeply enmeshed in and contributed significantly to the alternative political visions crystalizing during the "red years" of the 1920s and 1930s—when the Bolshevik Revolution, anticolonial and labor insurgencies, and the circulation of people, newspapers, and ideas all expanded the realm of possibilities for battling exploitation and subjugation.[27] Activists in northern Oriente were acutely aware of how international developments affected their own lives, and they had big-picture ideas of how to tackle structural injustices. They joined and built Black-nationalist, communist, antifascist, and related networks that spanned the Caribbean and reached across the western world—all from a small corner of Cuba dominated by powerful agricultural companies.

Sources and Terminology

This study began with a surprise I found in the Archivo Histórico Provincial Santiago de Cuba's associational records. I had planned to study the organizing traditions of foreign sugar workers in the US-dominated sugar zone of the east but understood the task would be difficult, as they were so famously subjugated and removed from the centers of Cuban political action. Knowing about Garvey's UNIA, I began in the associational records and soon noticed something odd; file after file was filled with other organizations whose roots, branches, and aims spanned the globe: a masonic lodge whose letterhead printed a Brooklyn address in ornate cursive; the Seventh-day Adventist group planning a meeting in Mexico; and the Círculo Republicano Español collecting sugar and money for the Spanish front. Where were the isolated workers? The project grew from there, as I revised my understanding of sugar towns. While Cuban historiography has emphasized their relative isolation, from the perspectives of labor migration and the global commodities trade, company towns were anything but backwaters.

To research this locally rooted, transnational history, I consulted archival records in four countries. Authorities kept tabs on workers, especially rebellious ones, so US, Cuban, and British diplomatic correspondences found in national archives proved essential to understanding strikes and other labor disturbances. Consuls in the field corresponded regularly with home offices, local authorities, and company administrators about labor supply and demand, wages, political climate, repatriation matters, and much more. As Jorge Giovannetti-Torres has demonstrated, British West Indians in particular were prolific letter writers and strong self-advocates for their rights as colonial subjects, so the UK National Archives contain a rich collection of accounts documenting Antillano experiences in Cuba. I also consulted company records housed in the US and Cuba. These illustrate the operating principles of powerful employers as well as how they handled threats to production. As one can imagine, the United Fruit Company (now Chiquita) does not allow researchers into its archives, and much of what remained in Cuba after 1959 had deteriorated significantly before I visited.[28] I have filled in the gaps using administrators' correspondences with other parties, public records like annual reports, and trade publications. Additionally, I am tremendously grateful for the Cuban practice of including lengthy appendixes of documents in historical monographs, such as in Zanetti and García's masterful account, *United Fruit Company*.[29]

For the perspective of workers and their organizations, Cuba's associational records are a rich source. During the republican period, clubs and associations were required to register with the state, and their paperwork remains in provincial archives. These documents reveal local residents' interests and priorities, organizing goals, club membership numbers, and day-to-day activities. Additionally, the Workers Collection at the Instituto de Historia de Cuba in Havana houses a treasure trove of information about leftist labor unions and political parties as well as difficult-to-find newspapers. While I did not travel to Moscow, I was able to hire a researcher who photographed files from the Russian State Archive of Socio-Political History (RGASPI), which has a collection on the Communist International and its many sister organizations, including the Partido Comunista de Cuba (PCC). The RGASPI has also digitized and made public much of its collection, a source I used for research on the Caribbean Bureau and the International Brigades.

I also consulted a wide range of newspapers and other periodicals published on and off the island. Almost every issue of the *Negro World* newspaper between 1920 and 1928 contains multiple reports from Cuba. The international leftist press was particularly interested in the revolution of 1933. Finally, special mention should also be made of the superb thirteen-volume *Marcus Garvey and Universal Negro Improvement Association Papers* series edited by Robert Hill. Hill and his teams of researchers have compiled an invaluable collection about the international movement, upon which the chapter on Garveyism relies.

All this talk of published and digitized records, however, should not suggest that I could have possibly skipped researching in the provincial archives of eastern Cuba. No published or digitized document can compare to the surprises of provincial archives nor to what Lara Putnam has called the "place-specific learning" of research in the field. Standing under the colossal remnants of a sugar mill or chatting with a coffee vendor whose Jamaican grandparents had immigrated decades ago are the moments of "forced contextualization" that give texture and meaning to documents in archives.[30] Only in *being there*—reading though hundreds of documents and learning from archivists, librarians and local residents—could I even begin to grasp the messy, complicated, and vibrant history of northern Oriente.

Finally, a brief note on terminology. There are, perhaps, as many definitions for words like "internationalism" and "cosmopolitanism" as there are people who use them. As John French points out, transnational histories thus risk a certain "analytical slackness."[31] To avoid that pitfall, I offer here a few explanations of how I understand these terms for the purposes of this book. First, as I use it, "transnational" simply means crossing national borders. It is not a politically loaded term, but rather describes a geographical range that can be applied to goods, human networks, ideas, and more. By contrast, "internationalism" is a term used to describe solidarity struggles articulated across borders, rooted not only in common experience (such as racial discrimination or labor exploitation) but also in a shared political agenda (such as racial uplift or socialism).[32] Garveyite pan-Africanism, communism, and transatlantic antifascism are all considered here forms of internationalism. Internationalism, as it is used in this book, leans to the left. Recently, scholars have pushed against the association between "internationalism" and older Marxist calls for proletarian unity, instead centering feminism, religion, or interstate institutions.[33] By contrast, this book embraces the term's connotations and connection with the Old Left, especially communism and antifascism.

Finally, I argue that the working-class women and men of northeastern Cuba, as well as their multiple and overlapping internationalist mobilizations, were nothing short of cosmopolitan. By "cosmopolitan," I wish to emphasize both the nationally diverse nature of the setting—company towns and their vicinities—and the fact that the personal experiences of individuals in northeastern Cuba and their political organizing strategies were global in origins and outlook; they were motivated by a broad spirit of human solidarity not limited by geography.[34] Cosmopolitanism, in this sense, is the condition and process by which men and women developed outward-looking world visions as well as a conscientious commitment to wider transnational communities.[35] Much like others have argued about diaspora, cosmopolitanism is not simply a state of being; it is made in place and over time, as individuals share news, form networks, and mobilize in defense of causes bigger than themselves.[36]

Book Structure

Cuba's Cosmopolitan Enclaves details the proliferation of internationalist movements in northeastern Cuba during the 1920s and 1930s. Chapter 1 begins by tracing the process by which United States sugar companies set up shop in northern Oriente on the heels of US military invasion and occupation. Foreign companies displaced the racially mixed peasantry of the region. The chapter then describes how sugar companies attempted to build self-sufficient, closed plantation complexes and to maintain subjugated workforces in the early twentieth century. They did so largely by recruiting immigrants, but also through tools like worker debt, collaboration with local authorities, and private armed guards. Subject to new labor regimes, Cuban and foreign workers nevertheless built vibrant civic societies engaging with pressing issues and connecting residents to transnational networks. Far from isolated, sugar towns in the east were cosmopolitan spaces deeply embedded in wider flows of trade, migration, and ideas.

Chapter 2 illustrates how British West Indian immigrants and Cubans used the Universal Negro Improvement Association to meet their specific needs as Black women and men laboring in sites of US imperialism. The very conditions arising from US economic expansion—including labor migration, ubiquitous Black exploitation, segregated enclave societies, and anti-immigrant nationalism—gave the UNIA tremendous appeal among mobile Black workers, and northeastern Cuba was home to some of the most popular and vibrant UNIA chapters in the world. Garveyites in Banes and the nearby sugar towns took a pragmatic approach to their dealings and with company and state. Operating in the shadow of terrible anti-Black violence, they nevertheless managed not only to keep their association alive but also to become regional and international leaders in the Garvey movement. In so doing, they played a major role in shaping the sense of Black diasporic solidarity that cohered globally in the 1920s.

Chapter 3 investigates labor organizing and communism in Cuba's eastern sugar zone. Labor unionization in the sugar industry proceeded in fits and starts during the first part of the twentieth century; there was nothing straightforward about uniting nationally diverse sugar workers, whose tasks ranged from cutting and hauling cane in remote fields to metallurgical work on railroads and factories in town. By the mid-1920s, however, sugar workers increasingly organized across labor sectors and nationalities, articulating their grievances in terms of Cuban sovereignty and anti-imperialism. They received a tremendous boost in doing so when the Communist International in Moscow and American communist parties turned their attention to the "yankee fiefdoms" of US corporations exporting fruit and sugar in Latin America. In a dramatic about-face from overlooking Cuba's "remote sugar towns" to prioritizing the island's number one industry, in 1932, communists on and off the island came to see revolution in Cuba as hinging on sugar workers laboring in the heart of US imperialism.

Chapter 4 details the 1933 sugar insurgency, when diverse groups of workers—including Cubans, Spaniards, Haitians, and British West Indians—put ideals of internationalism into local, revolutionary practice and seized one third of the island's sugar mills. In this moment, northern Oriente was the site of a standoff between national sovereignty in the name of workers' rights and accommodation to foreign imperialism. The global left paid close attention, and in particular, looked to sugar workers in this corner of Cuba as forerunners in an international movement against capitalist exploitation and imperialism. Their insurgency was so effective at cross-national revolution that the Cuban Communist Party took the rare position of ardently defending Afro-Caribbean immigrants. As sugar workers proved themselves to be the vanguard of revolution, they pushed communists across the Americas to the left.

By the late 1930s, workers in eastern Cuba were ardently defending the Spanish Republic, the subject of chapter 5. Local organizers founded antifascist clubs and associations that collected funds and supplies for the Republic's struggle against Francisco Franco's fascist insurgency. Many men hailing from northeastern Cuba enlisted in the International Brigades and risked their lives for the distant cause. Hardly considering their day-to-day lives peripheral to world events, men and women in the sugar towns of eastern Cuba saw themselves as once again taking part in a global battle, donating their time, energy, and money accordingly. Politicized in company towns and especially in the insurgency of 1933, volunteers drew connections between their experience with foreign power and labor organizing to their antifascist commitment.

The conclusion addresses the legacies of northeastern Cuba's interwar internationalism. Key political figures, who would define Cuba's political landscape for generations, cut their teeth in and around Banes during the revolution of 1933, and the strands of populism that emerged in the 1940s stemmed from ideological battles that played out in the sugar fields and factories of northern Oriente. Cuba's 1959 Revolution fundamentally altered the island's relationship with the outside world, but Cuba did not abandon internationalism. On the contrary, it became a global leader in the Third World struggle against imperialism. Yet, the new internationalism was state mandated and a far cry from the popular, diverse, and messy coalitions of interwar Oriente. The single-party, communist state has also shifted interpretations of previous eras of transnational solidarity, emphasizing the communist contributions and downplaying other kinds of activism.

Zooming into—and out of—Cuba's sugar enclaves illustrates the many ways that the arrival of foreign capital engendered internationalism in eastern Cuba. But this dialectical relationship between "globalization from above" and "globalization from below" was never automatic nor straightforward. A close look at Banes and the towns around it reveals the historically contingent nature of this process. What aided international solidarity in one moment, hindered it the next. Evolving local, national, and international developments constantly shifted the realms of possibilities for, as well as the objectives of, activism. Yet, despite constraints of economic dependency and the threat of violent reprisal, the diverse residents of northern Oriente made their home into a major hub of internationalism during a high point in the history of global radicalism.

1

Constructing Oriente's Cosmopolitan Coast

In December 1909, Irene A. Wright visited the northern coast of Cuba's Oriente Province. On her train ride east from Havana, the US-born journalist traveled through jungle so thick that she was surprised it had not overtaken the rails. By contrast, upon her arrival in the Banes-Nipe region, she encountered order and what she called the "Cuba of to-morrow." From the veranda of her hotel in the Pinares de Mayarí, Wright could take in the land surrounding Cuba's Banes and Nipe Bays, a view that encompassed the United Fruit Company's Boston sugar mill and the nearby town of Banes, another United Fruit mill called Preston on a peninsula jutting into Nipe Bay, and the port of Antilla. Surrounding these settlements were vast expanses of cane fields crisscrossed by tidy fire lanes so that the scene resembled "green checked gingham cloth."[1] To Wright, the view illustrated progress and modernity wrought by US investment. As she saw it, sugar companies had "replaced defective and picturesque paternalism" with a system of "'enlightened selfishness' . . . the very best business policy."[2] Just a few years later, the former muckraker Frederick Upham Adams was similarly impressed with United Fruit's operations in Cuba. In his 1914 account of the company, *Conquest of the Tropics*, he hailed the "industrial revolution, fomented and headed by American investors and officered by engineers, mechanics, and men skilled in agriculture" that brought development to Cuba's "squalid little native settlements" and "neglected wilderness." Of Preston, he wrote, "Where a few years ago there was nothing but waste land and fever-breeding jungles there has arisen, as if by magic, a flourishing and attractive little city."[3] These laudatory accounts of US industry praised United Fruit and other companies for building modern agricultural-export enclaves in Cuba's neglected tropical jungle. United Fruit, too, claimed that "the properties of the Company were carved out of the wilderness" and on "unimproved jungle land."[4] As Marixa Lasso writes, such visions of "the tropics" as unpopulated jungle served to erase the local residents and to diminish any sense that they might have been just as modern as the foreign forces that displaced them.[5] Indeed, conceptualizations of United Fruit's territory as built from nothing in the jungle erased both that which came before it and, as this book demonstrates, the cosmopolitan local communities thriving at the height of US imperialism.

Eastern Cuba was hardly untamed wilderness prior to the arrival of US sugar companies. Rather, it was home to a mixed agricultural economy, a robust and racially diverse peasantry, and a handful of large businesses already trading extensively with the United States. In the aftermath of Cuba's independence struggle, however, US military occupation and economic imperialism drastically altered the region's land tenure and economy. During the first two decades of the twentieth century, US sugar companies set up shop in northern Oriente, where they built the world's most productive sugar enclaves. These companies displaced small farmers and peasants, and the economy grew almost entirely dependent on sugar. By 1920, the stretch of land between the Nipe and Banes Bays to the east and Oriente's western border with Camagüey was well established as a prototypical zone of imperialist monoculture.

US-incorporated sugar corporations aimed, above all, to ensure a smooth process of continuous production and export. Characterized by vast expanses of foreign-owned land, privately held and managed ports and railroads, company-controlled essential facilities, and immigrant labor, agricultural enclaves typified the system of imperialist resource extraction spreading across the Caribbean basin during the age of US imperialism. Enclaves, however, relied on a contradiction; they were closed yet open, isolated yet deeply connected to the wider world. On the one hand, sugar towns were designed to be self-contained "factories in the field."[6] Companies aimed to insulate production from labor instabilities by importing workers from overseas, controlling their access to cash and kin, and monopolizing commerce, transportation, and infrastructure in their jurisdictions. On the other hand, their business model required constant movement between sugar territories and the rest of the world; sugar was shipped out, equipment and manufactured goods were shipped in, and laborers arrived seasonally. The largest migration to the eastern provinces of Camagüey and Oriente was that of Afro-Caribbean workers arriving from Haiti and the British West Indies to labor in sugar fields and factories. These workers formed the backbone of Cuba's sugar economy, and many had already traveled widely in the region, building the Panama Canal and harvesting bananas in Central America. They maintained contact with friends and family overseas through letters, print journalism, and fellow sojourners, all of which belies the idea that they were isolated.[7]

Others came too; missionaries, professionals, tradespeople, domestic servants, merchants, and more arrived from across the Americas, certainly Spain, and as far as China and Lebanon. These individuals of diverse nationalities were taking advantage of new pathways created in the wake of imperial expansion. Steamships, regional schooners, railways, telegraph lines, newspapers, and trade journals put the region into close contact with the wider world. In short, the very developments that facilitated US military power and corporate investment in Cuba also paved the way for smaller projects of individual men and women hoping to carve out a living in this new space of economic opportunity. Cuba's eastern sugar enclaves were deeply enmeshed in international flows, not only of capital and commerce, but also of people and politics in a process that generated heterogeneous local communities. Residents—Cuban and foreign alike—built rich associational and civic lives. They maintained connections with international associations and kept abreast of global developments, albeit in spaces dominated by private companies. While foreign capital kickstarted the circulation of people in the circum-Caribbean, local residents themselves built cosmopolitan enclaves.

War, Occupation, and US Capital

Until the twentieth century, eastern Cuba developed relatively independently from the western part of the island. Havana and the *oriental* capital of Santiago de Cuba were separated by 700 miles of land and uncooperative sea routes. The eastern provinces of Camagüey and Oriente (known respectively as Puerto Principe until 1899 and Santiago de Cuba until 1905) experienced little of the sugar growth that characterized Havana and Matanzas provinces in the eighteenth and nineteenth centuries. Contraband trade with neighboring Jamaica and Hispaniola sustained the east during Cuba's early colonial years, and in the nineteenth century, cattle ranchers, coffee growing, and provision farming prevailed.[8]

Without large-scale sugar plantations, Oriente Province had the most diversified agricultural sector on the island. Whereas planters dominated in the west, relying on slave labor until 1886, peasants and small farmers tilled the land in the east. In a system of land tenure called *haciendas comuneras*, which originated in royal land grants centuries earlier, landholders communally owned estates and farmed allotments of sizes determined by share numbers. The system was messy, but it enabled land to stay in families for generations, even as they expanded, and facilitated small-scale agriculture.[9] Oriente had the largest number of small properties in 1899 and those averaged the smallest acreage on the island.[10] Oriente also had the greatest number of Afro-Cuban landholders; 43 percent of Oriente's farms were held by nonwhites. By contrast, Havana's white landholders outnumbered Black and mixed-race landholders by a ratio of sixteen-to-one. In short, Oriente was one of the most racially equitable agricultural regions in the Americas at the close of the nineteenth century.[11]

Large-scale agricultural and mining businesses also dotted the eastern landscape. In fact, the United Fruit Company's first foray into Cuba began, not in "unimproved jungle land" as the company would later claim, but as a collaboration with one of the largest banana businesses in the Caribbean, owned by the Dumois family.[12] Born in 1837 and 1839, Hipólito and Alfredo Dumois were the eldest of five brothers descended from French planters who had made their fortune in Saint Domingue and fled during the Haitian Revolution. The Dumois family built a successful coffee business in eastern Cuba but moved into a fruit-export partnership in 1870. Hipólito had attended St. John's College in New York and worked mainly from his offices in the tropical-fruit trading district of lower Manhattan, while Alfredo ran the family's operations on the island. In 1887, the Dumois brothers launched their own fruit business and purchased one third of a hacienda comunera near the Banes Bay called Hacienda Banes. The hacienda was owned by several families of subsistence farmers. The Dumois properties expanded such that, by 1895, the family owned 1,000 Cuban caballerías (over 33,000 acres) in the Banes and Nipe region.[13] They ran three business. The Banes Fruit Company built a port, warehouses, fifteen miles of railroad, and train stops for each farming unit. The Samá Fruit Company purchased bananas from independent farmers nearby. And the Dumois Fruit Company managed the importation business from offices in Manhattan. The majority of their land was used to cultivate bananas, but the family also grew sugarcane and maintained pastureland.[14] The Dumois enterprises, incorporated in New York and financed with US capital, supplied 15 percent of bananas consumed in the US in 1895. Ariel James writes that, by 1899, the Dumois banana territory was twelve times the size of a typical Cuban sugar plantation during the 1860–70 period and was one of the largest banana plantations in the Caribbean, a far cry from the "wilderness" United Fruit would later claim prevailed in the region.[15] Like most Cuban plantations, however, Banes Fruit properties were destroyed during Cuba's final independence war, and Hipólito Dumois entered the twentieth century not as a landholder but as a Cuban agent for a US company.[16]

Cuba's independence struggle lasted three decades and spanned three wars with Spain. Each step deepened ties between Wall Street and the island. The Ten Years' War (1868–1878) began in southeastern Oriente and ended with the island in a state of ruin. Cuban planters found themselves faced with destroyed properties, rising international competition, sinking sugar prices, and new taxes levied by Spanish colonial authorities recouping funds lost during the war. Few could resume production. Some large planters borrowed from foreign banks to turn antiquated and damaged mills into large sugar factories, which became *ingenios centrales*, or simply *centrales*. Many traded their roles as Cuban planters for seats on the foreign corporate boards that now held their old properties. Meanwhile, smaller planters were unable to upgrade their mills and turned exclusively to cane growing. These cane farmers, or *colonos*, sold cane to the new, large centrales, as the sugar industry consolidated into fewer and fewer hands in the 1880s, all with deep ties to US capital. A series of agreements encouraged trade between the US and Cuba such that, in 1895, the United States received almost 90 percent of the island's exports.[17]

After a brief and unsuccessful independence war from 1879 to 1880, known literally as the "Little War," Cuba's final independence war began in 1895. The violence was devastating, especially in the east where, like the other anticolonial struggles, it began and much of the fighting took place. Spanish General Valeriano Weyler's "reconcentration" policy forced approximately half a million noncombatant Cubans into overcrowded urban centers and settlement camps, where an estimated 100,000 individuals died of starvation and disease while cane fields and mills stood idle in the depopulated countryside. The population, slightly under 1.8 million people just before the war, suffered an estimated loss of 200,000 lives. For their part, nationalist generals ordered that any properties potentially of use to the enemy be destroyed. Of Cuba's 1,100 mills active in 1894, only 207 survived the war. Sugar production fell by nearly 67 percent from 1895 to 1899. Smaller planters, unable to pay cash for protection, bore a disproportionate share of the destruction. Agricultural supplies such as fuel and tools were diverted to the war effort. Other industries were devastated too; livestock slaughtered, tobacco unplanted, and coffee left to rot on the trees. Combatants destroyed railroads, bridges, and roads.[18] In August 1896, Cuban *mambises* (nationalist fighters) burned the town of Banes and the Dumois properties. The Dumois brothers boarded steamers flying neutral flags and left for the United States.[19]

In February of 1898, the United States entered the conflict and relegated the Cuban army to a supporting role in their own independence. Upon Spanish capitulation, the US army denied Cubans the right to celebrate, as the US flag—not the Cuban—was raised over Santiago de Cuba and Cubans were excluded from ceremonies. What became known as the Spanish-American War ended with the Treaty of Paris between the US and Spain (with Cuba notably absent), and Spain ceding Puerto Rico, Guam, Cuba and the Philippines to the United States. Cuba thus ended its colonial period under the thumb of another foreign power when the US occupation began on January 1, 1899.[20]

Anglo-American "manifest destiny" promptly turned south. US economic and political leaders had eyed Cuba since 1820, when Thomas Jefferson suggested annexing the island, which presidents James Polk and Franklin Pierce both tried to purchase. By the closing of the western frontier in the 1890s, ordinary US citizens were enthusiastic about expansion into the Caribbean.[21] Trade publications, diplomatic correspondences, missionary reports, and a range of contemporary writings dubbed Cuba "the new frontier."[22] Conveniently, wartime destruction had cleared the path for US expansion.

For Cubans, the ruin of war was devastating, but Wall Street investors waxed enthusiastic. As a trade report later described it, "The destruction of many of the sugar plantations and mills had its brighter side, for it paved the way for modern improvements."[23] In 1900, the leading trade journal covering sugar, *The Louisiana Planter and Sugar Manufacturer*, wrote of "confidence on the part of some American capitalists that investments there in sugar properties are not only safe, but likely to prove profitable." After all, Cuba was secure in US hands and open for business, thanks to what the *Louisiana Planter* called "the conquest of Cuba by the United States."[24] Cubans were not in a position compete with US investors. Local capital was already scarce, a situation worsened by debt and capital flight during the war. Moreover, US occupation policies did not facilitate Cuban reconstruction. For instance, US military governor General Leonard Wood did not reduce interest rates for Cubans rehabilitating their properties nor did he develop an aid program for local farmers. Rather, just six weeks after the occupation began, the military started awarding franchises to US companies in the railroad, electricity, and streetcar industries.[25] Anti-imperialist legislation in the US Senate prohibited outright commercial concessions, but Wood and US investors found work-arounds.[26] For foreign investors, the war was not fought to aid neighbors in achieving independence, but rather to pave the way for US tutelage and the steady advance of "industry." Adams summarized: "For a hundred years Cuba had been desolated by wars and revolutions, but the strong arm of the United States had reached out and the mandate had been given that anarchy should end and that industry would be protected. This was an artful blow to the professional revolutionists, but it meant prosperity for Cuba and cheaper food products to the United States."[27] The "strong arm of the United States" came in the form of military occupation and policies that encouraged foreign investment.

As a first order of business, "professional revolutionists," political instability, and other threats to private property had to be curtailed. In 1899, US officials disbanded the Cuban Liberation Army and thereby ridded the island of an armed, multiracial threat to US authority. In its place, they formed a Rural

Guard tasked with protecting private property in the countryside. Guardsmen were required to take oaths of allegiance to US authorities. Landowners supplied rent-free land for Rural Guard outposts, which were located on or close to tobacco, coffee, and sugar plantations. Unlike the Cuban Liberation Army, which had been composed of a racially integrated officer corps and rank and file, the Rural Guard was almost exclusively white, thanks to literacy and "good standing" requirements. For the next half a century, the Rural Guard intimidated workers and suppressed labor uprisings.[28]

The famous Platt Amendment was an additional step to curtail instability and protect property. At Cuba's Constitutional Convention of 1900, US authorities made it clear that they would not evacuate the island unless the convention ratified an amendment proposed by US Senator Orville H. Platt granting to the United States the right to intervene in Cuban affairs "for the preservation of Cuban Independence, the maintenance of a government adequate for the protection of life, property, and individual liberty." This sweeping justification for intervention amounted to a surrender of Cuban sovereignty and was deployed during several moments of political uncertainty in the next decades, an era historians call "the Plattist state."[29]

Also paving the way for US economic expansion was US Military Civil Order number 62 in 1901, called Demarcation and Division of Rural Properties. The order privatized public lands and reversed the system of haciendas comuneras by converting shared estates into private property, which was often declared vacant. While the law stipulated that residents had a right to land they had been using productively, Cubans needed literacy, time, and money to defend their land, and they rarely succeeded.[30] Even those landholders who possessed deeds to their properties were so cash-strapped and indebted in the war's aftermath that they had no choice but to sell. Civil Order 62's effects were most widespread in the east, where communal lands had been common and wartime devastation extensive.[31]

Thus assured of a politically stable environment and abundant land for sale, US investors—both corporate and individual—began buying property. Initially, a vibrant North American settler movement took off.[32] Real estate companies bought tracts of land and circulated pamphlets praising the island's natural resources, suggesting settlers would sell tropical fruits year-round to US consumers. Optimistic colonizers arrived by the hundreds. By 1905, 13,000 North Americans had purchased Cuban land, with 7,000 of those in the eastern province of Camagüey.[33] Leland Hamilton Jenks, author of the 1928 *Our Cuban Colony*, explained that at the dawn of the century, "Scarcely an account of Cuba or a congressional speech failed to voice the expectation that the tide of migration which had been flowing westward would turn to

Cuba...." He added, "It was the eastern part of the island, where agricultural life had been virtually destroyed by Cuba's wars for independence, that Americans made particularly their own."[34] One writer dubbed Oriente "the California of Cuba."[35] Gradually, however, these enterprises developed more of a reputation for their failures and for the deceptive literature propagated by land companies—"misrepresentations, swindles, sufferings, and losses," as a trade report put it—than for their success.[36]

In the end, large agrobusinesses—not smallholding colonists—entrenched themselves in eastern Cuba, and they did so with help from US policies.[37] The 1902 Reciprocity Treaty reduced US tariffs on Cuban sugar, molasses, tobacco, iron ore, and some fruits and vegetables by 20 percent and reduced Cuban tariffs on a broad range of US manufactured, industrial, agricultural, and textile goods by between 20 and 45 percent. These terms disincentivized Cuban economic diversification and local manufacturing while incentivizing foreign investors to focus on the few products that entered the US at preferential rates. Cuban sugar grew dependent on US buyers, with the United States importing over 99 percent of Cuba's raw sugar until 1910 and over 90 percent until World War I.[38] Whereas monopolistic business practices in the United States were somewhat curtailed by antitrust legislation, no such legislation hindered US agrobusinesses in Cuba. By the late 1910s, it was clear that agricultural-export corporations had prevailed in northern Oriente. When a potential colonist wrote to the US consul at Antilla in 1919 inquiring about the possibility of starting a modest pineapple plantation near the Nipe Bay, the consul replied that the area is now "devoted entirely to the growing of cane and manufacturing of sugar."[39]

Sugar companies preferred eastern Cuba for several reasons. First, land there was cheap in the wake of wartime destruction. Sugar interests with links to US banks and refineries easily bought out small Cuban farmers, who predominated in the east and lacked the means to resuscitate their properties.[40] Second, new land made available through Civil Order 62 was most abundant in the east with its substantial public lands and haciendas comuneras. Third, eastern Cuba contained the island's most fertile soil. A relative dearth of sugar planting (which exhausts soil), as well as generations of cattle ranching and extensive forests (which enrich soil) made the area an attractive frontier for new growth.[41] Finally, the construction of the Ferrocarril Central linking Santa Clara in central Cuba with Santiago drew investors east. Railroad magnate William Van Horne, famous for the Canadian Pacific transcontinental project, began buying land in 1900 and completed construction in 1902 under the auspices of the Cuba Company, incorporated in New Jersey. Initially Van Horne hoped to profit from small-farm and family colonization, but he quickly recognized that freight was more profitable than passenger travel.[42] Van Horne's Cuba Company acquired several sugar farms, mills, and estates, and built two new mills—Jatibonico in 1905 and Jobabo in 1911—eventually becoming one of the largest sugar producers in Cuba.[43] Historians Zanetti and García write that "[t]he Ferrorcarril Central brought civilization to the eastern regions of Cuba—only, in this case, 'civilization' took the form of a gigantic imperialist plantation."[44] Whereas sugar development in western and central Cuba had taken place over the course of two centuries, sugar's dominance in eastern Cuba was accomplished in under two decades.

The northern coast of Oriente Province emerged as a major site of US economic imperialism by the late 1910s. The mills there were built with US capital and were the largest and most productive on the island; of Cuba's seven mills producing more than 300,000 sacks of sugar in the 1917 crop, six were located along Oriente's northern coast.[45] Preeminent among these sugar companies was United Fruit.

When the Banes Fruit Company properties were burned to the ground in 1896, the Dumois brothers fled to the United States and sold shares of their business to the Boston Fruit Company, an enterprise specializing in West Indian bananas and run by a merchant named Andrew Preston. Shortly after, the United Fruit Company was incorporated in New Jersey in 1899 with a merger between Boston Fruit and several operations run by Minor Cooper Keith, who was in the railroad and banana businesses in Central America. This new corporation immediately controlled 80 percent of banana imports to the US. Andrew Preston headed the conglomerate as well as its subsidiaries, including the Banes and Samá Fruit Companies previously owned by the Dumois family. Hipólito Dumois served on the Boston Fruit and United Fruit boards of directors. In 1899, he returned to Cuba as an agent of the new company and used his familiarity with the region to help it expand. United Fruit quickly pivoted to sugar in Cuba and, by 1900, owned over 60,000 acres on the island.[46] That year, the company built the massive Central Boston on the Banes Bay. In 1904, United Fruit purchased almost 200,000 acres on the Nipe Bay and established the Central Preston. United Fruit continued buying out adjacent farms, such that by 1937, the company owned 282,000 acres on the island.[47]

Fifty-five miles west of Banes, the municipality of Puerto Padre and surrounding lands were dominated by the Cuban American Sugar Company (CASC) and its two massive mills, Chaparra and Delicias. Former Texas congressman Robert Hawley and a group of investors affiliated with New York refineries had launched CASC at the start of the occupation in 1899 when they purchased 66,000 acres of land near Puerto Padre. The Chaparra mill was completed in 1900 with the support of General Mario García Menocal, a veteran of the Cuban Independence War, who went on to become the company's general manager for over a decade and, later, president of Cuba. Chaparra's output constituted 10 percent of Cuba's sugar harvest in its first year of production.[48] This "gigantic" enterprise, the *Louisiana Planter* maintained in 1900, "is without precedent in the history of Cuba and probably of the entire world."[49] In 1909, CASC bought 92,000 acres adjoining the Chaparra zone and soon built its second mill, Delicias. According to their annual report, this purchase included "the greater part of the town of Puerto Padre" and consolidated the company's position as a forerunner in sugar production.[50] The company outsourced risk by leasing lands to colonos.[51] CASC's eastern holdings, which together formed the world's most productive sugar estate, were considered a model enclave.[52] The Cuban American Sugar Company and its subsidiaries owned the enclave's entire infrastructure, mills, supporting industries such as livestock and construction, and health and housing facilities.[53] By 1937, the company owned a combined over 331,615 acres in the Puerto Padre region in addition to properties elsewhere on the island.[54]

Many of the largest US companies in the region were part of interlocked networks of business interests ultimately controlled by a small number of shareholders, as César J. Ayala has demonstrated. As a holding company with four centrales in Cuba, CASC was but one component of the National Sugar Refining Company (NSRC) headquartered in Brooklyn. NSRC also owned several other companies operating in Cuba, including the Guantánamo Sugar Company (with three mills), the New Niquero Sugar Company (one mill), and after World War I, the Sugar Estates of Oriente (four mills) and the Cuban Dominican Sugar Corporation (three mills). NSRC's holdings were concentrated in the Cuban frontier zone of Oriente. A tight-knit group of directors, board members, and managers controlled this conglomerate and provided its companies and their subsidiaries with close ties to North American banking interests, especially National City Bank, the leading financial house supporting US investments in the Caribbean.[55] City Bank itself acquired several mills in the 1920s.[56] This vertical integration—from cane field to factory to ship to refinery to bank—insulated large corporations from fluctuations in input costs and sugar prices. Cuba's old planting class was unable to compete, and US corporate interests increasingly bought out Cuban planters such that by 1924, US companies produced 64 percent of Cuba's sugar output.[57]

On the western end of northern Oriente's sugar zone—near the border with Camagüey, the Rionda group ran its largest mill, the Central Manatí, with lands stretching into Camagüey Province. Born in Spain in 1854, the "Sugar Baron" Manuel Rionda had moved to Cuba at a young age and incorporated the Tuinucú sugar mill in central Cuba in 1891. Like other planters, he joined a sugar brokerage firm in New York in 1897, which would eventually become the Czarnikow-Rionda house. In 1911, Rionda gathered a group of investors and a legal team from the New York firm Sullivan and Cromwell to launch the Manatí Sugar Company.[58] Manatí was the group's largest mill when it was completed in 1912, a venture so successful that the conglomerate purchased seventeen more sugar plantations in just one month in 1916. The group was incorporated that year as the Cuba Cane Sugar Corporation and was the largest sugar enterprise in the world by 1918.[59]

By the mid-1910s, Cuban and Spanish investors were following suit and taking advantage of new infrastructure to establish sugar centrales. This second wave of mills tended to have lower production numbers and fewer North American residents, though US chemists and engineers still filled the ranks of their professional staff. In this manner, a group of Cuban, Spanish, and US investors (including the Dumois brothers) built the Tacajó sugar mill west of the Nipe Bay in 1916. The Alto Cedro and Báguanos mills were constructed along similar lines in 1917. It was not long, however, before US capital acquired these properties. The Antilla Sugar Company purchased Tacajó and Bágunos in 1924 and purchased a nearby mill at San Germán the next year.[60]

In short, a massive amount of land, especially in the east, transferred to US hands during the military occupation and first decades of the Cuban Republic. The center of Cuba's sugar economy moved east to Camagüey and Oriente as control of the industry shifted to US corporations. Ayala writes, "The movement from west to east represents a parallel movement from the small central to the large one, from the heartland of the slave *ingenios* of the *ancien régime* to the new economic order established by US sugar agribusiness."[61] The area in which this US-concentrated *latifundia* was most extensive was the northern coast of Oriente. There, seven enormous sugar centrales operated in the 1910s, but only one was run by Cubans.[62] Boston, Preston, Chaparra, and Delicias were Cuba's four largest mills in 1913.[63] Together Cuba Cane, Cuban American, and United Fruit made northern Oriente the "sugar bowl of the world."[64]

For some, these changes meant progress. Eastern Cuba's well-to-do reaped the benefits of US-led development. Large landowners went into business with the new companies, and many saw their quality of life improve. With the Ferrocarril Central completed in 1902, a trip to Havana that used to take seven-to-ten days had been shortened to twenty-four hours.[65] New railroads and roads improved large farmers' access to markets, and the development of lively urban centers offered employment, educational, and leisure opportunities. A wide range of consumer goods were available in well-provisioned company stores for those with the cash. Cuban mayors, municipal councilmen, judges, and Rural Guard officers all cooperated with powerful companies and benefited accordingly. In Banes, residents celebrated the town's transition away from a "pigsty" with streets that became practically useless "muddy mires" during the rainy season to an orderly city with a strong infrastructure. For them, the "magnificent relationship" that existed between municipal authorities and United Fruit ushered in "a good aqueduct, a great electrical plant, splendid streets, luxurious promenades, big well-ventilated theaters, elegant instructional and recreational societies, an extensive and well-constructed sewage system, and a highway uniting Banes with the rest of the country."[66] Cuban children from wealthy families attended good, often missionary-run schools and found a range of employment possibilities with US firms.

Some cane farmers carved space of relative power and prosperity in the face of massive changes to northern Oriente. Ranging in status from the humble to the wealthy, these colonos supplied cane to the nearest central, hired their own labor, and sometimes ran their own commissaries. Unlike colonos in western Cuba, colonos in the east generally leased their land and were subject to company-set rail transport, sugar, and supply prices. Nevertheless, as Gillian McGillivray has demonstrated, big mills, like CASC's Chaparra and Delicias, depended on cane farmers, who came to form a powerful political block and to amass considerable bargaining power in Cuba.[67]

The vast majority of peasants and small farmers in northeastern Cuba, however, were unable to become prosperous colonos. For them, the dominance of sugar companies meant land loss and displacement. In the aftermath of Civil Order 62 and a boom in land speculation, large-scale investors bought out small farmers. Cattle ranchers, small-scale cultivators, and peasants could not compete with corporations in securing titles, legal assistance, and the favor of judges. Rural Cubans moved deeper and deeper into the eastern mountains.[68] In a drastic reversal from having had the smallest farms and the most robust and racially equitable peasantry at the turn of the century, Oriente was home to the largest sugar estates on the island by the 1920s. As Alejandro de la Fuente puts it, in Oriente "there was a good chance that each acre acquired by foreign investors and devoted to sugar production represented an acre lost to Afro-Cubans' subsistence and independent farming."[69] Displaced peasants joined eastern Cuba's rapidly growing agricultural proletariat, searching for seasonal employment in sugar fields and factories.

In short, by 1920, foreign capital had dramatically altered northern Oriente's social and economic landscape. Instead of a racially diverse peasantry, the zone was now in the hands of US-incorporated sugar companies.

Agricultural-export enclaves became the dominant mode of production, as powerful investors and company administrators believed tightly controlled zones of operations would ensure the smooth and uninterrupted export of sugar. Enclaves, their argument went, were the most efficient way to tame the tropics and usher in a new age of US industry, efficiency, progress, and modernity.

"Self-Contained" Enterprises: Company Control and the Model Enclave

In the early twentieth century, company administrators and their supporters argued that US investment was rescuing Cuba from centuries of inept Spanish governance. The previous colonizers, they claimed, had sat idly by in their dominion, ignoring the commercial opportunities of Cuba's fertile lands. In contrast, US capitalism brought modernity and prosperity. "Cuba's great opportunity ... will belong to Capital—fearless Capital which shall lift her chief industry out of its Spanish lethargy," explained a 1916 sketch of the sugar industry.[70] Another wrote, "The Spanish administration of Cuba had been notoriously incompetent ... The [sugar] industry was given a new life by the influx of American capital into the island."[71] To achieve modern production standards, corporations aimed to build "self-contained enterprises," as one United Fruit account put it, model spaces where US ingenuity flourished unhampered by Spanish ineptitude or Cuban political turbulence.[72]

Sugar enclaves had to be, first and foremost, tremendous in size. Observers frequently contrasted sugar agriculture in Cuba with farming practices in the US. Writing for United Fruit in 1924, Philip K. Reynolds explained, "The number and magnitude of the operations involved in preparing and equipping a large and efficient sugar plantation in Cuba are not usually comprehended by anyone whose basis may be the general farming operations in the United States."[73] Reynolds had a point. By the mid-1920s, United Fruit and its subsidiaries owned over 280,000 acres in Cuba.[74] Meanwhile, the average farm size in the United States was 145 acres and, even in California where agribusiness was well established, properties still averaged 201 acres.[75] The enormous sugar enclaves of northern Oriente incorporated everything required to plant, grow, harvest, manufacture and ship cane, as well as to maintain local infrastructure, workers, and a managerial class. United Fruit owned cane-growing land, undeveloped land for future crop rotations, pasture for livestock (that hauled cane carts and provided milk and meat), forests for timber, railroads, locomotives and machine shops, hauling equipment, fire lanes (which also served as paths for laborers and work animals), sugar mills, warehouses, ports, electrical plants, dairies and bakeries, commissaries and shops, housing, medical facilities, water towers, and more.[76] Sugar companies thus aimed to exert tight control over the supply chain, its vast and diverse inputs, and sugar-export operations. Expansiveness, in other words, was the goal.

Another key feature of these "self-contained enterprises" was imported West Indian labor. Like US imperialist operations across the Caribbean and Central America in the early twentieth-century, sugar companies in northern Oriente recruited foreigners, largely from the British West Indies and Haiti, to meet their labor needs. Since the turn of the century, United Fruit had brought Jamaicans and Haitians to Cuba to help with railroad construction and sugar harvests.[77] Hundreds of "non-specified Antilleans" were living in Oriente Province in the early 1900s.[78] Initially, Afro-Caribbean immigration was illegal. In an effort to "whiten" the island, Governor Wood issued Military Order 155 in 1902, which explicitly outlawed Chinese immigration and implicitly outlawed Afro-Caribbean immigration by prohibiting contract migration.[79] In its early years, the Cuban state and several large employers encouraged European families to settle in Cuba to meet the island's agricultural needs. Van Horne recruited Galicians and Canary Islanders for his railway project, and United Fruit had imported some 300 Canary Islanders to harvest cane in 1907.[80] These colonization endeavors, however, were short lived.

In the early 1910s, with their enormous scale of operations, sugar companies complained regularly of labor shortages and claimed that Antillano contract immigration was essential to the harvest.[81] In 1912, President José Miguel Gómez issued the first major exception to immigration restrictions when he authorized the Nipe Bay Company, a subsidiary of United Fruit, to import between 1,000 and 3,000 Antillano workers for the harvest.[82] In 1917, during the Great War when Cuba allied with the US, Cuban President Mario García Menocal (who helped found and managed the Chaparra mill) authorized the CASC to import contracted cane cutters in order to support Cuba's chief contribution to the war effort: sugar production.[83] This decree effectively lifted legal prohibitions of contract labor, and Antillean immigration rose and fell with the tides of the sugar industry. Whereas approximately 2,500 Haitians arrived in 1915 and just under 5,000 arrived in 1916, the number jumped to well over 10,000 in 1917, peaking at almost 36,000 in 1920 with the "dance of the millions" sugar boom. Immigration from Jamaica also steadily expanded, from under 8,000 per year in 1915–1917 to over 27,000 in 1920.[84] These figures plunged in 1921 after a postwar drop in world sugar prices paralyzed Cuba's economy, leaving workers homeless and hungry and sending thousands of migrants home. In 1922, the numbers had fallen to 848 Haitians and 5,016 Jamaicans arriving.[85] Although immigration gradually picked up in the mid-1920s, sugar quotas limited the crop and thus kept figures lower than the 1920 high despite a modest economic recovery.[86] In all, an estimated 600,000 Caribbean workers arrived in Cuba during the first third of the twentieth century.[87]

Sugar companies preferred Antillano labor for several reasons. Publicly, they claimed that there simply were not enough Cuban laborers to harvest their massive crops annually. Labor shortages—to the extent that they even existed—however, were a problem of their own making. With large agribusiness dominating northern Oriente, few independent cultivators remained in the region. In other words, the men who might have used harvest seasons to earn extra cash had been displaced.[88] In reality, sugar administrators hired foreign laborers because they believed Antillanos could be paid less than Cubans and were more easily exploited. An investigation into labor immigration carried out by the Cuban Interior Ministry in 1934 concluded that, since 1900, planters and sugar company administrators preferred Antillano laborers because they paid foreigners less than local workers.[89] Caribbean labor, wrote one US official, arrived "in shiploads principally from Haiti and Jamaica, the well-known breeding spots of negro labor which perennially circulates about the shores of the Caribbean," echoing the language of chattel slavery in signaling Black laborers' mobility and expendability.[90] Large employers also preferred foreign laborers because they were protected by neither Cuban nor US laws.[91] Finally, like their counterparts in Central American banana plantations, on the Panama Canal, in New England textile mills, and company towns across the globe, sugar company administrators believed labor segmentation—recruiting nationally, racially, and ethnically diverse workers—discouraged labor solidarity.[92]

Immigration from Haiti and the British West Indies contributed to significant population growth in Cuba's eastern provinces. At the height of immigration to Cuba in 1920, most arrivals to the island were from Spain (54 percent), but 21 percent of immigrants were from Haiti and another 16 percent were from other Caribbean islands.[93] Whereas the population of Cuba as a whole grew by 33 percent between 1907 and 1919, the populations of Camagüey and Oriente grew by over 93 percent and over 60 percent, respectively, during this period. Oriente and Camagüey had significantly higher non-Cuban, non-Spanish populations (at 7.5 percent and 7.1 percent, respectively) than the rest of the island, where the non-Cuban, non-Spanish population stayed below 3 percent, except in Havana where it was approximately 4 percent.[94] The trend continued from 1919 through 1931, when Camagüey grew by 78 percent and Oriente by 46 percent, while Cuba's other provinces grew by between 7 and 41 percent.[95] In short, the provinces of Camagüey and Oriente were growing at a rate that significantly exceeded the island as a whole, and the difference was attributable to an influx of foreigners, especially Antillanos. In other words, in early-twentieth-century Cuba, the sugar towns of the east were growing faster and filling with more foreigners than the major cities of the island.

In authorizing the importation of Antillano laborers, the Cuban state attempted to balance the wishes of sugar companies against popular sentiment. Cuban public opinion was increasingly hostile to Caribbean contract labor. Some simply opposed Black immigration on racist grounds while others objected to imperialist companies importing workers who undercut local wages. Others condemned the fact that foreign workers removed earned money from Cuba.[96] The Cuban state could not simply ignore these concerns. At the same time, sugar companies claimed that Antillano field hands were fundamental to the annual harvest and, therefore, the island's entire wellbeing. As a CASC administrator put it in a request to recruit laborers, "there is a scarcity of laborers in Oriente;" without foreign workers, the company would likely be forced to "leave sugar uncut in the fields, at a great loss to this company, to the territory where its enclave is situated, and for the state which will suffer the lack of income."[97]

The Cuban government solved this problem with a system in which the state acknowledged the economy's dependence on foreign labor while appeasing public opposition to immigration. Beginning in 1917, large sugar companies requested "special permission" to import West Indian workers, which the Secretary of Agriculture authorized while also stipulating provisions designed to prevent foreigners from settling in Cuba. Companies were to import migrants "exclusively for agricultural labor related to the cutting and processing of cane," pay local rates, return workers to their island of origin "promptly" at the end of each sugar harvest.[98] Cuban American was required to deposit twenty dollars for each worker into an account designed to cover expenses if foreign workers became public charges.[99] In practice, however, few of these provisions were met. Companies rarely complied and rarely suffered the consequences. Annually, Cuban American and others reported that several hundred workers had been "impossible to find" and had "not responded to [the company's] call."[100] Yet the Secretary returned the deposited funds in light of the fact that the company "made an effort" to locate all the men. With this arrangement, the state paid lip service to concerns about "undesirable" immigrants while still accommodating powerful sugar interest, and sugar companies secured their preferred labor. Both the state and the companies washed their hands of year-round care for the workers. For their part, the "missing" workers were likely finding dead-season work on fruit or coffee plantations or trying their luck in cities.[101] The next year, they would return to the sugar zone for the *zafra* (harvest), saving companies the trouble of recruiting a few hundred men from distant islands.

To recruit workers, sugar companies sent agents throughout the Caribbean and paid them by the number of workers contracted.[102] Laborers contracted abroad often arrived through privately held ports, over which the Cuban government had little authority, a system that enabled administrators to import more than their authorized number.[103] Large colonos also hired their own recruiters, usually Haitians or British West Indians.[104] Employers kept a close watch on each other's recruitment activities, with CASC's general administrator once requesting that his agents send reports on competitors' activities abroad.[105] Competition for *braceros* (field hands) was, at times, fierce, and employers were known to poach one another's workers directly from docks and railway stations.[106]

United Fruit recruited workers from nearby Haiti and Jamaica, where they signed labor contracts, and imported them through their private ports on the Nipe and Banes Bays, as well as through the state-run port at Antilla.[107] Some scholars have suggested that workers were hired directly from the company's banana plantations in Jamaica.[108] The Cuban American Sugar Company drew mostly from farther afield in the eastern Caribbean islands of Barbados, Grenada, St. Vincent, Montserrat, Antigua, Dominica, St. Kitts, St. Thomas, St. Martin, and Curaçao, islands which the CASC administration considered its "special preserve for labor recruiting."[109] In debt to the company for their transportation, these workers were especially subject to company and colono abuse due to the greater distance between home and Cuba. CASC alone brought 22,058 workers through Havana, Santiago de Cuba, and its private port near Puerto Padre between 1917 and 1923, mainly on company ships.[110] Other Antillanos traveled to the region on their own, responding to advertisements in local papers in their home islands announcing the availability of employment and supplying information about transportation and visa requirements.[111] Upon their arrival to Santiago de Cuba, migrants without company contracts were compelled to spend time in a quarantine station. Immigrant workers decried conditions at the station, which in the early 1920s, had become one of their chief complaints.[112]

Sugar companies took several measures to manage and control their multinational labor forces. First and foremost, armed personnel patrolled their properties. United Fruit supplied the land and buildings for Rural Guard outposts, as did CASC. Companies also provided horses and railcars to facilitate patrols in or near sugar territories.[113] Rural guardsmen protected company interests, intimidated workers, repressed strikes, and arrested and imprisoned trouble makers.[114] In 1923, for instance, an unarmed British West Indian worker named Moses Buchanan attempted to leave the Tacajó mill near Antilla, when he entered into a dispute with the local guardsmen, who shot and killed him. A British diplomat investigating the matter complained that the company deliberately obscured his work, denied him access to witnesses, intimidated Buchanan's friends, and tarnished his reputation. The guardsmen were exonerated of the crime.[115] Such incidents were common. Sugar companies also hired private security guards, who were known to use violence. As a third level of armed protection, army soldiers patrolled near sugar estates in the weeks before and during the harvest.

In addition to monopolizing violence, sugar companies dominated commerce in their territories. Employees were largely compelled to rely on company stores for provisions, which could charge higher prices than the open market. As chapter 3 details, by the 1920s, labor leaders in United Fruit territory were calling for free commerce in the company *bateyes* (settlements around a mill). During lean times, workers were often paid in credit at the commissary, a practice that became a chief grievance for labor organizers in the region, especially during the sugar insurgency of 1933.[116] Independent merchants needed permission to open shop on company land, and their trade was restricted. Shops could be removed with little notice, as in 1928 when CASC announced plans to remove a number of private stores from its batey in order to make room for a new warehouse. Several shop owners refused to leave, and a local truck driver dumped a shipment of merchandise in the plaza in protest.[117]

Companies like United Fruit, CASC, Cuba Cane, and others also controlled transportation in their jurisdictions, and many sugar towns were often only reachable by way of company-owned rails. Passengers traveling to the United Fruit town of Banes left the main Santiago-Santa Clara line at Alto Cedro where they joined the Cuba Company's line to Antilla. At Dumois, they disembarked and joined United Fruit's private line which, until 1938, ran on a different gauge system and required separate locomotives from the mainlines. The trip from Dumois to Banes was twenty-five miles long and passed entirely through United Fruit lands.[118] In CASC's territory, the rail service around Puerto Padre was entirely private, and the nearest public railroad was over forty miles via private lines away from the Chaparra mill.[119]

The built environment of enclaves also facilitated labor control. In US-owned properties, social and living arrangements were planned along national-racial lines, with segregated sleeping quarters, commissaries, hospitals, leisure facilities, churches, and schools.[120] Elite neighborhoods of company towns, typically called *el barrio americano* or *la zona americana*, were home to administrators and boasted pristine parks, recreational facilities such as tennis courts, paved streets, and screened-in houses. Screens, as Louis Pérez Jr. has pointed out, took on a special meaning and suggested "aloofness, a way that North Americans distanced themselves from the daily experience of living in Cuba."[121] Administrators were mainly North Americans, but included some Cubans, such as CASC's administrators Ernesto Fonts y Sterling, who had studied at the New York Military Academy, and Mario García Menocal, a Cornell University graduate and future president of Cuba. Cuban neighborhoods, in contrast, were neglected, often reliant on underfunded municipal services to serve rapidly growing populations.

United Fruit situated its company headquarters in Banes at a distance from the Central Boston. Doing so insulated the managerial class from the unpleasantness of the mill, which ran loudly twenty-four-hours a day during the zafra and emitted a powerful odor. El barrio americano of Banes was located on the eastern side of town, which in 1910, included the manager's house and a guesthouse, polo fields and tennis courts, and a manicured garden complete with a fountain, offices, and clean streets shaded by trees.[122] The company-run general store was well stocked with US canned goods, clothing, and sundries. By the 1920s, this district included housing, a hotel, social clubs, restaurants, offices, warehouses, bakeries, pharmacies, schools, churches, theaters, and a hospital, all constructed of the best materials.[123] In contrast, the "Cuban Banes" stood apart from el barrio americano on the other side of the Río Banes and was unpaved, lacking in sanitation facilities and parks, and poorly maintained. The hospital serving Cubans in town was underfunded and reliant upon an uneven stream of donations. As one commentator wrote, in Banes the Cuban "works barbarously. If he doesn't work that way, he doesn't eat."[124] Afro-Caribbean immigrants too had their own neighborhood, located in the hilly section of town called La Güira but often nicknamed Overtown or Jamaicatown. Their homes were built with rudimentary materials, including mud brick, wood (which was ever-more difficult to secure as sugar fields overtook forests), and thatch. As late as 1943, a visiting official remarked that he was "rather surprised to find an unimproved village and some measure of neglect on the outskirts of what is really a pleasing township of good streets, good houses, hospitals, stores, etc." As he explained of Banes, "the layout of the whole township is excellent but the contrast between the town and La Guira village is marked."[125]

About five miles away from Banes, on a stretch of land jutting into the Banes Bay, sat the town of Macabí, home to the company's Boston mill. The mill ran around the clock during the harvest season, which peaked in 1920 at nine months in length, as Cuban and immigrant men worked two long shifts to keep the operation going uninterrupted. The Boston batey contained worker housing, health facilities, and commissaries.[126] United Fruit's other mill, Preston, sat some thirty-five miles away from Boston around the Nipe Bay, on the Mayarí River. Like Banes, Preston was divided into neighborhoods known as the American Section, Cuban Section, and the Colored Section. The managerial neighborhood contained a pristine store with departments for groceries, hats and boots, dry good, and hardware. Some worker housing was sturdy enough to be featured in United Fruit publications, but most were ramshackle, lacking electricity and sewage.[127]

Banes, Boston, and Preston were surrounded by vast expanses of cane fields. Unlike CASC, which grew cane through the colono system, United Fruit leased very little land to colonos and instead grew cane in fields administered by the company in a system known as "administration cane." In this arrangement, braceros worked directly for the company in distinct "colonies." Each colony had a small settlement where braceros lived, far from towns, in rudimentary huts made of mud or bagasse (a composite material of compressed cane stalk after the sucrose has been extracted) bricks with dirt floors and thatch roofs. Cuban braceros, who tended to live with their wives and children, resided in huts called *bohíos*, while Haitians and Jamaicans built their shared housing from found materials—such as timber, cane stalk, and burlap—just before the start of the harvest season. That the Haitian and Jamaican workers lived in squalid conditions was beside the point for United Fruit, as it built its reputation as a harbinger of modernity. Photo albums maintained by the company focused on emblems of progress, such as industrial machinery (for instance, an enormous crane designed to tip oxcarts onto train cars) rather than on workers themselves. Only in the background of these photographs can one glimpse the mud huts with burlap or thatch roofs in which workers resided.[128]

US observers considered United Fruit's territory in northeastern Cuba a model agricultural-export enclave. In 1920, William Joseph Showalter wrote for *National Geographic*, "A visit to a big plantation like that at Preston is an impressive experience. It is a small empire within itself, having its own railroad system, its own police department, its own hospital, its own fire department. It covers 280 square miles of territory, possesses a population of nearly ten thousand, and has nearly twelve hundred buildings."[129] A 1926 travel guide also explained of United Fruit's Boston and Preston mill towns, "These towns are the nerve centers of an *imperium in imperio*."[130] This repeated notion of an "empire within itself" reflects the goals of sugar company administrators: enclaves were, in essence, attempts to remake Cuba's physical and social landscape in a modern, industrious, and, above all, orderly fashion. Such spaces were to be protected from the vagaries of Cuban society with its racially mixed population and, as Adams put it, "professional revolutionists." But residents of enclaves had other ideas. Constrained as they were by the overwhelming power of sugar companies, individuals from across the Americas and farther afield nevertheless formed heterogeneous local societies deeply connected to the world beyond Cuba's eastern sugar zone.

Cosmopolitan Enclaves

As much as company representatives hoped to build sovereign spaces within Cuba, their power was never absolute. As Catherine LeGrand, Lara Putnam, Matt Casey, and others have demonstrated, imperialist companies were hardly omnipotent in their enclaves.[131] It is true sugar companies dominated local infrastructure, built segregated facilities to discourage collaboration, and monopolized transportation and commerce in their territories. Life for most in sugar territories was arduous, working conditions terrible, and opportunities for redress limited or nonexistent. Yet, companies could not entirely impose their will on employees and residents. Individuals, from fieldhands to metallurgical workers, from laundresses to teachers, found ways to maneuver outside of company control. Nonelite women and men nurtured social and cultural networks that sustained them in good times and bad. Moreover, communication and involvement with the outside world was constant.

Baked into the business model of sugar companies in northeastern Cuba was a fundamental contradiction. On the one hand, enclaves were closed spaces, geographically removed from the centers of Cuban society in an attempt to remain insulated from political disturbances. They were meant to be self-sufficient, containing within themselves much of what was needed to grow, harvest, and ship cane and to sustain the men and women carrying out this work. Yet, on the other hand, they relied on constant movement and exchange with the wider world. Goods, people, and ideas traveled in and out of northeastern Cuba. Seasonal laborers, by definition, arrived and departed annually. And there were others. Individuals who were neither field hands nor company managers joined the influx to northeastern Cuba. Filling the ranks of the upper classes were chemists, engineers, architects, and other professionals from across Europe and the Americas. Domestic servants such as housekeepers, laundresses, nannies, and cooks—largely from the British West Indies—labored for those upper classes. Teachers, missionaries, nurses, doctors, and pharmacists took care of the educational, spiritual, and physical wellbeing of enclave residents. Finally, cobblers, tailors, watchmakers, bakers, chefs, and other tradespeople kept daily life running. These individuals established vibrant communities and maintained rich associational lives. In so doing, they built cosmopolitan enclaves, heterogeneous local societies actively contributing to the wider world of ideas, culture, and politics.

The diverse stream of immigration to northeastern coast began at the dawn of the century. North American settlers were among the first to arrive in the region, and they were joined by teachers, entrepreneurs, and merchants.[132] Of the La Gloría settlement, near Nuevitas on Camagüey's northern coast, Jenks wrote, "They came from thirty states, two territories besides Canada, Prince Edward's Island, and British Columbia. They were physicians, a clergyman, a lawyer, an editor, small merchants, clerks, bookkeepers, locomotive engineers, carpenters, skilled mechanics, and many farmers."[133] In 1909 and 1910, when Wright visited North American colonies in Oriente, she encountered US citizens and Canadians, as well as Swedes, Britons, Finns, Norwegians, and Jamaicans who worked as hired hands on farms, and Spanish and Cuban merchants. Encouraged by land-company literature, she claimed, most had given up property at home only to find "hard luck" in Cuba raising fruits, coffee, and tobacco. Some moved to sugar enclaves to build a new life in the expanding sugar economy.[134]

Spaniards too moved into northern Oriente in the early twentieth century. Although Afro-Caribbeans formed largest immigrant group in the eastern provinces of Oriente and Camagüey, Spaniards were the foremost immigrant group to the island as a whole in the first two decades of the twentieth century. US occupation policies encouraged Spanish immigration in an attempt to "whiten" the island, and the new republic followed suit. By 1931, Spanish-born residents represented 16 percent of Cuba's population.[135] In United Fruit's territory, most Spaniards came in the company's early years, including the 300 Canary Islanders recruited to work the sugar harvest in 1907.[136] Others from Galicia, Asturias, and León joined them. The Cuban American Sugar Company also had a significant Spanish population, who worked on the company's railroad lines, in construction, and in the boiler rooms.[137] Spaniards in northeastern Cuba worked as field laborers, tradesmen, professionals such as teachers and accountants, and, as in the rest of the country, shopkeepers and merchants.[138]

As they often did in zones of imperialism, Protestant missionaries joined the influx to northern Oriente.[139] Their objectives extended beyond spreading God's word; missionaries hoped to help build a new Cuba based on Anglo-American values, to encourage locals to shed their Spanish Catholic heritage, and to prepare the island for US-led modernity.[140] Some of the earliest missionaries to Cuba were from the American Friends Board of Foreign Missions, and when the Quakers launched their Cuban missions, they chose northern

Oriente as their base of operations. From the start, missionaries and sugar companies worked together. In 1900, on a ship from Jamaica to Cuba, Captain Lorenzo Baker of the United Fruit Company offered the experienced missionary Zenas Martin $2,000 toward a mission in the company's Cuban territory.[141] Martin and Baker were close friends, and Martin's mission in Jamaica was also on United Fruit land.[142] By 1904, five Quaker missions were operating in Cuba, with four located along Oriente's northern coast; in Gibara, Holguín, Puerto Padre, and Banes.[143] Martin himself became a cane farmer and, by 1920, employed around 40 Haitian, Jamaican, and Cuban workers seasonally. At least once, he put down a labor action with strikebreakers.[144] The Quakers were hardly alone in cooperating with powerful imperialist employers. Companies often paid missionary salaries, offered religious workers jobs, and funded mission schools. Company administrators served on the boards of directors of church schools, and missionaries relied on company hospitals, transportation, tuition funding, donations, and social and sports clubs for leisure activities.[145]

Many Protestant schools charged tuition and educated middle and upper-class Cubans to develop skills well suited for employment with US businesses.[146] Students learned English.[147] Girls were taught to become good homemakers and boys to be company men. Many graduates were hired directly into positions with foreign companies.[148] As one Quaker missionary put it, teaching in Cuba presented "greater opportunities for influencing those who must become the history makers of their nation."[149] Future Cuban President Fulgencio Batista graduated from the Quaker school in Banes in 1913 and immediately began working for United Fruit.[150]

Seventh-day Adventists also established schools at the American colony of Bartle in northern Oriente and in Chaparra and Delicias where they operated with support from the Cuban American Sugar Company.[151] By the 1930s, the Antillean Union of the Seventh-day Adventists was opening schools and sanitariums, and organizing churches.[152] A group called the West Indies Mission was also active throughout Cuba, Haiti, and the Dominican Republic by the 1930s. With eighty-three "preaching centers" across Cuba, the mission had so many locations in CASC territory that they required a special rail pass from the company to reach them all.[153] The West Indies Mission served primarily the poor and working men and women of the area.[154] Matthew Frye Jacobson has argued that US efforts to Christianize and "civilize" the world were, in many ways, an economic mission, with missionary work closely linked to the expansion of American "property relations, . . . modes of production, and patterns of consumption."[155] In Cuba, "civilizing" missions not only spurred material wants (and thus expanded the market for US exports), but they also aimed to create a well-disciplined worker.[156] In requests for support from CASC, the West Indies Mission organizers claimed their work produced "a better, faithful, and more loyal employee."[157]

Other professionals arrived in sugar enclaves. Sugar companies drew upon the experience of seasoned imperialists, and men of far-reaching backgrounds filled upper-level positions such as company administrators, engineers, and chemists. As Wright put it about the Central Preston, "It is managed by an American, assisted by men of other nationalities, especially English with wider tropical experience and more thorough training to their duties than Americans have hitherto had time or opportunity to attain."[158] In 1929, a Swiss applicant to a manager position at CASC, named A. F. Paris, had a resume that included running a sugar beet farm in Germany, managing sugar plantations in Peru, touring sugar and coffee plantations in British East Africa, working on staff of the Hawaiian Sugar Planters' Association, and managing two Hawaiian plantations.[159] Paris and other such professionals were akin to those whom James W. Martin calls "banana cowboys," white collar professionals making their livings in the agricultural-export zones of Central America.[160]

By the 1920s, northeastern Cuba and especially its company towns were nationally diverse spaces. In 1924, the Cuban American Sugar Company listed Cubans, Spaniards, and others of "various nationalities" in its labor records.[161] In the 1930s, these included Virgin Islanders, Puerto Ricans, and other US imperial subjects.[162] Chaparra and Delicias were also home to Chinese residents, including Francisco Chiong who worked for the company for over thirty years and had traveled to Jamaica and China recruiting laborers. Many of his compatriots had worked for Cuban American for decades.[163] As for United Fruit, women and men from across the Americas, Europe, and China settled in Banes. From the Spanish Caribbean, several Dominicans were living in Banes by 1919.[164] That year, a company agent in Puerto Rico recruited 600 men for work in the cane fields, and by the 1920s, several dozen Puerto Rican families lived in town.[165] An Anglo-American raised in Banes, Jack Skelly, remarked in his memoir that Chinese cooks were common, with the managerial class considering it a matter of prestige to hire them.[166]

Antillanos, who sugar companies imported precisely because they were thought to be easily isolated, were themselves a diverse and well-traveled group. They hailed from not only the British West Indies and Haiti, but also the Dutch Caribbean, French Caribbean, and what was after 1916 the US Virgin Islands.[167] Many British West Indians, who were often called *ingleses* or *jamaicanos* (even when they were not Jamaican), had labored on the Panama Canal or in Central American banana plantations before coming to Cuba. In the 1910s and 1920s, several thousand British West Indians arrived in Cuba directly from Central America.[168] Moreover, as Giovannetti-Torres details in his definitive account, British West Indians were an internally diverse group, with significant differences in background and immigration experiences between those arriving from the smaller islands of the eastern Caribbean and those arriving from Jamaica. *Ingleses* were prolific letter writers, often sending word to newspaper editors, British officials, and families back home. Their "epistolary journeys" spanned the globe and kept them in touch with the world beyond Cuba.[169]

Many Antillanos declined to stay in their designated roles, moved up within the sugar economy, or found work other industries altogether. As Casey describes, Haitians, who were Kreyol-speaking and largely without formal education, often remained in rural employment, yet they still managed to work varying jobs within the sugar economy, strategically negotiate labor conditions, cultivate religious communities, and interact regularly with members of the many other national groups living in the region.[170] For their part, British West Indians arrived in Cuba with relatively high levels of literacy and education (94.5 percent of Jamaican migrants in the mid-1920s were literate) and with previous work in skilled or semi-skilled occupations, both of which gave them slight advantages in terms of social mobility. As native speakers of English, British West Indians were the favored domestic employees of the North American managerial class.[171] In fact, domestic service with US families was one of few employment options open to foreign Black women, and many a manager's house was staffed with British West Indian laundresses, nannies, housekeepers, and cooks. Antillano men also worked as gardeners, chauffeurs, and household staff for North American families and in leisure facilities such as the American Club.[172]

Antillano field hands moved from company to company in search of better wages.[173] That workers used mobility to their advantage is demonstrated by the facts that employers competed over labor and that every year companies like CASC were unable to account for at least a few hundred workers. While many immigrants arrived in northeastern Cuba directly through company ports with bracero contracts, others came on their own with a bit of cash and different goals. In 1923, for instance, only 5 percent of Jamaican immigrants to Cuba were unable to pay the required migration deposit, and that year all Jamaican immigrants paid their own passage.[174] These individuals moved throughout the region in search of opportunity and an agreeable community. As I demonstrate in chapter 2, men and women did not travel exclusively for the purpose of finding work; many journeyed in the service of transnational civic and religious associations like the Universal Negro Improvement Association, spreading messages of racial uplift and religious redemption.

While braceros generally left sugar enclaves for home or for work in coffee plantations at the end of the harvest, some foreign workers and their families remained in the sugar zone and formed vibrant communities in the region's towns, like the La Güira neighborhood of Banes.[175] By the mid-1920s, British West Indians living in La Güira worked as watchmakers, tailors, cobblers, shopkeepers, coal stokers, bricklayers, train conductors, carpenters, plumbers, tinsmiths, butchers, mechanics, and bookbinders.[176] La Güira had its own restaurants, bakeries, and boarding houses. This range of professional positions and the local economy of British Antilleans in Banes made for a diverse and lively setting, remembered to this day in memoirs and novels.[177]

British West Indians also worked in professions such as teaching or nursing. United Fruit's Preston batey had housing designated specifically for "Jamaican nurses."[178] One such nurse, Elise M. Forbes, was born in Kingston and carried a Jamaican passport but spent her early years in New York City where she earned her nursing degree. During her time in New York, she visited Jamaica and Cuba on multiple occasions. Immediately after graduating in 1918, she moved to Preston. When Forbes lost her right leg in a train accident, she submitted an application to return to New York where she had a sister.[179] Forbes' story is characteristic of the ongoing movement between locales such as New York, Jamaica, and eastern Cuba that characterized life for Antillanos in the circum-Caribbean.[180]

Passenger and freight shipping throughout the region facilitated travel in this new "American sea." Early in the century, Munson steamships sailed three times a month carrying passengers and freight directly between Antilla and New York, with no need to stop in Havana. Later, Munson ships on the Antilla route also stopped directly in Banes and Preston, saving passengers the trouble of traveling by land to Antilla.[181] By the 1920s, cargo ships traveled directly from Antilla carrying sugar to Baytown in Texas, Boston, New York, Philadelphia, and Wilmington.[182] United Fruit maintained its own fleet, the Great White Fleet, which made weekly trips carrying cargo and passengers between eastern Cuba, Havana, New Orleans, and New York, with many routes connecting directly to Banes, Boston, and Preston.[183] Ships sailing under other flags also docked at Antilla, Banes, and Preston; in 1931, reports listed British, Danish, Dutch, German, Norwegian, Panamanian, Swedish, Italian, and Japanese ships as all docked in one of the three United Fruit ports.[184] Similarly, the docks at Puerto Padre connected Cuban American's territory with the National Sugar Refinery Company sites in New Orleans, Boston, and Brooklyn. Passenger steamers sailed regularly between northeastern Cuba and the wider world. Less glamorous, crowded schooners ferried Antillanos to multiple ports of call in the greater Caribbean. Each of these ships, of course, was staffed by crews who spread information verbally and through the printed word by bringing newspapers and political pamphlets. When Cuba exploded in revolution in 1933, Cuban authorities routinely seized "inflammatory" literature from crew members on cargo ships.[185]

In this sea-going culture, travel between centers of US economic influence was common and fluid. White US citizen Morton Franklyn reported that he "dropped off" in Delicias during a time when he was "traveling around on ships." Authorities spent considerable time tracking down another white North American, Donald Armour, who traveled through the Caribbean and Central America swindling women and fellow US citizens wherever he went—including to eastern Cuba where he married a Cuban woman and fathered four children before disappearing again. A skilled and enterprising "rogue," Armour arrived in most places destitute but departed a "man of ample funds," thanks to the generosity of "kindly Americans."[186] Throughout his travels, Armour was able to take advantage of (and evade responsibility in) the interconnected space created in the wake of US economic expansion.

Some, like Franklyn and Armour, kept moving, while others stayed put. Take, for instance, the story of an African American man named Fred Roberts. Born in Reconstruction-era Georgia, Roberts had worked cleaning engines as a young man in a railroad shop near Atlanta. At the outbreak of war with Spain in 1898, he left for Tampa with the intention of enlisting in the army. Instead, Roberts found work as a teamster with a private contractor with whom he traveled to Cuba. After the war, when he was involved in the disarmament of Spanish forces in Havana, a Spanish soldier insulted him, and a fight ensued. The soldier used a bayonet to stab and beat Roberts, who suffered permanent injuries and was rendered unable to engage in vigorous manual labor. Roberts eventually headed east and found a job with United Fruit in Banes, where he satisfied his employers as a "well-behaved" worker and was a well-known member of the community. Regarding his nationality, a United Fruit official explained, "That he is an American negro there is no doubt, as anyone who has lived in these parts of the world could testify at once." Years later, in 1936, when Roberts was sixty years old, he petitioned the local American consul for assistance returning home but lacked documentation proving his US citizenship. Several company managers wrote to the consul on his behalf, but no one provided him with cash for passage.[187]

Roberts was one of many African Americans who had joined the war effort and headed to Cuba.[188] Most returned home and were disappointed to find that not even military service could relax the color line in a nation legally and extralegally segregating and disenfranchising Black citizens. Some, however, like Roberts, settled in Cuba and sought to carve out a life in a zone newly opened to US citizens and promising prosperity in booming agricultural industries. African Americans may have imagined Cuba as a place where they could leave behind the daily struggles of Jim Crow, though they were likely disappointed. Whereas Donald Armour had survived on funds swindled from kindly strangers, Fred Roberts secured no such assistance, despite being a fixture in his community. In short, while the color line was somewhat fuzzier in Cuba, it nevertheless existed and would harden in company towns during the first decades of the century.[189]

In the multinational, multiracial space created in the wake of US expansion, residents formed romantic unions across national and ethnic lines. People most often married individuals with whom they shared a native tongue, such as Puerto Rican Julio Ramos Rivera, who married and grew a family with a Cuban woman, and Juan de Jesús González, who married a Spanish woman.[190] As for English speakers, Amanda Isaroon from the Virgin Islands lived with a Jamaican for ten years near Cueto ten miles east of the Nipe Bay where they raised their five children.[191] In 1923, a wedding ceremony near Delicias involved a British West Indian bride who was raised in the Dominican Republic, an Antiguan groom, and a Jamaican host.[192] Individual backgrounds and households, however, often resisted easy classification, and intermarriage across languages and ethnicities was common. Many male US citizens married Cuban women and acclimated to local society.[193] When the white settler William Boitel died in the mid-1930s, a conflict ensued over who was to inherit his small orange grove—either his wife, about whom "it is generally understood among the Jamaican element that she was born in Jamaica" but who claimed to be English, or his children in the US. Complicating matters was the fact that "he associated so much with the Cubans one forgets he is an American citizen."[194]

All of this movement to and intermingling in northeastern Cuba took place during a peak period of civic organizing in the Americas and worldwide. Newspapers and letters circulated internationally thanks to improvements in printing and travel technology. Mutual aid societies, masonic lodges, and youth clubs took off during the first third of the twentieth century, and Cuba's eastern sugar zone was hardly an exception. Historians Lara Putnam, Tyesha Maddox, Kaysha Corinealdi, and others have written of the rich associational life and activism sustaining Caribbean migrants and immigrants in the Americas.[195] In northeastern Cuba, these civic organizations often had transnational memberships and maintained regular contact with overseas communities through correspondence and travel.

Religious organizations brought members into a transnational orbit. The Quaker missionaries who settled in northern Oriente hailed not only from the US but also from Jamaica and Mexico, and they had a wealth of experience in other overseas missions.[196] The Antillean Union of the Seventh-day Adventists maintained interconnected missions in Haiti, Puerto Rico, Santo Domingo, and the Bahamas, and had branches throughout Cuba. Members gathered annually, with conference locations alternating between the Caribbean and North America.[197] International meetings, the wide circulation of pamphlets and other reading materials, the movement of missionaries and their families, as well as the training of local preachers all brought Cuba, and in particular the towns of northern Oriente, into regular contact with the outside world and helped keep local men and women abreast of international concerns.

Associational rosters from the 1920s in United Fruit's territory reveal the area's national diversity. In addition to elite clubs like the American Club, the Anglo-American Association, the Union Cuba, and the Pan-American Club found in most company towns and Cuban cities, Banes, Mayarí, and Antilla hosted groups, such as the Haitian Club, Unión Haitiana, Jamaican Club, a Jamaican Seventh-day Adventist group, West Indian cricket clubs, sporting associations, and youth clubs.[198] The Universal Negro Improvement Association had strong branches in all United Fruit company towns, as I detail in chapter 2. Similarly, the Cuban American Company strongholds at Puerto Padre, Chaparra, and Delicias hosted dozens of civic organizations, including the UNIA, sporting clubs, mutual aid societies, and religious organizations. Occasionally, the roles of different associations merged, as in the case of the Jamaican-run Banes Union Church, which established a mutual aid society in 1923. Their Relief Association charged dues and paid sickness and death benefits to its members.[199] Upon the society's dissolution two years later, the society's remaining funds were designated for a local Spanish-speaking Catholic organization, indicating linkages across religious and linguistic lines.[200]

By the late 1910s and the 1920s, masonic temples and lodges also operated in the sugar towns of northern Oriente. A masonic group called the Kane Lodge, founded in 1923 at Preston, served a largely West Indian community and maintained several permanent committees, including financial, charity, and grievance committees.[201] With a diverse membership, the lodge had Spanish- and English-speaking officers, and although they carried out most of their business in English, they kept meeting minutes in Spanish in compliance with national laws. This would not have been a tremendous difficulty as both the master of ceremonies and the master of rules had Spanish surnames. Kane members were largely men of some means as the initiation fees were high, twenty-five pesos, and membership dues were five pesos, significantly more than the two pesos required by more popular associations like the UNIA. Membership numbers are unavailable for the 1920s, but by 1931, after economic collapse had sent many foreigners home, the lodge still had forty-three members, indicating lasting strength.[202] In nearby Antilla, an Oddfellows lodge known as Luz Unida was founded in 1926, also with a primarily English-speaking leadership; it was later described as a "Society of Jamaicans."[203] The stated aims of the group included "collecting contribution and membership fees and redistributing them along the principles of benevolence and charity."[204] Both the Luz Unida in Antilla and the Kane Lodge in Preston included in their rules mechanisms by which members of related lodges could join, suggesting that new members routinely arrived with affiliations from elsewhere.[205] Both lodges maintained formal ties to their national and international leadership councils, established liaison positions, and corresponded regularly with wider affiliates.

This rich civic life built in northeastern sugar towns supported Cubans and immigrants as they navigated the challenges of a community dependent on a single agricultural export. Mutual aid societies abounded and provided members with a cushion in times of economic instability, a small but important safety net unavailable through employers or the Cuban state. The region's strong associational life and civic society provided the foundation for more explicitly activist groups with internationalist aims and agendas.

One such endeavor, a preview of the transnational solidarity movements that would follow, was the "Pro-Santo Domingo" campaign of 1919. In January, Dominican nationals living in eastern Cuba demanded an end to the United States' occupation of the Dominican Republic, which had begun in 1916. They and their supporters formed committees and elected officers to host speeches, concerts, festivals, and public meetings raising awareness of atrocities committed by US troops in nearby Hispaniola. Pro-Santo Domingo leaders denounced the US for claiming to support self-determination in the aftermath of the Great War while simultaneously occupying sovereign nations. They called the US the "most tyrannical state in the world." Organizers contributed funds toward sending a Dominican delegation to the Paris Peace Conference where they lobbied allied forces for an end to the intervention.[206]

The campaign proved particularly popular in Banes, where the Dominican Consul to Santiago de Cuba made a controversial speech to a large audience. He compared the situation in his homeland to the German occupation of Belgium during the Great War and claimed that "a Germany greater than the European Germany existed on this side of the Atlantic, and was making Santo Domingo a second Belgium." After several weeks of organizing, campaigners reported that "a great success was everywhere met."[207] By early February, plans were under way for simultaneous Pro-Santo Domingo demonstrations on the 24th of the month in several *oriental* sugar towns, including Banes and Mayarí in United Fruit territory, Puerto Padre (CASC headquarters), Holguín, Gibara, Palma Soriano, Victoria de Las Tunas, and Bayamo, all in northern Oriente, as well Santiago, Guantánamo near the US naval base, and the copper mining town of El Cobre. Cuban authorities were alarmed to learn that support for the rallies was so widespread that several local mayors planned to participate.[208] Eventually, the administration of Cuban President Mario García Menocal, who had been the general administrator of CASC's Chaparra mill, ordered that municipal authorities prevent the demonstrations. The Pro-Santo Domingo group's plans were frustrated, and the campaign fizzled. Nevertheless, the fact that Dominican actors and their local allies were planning simultaneous demonstrations in response to US imperialism overseas speaks to the cosmopolitan and restive character of eastern Cuba's company towns during the interwar period.[209]

The Pro-Santo Domingo campaign in eastern Cuba shares several features with the solidarity movements that followed and that are detailed in this book. First, Dominican activists and their sympathizers in eastern Cuba were joining a rising tide of anti-imperialism in the Americas. Latin American nationalists were increasingly challenging US hegemony as the "American century" set in, and forging a common, pan-American cause as they did so.[210] Second, the Pro-Santo Domingo demonstrations highlight the region's internal heterogeneity, as there were substantial numbers of Dominican nationals in the region. Finally, the campaign against the US occupation of Santo Domingo suggests something of the internationalist outlook held by residents of eastern Cuba's sugar-producing territory. Local women and men shared many of the same concerns as their Dominican counterparts, and many likened the Dominican story to US interference in Cuban affairs. In fact, it was rumors of an agenda expanded to include US imperialism *in Cuba* that had drawn the attention of authorities.[211] In short, Pro-Santo Domingo organizers intertwined their local grievances with wider, transnational causes and mobilized accordingly. While their campaign was short lived, it was just the beginning of internationalist mobilizing in northern Oriente.

Conclusion

It is tempting to view agricultural-export enclaves in the Caribbean and Central America as closed-off spaces of near-absolute company control. Ironically, this picture of enclaves as sovereign corporate zones, removed from Cuban society and politics, was, for a long time, one shared by sugar companies and anti-imperialists. After all, both had a vested interest in emphasizing company sovereignty and power—either as hallmarks of modern efficiency and industry or as a quintessential form of imperialist oppression. As LeGrand has written, however, "enclaves are places with their own historical directions; socially complex regions in which people of different national, racial, ethnic, and linguistic origins have to deal with each other; porous areas with multiple connections to their own countries and the outside world."[212] In the story of northern Oriente, US economic expansion paved avenues for the movement of capital, technical expertise, commodities, and labor into and out of the region. Once pathways created by US capital were opened, however, enterprising individuals seized upon these circuits and used the new networks to their advantage. Men and women from all walks of life traveled to sites of US imperialist development in the Americas—from the Panama Canal Zone to the Standard Oil fields of Colombia and Venezuela to the banana plantations of Central America, and to sugar towns like Banes.

Each aspect of US imperialism in Cuba—military, political, and economic—was accompanied by a dynamic movement of women and men. With war and military occupation, some like Fred Roberts stayed behind, building a new life in a region that promised prosperity (even if it didn't deliver). Other US citizens, assured by the political stability imposed on Cuba by the Platt Amendment that the island would be stable and safe for migration (and perhaps ultimately annexed to the US), moved to Cuba as colonists. Technicians, with experience spanning the world of resource-extraction imperialism, brought their expertise to the booming sugar industry. Missionaries, some bringing with them years of experience overseas, spread God's word and established schools. Company towns depended on a host of domestic servants, tradesmen and tradeswomen, and vendors, many of whom arrived from elsewhere.

Most of all, with foreign capital and the rise of multinational corporations on Cuba's northeastern coast, came hundreds of thousands of laborers in need of jobs. Many of these individuals had already traveled extensively throughout Central America, the Caribbean, and North America. Subject to company and Rural Guard abuse, living under the constant threat of eviction and deportation, underpaid, and derided by many, Afro-Caribbean immigrants were not the cut-off and isolated laborers described in some historical literature.[213] Antillanos used mobility to improve labor conditions, and they interacted regularly with women and men from across the globe. Some took advantage of their relative social capital to move up within local society and establish settled communities, which would form the backbone of the Universal Negro Improvement Association, the subject of chapter 2.

In northern Oriente, nationally and racially diverse women and men found themselves in a space run largely according to the dictates of the sugar economy, yet never monolithically controlled by any single company. In dynamic interaction with foreign capital, local residents—both Cuban and foreign—came to understand their daily struggles in transnational terms and to formulate connections with their counterparts overseas. People of diverse nationalities deployed a cosmopolitan sensibility in Banes and towns like it to make their way in a changing global economy. But cosmopolitanism entails more than worldly experience and background; it is also a matter of one's worldview and ambitions for global belonging. The next chapters illuminate how the men and women of Cuba's northeastern coast engaged with transnational struggles for racial solidarity, working-class revolution, and against the growing threat of fascism.

2

Garveyism, Community Building, and Forging Diaspora in Company Towns

On July 23, 1921, the SS *Munamar* set sail from Antilla, Cuba, bound for New York. Aboard were five British West Indian members of the Universal Negro Improvement Association (UNIA) on their way to attend the organization's second International Convention. The contingent included a Jamaican couple, Harold and Anita Collins, who were living in the United Fruit Company town of Banes, where Harold was a pharmacist. They were joined by a fellow Jamaican, Arnold S. Cummings, who also lived in Banes and had made a name for himself as a successful fundraiser for the association. A carpenter from Grenada named George Taite represented the nearby United Fruit mill town of Preston. Finally, UNIA Chaplain General Reverend George Alexander McGuire also boarded the *Munamar* that day. The Antigua-born pastor was returning home from his second two-month tour of Cuba, which had more UNIA chapters than any country besides the United States. Speaking before packed audiences across the island, McGuire had successfully recruited new members to the organization and raised funds for the association's two great enterprises, the Black Star Line (BSL) shipping company and the Liberian Construction Loan program to finance Black settlement in West Africa.[1] When the UNIA delegates disembarked at Pier 9 of New York's East River on July 27, they had every reason to be enthusiastic about the progress of their association.

An estimated 50,000 people were expected to attend the UNIA convention that August (though reports indicate the actual number was closer to 10,000).[2] Harold Collins and his fellow travelers from Cuba joined delegates from across the Americas and as far afield as West Africa to discuss current events, share news of their local branches, and collaborate in shaping the international UNIA program. Over the course of thirty-one days, speaking topics ranged from poor medical and educational facilities in Spanish Honduras to suppression of the UNIA newspaper, *Negro World*, in the British West Indies to the atrocities of lynch justice in the US South. Anti-imperialism and the struggle for a "free and redeemed Africa" loomed large throughout the conference, with participants frequently criticizing the League of Nations for having recently turned over Germany's colonies to France and England without consulting African representatives. Attendees praised Moor resistance against the Spanish in Morocco and passed a resolution condemning Spanish colonial aggression. A white suffragette name Helena Hill-Weed spoke on behalf of the Haiti and Santo Domingo Independence Society, urging US voters to demand an end to Marine occupations in those countries.[3]

Representatives from Cuba, too, shared their vision for racial uplift. On the penultimate day of the convention, Harold Collins, who was formally inducted as a UNIA officer with the title "West Indian Leader of the Eastern Province," introduced a resolution suggesting that the association "publish schoolbooks from which all children of this organization shall be taught racial pride" and that local chapters establish schools. He said, "our race has suffered materially by being instructed from books written by alien teachers, and. . . . such instruction has tended to a great extent to destroy our racial pride and progress." His resolution passed unanimously.[4] In his closing address, Marcus Garvey, the founder and President General of the UNIA, delivered a message for delegates to "take home and propagate among the scattered millions of Africa's sons and daughters." After condemning the League of Nations and praising Indian and Irish nationalism, he called on attendees to "Go back to your respective corners of the earth and preach the real doctrine of the Universal Negro Improvement Association—the doctrine of universal emancipation for Negroes, the doctrine of a free and a redeemed Africa!"[5]

Anita and Harold Collins did just that when they returned to Banes in mid-September. The local UNIA branch, called "Division #52," hosted several mass meetings in which Harold delivered speeches reporting on the convention and summarizing UNIA laws and regulations. He dwelled especially upon the UNIA Bureau of Passports, which facilitated members' travel between branches of the organization, a topic of particular interest to his fellow immigrants in the audience. Unsurprisingly, given his popular resolution on education, Collins addressed plans to establish "schools for children of African descent." The UNIA women's auxiliary unit, the Black Cross Nurses, welcomed Anita Collins home with a night of entertainment, including a formal ceremony, speeches, and a dinner-dance. Harold and Anita opened the ball with a waltz, he "neatly clad in black and with gloved hands" and she in an orange taffeta dress with cream lace, items likely purchased in New York or at United Fruit's well-provisioned department store.[6] The elaborate events reflected the couple's esteemed stature in UNIA Division #52; Harold was the executive secretary and regularly delivered lectures on health and disease for audiences in town, and Anita had founded the Black Cross Nurses and served on the Ladies' Division Advisory board.[7]

From their home base in Banes, then, Harold and Anita Collins traveled in service of the UNIA, heard and spread news of global events pertinent to the Black race and anti-imperialism, and collaborated toward racial uplift. In Jamaica, New York, and Banes, they developed a cosmopolitan worldview and shared it with their neighbors, those whom Garvey called the "scattered millions of Africa's sons and daughters." The Collins story was emblematic of wider patterns developing in the early-to-mid-twentieth century. Harold was born in Brownstone, Jamaica, in 1893. He and Anita married in 1919 and soon moved to Banes. Harold's brother Frank also lived in Banes in the 1920s, where the Collinses were prominent members of La Güira's Antillano community. Another brother, Ivan, had immigrated to Canada and served in the Canadian Regiment during the Great War. Their sister Ethel lived in Harlem and hosted Anita and Harold during their visit for the 1921 convention.[8] There, she made her "social debut" into the UNIA along with three other young women.[9] Ethel Collins remained active in the UNIA for two decades, serving as the organization's Acting General Secretary in 1929.[10] During the interwar period, British West Indian families like the Collinses formed a diaspora within the African diaspora, as they served the crown, traveled the Caribbean and Central America searching for work, and moved to the US north. A booming international Black press, prominently including the UNIA's official organ, the *Negro World*, strengthened ties between these locales and facilitated a sense of shared experiences among far-flung individuals.[11] The sugar towns of northern Oriente were key nodes in these overlapping networks of labor migration and activism that came of age with the international New Negro Movement of the 1920s.

As much as sugar towns were shaped by a rising tide of diasporic sensibility and internationalist activism, they were also spaces of single-crop economic dependency, imperialism, and racial subordination.[12] Disembarking the *Munamar* at Pier 9 on July 27 were the wife and young children of Robert V. Howley, general manager of United Fruit's Preston mill, returning home to Newton, Massachusetts.[13] In fact, at the same time that George Taite was representing the Preston branch at the UNIA convention, Howley and his fellow manager F.W.B. Hogge were busy shutting down the UNIA in Preston. According to the *Negro World*, "members have been turned out of their jobs and houses which they rent, while others have been ill-treated" and blackballed from future employment. The local division's General Secretary, G. R. Christian, was questioned in Howley's office and detained by the police. Under arrest, Christian was "grossly assaulted and beaten" and remained in police custody for several hours.[14] Howley's move against the UNIA in Preston took place during a time of dire economic straits in Cuba, as the sugar market had recently collapsed, taking the island's economy down with it and leaving laborers across the island out of work and destitute. Foreign workers were particularly hard hit, and Howley worried that any gathering of workers spelled trouble for the company. As Christian later recalled, it was fear of a strike that had stirred the UFC managers to action: "Because of the great strides we were making, the powers that be in Preston . . . got uneasy by thinking the UNIA would cause strikes if allowed to go on at the rate we were going."[15] In short, the island's dependence on sugar—and its consequent crash—put the Black-uplift association in a precarious position, as company managers and state authorities suppressed activities they deemed suspicious.

On its trip between Antilla and New York every other week, then, the *Munamar* traveled along one route with multiple meanings. On one hand, the ship was a passenger-cargo vessel, and it sailed in service of imperialist capitalism. Not only did it transport company managers and their families in its first-class cabins, but the ship had been specially retrofitted to carry up to eight million pounds of raw sugar in its hold, and it made additional stops at refineries in New Jersey after passengers disembarked at Pier 9.[16] On the other hand, the ship traveled between northern Oriente, a leading hub of UNIA activism, and New York, the heart of a Black cultural and political renaissance taking shape in the interwar years, bringing with it people (and their newspapers) deeply engaged in the work of building diaspora. This chapter tells the story of how the Universal Negro Improvement Association flourished in this contradictory space, forging international alliances and fighting for Black uplift. Making sense of the close ties between Cuba's sugar economy and Garvey's diasporic movement—and by extension, between US economic imperialism and the international New Negro Movement—requires refocusing our attention away from well-known metropolises like Harlem and Havana and toward the sugar enclaves of northern Oriente. As Sidney Mintz has written, if urbanization is defined by technological advancement, heterogeneity, and modern services, then "for many Caribbean societies, the most 'urban' communities are not cities but plantations."[17]

Northern Oriente was a powerhouse of Garveyism at the movement's height from 1919 to 1927. Three of the four men representing Cuba at the UNIA convention in 1921 were from United Fruit territory, and Banes was the leading branch of the UNIA in Cuba.[18] Zooming into sugar towns like Banes reveals not only the surprising role of "outpost" Garveyites punching above their weight in the global movement but also the ways individuals of different national backgrounds collaborated.[19] While the UNIA in Cuba was best known as a British West Indian affair, Cubans also took an interest, and many joined the movement. In fact, the most famous account of Afro-Cuban Garveyism comes from northern Oriente. María "Reyita" de los Reyes Castillo Bueno grew up at Cueto near the Central Alto Cedro, just a few miles west of United Fruit lands, and joined the UNIA as an adolescent. She later recalled connecting Garveyite messages of Black unity and African redemption to her formerly enslaved grandmother's stories about the Kingdom of Congo. Castillo Bueno recruited fellow Cubans to the organization and fondly remembered events like Marcus Garvey's visit to Banes. She enjoyed the friendly jockeying over whose music—Jamaican or Cuban—was to be played at UNIA festivities, as the movement bridged linguistic, cultural, and national divides.[20]

When the UNIA arrived on the scene in northern Oriente in the late 1910s, Castillo Bueno and her fellow Afro-Cubans already had significant experience with Black clubs and associations. Since the earliest days of slavery, Africans and Afro-Cubans had supported one another through *cabildos de nación*, organizations of individuals with a shared African heritage and language. In addition to maintaining ancestral traditions, these early mutual aid societies provided illness and burial benefits and occasionally purchased the freedom of their members. By the middle of the nineteenth century, Afro-Cubans were also forming *sociedades de color*, which continued though the twentieth century and promoted the educational, economic, and social uplift of their members through newspapers, education, and political advocacy.[21] Later, these sociedades collaborated with UNIA chapters in eastern Cuba.

The path between *cabildos* and the UNIA, however, was interrupted by racial violence. In the early twentieth century, Blackness as an organizing principle ran up against Cuba's national ideology of racial harmony. Black participation in Cuba's nineteenth-century independence wars, the prominence of several Black generals (including the "Bronze Titan" Antonio Maceo) in those struggles, and the pressing need to counteract Spanish claims that independence would result in "another Haiti" had all generated a powerful rhetoric of *cubanidad* as racially inclusive. José Martí, the ideological leader of Cuba's War of 1895, had famously declared that "there is no race hatred, because there are no races."[22] Ideologies of a "raceless nationality," as historians have demonstrated, had contradictory effects in the Cuban Republic.[23] On the one hand, the ideal of racial brotherhood gave critics language with which to condemn the state for not living up to its ideals. On the other hand, the idea of Cuba as "raceless" had a silencing effect, as it posited racial animosity as a thing of the past, born of the now-overcome conditions of Spanish colonialism and slavery. "Stirring up" racial tensions was, in this interpretation, anathema to what it meant to be Cuban.[24]

When the Garvey moment was taking off in Cuba, however, Black organizers had more to worry about than rhetoric and ideology. Weighing heavy on their minds, especially in Oriente, was the very real threat of racial violence. Less than a decade earlier, the Cuban state had massacred thousands of Black Cubans in the east, the vast majority of whom were unarmed civilians, in an event that came to be known as the "race war" of 1912. In the early 1900s, Afro-Cubans were frustrated by unmet independence-era promises to end racial discrimination. They were excluded from unions and underrepresented in public-sector positions, like teachers and soldiers. Adding insult to injury, private employers often preferred immigrants from Spain—the former colonizer—to Black independence veterans who had fought to liberate the country. In Oriente, their discontent was especially acute, as foreign companies pushed Black landholders off their properties. Afro-Cuban participation in the 1906 Liberal Party revolt did not improve matters. Disillusioned by mainstream politics, Black independence veterans, led by a former Liberal Party leader named Evaristo Estenoz, established the Partido Independiente de Color (PIC) in 1908. The party called for access to employment, education, and land, and for hiring preferences for Cubans over foreigners. By 1910, the PIC had municipal committees across the island, thanks to its newspaper *Previsión*. Predictably, PIC opponents and the Liberal government of President José Miguel Gómez branded the group "racist" and moved to suppress the party. Afro-Cuban senator Martín Morúa Delgado led the passage of a law prohibiting political parties composed of a single race, effectively outlawing the PIC.[25]

In response the outlawing of their association, PIC leaders launched an armed protest of a few hundred men in Oriente on May 20, 1912, the tenth anniversary of Cuban independence, calling for the repeal of the Morúa law in time for elections. Newspapers depicted the *independistas* as practitioners of witchcraft threating white women and launching a race war. The PIC protest—a standard maneuver for aggrieved political parties in republican Cuba (after all, the governing Liberal Party had led an armed revolt just a few years earlier)—was met with the full force of the Cuban state. Constitutional rights were suspended in Oriente, over 4,000 soldiers mobilized, and arms distributed to white militias. The United States landed the Marines to protect foreign properties and assembled a naval force in Cuban waters. The presence of US soldiers freed up the Rural Guard to suppress the rebellion, and it encouraged President José Miguel Gómez to demonstrate that his administration could take care of matters on its own and avoid another US intervention.

The "race war" that the government accused the PIC of fomenting actually came to pass with the brutal suppression of the group. Oriente was the site of a bloodbath in which the Rural Guard and white militias indiscriminately attacked Afro-Cubans, including women and children, regardless of any known or suspected affiliation with the PIC. Reports of summary executions and the slaughter of prisoners were common. Estenoz and another prominent PIC leader, Pedro Ivonet, were killed and their bodies publicly displayed. Estimates range from 3,000 to more than 6,000 murdered, far exceeding the few hundred who participated in the rebellion. Even though the PIC was thoroughly squashed, the Cuban state continued repressing Afro-Cubans after the violence subsided. Afro-Cubans remained in prison without charge, and in Oriente, site of the worst violence, Black civilians continued to be arrested on the mere suspicion of sympathizing with the PIC. Despite calls for amnesty, the government did not release the prisoners until years later in March of 1915.[26]

It is unlikely anyone in Cuba in the 1920s, let alone a Black organizer, was ignorant of these events. British West Indians probably had also heard of a 1917 massacre at the Central Jobabo in Camagüey.[27] In the midst of another political rebellion, this time led by now-former President Gómez (who had squashed the PIC's revolt) army soldiers entered Jobabo on April 4, 1917, and began harassing Afro-Caribbean braceros. The next day, soldiers executed several Antillano men in Jobabo, killed two more in a neighboring town, and shot yet another on the road nearby. Information circulated that they had also murdered four Jamaicans at the Central Santa Lucía. At least fourteen Black immigrants were killed during this episode, though some remember the number being closer to thirty.[28] The murdered men were not affiliated with the Liberal Party or its rebellion; rather, they were victims of longstanding racism, hatred toward Black immigrants, and scapegoating of foreigners (especially Black foreigners) during times of political turbulence.

These moments of violence were potent reminders of the dangers of organizing along racial lines in Cuba. UNIA members had to tread carefully, and they knew it. Yet, despite living in a state of economic precarity, under the thumb of monopolistic companies, and facing the ever-present threat of violence, Afro-Caribbean immigrants and their Cuban allies in northern Oriente managed to preserve and expand their organization against the odds. In this way, the Garvey movement was "both a product and a catalyst" of the diasporic consciousness generated by migration in the world of US empire.[29]

Members used the UNIA to build a place for their community in northern Oriente, counteract Cuban hostility to Black foreigners, and even to secure a degree of protection from state violence. In so doing, they made northeastern Cuba a leading region in the global Garvey movement, which in turn placed them front and center in a wider world of diasporic political engagement.

Rise of the Garvey Movement in Eastern Cuba

In 1914, Marcus Garvey founded the Universal Negro Improvement Association in his native Jamaica, and three years later, he moved the organization to Harlem. The association spread in Cuba along with readership of the *Negro World*, disseminated by migrants and merchant mariners. The first UNIA local chapters, known as "divisions," in Cuba opened in late 1919, and three delegates from Cuba attended the first UNIA international convention in August of 1920, two of whom were from United Fruit territory. Interest in the organization's shipping company, the Black Star Line, and in the speaking engagements of UNIA high officials touring the island in 1920–1921 boosted the organization's popularity in these early years.[30]

While its particular character varied from place to place, a few general principles characterized the UNIA and are captured in the association's name. First, Garvey's *universal* message promoted Black unity across differences of origin, class, and color. The movement strongly discouraged insular chauvinism and colorism, both of which Garvey had experienced during his early sojourns among West Indian communities in Costa Rica and Panama. Second, as a *Negro* association, the UNIA promoted race consciousness and Black uplift. Garveyites prioritized racial solidarity (as opposed to the class solidarity promoted by Marxists) in their organizing efforts and championed race pride. Finally, the UNIA was an *improvement association*, part of a panoply of Black mutual aid associations, masonic lodges, temples, churches, and scouting troops working across the African diaspora to "uplift the race" in the early-to-mid-twentieth century.[31] Garvey's movement is also remembered as a "Back to Africa" campaign—and the UNIA's program included a plan to establish a base in Liberia—but in the greater Caribbean, emigration was not central to the UNIA program. Rather, a "free and redeemed Africa" was more of a distant objective, to be achieved through generations of struggle.[32]

In 1920, UNIA divisions opened in Havana, Santiago de Cuba, and several export towns, including Banes.[33] By the early 1920s, Cuba had fifty-two divisions, more than any country besides the United States and more than any US state except Louisiana.[34] British West Indian migration was essential to the expansion of Garveyism, and the Garvey movement was an essential component of British West Indian life overseas.[35] Preeminent scholar of Garveyism, Robert Hill writes, "Without the emigrant base, the Garvey movement would never have arisen and flourished to the extent that it did. The two were symbiotic. . . ."[36] The interwar years were a highpoint for British West Indian civic organizing at home and in the diaspora, and the UNIA harnessed that enthusiasm in a reliable, portable form that migrants could take with them as they traveled. In Cuba, the organization became a means of building social capital in new and unfamiliar places. Members often reported arriving in town not knowing a soul but carrying a UNIA membership card.[37] Unlike other major destinations of British West Indian migration, such as Panama and Costa Rica, Cuba had no newspaper specifically geared toward a British West Indian readership, making the *Negro World* all the more essential to Black speakers of English on the island and further boosting the popularity of the organization.[38] Readers in Cuba often sent money to the parent body, asking for copies of the paper, the spread of which generated further interest in the association.[39]

The association's Cuban base of operations was the mill towns of northern Oriente where Antillanos had migrated to labor in the sugar industry. The United Fruit towns Banes and Preston both had UNIA divisions in early 1921, as did the town of Guaro near the company's cane fields. Other divisions were located in the Cuban American Sugar Company (CASC)-dominated city of Puerto Padre and near their Chaparra and Delicias mills, the Cuba Cane Company's largest mill at Manatí, and the Antilla Sugar Company's Tacajó and San Germán mills, to name but a few. The association between the UNIA and company towns in eastern Cuba was so close that the UNIA's High Commissioner to Cuba, Eduardo Morales, made a point of noting that the Antilla division's situation was exceptional; Morales explained, "you in Antilla have all the opportunities to work owing to the fact that you are on a governmental spot . . ."[40] In other words, while most UNIA chapters operated simultaneously in two jurisdictions—that of the Cuban state and that of the company—Antilla's Garveyites only had to contend with only one.

Banes hosted one of the strongest UNIA divisions in the Caribbean, widely recognized as a regional leader. Garvey himself called Banes a "great stronghold" of the movement, and Chaplain General McGuire referred to Division #52 as the "model division in Cuba," once remarking that when "he is in Liberty Hall at Banes, he feels as if he is in Liberty Hall, New York."[41] Local observers also commented on Division #52's strength, including a UNIA representative from nearby Cayo Mambí who referred to the Banes branch as "the beacon light of all divisions on Cuba."[42] Division #52 maintained high membership numbers throughout the 1920s. They built their own Liberty

Hall in December of 1920 and, just a few months later, increased its seating capacity from 300 to 500.[43] At its height, the Division claimed as many as 940 members, rivaling chapters in US cities.[44] A regional leader, Division #52 hosted a meeting of *oriental* Garveyites in 1923, calling on all delegates to devise "plans for closer relationship among divisions" and invited representatives from Santiago, Guantánamo, Miranda, Cueto, Cayo Mambí, Antilla, and San Gerónimo.[45]

Northern Oriente was an essential stop for UNIA high officials drumming up support for the organization. Chaplain General McGuire spent January and February of 1921 traveling across Cuba and, in northern Oriente, he visited Puerto Padre, Preston, Banes, and several other mill towns.[46] Between mid-May and mid-July that year, McGuire completed a second, two-month tour of Cuba. He sailed in and out of Antilla—not Havana—and traveled widely in the east. While the Chaplain General visited Havana Province for four days, he stayed on the northeastern coast for over twenty-six days, spending twelve nights in United Fruit's territory alone.[47] Touring UNIA leaders generated considerable enthusiasm for the organization, and members frequently commented that high-profile visits had moved them to join. At a 1921 farewell meeting for Harold Collins and other delegates heading to the New York convention, a woman named Catherine Richards explained that she was drawn to the UNIA after hearing McGuire speak in Guantánamo.[48] Of McGuire's speeches in Banes, a reporter commented, "He has electrified and stimulated us and we are going to show it. Just watch us grow."[49]

In March 1921, Marcus Garvey himself traveled through northeastern Cuba. Having begun his tour in Havana, he soon headed east, visiting Santiago, followed by the northern coasts of Camagüey and Oriente, where he stopped in Morón, Nuevitas, Preston, Banes, and Antilla before heading to port cities of the east and sailing for Jamaica. To get to Banes, Garvey and his personal secretary took a special rail car to the terminus at Dumois and were then met by a contingent of UNIA officers who led a motorcade into town. Division #52 had rented out the Teatro Heredia, the town's largest venue, because their Liberty Hall could not hold the expected crowd. After a formal procession, opening songs, and no fewer than a dozen presentations, Garvey spoke about the interconnected African diaspora—"the population of Negroes everywhere"—and the goals of the UNIA. He suffered from a cold the next day, and Anita Collins directed the Black Cross Nurses in caring for the leader. Garvey claimed to have sold thousands of dollars of Black Star Line stock and collected hundreds in entrance fees during his stay in Banes.[50]

From mid-1921 to mid-1922, UNIA High Commissioner Eduardo Morales traveled across the island, spoke at UNIA meetings, and opened new divisions. With an international and bilingual background, Morales was born in Cuba but raised in Panama, where he became a labor organizer and a UNIA leader before moving back to Cuba. By May 1922, he had visited *oriental* mill towns several times.[51] In June, Morales submitted to the *Negro World* a description of Cuba's geography, dwelling especially on the Province of Oriente which, he claimed, was three times the size of Jamaica.[52] He treated Banes as a home-base of sorts, returning frequently to town, corresponding regularly with local members, and dubbing Division #52 the "shining star of the other divisions throughout Cuba."[53]

Lesser-known field organizers also helped spread the UNIA across Cuba. Two such men, Samuel P. Radway and Dave Davidson, opened chapters in Costa Rica and Panama before moving onto Cuba, where they focused on the eastern part of the island.[54] In February 1921, the pair visited Jobabo, where British West Indians were massacred just four years earlier. They were careful to first secure permission for a meeting from the Rural Guard and the town magistrate. With permission in hand, they posted placards in Spanish and English and spread word about an informational meeting. At 7:30 p.m., they claimed, they had gathered over 500 "Cubans, Haytians, and other West Indians, and a few Canadians" to whom they explained the aims and objectives of the UNIA in Spanish and in English and discussed the history of the African continent. The whole the process was repeated the following day.[55]

Here we see both the pragmatism of the organizers and the cosmopolitan appeal of the Garvey movement; after obtaining permission to operate, Radway and Davidson gathered individuals of many nationalities and discussed—in two languages—African history. They offered a redemptive vision of Black solidarity, specifically addressing the migrant experience. Looking ahead, Davidson said, Black women and men would not travel the world as migrants in search of work, but as well-heeled tourists traveling aboard Black-owned ships. Over the course of those two days, new members enrolled, a division was formed, and officers were elected.[56] On at least one occasion, Garvey attempted to suppress Radway and Davidson's activities, but they carried on anyway, suggesting that organizers in the field could and did act independently of Harlem headquarters.[57] In other words, the UNIA's expansion was not a product of dictates from Harlem; the grassroots movement also spread through the enthusiasm of local residents.

Garveyites based in northern Oriente, especially Banes, were key figures within the international association. Men from United Fruit's zone represented half or more of the delegates from Cuba at the UNIA's first three international conventions.[58] From his base in Banes, Arnold Cummings in particular traveled widely and frequently in service of the organization. Harlem headquarters relied on his leadership not just in Cuba but also internationally.[59] Jamaican by birth, he had become a "heavy stockholder in the Black Star Line and a liberal purchaser for the Liberian Construction Loan" by the late 1920s. He was known as a UNIA "Deputy of Cuba" and served as personal secretary to UNIA Chaplain General McGuire during his tours of the island.[60] McGuire sometimes tasked Cummings with re-organizing divisions that had suffered from mismanagement.[61] Cummings also joined Garvey for part of his Cuban travels and spoke at several events with the president general.[62] He was such a successful UNIA organizer that the parent body sent Cummings on multiple recruiting tours in the United States, beginning in 1920.[63] In 1922, he was in Winston-Salem, where he stayed at least four months delivering speeches about the association.[64] Based not in Harlem but in Banes and traveling widely, Cummings stayed active in the association through the decade.

In short, UNIA divisions in northeastern Cuba's sugar towns figured prominently in the global Garvey movement, not just as spaces where the movement was immensely popular, but as home to regional and international leaders of the association. Officers from Division #52 in Banes—and not, say, Havana or Santiago—represented Cuba at the international conventions, and Harlem sent men like Cummings on recruiting tours in the Unites States. Garveyites in northern Oriente not only *joined* the transnational uplift association from their "outpost" in eastern Cuba, but they also *led* the movement from a nexus of global trade, labor migration, and popular internationalism. In so doing, they expanded an organization that met their specific needs as Black men and women building and sustaining community in sites of economic uncertainty and imperialism.

UNIA Community Life

For Garveyites in northern Oriente, the UNIA was a crucial—if not the most important—mainstay of community life. At once a mutual aid society, a religious organization, and a racial-uplift association, the UNIA offered social capital and community to Antillanos on the move throughout the greater Caribbean. As a mutual aid society, UNIA divisions collected dues toward sickness support and burial.[65] In Antilla, the vice president was assigned the job of "visiting sick, isolated, and unemployed members" as well members who "need any manner of social support." The organization's mission also explicitly entailed helping readers stay abreast of global events; Antilla's UNIA maintained a lending library which collected "books, articles, newspapers and similar items."[66] Care for the sick, death benefits, and libraries were services that sugar companies and the Cuban state certainly did not provide, making the UNIA's work all the more essential.

Christianity was an essential component of the UNIA uplift agenda, and meetings entailed opening and closing prayers, hymns, and sermons. Together, Black churches and the Garvey movement provided spiritual sustenance for British West Indians away from home. Local ministers often supported the UNIA, as when "Brother J.T. Parris and his committee of the church were . . . very instrumental" in helping get the UNIA division sorted out with local company and state authorities at the Central Manatí.[67] In another example, when president of the Cayo Mambí division, R. A. Bennett, traveled 120 kilometers west to Banes, local UNIA officers made sure his first stop was the Baptist Church. That Sunday, Reverend H. Thompson's sermon addressed the prodigal son, but rather than interpret the parable as about being "lost and found," he related the story to migration; Thomson asked parishioners, "What man of good character . . . would covet the reception of a brother who was stranded in a foreign land?"[68]

As Randall Burkett has argued, the Garvey movement was a "civil religion" in that it was a nationalist ideology with a sense of divine mission, which Giovannetti-Torres argues was certainly the case in Cuba.[69] Indeed, religiosity was a major component of the UNIA's appeal. Chaplain General McGuire's two tours in 1921 gave the organization a significant boost on the island and may have been even more popular than Garvey's visits. (Garvey admitted as much, explaining that he often arrived in Cuban towns only to find that McGuire had left few funds to collect.[70]) McGuire's speeches in Cuba highlighted the divine nature of the UNIA's mission. In Banes he offered "A New Creed for a New Negro," which, according to a *Negro World* report, he summarized as "I believe in God, my father, and in the Hon. Marcus Garvey as my leader; the Black Star Line as the ark of safety and the land of Africa my home."[71] As interviews conducted later revealed, British West Indians in Cuba were religious, but not dogmatically attached to any particular denomination.[72] In this way, the religious nature of the Garvey movement did not contradict religious devotion to a specific congregation or church. Rather, the line between the UNIA as a civic organization and religious institutions would have been a blurry one, if it existed at all in the eyes of UNIA members.

In fact, the UNIA *was* a church to many of its members. In Cuba, McGuire "pinned medals of African redemption" on members in one moment and baptized babies into the organization the next.[73] According to the UNIA charter, every division was required to have a chaplain who served the spiritual needs of its members. The UNIA meeting place, Liberty Hall, hosted weddings, as when Thomas Campbell and Bonita Scarlet were married in Preston on January 23, 1921.[74] UNIA members were also buried under the UNIA flag of red, green, and black at funerals presided over by UNIA chaplains. UNIA Chaplain Robert Blake oversaw the funeral of Beatrice Bradshaw, who died leaving behind a husband and five children, including a days-old infant. Bradshaw's death and funeral illustrate poignantly the UNIA's role in sustaining the Banes community during times of hardship.[75]

Another mainstay of life in the Garvey movement was its many auxiliary groups. Banes Division #52's subgroups included the African Legions, a men's group that "maintained order within the society" and practiced "military skill and discipline"; the Motor Corps who provided instruction in the maintenance of automotive vehicles and driving lessons; a band, a choir; and boy scouts. Banes Garveyites had plans to organize a "juvenile dime bank" to "encourage the spirit of saving among our children" and a medical society to care for the sick.[76] Other UNIA divisions worked to establish grocery stores and health clinics, and many ran Sunday schools and day schools.[77] For women, the principle means of affiliation was with the Black Cross Nurses, who cared for the sick, provided relief during emergencies, and educated the public in first aid, sanitation, and disease prevention. Whether in Harlem, Detroit, New Orleans, or Limón, Panama, the nurses were famous for their sharp uniforms, orderly participation in parades, and fundraising. Reports from Cuba repeatedly emphasized the important role of this women's group, and Garvey himself praised the well-run Black Cross Nurses of Banes, founded by Anita Collins.[78]

Women Garveyites in Cuba, however, were not relegated to the Black Cross Nurses or limited leadership positions like "Ladies' President" or "Ladies' Secretary," as was common in the US. Rather, they were integrated into the main leadership structures of local branches. Women performed the work of record keeping, correspondence with Cuban officials and UNIA headquarters, and planning meetings. Marc McLeod writes "women tended to form the backbone of UNIA branches in the sugar mill towns, as they provided a permanent, stable presence throughout the year, especially when many men were away working the sugar zafra."[79] Women were respected leaders in Cuban branches of the UNIA, with some divisions founded by women and many a mass meeting run by a "mistress of ceremonies."[80] In Guantánamo, Theodora Thomas was credited with establishing the local UNIA branch. She "came from across the seas and preached the doctrine of the U.N.I.A. and A.C.L. on the streets and corners" until there was enough interest to start a division.[81] On Oriente's northern coast, women served as chairpersons of mass meetings, program organizers, secretaries, and *Negro World* reporters.[82] Banes's Jemima Kelso stands out. Initially, she served as the assistant secretary of the Ladies' Division, but in 1921, she ran for the position of executive secretary. Up against two men, Kelso received the overwhelming majority of votes (she earned 116 against 8 for one candidate and 32 for the other) and was duly installed in the position.[83] Kelso often contributed reports on Division #52's progress to the *Negro World* and oversaw her division's registration with the Cuban registry of associations in 1922.[84] She corresponded regularly with High Commissioner Morales, whom Division #52 supported financially during his tour of the island.[85]

For Garveyite women, the organization offered paths to leadership that were otherwise closed to them in Cuban society.[86] UNIA officers—in positions like president, vice president, secretary, or treasurer—were respected members of the community, and many rose to local prominence through the association. While the association promoted Victorian ideals of women as helpmates and mothers, in practice women developed leadership experience through the UNIA and became influential public figures in their own rights, as Barbara Bair and Honor Ford-Smith have explained.[87] Ford-Smith writes of Jamaica, "Garveyite women both participated in and led a movement which drew women out of the home and immersed them in public life."[88] Bair argues that leading Garveyite women created "modified positions of authority for themselves," thereby challenging limited notions of womanhood. In Bair's widely cited article on the subject, she points to Ethel Collins as a "woman who developed organizational skills and rose within the movement, networking with other women and men and participating in, or personally shaping, some of the key elements in the organization's history." Ethel Collins was none other than the sister of Banes's Harold Collins.[89]

Community life in the Garvey movement had its own geographical center, Liberty Hall, and calendar. In Cuba's smaller divisions, Liberty Hall could be the home of a prominent member or "no more than a selected spot of ground with benches arranged out in the open air," as McGuire reported.[90] Some divisions met in rented or borrowed spaces, such as a schoolhouse, while a select few managed to secure a proper meeting hall or theater, as did Banes Division #52.[91] Meetings took place on Wednesday and Sunday evenings, and entailed prayers, speeches, musical performances, and singing—especially the UNIA's official song, the Ethiopian National Anthem, and religious hymns. The Garveyite calendar was filled with parades and dances on important religious holidays and secular dates, such as Cuba's Independence Day, Garvey Day, and the British Empire's Emancipation Day.

One of the most fundamental tasks of the Garvey movement in Cuba was showcasing Black respectability. Hostility to Black immigrants was often expressed as fear of rebellion, disease, and witchcraft. Many Cubans believed

Black immigrants introduced contagious diseases to the island.[92] Stereotypes about witchcraft-practicing immigrants circulated widely, with sensationalist headlines like "Savage Haitian Murders a Boy and Eats His Body" and "Haitians Caught in Grotesque Witchcraft Practices" appearing in Cuban newspapers.[93] In the face of such stereotypes, UNIA rules and regulations in Cuba required that the organization be one of "polite society." Selling and drinking alcohol was prohibited in Liberty Halls, and violators were expelled. Seven or more people could form a new division, but "these people have to be sufficiently educated and respected in order to command the attention of the other respected and educated members of their community."[94] During his travels, Commissioner Morales exhorted UNIA members "to maintain the highest order of respectability."[95]

While behaving respectably was important in and of itself, so too was ensuring that the wider community noticed. The formal pageantry of mass meetings, religious services, parades, and holiday events were means to display Christianity, erudition, and respectability for the wider republic. Garveyites in Cuba often commented on the reception of UNIA activities, especially members of Banes Division #52. Of a parade held in honor of Chaplain General McGuire's visit, Robert Blake wrote, "The spectacle was inspiring and the Division has again scored another point in the estimation of the public."[96] Another Banes reporter noted of a Mother's Day celebration, "the hall was comfortably filled with the most influential element of this municipality."[97] In short, Harold and Anita Collins's public lectures on hygiene and disease prevention, Christian Sunday schools, orderly parades, and the affiliation of prominent community members all flew in the face of stereotypes about Black immigrants as diseased and illiterate practitioners of witchcraft. These performances left their mark in the minds of observers in eastern Cuba, as memories of "Jamaican" immigrants often commented on their parades.

The UNIA's membership composition varied from place to place. In northern Oriente, the officer corps were largely skilled workers, domestic servants, tradespeople, and professionals living in the Antillano neighborhoods of company towns. The Banes UNIA was led by independent tradesmen and artisans (such as tailors or watchmakers) and skilled workers laboring for United Fruit in positions such as coal stoker, train conductor, driver, mechanic, and bricklayer. Some UNIA officers in Banes worked in the professions. John A. James was a teacher who served as a UNIA officer until 1937, and Harold Collins was a pharmacist. Cummings appears in the records as an "agent," likely a reference to selling shares in the Black Star Line, and was later listed as a bookseller.[98] Sometimes president and sometimes chaplain, Robert S. F. Blake, a carpenter, wrote to the *Negro World* in 1923, "In this division you will find men in all walks of life, men of the medical profession, engineers, tradesmen, mechanics, and others, all united, standing firm, with one watch-word 'a new and redeemed Africa.'"[99] Women officers were, with few exceptions, domestic servants in the homes of North American managers.[100] Rank-and-file members in eastern sugar towns were most often sugar factory and field workers. The Jobabo Division that Radway and Davidson established in early 1921 was composed of field workers. Reports to the *Negro World* often noted that male members had left town in search of work, indicating manual labor given the seasonal nature of the sugar economy.[101] Upon his return to New York, Chaplain General McGuire noted the humble conditions of most UNIA members in Cuba, remarking "most of them live and work on estates, with very few having houses of their own."[102]

The UNIA in Cuba was not restricted to British West Indian immigrants, but the extent to which Afro-Cubans were drawn to the Garvey movement has been difficult for historians to measure. Aline Helg and others have suggested that the massacre of 1912 effectively ended race-based mobilizing in Cuba.[103] Sandra Estévez Rivero argues that memories of 1912 limited the UNIA's appeal among Afro-Cubans, especially in Oriente where the violence of that year had been concentrated.[104] While some Cubans surely feared violent reprisal, others simply disagreed with the race-first premise of the movement. In March of 1921, Marcus Garvey met with Miguel Ángel Céspedes, president of the Club Atenas, an Afro-Cuban society in Havana. Regarding Garvey's Back-to-Africa program, Céspedes told Garvey that Black Cubans "cannot conceive of having a motherland other than Cuba."[105] Some have concluded that this exchange suggests that the UNIA fundamentally conflicted with nationalist ideologies of *cubanidad,* and Cubans would not support the UNIA.[106]

Political organizing exclusively focused on race was indeed rare in Cuba after 1912. As Melina Pappademos, Alejandro de la Fuente, and Takkara Brunson have demonstrated, Afro-Cubans mobilized around a wide range of political, ideological, gender, and social circumstances that included—but were not limited to—race. This does not mean, however, that Black racial consciousness disappeared in 1912. A robust collection of Black associations remained active through the republican period.[107] Moving beyond Garvey's encounter with Céspedes, historians—especially Marc McLeod and Frank Guridy—have demonstrated that Afro-Cubans did in fact join the UNIA in significant numbers. Guridy argues that the movement's embodied performances of diasporic belonging—including parades, uniform wearing, and mass meetings featuring music and elocution—facilitated the "UNIA's appeal across linguistic and cultural differences."[108]

For their part, local UNIA organizers were acutely aware of Black Cuban patriotism and of the dangers of racial organizing on the island. They largely avoided the appearance of political entanglements and violations of the Morúa law, which prohibited political groups "exclusively made up of individuals of one race or color" and was still on the books in the 1920s.[109] The most obvious mechanism for compliance was simply omitting mention of race from the association's title, which a handful of divisions did. When the Havana division registered with the Cuban state, its title was "Universal Improvement Association and Communities League" rather than "Universal *Negro* Improvement Association and *African* Communities League." On correspondences over minor matters (a change of address, for instance) written on the parent body's letterhead, local officers simply drew a line through the words "Negro" and "Africa," leaving them plainly visible to readers.[110]

With such precautions in place, international and local leaders aimed to recruit Cubans to the cause. Encouraged by British West Indians in Cuba, the *Negro World* launched a Spanish section of the paper.[111] The parent body also named a Black Star Line ship after Afro-Cuban Independence hero, Antonio Maceo. Cubans did formally enroll and lead the uplift association, especially in Cuba's larger cities and towns. Early on, Havana's Division #24 was run by influential Afro-Cubans. The Guantánamo division had many Cuban members, and its second vice president Ernest Peterson often delivered speeches in Spanish.[112] By early 1922, there were two Guantánamo divisions, Spanish-speaking and English-speaking.[113] Both worked closely with the Afro-Cuban *sociedad*, Club Moncada, which hosted Garvey during his stay in town.[114] In 1927, when international UNIA organizer and fundraiser Henrietta Vinton Davis visited Cuba, Santiago's Garveyites were also divided into two sections, known locally as the "English-speaking division" and the "Spanish-speaking division," which co-hosted a mass meeting in her honor.[115] Similarly, in central Cuba, close to Santa Clara, the Remedios division had parallel bodies, a Cuban section and an English-speaking section.[116] These moments of cooperation and separation into language-based sections suggest that the relative absence of Afro-Cubans Garveyites in the archival record might have less to do with fundamentally incompatible notions of racial belonging than with practical matters such as language barriers.

In the sugar towns of Oriente, British West Indians mainly led the movement, but they put forth an inclusive vision of racial uplift and connected with the wider Cuban public. In recognition of Cuban patriotism, UNIA meetings almost always entailed singing the Cuban National Anthem and use of the Cuban flag.[117] Reports to the *Negro World* often mentioned speeches in Spanish and Cubans in the audiences of meetings.[118] In July of 1921, at the Río Cauto mill a mass meeting included "a great crowd of Cubans" prompting the chairman to address the crowd in Spanish, explaining that it is "not a partial movement; it involves the Cuban Negroes, as well as the American, Jamaican and all the Negroes existing in the world," emphasizing the cosmopolitan spirit of the organization.[119] The chairman's impromptu speech highlights the ways Garveyites bridged national divides and constructed a diasporic vision from the sugar towns of eastern Cuba.

Eduardo Morales, high commissioner to Cuba, was particularly effective at recruiting Cubans to the cause in the eastern part of the island. He often addressed audiences in Spanish, as he did in the CASC town of Puerto Padre, where he "delivered several speeches in Spanish and captivated the Cuban element in the population," and in Banes.[120] In November of 1921, there was a commotion outside of a meeting in Banes, and "when we looked out to see, some thirty Cubans came rushing in to hear their friend Mr. Moralis [sic], who in his fine style did entertain them to the best." At the same meeting, a Cuban member from Preston, Aurelio de Lara, addressed the audience in his native tongue "and was applauded by all for his illustrious manner," suggesting that Cubans, too, valued the elocution for which the association had become famous.[121]

"Reyita" de los Reyes Castillo Bueno remembered well the Jamaican Molvaina Grand ("Miss Molly") and her husband Charles Clark, who led the Cueto UNIA division and who hosted meetings in their home. Castillo connected Clark's speeches about the UNIA's mission to be "one big family" to her grandmother's recollections of the Kingdom of Congo. As a teenager, she helped recruit fifty or so Cubans who were active in the Cueto division. Castillo described UNIA life in town as full of meetings, parties, and fundraising fairs, where food, candies, and nonalcoholic drinks were sold. Although Castillo herself wasn't able to, many members of the local division went to hear Marcus Garvey speak during his 1921 tour, "and how happy they were when they came back to Cueto, such excitement and high hopes they brought back with them."[122] As Castillo's stories of widely attended, festive celebrations indicate, it is no simple feat to measure Afro-Cuban participation in the UNIA; paying one's monthly dues and attending Sunday night meetings were not the only ways individuals connected to the movement.

In order to keep the organization afloat amid Cuba's restrictive environment around race, Garveyites carefully distinguished between political interference and the religious, entrepreneurial, and respectable work of racial uplift. This distinction—as well as the UNIA's work supporting the local community—was especially important when Cuba entered into an economic crisis in 1921. At that time, Morales, more than anyone else, helped the movement thread the needle of surviving as a Black-uplift organization amid dark economic times and increasing attention from authorities.

"Putting the Program Over" during Cuba's 1921 Crisis

No sooner had the UNIA established a firm foothold in Cuba than the economy collapsed. The US government had tightly controlled wartime sugar prices, but when those restrictions were lifted after the war and refiners were free to purchase on the open market, sugar prices had soared. During Cuba's "Dance of the Millions," the cost of sugar rose from 6.5 cents per pound in September 1919 to a high of 22.5 cents in May 1920. Owners upgraded mills, expanded production, and hired more workers, taking on significant debt with the promise of continued prosperity. These boom times were short lived, however, as Europeans resumed beet-sugar production and cane overproduction threatened global prices. In mid-1920, the bubble burst, and prices plummeted, landing at 3.75 cents by Christmas of 1920 and causing a run on banks. To compensate, mill owners initially increased production, a decision that forestalled for a few months the brunt of the disaster. The 1920–1921 sugar harvest was the second biggest in Cuba's history at just under four million tons.[123] But after the harvest of 1921, the situation was grim and the picture clear: crisis had set in. US banks took over mills with owners who could not pay boom-era debts, further consolidating the US hold on the Cuban sugar industry. The National City Bank of New York acquired the mortgages and debts of some sixty mills in 1921 alone. The US and UK governments raised tariffs to protect growers at home and in their overseas territories. Colonos and mill owners cut back drastically. Sugar sat unsold in warehouses, and what to do with the massive crop became a pressing question about Cuba's economic wellbeing in the second half of 1921.[124]

By mid-1921, sugar workers found themselves in a desperate situation. Pay dropped precipitously, from a 1919 high of over 1.4 dollars per 100 *arrobas* (25,000 pounds) of cane cut to 80 cents in January 1921 and a low of 60 cents in 1922.[125] As US government reports from June and July of 1921 explained, sugar growers and mills "have discharged a large part of their laborers, and the Island is now overflowing with the unemployed. Many people are working for food alone," and "actual starvation is reported from many localities." Foreign workers were hardest hit; "thousands of these immigrants are making the greatest effort to return to their native countries but they lack sufficient funds to pay their passage."[126] British West Indian and Haitian field hands found themselves out of work and hungry. Many traveled to eastern ports, often on foot, in search of passage home. They encountered hostility from similarly destitute Cubans, price gouging from shopkeepers, and abuse from the Rural Guard and police.

In August 1921, a critic of the Garvey movement following the news in Cuba from Panama condemned the UNIA. He contrasted upbeat *Negro World* accounts of UNIA fundraising successes in Cuba with *Kingston Gleaner* reports of Jamaicans stranded on the island without work or food. The writer pointed out that Garvey boasted of McGuire having "cleaned up all of Cuba and left not even a brass nickel there" around the same time that the Jamaican paper reported, "there are not only thousands of Jamaicans out of work [in Cuba] but large numbers of them are threatened with starvation and other hardships."[127] The critic suggests that Garvey and his fellow UNIA leaders were charlatans who skimmed resources from a desperate population. His criticism raises a number of questions, especially what role the UNIA played in the lives of Garveyites in Cuba and how the movement, which remained strong until the end of the decade, managed to weather this economic storm. Giovannetti-Torres has pointed out that UNIA high officials in Harlem—many of whom visited Cuba in 1921—did not make any formal statement about the plight of Afro-Caribbean workers on the island.[128] Had the critic in Panama known about the welcome gala for Anita and Harold Collins in Banes that September, in which attendees donned white gloves and taffeta dresses, he certainly would have condemned local leaders in addition to Harlem officials. Later, Cuban communists would agree that the UNIA failed to serve the real needs of its members. In 1929, Sandalio Junco, a prominent Afro-Cuban communist claimed that Garveyism—and its entrepreneurial message—offered false hopes of African redemption and only served to divide and distract the working classes.[129] Yet closer examination reveals significant distinctions between worker experiences in different locations. In fact, in some cases, the association actually proved useful to both its members in company towns and powerful employers during times of hardship, which helps explain the Garvey movement's enduring strength in Cuba.

In some ways, the critic in Panama exaggerated the contrasts between UNIA fundraising and Antillano destitution by overlooking particulars of place and time. The worst of the economic crisis came later to the towns run by US corporations with enough capital to keep grinding cane, such as those of northern Oriente. The critic in Panama contrasted newspaper accounts from July 1921, but Garvey's July speech described his travels in March, when the island was still in the midst of grinding the massive 1920–1921 crop. Chaplain General McGuire's second fundraising tour lasted well into July, but he spent most of that month in the large mill towns of northern Oriente, where several mills continued griding through June and July—one as late as November. In fact, on September 9, the Central Delicias, home to a robust UNIA division, had "finished the most colossal cane sugar crop that has ever been recorded," according to a trade journal.[130] United Fruit's Boston mill ground through the end of September, and Preston ground through mid-October, also finishing with the largest crop in the mill's history.[131] Workers for these vertically integrated US sugar corporations were in a better position than their counterparts working for smaller colonos, many of whom simply fired laborers and closed commissaries, even though workers had often been paid in company-store credit. Many of these smaller properties transferred from Cuban to US hands during the crash. In other words, working for a vertically integrated US firm insulated employees from the worst of the crisis, at least for a time.

When hard times hit all of Cuba (including the colossal mills of northern Oriente), the UNIA remained strong—and even expanded—in towns like Banes and Puerto Padre. The association thrived in the early 1920s precisely because it helped members weather the storm. Additionally, Garveyites in northern Oriente took great pains to protect their association and a pursued pragmatic approach in their dealings with company and state to keep the organization running. For their part, company administrators recognized that the UNIA was extremely popular. For them and even some Cuban politicians, maintaining good relations with the UNIA could prove useful.

Historians have long attempted to characterize the ideological nature of the Garvey movement. Was it a working-class or bourgeoisie affair? Radical or accommodationist? In his account of the global Garvey movement Adam Ewing writes, "Garveyism was radical in some moments and reactionary in others, strident in some places and cautious in others."[132] The UNIA was associated with labor radicalism in its early years when Socialist W. A. Domingo edited the *Negro World* and ran articles calling for armed resistance in the aftermath of race riots in the US.[133] In 1919, Garveyites were involved in labor strikes in Trinidad and were among the leadership of the island's most important labor organization, the Trinidad Workingmen's Association.[134] In 1920, the UNIA and a US-based labor union co-organized a strike in the Panama Canal Zone, with none other than Eduardo Morales at the helm.[135]

In late 1919, however, a change in approach was beginning. At that time, United Fruit managers in Central America worried about a visit from UNIA international organizer Henrietta Vinton Davis. "She has only to lift her finger when she gets here to start trouble that might take months to smooth over," claimed one official, indicating how popular the organization was and how much United Fruit feared its influence.[136] While company administrators weighed the pros and cons of attempting to suppress the organization, representatives from the Black Star Line reassured them that the UNIA "will in no way create disturbances or interfere with the Company's business."[137] After all, an administrator reported, "the main object [of their trip] is the sale of stock. Stock can only be sold to those who are earning money."[138] United Fruit agreed to host the visitors. When Davis returned a few months later, the company went so far as to give workers the day off and offer them cheap rail transportation to hear her speak.[139] Garvey himself bragged of organizing his Central American schedule in 1921 around United Fruit's needs so that workers could have "a special pay day."[140] A United Fruit manager reported that Garvey claimed "he too is an employer of labor, understands our position, is against labor unions, and is using his best behavior to get the negro race to work and better themselves through work."[141] During his travels, Garvey emphasized that he had no wish to disrupt local governments. Hill calls Garvey's 1921 position a "retreat from radicalism," as the leader was not interested in picking fights with state authorities or major employers. The Black Star Line's financial troubles and the fact that the US State Department repeatedly refused to grant Garvey a re-entry visa were powerful disincentives to agitating against regional authorities.[142] Upon his arrival in Cuba in March of 1921, Garvey announced "I do not come here to interfere with the labor question or the political question where governments are concerned."[143]

In northeastern Cuba, local UNIA divisions, too, were pragmatic with authorities, a move that helped safeguard their association. In this effort, UNIA High Commissioner Morales led the way. In Panama, he had been a leader in both the UNIA and the United Brotherhood, which together led the 1920 Canal Zone strike.[144] The strike, however, was unsuccessful. Garveyism continued to thrive in Panama, but the movement avoided labor agitation thereafter.[145] Morales and his fellow-organizer William Preston Stoute left Panama for Cuba, having learned a valuable lesson: better to work with authorities in order to keep the racial-uplift organization alive than fight against them and risk having the association shut down entirely. In Cuba, Morales oversaw "efforts to have the branches registered under the laws of Cuba," an endeavor aided by support from Oriente's governor, Alfredo Lora.[146]

In June of 1921, Governor Lora appeared unexpectedly at a UNIA meeting in the provincial capital, Santiago de Cuba. According to a *Negro World* report, he had heard rumors that the UNIA was a "political organization" and that "a Cuban is identified as its leader and that he is making fiery speeches to excite the Cuban Negroes." Alarmed, he decided to see for himself. The afternoon the white governor showed up in Liberty Hall, Santiago's UNIA Lady President Clarise Walters was overseeing unpleasant business: addressing accusations of financial mismanagement against the division president. The meeting attendees swiftly changed course, welcomed the visitor, and sang the Cuban national anthem. Morales gave a short address explaining that the UNIA was "gathering under its wings the 400,000 Negroes that are scattered all over the world[,] teaching them to look upward, to take an active part in the commercial and industrial world, teaching them how to love and appreciate their own race even as the other races love and appreciate their own and finally to prepare them for the redemption of Africa, our inheritance." Evidently satisfied that the association was not provoking social or political disorder, the Governor expressed his approval, stating, "You can count on my wholehearted support." According to the report, he was "pleased to see Negroes striving for their uplift."[147]

The next day a delegation of five UNIA officials, including Morales and Walters, visited the Governor's palace, and Lora again expressed his support. Morales took the opportunity ask for written authority to conduct UNIA business. Not only was the authorization granted, but the governor also offered Morales "a police escort for his personal protection through the island and to assure the natives that authorities are in favor of the movement." (Lora invited Morales to choose the "color" of the policeman who would accompany him, but Morales astutely replied that he "had no special choice as to the color of the guard as we were not especially antagonistic to any race.") The delegation enjoyed refreshments and exchanged pleasantries, especially about the Black Star Line.[148] The governor ultimately granted the UNIA "free and unmolested doings in the Province of Oriente."[149] According to the (none too pleased) US consul in Santiago, Lora sent letters of introduction to local mayors encouraging them to work with the association.[150]

Lora's support of the UNIA is curious, and his visit to Liberty Hall reveals three important aspects of the organization's relationship with authorities. First, the exchange between Lora and UNIA officials indicates that all parties involved knew very well that Afro-Cubans feared retribution from Cuban authorities if they affiliated with the movement. Morales explained to Lora that written permission to operate would be especially useful in recruiting Afro-Cubans, "as they were afraid the authorities would misinterpret their motives and have them arrested."[151] In Cuba, the UNIA walked a thin line between the longstanding racial-uplift culture of sociedades de color and the Morúa law prohibiting race-based political parties, which Afro-Cubans had good reason to fear violating in light of the violence of 1912.

Second, as Frank Guridy has demonstrated of the late 1920s, it was Afro-Cuban participation in the UNIA that most alarmed Cuban authorities.[152] The governor himself explained that rumors of a Cuban leader "making fiery speeches to excite the Cuban Negroes" initially troubled him, yet he quickly came around to not only tolerating the association but also offering his assistance. Morales and Walters probably convinced Lora that the UNIA was committed to staying out of Cuban politics and had no intention of stirring up racial antagonism. Rather, as they must have explained, the organization's goal was Black uplift through economic development. The UNIA rulebook in Cuba clearly stated that members "have sworn to respect the rights of all humanity and the government under whose jurisdiction it falls, to not interfere in political affairs of the state, to not speak against any other race, to not concern itself with any discussion that could alter the peace, union, and harmony that must serve as the fundamental base of all well governed societies."[153] With its largely British West Indian membership, religious overtones, and commitment to staying out of local politics, the UNIA did not threaten Lora's political interests.[154]

Finally, there were political gains for Lora in cooperating with the association. Thanks to universal male suffrage, Black Cubans, in fact, did have some political influence. As Pappademos explains, "No party dared to publicly reject Black voters."[155] Lora likely saw supporting the UNIA as an opportunity to display a longstanding friendliness toward Black causes. He had fought in the War of 1895, a multiracial struggle for Cuban independence, and could now claim to be lending a hand to a widely popular Black organization in his jurisdiction. Cuban President Mario García Menocal, former manager of the CASC's Chaparra mill, had made a similar conclusion the year before when the Black Star Line's *Frederick Douglass* sailed into Havana's harbor. The captain and crew were invited to meet with García Menocal, who then asked to have his photo taken with the group.[156] Displaying friendliness toward Black causes—at least, those considered nonthreatening to Cuban political interests—was an electoral strategy for white politicians. This was especially the case in the shadow of the 1912 massacre; Liberal Party President Gómez's brutal overreaction to the PIC uprising was said to have cost his party the election that year.[157]

Securing Governor Lora's support paid off for Garveyites in northern Oriente. In 1921, company administrators at the Central Marcané—twenty-two kilometers southwest of the Nipe Bay—had granted the UNIA a building to use as a Liberty Hall, but, in July, when rumors circulated that they were "forming plots to be white people's haters," local authorities erected bureaucratic hurdles to the association's activities. Even after the magistrate received a declaration that the organization was not a "political one which is against the government," he issued so many restrictions that UNIA operations were untenable. The division's acting secretary, Theo Webley, headed to Santiago to locate Commissioner Morales.[158] When the pair returned with written authority from Lora in hand, Morales spoke with the magistrate who, in turn, promised to give the Garveyites "every protection."[159]

One can only imagine what Morales said to smooth things over with the Marcané magistrate, but the point to be made was that the UNIA had Governor Lora's permission to operate and was uninterested in political affairs. Morales repeatedly emphasized to authorities the apolitical nature of the movement, that it was not hostile to any other race, and that it promoted racial uplift through economic development. On October 30, 1921, for instance, Division 52 welcomed the Banes mayor at a mass meeting. According to Kelso's *Negro World* report, the mayor "addressed the audience in Spanish, encouraging us in the good fight, and promised his assistance in whatever lies in his power," and Morales followed with a speech in Spanish for the benefit of the mayor and Cuban members.[160] Such overtures to local officials went a long way toward enabling the long-term survival of the association.

For their part, company administrators used tolerance of and even support for the UNIA for their own ends. Just as United Fruit officials in Costa Rica concluded that the safest course of action for dealing with Davis's visit was to maintain friendly relations with the popular organization, some company administrators in eastern Cuba worked with the UNIA to build good will among workers during a time that Gillian McGillivray has called the era of the "patrons' compact." She explains that in addition to "time-honored repression" and progressivism with the building of roads and electrical supplies, administrators used patronage to "establish social peace at their mills."[161] In a manner similar to that of administrators' wives distributing meat to workers on holidays, company authorities in the mill towns of eastern Cuba often gave the UNIA a building to use as a Liberty Hall or included the organization in company events.[162] For example, when Garvey visited United Fruit territory, Division #52 officers obtained a special railcar from the company.[163] Garveyites were not unaware of the conceit and played up cordial relations with sugar companies; reports to the *Negro World* from Cuba often thanked individual administrators as a "friend of the Negro."[164]

UNIA organizers in Manatí were particularly astute at using patronage to their advantage. Part of the Czarnikow-Rionda holdings, the Central Manatí was ultimately controlled by Manuel Rionda, the "sugar Baron" whom McGillivray has described as a "super patron." Rionda liked to be seen distributing gifts and favors to workers, and employees figured out how to "work the system" playing up managers' wish to seem benevolent.[165] In April of 1921, Manatí's UNIA Division President William Bennett drafted a petition for the company administrator, informing him about the UNIA and asking for permission to hold meetings, as well as for help with the local police. The petition was submitted, and the company administrator granted all requests and added "the free use of a building for our meetings."[166] The good relationship between the UNIA and the company reached a high point at a Cuban Independence Day celebration on October 10, 1921, in the midst of Cuba's economic crisis. The company and the UNIA co-organized the town's festivities, which began with a procession through town; the municipal band led the way, followed by the UNIA officer corps, Black Cross Nurses, African Legions, and rank-and-file members who carried the Cuban and UNIA flags. In the town's Central Square, the mill administrator and other managers greeted the crowd, and the Cuban and UNIA anthems were sung. UNIA First Vice President B. B. Sims "spoke in Spanish on behalf of the association and congratulated the Cubans on their achievements and thanked the Manatí Sugar Co. for their courtesy towards us." The crowd gave three cheers for the Cuban Republic, the Cuban President, and the Manatí Sugar Company. "The cheers were retuned for Jamaica for Marcus Garvey and the UNIA." The crowd then gathered near the commissary for refreshments at the invitation of the administrator. That evening at Liberty Hall, an administrator likened the friendly relations between the company and the UNIA with those between Jamaica and the Black Cuban independence hero, Antonio Maceo, who stayed in Jamaica on several occasions. Fifteen new members were enrolled.[167] In short, Manatí Garveyites understood the importance of Cuban patriotism and deployed mutually recognizable symbols of nationalism in their attempt to forge harmony between the association and the sugar company, and the company responded in kind. This pragmatic approach to staying afloat despite unequal power relations seems to have worked in especially well in many of Cuba's northeastern sugar towns run by vertically integrated companies whose holdings were extensive enough to weather the 1921 crash.

Elsewhere, however, the relationship was more contentious, as authorities maintained that *any* gathering of workers—especially of Antillanos—was a risk to the already-precarious social order. As the full effects of the crisis set it, Garveyites repeatedly ran into trouble with the police and Rural Guard during the second half of 1921. Police officers disrupted UNIA meetings in the town of Florida.[168] In Camagüey, police raided a gathering, assaulted members, and "forcibly disbanded" a UNIA meeting in December.[169] Even without violence or intimidation, however, local authorities could make things difficult by denying the organization a permit to meet or hold a parade.[170]

Good relations with company officials were not a guaranteed strategy to protect the association. While Division #52 in Banes stayed afloat until 1960, closing only a year after the Cuban Revolution, the UNIA branch at United

Fruit's Preston mill was shut down. Administrators Howley and Hogge suppressed the association just as the 1921 UNIA Convention was getting under way in New York.[171] Christian, whom Howley had arrested, later recollected that it was fear of a strike that had stirred the UFC managers to action.[172] Although the town remained home to enthusiastic supporters of Garvey and his movement, individuals who continued to write to the *Negro World* and attend events elsewhere, there are no further reports of a Preston Division.[173] In this climate of uncertainty, efforts to maintain cordial relationships with employers were imperative.

Garveyites did not sit idle during the 1921 crisis. They pursued several strategies in advocating for their members and supporting their community. First, they used the *Negro World* to warn overseas readers about the situation on the island, list grievances against specific employers, and protest the fact that mills and colonos continued to recruit British West Indians into a desperate situation.[174] Writing from Camagüey Province, Charles S. McKenzie reported to the *Negro World* that the situation for Black foreigners was such that men were physically assaulted and then denied police protection and medical treatment. One man, Richard Dexter, died from his wounds after such an attack. McKenzie also reported that workers were mistreated at the Central Estrella, where Antillanos were working for meals alone, and at Central Céspedes, where "there are about fifty Negroes who were laid off without any payment of wages and after five months of work . . ."[175] In contrast to the large company towns of northern Oriente, these two mills were smaller and would change ownership before the crisis subsided; the following year, Estrella was acquired by a larger sugar company and Céspedes joined the Rionda group. From the Cuban American Sugar Company's territory, the Chaparra UNIA President, Gordon Procope, singled out the mill for paying in promissory notes. He also accused the company of hiring an agent who recruited workers from Jamaica under false pretenses; laborers were told that they could work anywhere, but, upon arrival, were compelled by debt of their passage to work for Central Chaparra. They were completely abandoned by mid-1921.[176] Elsewhere in Cuba, a man named J. A. Thorpe wrote to the paper contesting the negative stereotypes about Black immigrants in the Cuban press. Highlighting the importance of cross-national Black unity, Thorpe explained, "In my opinion, Mr. Editor, these printing presses are willfully doing these things to prejudice the minds of the Cuban Negroes against we, the West Indian Negroes, and to keep us at variance all the time."[177]

UNIA field organizer Samuel Radway wrote one of the most striking accounts of the conditions facing Antillanos in Cuba in 1921 and warned British West Indians against emigrating. "Starvation stares us in the face," he explained. Workers were abandoning their homes and traveling on foot in search of employment, relief, or a means of returning home. "Laborers have walked hundreds of miles looking for work and found none." West Indians were "mocked by the Cuban peasantry" and paid in worthless *vales*, or company-store credits. Radway described price gouging and the routine practice of overcharging Antillanos for everything from food to railway tickets. West Indians searching for work were subjected to brutal violence, including the murder of one man named Abraham Leslie. For Radway, however, the UNIA was a source of succor and support during these hard times. He criticized Leslie's companions, who had fled the scene, in the following way: "Why did these five other men run? Because they were not members of the U.N.I.A. I would advise right here that, if young men want to be men with backbones, they must join the U.N.I.A." In other words, as Radway explained, conditions were terrible in Cuba, yes, but the UNIA offered a path to survival and resistance.[178]

Santiago de Cuba's UNIA Division #71 was the most ardent defender of British West Indians during the 1921 crisis. Division #71 provided relief to distressed immigrants and advocated for better support from British diplomatic authorities. In September and October, William Walters, a leading Garveyite in town, provided food to immigrants and later billed the British consulate. The UNIA insisted that the consul should help with food, clothing, and passage home. Santiago's Garveyites condemned imperial authorities for permitting ongoing migration to Cuba. Perhaps most dramatically, the UNIA led demonstrations outside the British consulate, prompting the consul to request police protection.[179] US diplomats were concerned with the UNIA's ability to mobilize immigrants in Santiago, noting that the association "seems to be doing its best to keep these people stirred up and to arouse an unruly spirit in them."[180]

British Antilleans persistently sought representation and protection from British colonial and diplomatic officials, especially in the aftermath of the 1917 Jobabo massacre.[181] Yet in 1921, British colonial and diplomatic officials declined to work with the UNIA. The UK Foreign Office told a diplomat in Cuba not to give the association any "encouragement," and the *Negro World* was banned in several British colonies.[182] That British authorities were alarmed by the UNIA's popularity is unsurprising; the organization, after all, stood proudly for a "free and redeemed Africa" at the height of British imperialism on the continent. In contrast, Cuban authorities like Governor Lora largely viewed the UNIA as an entrepreneurial, Christian, "immigrant-protection," and Black-uplift organization and were willing to work with the association—as long its members stayed out of Cuban affairs.

In short, Garveyites in eastern Cuba's mill towns deployed authorization from Oriente Governor Lora, the tolerance local magistrates, and company administrator's self-styled images as benevolent patrons to keep their organization afloat through the 1921 crisis and beyond. Their pragmatic approach to working with authorities had its limits, though, as the British consular services largely declined to take up Antillano demands for assistance in 1921. Hardly sitting idly by during a time of acute crisis, Garveyites directed their energy where it might be most effective: "epistolatory activism" and sending word through the international Black press.[183] Diasporic connections, in other words, were front and center of Garveyite activism in Cuba.

Black Uplift and Building Diaspora in the US-Caribbean World

Far from collapsing in the aftermath of the 1921 crisis, the UNIA thrived in Cuba, as economic insecurity and anti-immigrant hostility enhanced the need for the mutual aid association. As Giovannetti-Torres explains, "The sugar crisis revealed the enduring hostility against foreign blacks in Cuba. Once the island had felt the impact of the market crash, Afro-Caribbean migrants became racialized scapegoats, diseased aliens, and damaging to the nation."[184] In response, UNIA members came together, provided material support for one another, and built a strong and reliable community. Garveyites harnessed and grew the UNIA infrastructure to connect with the wider world of Afro-diasporic politics. From the sugar towns of eastern Cuba, they contributed to the global sense of diasporic solidarity cohering in the interwar period.

The association expanded in 1922; more UNIA divisions opened that year than in any other, especially in the east.[185] There are several explanations for this growth. First, Garvey's arrest on mail fraud charges in the US in January of 1922 increased the organization's popularity on the island, as many came to his defense. Jemima Kelso in Banes wrote, the UNIA was "boosted more than ever [now that the Garvey] Defense Fund is started."[186] Second, this expansion coincided with Morales' great organizing push, which continued through the middle of the year. Finally, in eastern Cuba, word had spread that the association had recently provided material relief to distressed immigrants in Santiago, illustrating the benefits of affiliating.[187] The association's plans to establish grocery stores, health clinics, and a shipping line made good sense in light of the price gouging, lack of access to healthcare, and difficulties returning home that Antillanos faced during the crisis. While the struggle for a redeemed Africa and an uplifted race undergirded routine organizing in Cuba with a sense of wider purpose, the day-to-day work of visiting the sick and running Sunday schools also provided members with tangible benefits.

In short, the UNIA improved their lives. As Charles McKenzie, who wrote to the *Negro World* about terrible working conditions in Camagüey during the 1921 crisis, put it, "Join the U.N.I.A., the only way for Negroes to be happy."[188]

British West Indians, away from home and without local kin networks for support in times of crisis, appreciated the mutual aid and community-building aspects of the association. Throughout the early 1920s, Garveyites "put the program over" despite—or perhaps more accurately, *because of*—hardships in eastern Cuba.[189] This "dogged determination" to continue Sunday night mass meetings and monthly parades, to keep sending reports to the *Negro World*, and to participate in the formalities of UNIA life served a key purpose: maintaining a strong associational infrastructure despite the precarity that characterized life in Cuba.[190] Even when individual members left town in search of work, local branches of the UNIA remained a bedrock of community life.[191] In 1923, Banes Division #52's President Blake wrote to the *Negro World* describing a monthly parade they continued despite the fact that "many of our male members have left this locality in search of employment." Those still in town, he explained, maintained a position of "no surrender," concluding that "the race-loving Negroes of Banes have built up a lovely division. It's only for them to keep together . . ."[192] To Blake, "keeping together" UNIA activities, even as the community shifted around them, was a responsibility that members proudly assumed. From the perspective of company towns, then, the infrastructure created through the UNIA kept local communities strong in good times and bad, even when individuals were forced to leave.

Similarly, from the perspective of the individuals who traveled the region in search of work, the UNIA provided a welcoming community and a degree of social capital in new homes. At a 1921 meeting in Marcané, a young woman named Irene Richards told her UNIA story. She showed the audience her UNIA card from Santo Domingo and explained that, upon arriving in Cuba, she had "first inquired if there was any society of the UNIA here." When she heard that, yes, there was a local branch in town, she felt "good and comfortable for, she said if there wasn't any, she would have to leave for another place where there was."[193] In other words, Richards was unwilling move to a town without a UNIA chapter, such was her dedication to the organization. Putnam has written that British West Indians in the greater Caribbean used the UNIA and other associations to "cushion the risks and loneliness of an economic system built on extreme mobility."[194] In the sugar towns of eastern Cuba, where seasonal unemployment was the norm and where livelihoods were subject to the whims of Wall Street, this cushioning was essential. For women, the UNIA was especially helpful in offering a means of quickly securing local connections, receiving vital information about safe places to stay and prospective employers, and affiliating with a respected local association.

The Garvey movement also facilitated network building. Rather than a world of chapters and divisions orbiting around the New York headquarters, the UNIA in the Caribbean was a web of interconnected men and women who moved throughout region in search of a livelihood, yes, but also to advance the reach of the organization.[195] Ceremonial activities—such as new division openings, charter unveilings, division anniversary or Emancipation Day celebrations, flag raisings, and dedications—almost always occasioned the arrival of speakers and guests from other eastern sugar towns.[196] Some traveled from farther afield, as when Garveyites from Montego Bay and Kingston attended a November 1921 meeting in Banes.[197] With every ceremony attended by out-of-towners, Garveyites were fostering regional connections and building networks they knew could later come in handy.

Reading, sharing, and contributing to the *Negro World* were also acts of network building and forging diaspora. Robin D. G. Kelley and Sidney J. Lemelle have written that Black nationalism is a form of what Benedict Anderson calls "imagined community."[198] In this sense, UNIA symbols—including a flag, anthem, and constitution—cohered a sense of belonging among Garveyites the world over. Just as important as symbols and pageantry in imagining a shared community was the circulation of newspapers. Putnam writes, "the international circulation of black-run periodicals, and their integration in communal discussion at multiple sites, generated a transnational black public."[199] For Black speakers of English in Cuba, the *Negro World* was essential to the work of imagining—and building—diaspora. Reading and writing reports about the Ethiopian National Anthem, the "smart" uniforms of the Black Cross Nurses, and the Garvey movement's colors of red, green, and black reminded readers that others were also holding Sunday-night mass meetings and staging parades, singing familiar songs, and waving the same flag. Contributors and readers were assured that, should they have to pick up and leave, they might find a familiar organization awaiting them in their new destination, as did Irene Richards in Marcané.

In the "News and Views of UNIA Divisions" section of the paper, reports from across the Caribbean listed the names of individuals performing solos at mass meetings, leading processions, and presiding over weddings. The practice of naming individuals kept readers abreast of the activities of family and friends. Contributors also issued specific warnings, as when a reporter from Banes warned readers about an Irish priest who had settled in town and was spreading false information about the Garvey movement.[200] Almost every issue of the *Negro World* contained multiple reports from Cuba. (On page 10 of the January 28, 1922, edition alone, five of the eight "News and Views" reports were from Cuba, and on July 29 four of the eight reports were from Cuba.[201]) As the written embodiment of the UNIA's international community and as a forum in which rank-and-file members communicated, the *Negro World* was the means through which readers and writers did more than *imagine* community; they constructed diaspora in the pages of the paper.

Far from considering themselves peripheral actors watching global events from the sidelines, the Garveyites of northern Oriente were featured widely in the *Negro World's* coverage, as was news important to them. The paper kept its readers abreast of international developments, and any given issue of the paper covered events from across the globe, with a special emphasis on struggles against racism and imperialism. In July of 1926, a single edition covered Jewish settlement in Palestine, racist mistreatment of Japanese journalists in South Africa as well as the "plight of Indians in South Africa," Anglo-Italian cooperation (which threatened Abyssinia but was nevertheless was sanctioned by the League of Nations), and a petition signed by Haitians in Havana condemning Haitian President Eustache Antoine François Joseph Louis Borno for operating at the behest of foreign economic interests and US occupying authorities. In fact, this anti-Borno sentiment was covered in three places in the issue, including a full Spanish reproduction of the petition and an opinion piece that ended "Haiti is a black country; it belongs to black people, and they should be allowed the rule it unhampered by outside influence, such as the United States imposes upon it."[202] For readers in Banes learning of the anti-imperialist sentiment of Haitians across the island in Havana, and for countless others, the paper facilitated local-global connections and wider diasporic consciousness.

Perhaps more than any other aspect of the UNIA program, the Black Star Line encapsulated the Garvey movement's dual mission: an ideological commitment to Black redemption and a pragmatic diasporic program for achieving it. Garveyites in northern Oriente invested heavily in the Black Star Line; McGuire claimed that some of the most enthusiastic investors in the BSL were in Cuba. In Banes, both he and Garvey and raised significant funds for the line.[203] As Garvey put it, the BSL enhanced the Black race's reputation, spread the UNIA's message, and increased its membership. He claimed the *Frederick Douglass's* 1919 and 1920 voyages through the West Indies and Central America "brought into the fold of the Universal Negro Improvement Association hundreds of thousands of Negro men and women who never could have been reached otherwise, who would never even have been convinced of the possibility of a race scattered through the world coming together under one program, one definite platform."[204] (The *Frederick Douglass* had traveled to northeastern Cuba before; as the *Yarmouth,* the ship had delivered the first US colonists to the settlement at La Gloría in 1900.[205])

Beyond the pride that Caribbean men and women must have experienced upon seeing an impressive Black-owned carrier like the *Frederick Douglass,* material realities fostered enthusiasm for the BSL. In Guantánamo, Garvey promoted the line in the following terms: "When you are going to leave Cuba[,] we want you to leave in no other ships but the steamships of the Black Star Line . . . You will be better treated, [and find] better facilitates on your own steamships. Black captains, black crews."[206] West Indians in Cuba understood intimately the benefits a Black-owned shipping line. In fact, several had personally taken advantage of the BSL's tours to change their circumstances. According to the captain of the *Frederick Douglass,* when the ship arrived in Colón in April of 1920, hundreds of West Indians fed up with racism in the Canal Zone boarded hoping to try their luck on Cuba's sugar estates.[207] In Cuba, immigrants had personally suffered through the high cost of travel, overcrowded and unsanitary conditions on regional schooners, and debts owed to companies for passage. Making matters worse, employers were known to deny passage on company-owned ships so that their workforce would be retained.[208] By late 1921, many Antillanos had also experienced being stranded and destitute in an unfriendly land in which they were dependent on unreliable consular authorities for a slim chance of getting home.

Garveyites in Cuba remained hopeful about the prospects of the Black Star Line even as one of its ships lay in ruins off the coast of northern Oriente. On August 24, 1921, the crew of the SS *Kanawha,* renamed the *Antonio Maceo* after Cuba's independence hero, abandoned ship at the port of Antilla. It was the sad end of the *Maceo's* history, which began in May of 1920 when the BSL purchased the ship that Tony Martin described as "the most ill-fated of the line's vessels."[209] The former luxury yacht had been requisitioned into service during the Great War but was in poor condition by the time it was acquired by the BSL. The *Maceo* never made it anywhere according to plan. The vessel, intended for a New York-West Indies route, suffered engine breakdowns, damaged machinery, and the introduction of harmful saltwater into its boilers. The maiden voyage was interrupted twice for repairs, but the ship eventually made it to Havana in April 1921, and thanks to several more urgent repairs, to Kingston in May. After an unsuccessful start for Colón, the *Maceo* arrived in Santiago, where it received a warm welcome, including from Governor Lora. As it headed out again, however, the ship only made it as far as Antilla, where it broke down for good. The crew abandoned ship in August, and Garvey called on the US consul to assist its passengers in returning home at the BSL's expense. In 1925, a storm unmoored the ship, and it began to sink, remaining half submerged off the coast of Antilla.[210]

Yet, despite the *Maceo's* disaster, the wreckage of which remained visible from Antilla, Garveyites in northern Oriente did not give up on the idea of a Black-owned shipping line. Ever pragmatic, Harold Collins proposed that the UNIA invest in sailing schooners rather than large, expensive steamships at the international convention in August 1922. He acknowledged that the BSL's failure had caused a loss of membership in Banes and proposed instead that the UNIA consider "operating a fleet of sailing vessels in West Indian waters." It would be easy to find crews for the ships, as there "were already a large number of experienced sailors who were capable of operating them successfully" from the West Indies.[211] This suggestion was built from his experience in eastern Cuba; interisland travel—not the longer voyages to New York or places farther afield, such as Liberia—was urgently needed, and a line of schooners could improve their lives in an immediate and tangible way.

Historians have pointed to the Black Star Line's failures as the Garvey movement's greatest weakness.[212] This argument, however, only holds water insomuch as we measure the line's success in terms of its ability to accumulate capital. Rather, suggests Jeffrey Howison, the line's great success lay in its power as a symbolic venture, "a vision of economic self-determination and black liberation."[213] As Charles V. Carnegie explains, the BSL ships were an important source of pride after the degradations of the middle passage: "This time around, the ships would be black-owned and navigated by a black crew. These liners would embody and promote black prosperity."[214] The captain of the UNIA's *Yarmouth* later wrote that, over time working with Garvey, he learned that commercial success was not Garvey's main goal. Rather, the image of ships "owned and operated by colored men" was what mattered.[215] Although at first glance, the Black Star Line's abandoned *Maceo* off the coast of Antilla represents the foolhardy commercial escapades of UNIA leaders in Harlem, Garveyites in Cuba had good reason not to give up on the idea of a Black-owned shipping venture.

In Cuba, the UNIA also connected individuals, often in geographically remote locations, with a wider world of Afro-diasporic politics and political imagining. Although room to maneuver for Black men and women in Cuban society—especially foreigners—was limited by the threat of violence and company control, Garveyites did not turn their attention away from global politics. Rather, they spread their vision for diasporic uplift. In July 1921, Samuel Augustus Richards, an ex-corporal of the British West India Regiment, wrote to King George V on behalf of "the English speaking Negroes who are suffering for want of employment in Cuba[,] in America and in Panama." He suggested that the crown "give the English speaking Negroes a portion of land of our own in Africa; so that we may be able to cultivate it and . . . be better off [to] settle down and do well."[216] Such assistance, of course, never happened. For this and many other reasons, Garveyites in Cuba condemned British authorities. In 1923 from the sugar town of Morón in northern Camagüey, Joseph A. Todd wrote a *Negro World* article entitled "British Rule Bad for Black People" and described his own move away from his native Barbados with the decline of the sugar economy there and the British government's failure to protect Caribbean cane sugar from competition from European beet sugar. He went on to argue that in both Panama and Cuba, the British government could not be relied upon to come to the aid of its subjects in need.[217] With these conversations, Garveyites embedded themselves deeply in the wider and increasingly interconnected world of Black diasporic politics and built lasting networks of likeminded strugglers for racial uplift and against imperialism.

Decline of Garveyism in Cuba

Garveyism remained strong in Cuba through the 1920s, outlasting the highpoint of the movement in the US. Throughout the 1920s, new divisions opened, officers sent reports to the *Negro World*, and mass meetings were held. Cuba sent delegates to the fourth, fifth, and sixth UNIA conventions. The tides of the movement in Cuba began to turn in the late 1920s, however, for several reasons. First, although things had stabilized, Cuba never fully recovered from the crash of 1920–1921. Immigration from the British West Indies, which peaked in 1920, slowed to a trickle by the end of the decade.[218] The Cuban government repatriated approximately 18,000 Antillanos in 1928 alone.[219] By the early 1930s, Arnold Cummings, who had represented Banes at the UNIA conventions and who was sent on recruiting missions in North Carolina, was back in Jamaica and active in the Harmony and St. Andrew Divisions.[220] Across the island, membership numbers in the UNIA dropped significantly with the declining population of British West Indians, the movement's biggest constituency.

Second, in 1929, Cuban President Gerardo Machado cracked down on the association. As Guridy has demonstrated, Machado was alarmed by increasing Afro-Cuban participation in the UNIA, which was particularly strong in Las Villas Province. By the late 1920s, the Sagua la Grande branch was a forceful advocate for Black rights, a situation which threatened Machado's image as a Black-friendly president. He sent informants to Sagua la Grande, and the police harassed members. In late 1929, Machado shut down the UNIA in Las Villas using the Morúa law. Garvey was banned from entering the country in 1930.[221] During this period of persecution, however, Banes Division #52 remained open, unmolested by the Cuban state, as did several other mill town chapters. In fact, Division #52 only closed in 1960. The hard work Garveyites in *oriental* sugar towns put into cultivating good relationships with company authorities protected many eastern branches of organization during this period of persecution.

The composition of UNIA divisions in the east shifted in this changed political and economic climate. In Banes, many officers from the early 1920s transferred their energies to a new association, the Jamaica Club, founded in 1927. Division #52's executive secretary James Lake and trustee Josia Frances both moved to the new club.[222] The professional composition of the UNIA officers also changed. By 1930, day laborers served as trustees, and in 1933 field laborers held leading positions, such as secretary, in an officer corps no longer dominated by tradesmen and domestic workers.[223] That the old officer corps gravitated to the Jamaica Club while factory and field workers moved into UNIA leadership suggests a changing class composition of the UNIA, which was not uncommon in the Caribbean and Central America. In 1930, British West Indian elites in Limón lamented that the local UNIA chapter had transitioned from the "classes" to the "masses of the Negro race."[224] By the end of the 1920s, UNIA Division #52 was no longer led by the relative elites within British West Indian society who had avoided confrontations with the company by focusing their energies on community stability and projections of respectability. Moving forward, the thrust of civic organizing in Banes would be labor organizing.

Conclusion

As US capital spread throughout the Caribbean in the early twentieth century, employers attempted to circumvent labor scarcities and prevent workforce instabilities by importing Antillano laborers. While they might have intended to create an isolated and stable workforce, and they did constrain workers' daily lives, early multinational corporations also opened circuits of travel and information exchange that took on a life of their own, as migrants and their families, associations, political ideologies, and grievances moved through them. Banes, the heart of United Fruit territory, staffed heavily by foreign laborers, epitomized the potentially totalizing power of an enclave company.

Yet it was there that the UNIA flourished, with a strong and influential membership not only serving their own needs, but also leading Black community life in town and spearheading the international Garvey movement's Caribbean arm.

Close examination of the UNIA in Banes and nearby company towns reveals on a local scale the dialectical relationship between global economic expansion and the formation of transnational-solidarity movements. Cuba was the last stop for many British West Indian migrants who had personally witnessed ubiquitous racial exploitation in the Panama Canal Zone, in Costa Rican banana plantations, and elsewhere. These men and women continually found themselves vulnerable to the economic shifts and sudden unemployment that accompanied monocrop economies, so they joined and spread a race-first organization that would function as a mutual aid society and a source of community strength in hard times. In this sense, the UNIA was both a product of and a response to the segregation and economic dependency that accompanied US power throughout the Caribbean. In turn, Garveyites shared a vision of racial uplift with Afro-Cubans who had their own long and complicated history of racial organizing.

In the aftermath of the 1912 massacre of Afro-Cubans, the 1917 massacre of British West Indians, countless acts of violence against Antillanos, and the economic collapse of 1921, Garveyites in Cuba carved out room to maneuver against the odds. When it came to capitalist exploitation, the UNIA was not an explicitly oppositional force. But, by building and strengthening transnational networks and facilitating a sense of diasporic belonging, the cosmopolitan women and men of eastern Cuba used the association as a tool for contending with the hardships of labor in sites of US-led commercial agriculture and for pursuing an inclusive Black-uplift agenda. That they never launched a head-on attack against the state or sugar companies does not mean they remained passive. Rather, they targeted their efforts where they might be most effective. In Santiago in September 1921, that meant directly confronting the powers-that-be, demanding that British representatives to do more for their destitute subjects, and feeding the hungry. In the large company towns of northern Oriente, that meant cultivating good relationships with local authorities, staying clear of political entanglements that would only jeopardize their already-precarious status, and projecting respectability in terms clearly relatable to local audiences. Across the island, it meant contributing to the diasporic paper, the *Negro World*. Those who could built an infrastructure that sustained their communities in difficult times, and, in so doing, joined—and led—a world of diasporic political engagement.

By the end of the decade, however, the patrons' compact was in a state of crisis. The Great Depression exacerbated Cuba's already-precarious economic situation; mill administrators no longer bestowed small gifts to workers; and workers no longer tolerated hollow gestures of benevolence. As the economic crisis deepened and the government of President Gerardo Machado moved toward authoritarianism, opposition movements across the island picked up speed and a new era of militant resistance was under way, especially in eastern Cuba.

3

"The Weakest Link of Imperialism's Chain in the Caribbean"

Sugar Workers, Organized Labor, and Global Communism

In February 1925, the Unión Obrera de Banes invited Julio Antonio Mella, a student leader and a rising star in Cuba's anti-imperialist left, to attend the town's carnival festivities as their guest of honor. Two years before his visit, several small guilds had come together in Banes to form the Unión Obrera, as eastern Cuba's laborers were consolidating into more and more inclusive organizations. The union had become a fixture in local community life; its *centro obrero* hosted a reading library and a night school. For his part, Mella would not have missed an opportunity to address workers in this United Fruit Company town, the heart of the US-dominated sugar industry in Cuba. By the time he visited, the young leader had traveled widely, including a 1920 trip to Mexico, which was still reeling from revolution. He had cofounded the Cuban branch of the Liga Antiimperialista de las Américas, and in 1923, organized the Universidad Popular José Martí (UPJM) in Havana. Influenced by the university-reform movement in Argentina and popular university initiatives in Peru, the UPJM held classes for workers on Cuban history, workers' rights, revolutionary theory, and recent history—especially the Mexican and Russian Revolutions. When Mella came to town in early 1925, he brought friends. Fellow anti-imperialist and poet Rubén Martínez Villena, student union leader Leonardo Fernández Sánchez, and the "Red Feminist" Mariblanca Sabas Alomá all joined him. They held classes at the Unión Obrera headquarters and organized a UPJM field campus. Mella spoke at a massive rally remembered as one of the most important in the town's history.[1]

Mella's background reflects the international forces shaping Cuba's generation of young radicals coming of age in the 1920s. Born Nicanor McPartland, he was the illegitimate son of an Irish American woman named Cecilia McPartland, whose family had immigrated to New York, and a successful Dominican tailor, who had settled in Cuba. Mella's paternal grandfather, Don Nicanor Mella y Brea, had been a leading general in the Dominican wars of independence against Haiti in 1844 and again in the 1860s against Spain.[2] Raised in upper-class circles of Santo Domingo, the future revolutionary's father studied his trade in Paris before marrying and moving to Cuba. According to family lore, Don Nicanor had joined fellow Dominican Máximo Gómez in Cuba's Ten Years War of Independence, which brought him to the island. After moving his business to Havana, he traveled regularly to New York to learn the latest fashions and purchase textiles. It was during one such trip that Mella began his affair with McPartland, who moved to Havana when she became pregnant. The young Nicanor was born in Havana in 1903. He and a younger brother spent their early years moving between Cuba and the United States, especially New Orleans, where he attempted to enlist in the armed forces before his father summoned him to Cuba. When his mother returned to the US for the final time, her still-young sons landed in the household of their father and his wife. The family had a well-appointed library, and Don Nicanor spoke excellent Spanish, French, and English. The boys, however, endured affronts and rejection in their home and wider community due to their illegitimate status. In around 1917, the future revolutionary began going by the name of Julio Antonio Mella, shedding a surname that reminded tutors and classmates of his questionable origins and taking on a name made prestigious in the Dominican independence struggle. In her excellent biography, Christine Hatzky, argues that Mella responded to his difficult youth with "rebellion and aggressiveness."[3]

In August 1925, six months after his trip to Banes, Mella participated in the founding congress of the Partido Comunista de Cuba (PCC). There, he raised the matter of exploitation in sugar centrales and, according to the meeting minutes, "especially in the Banes mill of the United Fruit Company." He proposed that a rural campaign become one of the party's main tasks and argued that mill bateyes should be considered state property in order to reduce sugar companies' monopolistic power. José Miguel Pérez of the communist group of Guanabacoa also spoke of the big mills in the east, especially the Chaparra mill adding that everything—right down to the shoe shiners—was controlled by the company and suggested organizing small colonos into the anticapitalist struggle.[4] Mella's weeks in northern Oriente, in other words, were decisive for the founding father of Cuban communism. As Sabas Alomá later recalled, "Mella's time in Banes not only had an impact on the local people, but, I believe, it also had a major impact on him ... Mella had never had such intimate contact with the tragic reality of imperialist exploitation. Certainly, he had deep theoretical knowledge of Marxism and student revolutionary practice. But such a brutal confrontation with the condition of our countryside and our people—I think, made him feel the naked reality..."[5]

For several reasons, it is unsurprising that Cuban communists would address the sugar industry at their founding congress. First, since the earliest days of Cuba's independence struggle, opposition leaders identified the island's dependence on sugar as the source of several societal ills, including racialized labor exploitation, social inequity, widespread unemployment, and imperialism.[6] Second, US economic power was strongest within the sugar industry so sugar estates would have been prime candidates for anti-imperialist struggle.[7] Third, in terms of Marxist theory, mill workers labored outside of urban centers, yes, but they also worked in Cuba's most industrialized sector and thus formed a proletariat in the classic sense.[8] Finally, because the industry encompassed industrial mill workers, agricultural braceros, and a peasantry (in the form of small colonos), a sugar campaign would facilitate a powerful agro-industrial or peasant-proletariat alliance, considered to be an essential building block of revolution since the recent Bolshevik victory in 1917. Yet, despite the theoretical and practical importance of the sugar proletariat, it took the Partido Comunista de Cuba over half a decade to make inroads among sugar workers.

Histories of Cuba often mark 1925 as a foundational year in the island's labor struggle because the PCC was founded that year. In its first iteration, however, Cuba's communist party was small, relatively isolated from the Communist International (or Comintern) in Moscow, and fighting an uphill battle for survival—not organizing workers in distant sugar mills and fields. From the perspective of sugar workers, however, the mid-1920s marks not the beginning but a pivotal point in a longer struggle against exploitive conditions that had been building since 1917. During a wave of strikes in 1924 and 1925, transportation and sugar workers formed national and industry-wide labor organizations, unions that reached multiple sectors, including for the first time field and factory workers. These were also the years that anti-imperialism was firmly entrenched in the workers' movement of eastern Cuba, well before the PCC took it upon itself to "advance the international education of the Cuban masses."[9] Northern Oriente's multinational sugar workers were hardly ignorant of the global economic system that exploited them as they cut, hauled, and ground cane, processed and bagged sugar, and loaded it onto ships heading north day after day during the zafra, and that left them unemployed when it was over. Workers, especially in the United Fruit town of Banes, linked local demands for better pay and working conditions to wider calls for Cuban sovereignty in the face of foreign, monopolistic power. Mella and his comrades were aware of these developments when they founded the Partido Comunista de Cuba.

This chapter tells two interrelated stories: first, of the organized labor movement in Cuba's sugar fields and factories, and second, of the PCC's slow move to recognize and harness the revolutionary potential of the sugar proletariat, including foreigners. These stories converged in the years between 1929 and late 1932 thanks to changes in Cuba's political landscape, conversations with international communist organizers, and the actions of sugar workers themselves. By the end of this period, the PCC regarded Cuba's sugar proletariat, especially the multinational workforces in foreign-owned agricultural-export enclaves, as fundamental not only to Cuba's revolutionary struggle, but also to that of the Americas-wide anti-imperialist fight. Ironically, the reasons communists initially neglected sugar workers—they were too rural and too foreign—would become the very motivations for an aggressive organizing campaign in 1932, thanks to pressures from within and without. Communists in Moscow, New York, Montevideo, and beyond claimed that Cuba's multinational, multiracial sugar workforce embodied communist ideals of international proletarian unity. By late 1932, the PCC was arguing that the industry's workers were the heart and soul of revolution in Cuba. Far from a backwater, the US-controlled sugar towns of eastern Cuba were central to communist formulations of the intertwined struggles against imperialism, racism, and capitalist exploitation. International organizers heralded the incipient strikes taking place in early 1933 as a model to emulate across the Americas. Little did they know that sugar workers would erupt in revolution later that year, the subject of chapter 4.

Labor Resistance in Eastern Cuba's Sugar Industry (1916–1925)

There was no shortage of labor resistance among sugar workers in the late nineteenth and early twentieth centuries, but organized labor as such proceeded in fits and starts until World War I. Strikes and unionization efforts took off in 1917, when workers were squeezed by wartime inflation, and the government stepped in at an unprecedented level. It was the 1924–1925 harvest, however, when workers united across sectors and began connecting their day-to-day fight against exploitation with the wider struggle against imperialism. In this sense, 1925 marked less a beginning than a culmination of years of labor agitation.

Several factors stood in the way of a thoroughly unionized sugar proletariat. First, sugar workers were geographically dispersed in mills and *colonias* (grouping of cane fields) deep in the Cuban countryside, most of which were reachable only on company-controlled railways. Even within a particular company's territory, the distances between mill bateyes and colonias could be significant. Second, many working for a given sugar company were not directly employed by the same entity; rather they were employed by intermediaries, individualizing the problems facing workers and enabling companies to deny authority over labor matters. Third, sugar is a compartmentalized industry, with *macheteros* (cane cutters), cane haulers, railway workers, coal stokers, mill workers, metallurgical workers, stevedores, and more, all performing distinct tasks with distinct pay. Fourth, it is highly seasonal work, with a "dead season" after the zafra ensuring that laborers were dispersed during a significant portion of the year. Yet a fifth factor discouraging labor organizing was that the power and reach of employers extended further in sugar zones than it did in urban centers, as companies controlled housing, education, commerce, the provision of basic goods, and healthcare, among other necessities. They could (and usually did) evict troublesome employees. Sixth, private police forces, the Rural Guard, the Cuban army, and sometimes even US Marines stood ready to intimidate workers or violently squash labor agitations.[10] Finally, like other resource-extraction industries in Latin America and company towns across the Americas, sugar companies segmented the workforce along racial and national lines, a policy intended to discourage labor unity.[11] This strategy often succeeded. In 1913, the Jatibonico sugar mill contracted Chinese laborers in response to labor actions and housed them separately. During labor mobilizations in 1917, administrators at the Central Francisco were pleased to report that Haitian and Jamaican workers had been their "salvation." Not infrequently, conflicts arose between workers of different nationalities, as when clashes erupted between Haitians and Cubans at the Jatibonico mill in 1916 and at the Atlantic Fruit Company's mill in 1922.[12]

The Cuba Cane Company's 1924 response to a threatened strike illustrated the obstacles facing organized labor. On Oriente's northern coast, workers for the company's largest mill, Manatí, attempted to organize a new union and presented management with a list of demands that year, including wage increases, an eight-hour day, and overtime pay. In response, the company fired the workers, evicted them, and shared a list of the unionizers with other employers. When workers complained about the unjust terminations, the manager explained that he had nothing to do with their labor arrangements, as they were in fact employed by contractors. If they were no longer needed by the contractors, however, their homes were required back for the company. Additionally, the manager reported that he had state support, as the army was "taking steps to avoid any paralyzing." Finally, Cuba Cane made plans to import 150–200 Chinese workers "as a precautionary measure."[13]

Given these conditions, an organized labor movement took over a decade to build in the sugar industry. The turbulent year of 1917 kickstarted the process. Internationally, 1917 saw the US enter World War I in April and the Bolsheviks seize power in Russia that November (the October Revolution, according to the Russian calendar). In Cuba, the year began with a political revolt, saw the landing of US Marines on the island midyear, and ended with a hallmark moment in Cuba's labor movement, when the presidential administration intervened in a massive strike not to violently squash the movement, as one might expect, but in fact, to mediate between employers and workers.

Early that year, the Liberal Party, led by former president José Miguel Gómez (who had severely repressed the 1912 PIC rebellion) launched an armed insurgency to contest the reelection of Conservative President Mario García Menocal.[14] Fighting during the Liberal Rebellion was especially intense in the eastern provinces of Camagüey and Oriente, where peasants displaced by sugar's expansion into the east supported the rebels. Gómez and his supporters attacked military posts and sugar properties. Bandits took the opportunity to ransack sugar estates. It was amid this rebellion that soldiers entered the mill town of Jobabo and massacred more than fourteen British West Indian workers under the pretense of squashing the uprising. The rebels received no support from Washington, which actually preferred President García Menocal to his predecessor; after all, García Menocal had managed the Cuban American Sugar Company's Chaparra sugar mill for years and was cozy with US interests. With the April declaration of war against Germany, Washington made it clear to García Menocal that the Liberal Rebellion was a dangerous threat, and any disruptions to sugar production would be considered hostile acts.[15] At the same time, the US had little appetite for another formal intervention in Cuba. Instead, Washington launched an informal operation that became known as the "sugar intervention." Between mid-1917 and late 1918, over 3,000 Marines landed in the eastern provinces of Camagüey and Oriente ostensibly for training purposes. In fact, the sites selected for "training" were all near sugar and mining properties and were designed to intimidate rebels and prevent strikes. US Marines stayed in eastern Cuba until 1923.[16]

Nevertheless, 1917 saw a surge in labor mobilizations. Cuban sugar was in high demand, and the island's economy thrived during the war, but rising cost of living due to wartime inflation and scarcity of basic goods sowed discontent among workers. Between 1917 and 1920, there were no fewer than 220 works stoppages, including several in the sugar industry.[17] In September of 1917, skilled workers in Cienfuegos formed the reformist Asociación de Mecánicos, Maquinistas, Herreros y sus Anexos, and struck, demanding an eight-hour workday and a wage increase. When President García Menocal mobilized armed forces to put down the stoppages, solidarity strikes erupted and spread east to the mills of Camagüey and west to Matanzas. Eventually, fifty centrales were involved and a quarter of the island's mills was paralyzed.[18] The strike wave encompassed other trades, including drivers, coachmen, carpenters, and masons—sectors that included Spaniards and West Indians—but was generally led by skilled workers and never reached fieldworkers, who were dispersed during the dead season. While laborers demanded better pay and shorter workdays, sugar companies had their own demands and called on García Menocal to take the opportunity to secure a guaranteed minimum price for sugar from the United States. The strike continued through October.

As John Dumoulin has detailed, rather than simply squash the strike, in early November, García Menocal's administration threatened to have the government carry out the harvest if the employers could not come to an agreement with their employees. Workers welcomed this prospect, declaring that they were "ready to return to work immediately if the government seized the mills."[19] In other words, sugar workers were taking the unprecedented step of demanding that the state take over production. This took place around the same time that workers, peasants, and soldiers were collaborating in Russia to ensure state control of production. In the end, the strikers did not obtain an eight-hour workday, but García Menocal oversaw a 20–30 percent increase in worker pay.[20] Dumoulin calls the strike "a formidable feat, a triumph of organization" and a "step from guild toward industrial union." At the same time, he writes, the movement ultimately failed thanks to the "fundamental weakness . . . of not organizing agricultural workers."[21] Organized labor would largely overlook agricultural workers for the better part of a decade.

In late 1918, railroad workers struck in Camagüey, and included political matters, such as the removal of US Marines, in their list of demands. The strike spread east and froze the national rail network from Santa Clara to Santiago de Cuba. When soldiers occupied the city of Camagüey, solidarity strikes began elsewhere.[22] Cuba's railway network was built to support the sugar industry, and the railroad strikes "embarrassed sugar factories." *The Louisiana Planter and Sugar Manufacturer* reported, "The sugar factories in the province of Oriente, Camagüey, and part of Santa Clara are being greatly inconvenienced by the continued strike of the employees of the Cuba Railroad Company." The author explained, "the damage to business in general is becoming very serious." He was particularly alarmed by the extent of sympathy strikes.[23] Cuba Railroad eventually made some concessions, but, as Zanetti and García point out, the "real importance" of the Camagüey railroad strike of 1918 lay in the advance in proletarian solidarity.[24] Cuba's labor movement was shifting away from occupational guilds toward wider forms of unity. Still, field workers remained largely unorganized. Occupational elitism, racism, and resentment toward Afro-Caribbean immigrants permeated the ranks of union leaders. For their part, laborers on rural properties probably weighed the benefits of labor unions against their chance of success with US Marines and the Rural Guard standing by.

In United Fruit's territory, labor actions during the 1910s were limited to specific sectors of the company, such as the 1916 strike of coal stokers at Boston. In that incident, the company ended up acquiescing to a small raise. In general, United Fruit was able to maintain the status quo by treating each action individually—usually evicting and replacing strikers, but also sometimes making incremental concessions. Toward the end of the decade, anarchism led by Spanish immigrants took a firmer hold among organized labor in Banes.[25] In 1919, anarchist Spanish and Cuban United Fruit metalworkers formed the Gremio de Obreros Metalúrgicos y Anexos (GOMA), and railroad workers formed the Gremio de Obreros Ferroviarios in 1920.[26]

In the mid-1920s, railway workers initiated more inclusive forms of labor solidarity in the sugar industry. They were the first to form a nationwide union with the Hermandad Ferroviaria de Cuba, founded in 1924 and bringing together engineers, stokers, and telegraphists from multiple rail networks.[27] The Hermandad's leadership was influenced by the American Federation of Labor (AFL) and not very radical. Nevertheless, the Hermandad led a twenty-one-day strike in mid-1924 that stopped much of the country's rail network. Although they did not achieve their demands, they succeeded in uniting diverse trades across public and private rail networks.[28]

During this time, the anarcho-syndicalist Enrique Varona led a railway union on the northern coast of Camagüey that stood out for its radicalism, inclusivity, and solidarity with field workers—including foreigners. The Unión de Morón served employees of the Ferrocarril del Norte de Cuba in the terminal town of Morón but declined to affiliate with the Hermandad, which Varona considered too reformist. He had worked with the anarchist Alfredo López, who cofounded the anarchist Federación Obrera de la Habana. According to Philip Howard, in 1924 the Cuban anarchist newspaper *Tierra!* declared that organizing Cuban, Haitian, and Jamaican workers on American-run sugar estates was a top priority.[29] So when sugar workers struck at several mills that continued to pay in tokens rather than cash in September 1924, Varona's Unión de Morón boycotted freight from those mills. He and other leaders were arrested, and sugar workers were fired and evicted, prompting a wider railroad strike. Stevedores and day laborers joined the strike. US Ambassador Enoch Crowder told President Alfredo Zayas the situation was harming US interests and must be resolved. With a presidential election and the sugar harvest close at hand, the strikers were successful, and their demands met.[30]

This success inspired others in Camagüey. Varona oversaw the creation of a new union, the Sindicato Provincial de Trabajadores de Camagüey (SPTC), which included for the first time field hands. Mill workers from several northern Camagüey mills struck in November, demanding the rights the earlier strikes had secured. The SPTC, the Unión de Morón, and railroad unions of Guantánamo and Santiago all supported the strike as did the Hermandad. Although sugar workers, under intense threats of violence, agreed to return to work on the factories' terms, railroad workers maintained their strike and railroad companies ended up conceding in a major victory for organized labor.[31] Varona's union, in short, had paved the way for widespread cross-sector solidarity in Cuba's sugar industry.

At the Cuban American Sugar Company's Central Chaparra, a fifty-two-day strike ended victoriously for workers in 1924. The year before, port workers at Puerto Padre had formed the Unión de Trabajadores de la Industria Azucarera de Puerto Padre, affiliated with freemasonry and anarcho-syndicalism. The union was open to all occupations, political groups, and ethnicities. In February 1925, company stevedores struck for the same wages that public employees enjoyed. When the company called in the military, sugar and railroad workers joined the strike. Solidarity strikes erupted across the region, as workers demanded the return of the dockworkers to their jobs, rent-free employee housing, and union recognition. Farmers and merchants supported the strike, and the workers received monetary contributions from as far as Havana. Fieldworkers too struck, though they were not yet unionized.[32] Gillian McGillivray points out that "there is no evidence that anyone broke *Chaparra's* 1925 strike—colono, field, or factory worker, Cuban, Inglés, or Chinese—before an official state mediator arrived in April," and the strike ended in the workers' favor.[33]

Afro-Caribbean immigrants too protested the labor regime in the mid-1920s, both individually and as part of organized labor efforts, but company and state authorities responded with repression and abuse. In 1924, a *colono* named Gutiérrez denied pay to British West Indians William Hines, Charles Sandiford, Leaman Higgins, Ruben Dailey, and Simon Wright in Camagüey. The men demanded their backpay and refused to work until it was handed over. In turn, Gutiérrez called in the Rural Guard to have the men evicted and orchestrated "frivolous" charges in local courts. The men spent considerable money suing for their pay and fighting to have the charges dropped, but, as the British consul noted, "it is hopeless for a West Indian, especially a penniless one to sue for anything in a Cuban court . . ."[34] Similarly, when Jamaican Henry Hayden protested working unpaid at the colony Puerco Gordo, the colono Hipólito Sánchez refused to pay. As Hayden detailed, Sánchez "threatened me with a revolver, explaining that if I did not leave his premise at once, he would shoot me." Sánchez then bought off witnesses.[35] In light of such abuses, West Indians supported organized labor during the strike wave of 1924–1925. According to Howard, on at least one occasion, British West Indians refused to scab when mill owners had attempted to break a strike by hiring them. Upon hearing of the situation (and probably under threats of violence from both sides), the men simply walked off the fields.[36] Others joined strikes with their Cuban counterparts, as did Llewellyn Porter and several of his countrymen, who struck at a sugar colonia in Oriente.[37] Along with Cubans, immigrant workers demanded the right to unionize, better wages, and an end to payment in vouchers and company-store credit.[38]

While some labor leaders considered Afro-Caribbean immigrants "unorganizable," this was hardly the case. Not only did British West Indians have a robust tradition of building churches, mutual aid societies, and masonic lodges, but they also made eastern Cuba a global hub of Garveyism, as chapter 2 detailed.[39] Additionally, British West Indians in Santiago de Cuba formed a union of their own, the Unión de Obreros Antillanos (UOA), with aims that stretched from local grievances to pan-Caribbean concerns. In 1924, Jamaican Henry Shackleton founded UOA. Shackleton was a Garveyite and had been involved in the 1921 distribution of food to distressed British West Indians. The UOA collaborated with Cuban organized labor, including Santiago dockworkers. The group also attempted to cross national lines by reaching out to Haitians and gender lines by reaching out to domestic servants.[40] The union took to task the unresponsive British imperial government, petitioning British officials for rights and protections in Cuba. The UOA corresponded with Cuban and British West Indian newspapers and disseminated news about working conditions on particular centrales.[41] Shackleton's group fought to lower travel expenses, to repatriate distressed immigrants, and to end abuse from recruiters.

The UOA connected local grievances to larger concerns over the British diplomatic services and questions about who had the right to represent imperial subjects. This was especially clear in their fight against terrible conditions at the quarantine station near Santiago de Cuba. In 1924, Shackleton sent to the British legation in Havana a petition he claimed had 2,500 signatories, individuals who had been "loyal subjects of His Majesty King George V" and taxpayers in their home islands but were then forced to emigrate to Cuba in search of work.[42] At the quarantine station, the petition claimed, immigrants were charged seven dollars for their fifteen-day stay, yet that money was not spent on services, food, or supplies, nor were they refunded the remainder when discharged early. Doctors and food peddlers overcharged immigrants, and authorities brooked no complaint. Further, "provisions made for our keep whilst under quarantine are inadequate, repulsive, unhealthy, and uncivilized ... No regard is given to cleanliness [, and] the sanitation is also horrible." In other words, the quarantine station was more likely to cause than to cure the illnesses it purported to keep out of Cuba. The petition described the practice of allowing labor recruiters to appear at the station, and "purchase from the quarantine authorities labourers who are taken away, in some cases by force, at night and sold to sugar centrales in different parts of the country, and that any show of resentment or refusal . . . results in the resenting parties being locked up in prison."[43] The situation facing West Indians was compounded by the fact that the British Consul in Santiago was himself involved in labor recruiting and would inevitably side against the workers. Indeed, Acting Consul Ernest P. V. Brice's conflict of interest was later confirmed by fellow consular officials.[44] Critiquing the British imperial state for failing to represent its subjects, Shackleton and the petitioners instead put forward the names of reliable Jamaicans for the office, thereby articulating a vision of self-rule for the colonies and their emigrants.

Immigrants were not the only workers putting local grievances in wider context during the mid-1920s. By this time, United Fruit's labor union was addressing questions of Cuban sovereignty in the face of US economic imperialism. In 1923, GOMA members founded the more inclusive Unión Obrera de Banes, which integrated several smaller trade guilds. The Unión was influenced by Spanish anarchism and anarcho-syndicalism and was largely (though not exclusively) composed of railroad and industrial workers.[45] Unión members supported labor campaigns elsewhere, including those of workers at the nearby Tacajó and Báguanos mills. In January 1925, the union sent a list of demands—including salary increases and a workday decrease from twelve to nine hours—to United Fruit, but the company managed to evade direct engagement by creating a mediation commission headed by a judge in the company's pocket. As the year went on, however, the Unión Obrera became more strident in its demands, which some have attributed to Julio Antonio Mella's visit in February.[46]

The main event of Mella's visit was to be a rally on the bridge dividing the barrio americano from the barrio del pueblo. The out-of-town guests, Mella, Martínez Villena, Fernández Sánchez, and Sabas Alomá, were all scheduled to speak, but as the rally was beginning on February 24, authorities ordered that the meeting be dispersed. Shots were fired, Fernández Sánchez was wounded, and the event fell apart. Undeterred, the workers reconvened at the Unión Obrera and decided to try again the following day—this time in the Parque Domínguez. A carpenter's union constructed a platform for the speakers, and plans were made to restage the rally. Of the four visitors, however, only Mella ended up speaking on that stage. Martínez Villena's tuberculosis kept him from participating, Fernández Sánchez was wounded, and Sabas Alomá had moved onto another engagement. A young worker named Delfín E. Mercade Pupo later recalled that the rally was a great success. According to Mercade Pupo (whose memory could be influenced by Mella's outsized legacy after 1959), the young student leader proclaimed, "one day, United Fruit workers will paint this barrio red!"[47]

Shortly after Mella's visit, the Unión Obrera de Banes received a boost in membership and picked up its labor agitation. On March 25, United Fruit fired twelve men who had refused to work amid a pay dispute. In response, some five hundred mill workers declared a strike, refusing to grind cane, and the mill was forced to suspend all cutting in its fields. The workers demanded the return of the fired men, a pay increase, reduced rent and provision prices, and unrestricted passage for local merchants to the batey of the Boston mill, a demand intended to reduce the company's commercial monopoly.[48] The company made some small concessions in the form of lower provision prices, but the status of the Boston batey became the sticking point in a two-year struggle over Cuban sovereignty that firmly planted the Banes region in the larger anti-imperialist movement.

In late 1924 and early 1925, Mella had been campaigning for Cuban sovereignty over the Isle of Pines, a small island off the southern coast of Cuba. In 1903, the Hay-Quesada Treaty had returned the isle, which was largely colonized by North Americans, to Cuba but the US Senate had not yet ratified the treaty by early 1925. As Cuban nationalism rose, pressure mounted to do something about this clear case of US imperialism. When Mella visited Banes, he connected this wider anti-imperialist struggle with monopolistic power of foreign companies and the pressing need workers had for improved pay and working conditions. The Unión too saw the bigger picture of US imperialism's effect on their daily lives and, shortly after Mella's visit, launched a campaign for Cuban sovereignty over a piece of land much closer to home.

The United Fruit Company's Boston mill sat on the Macabí cay in the Bay of Banes, which had been, for all intents and purposes, the company's private property since 1900. United Fruit controlled the entrance—with armed private police, no less—and did not allow free commercial enterprise there. Macabí's approximately 1500 residents lived in what was effectively sovereign company territory and were compelled to pay company-set prices for basic goods and necessities. Macabí, however, could be considered territory of the Cuban state thanks to a 1903 law that designated all outlying lands and cays state lands. The company, however, insisted that it was a peninsula—not a cay—because an inlet connected Macabí to the mainland, though the company itself had fortified that inlet to make it crossable in all seasons.[49] The matter of the Isle of Pines was finally settled after surveys revealed that it would never be appropriate for a naval base, and the US Senate ratified the Hay-Quesada Treaty on March 13, 1925.[50] The Unión Obrera de Banes's struggle for Macabí, however, lasted two more years and ended in the company's favor.[51] Nevertheless, the connection between workers' rights and Cuban sovereignty had been firmly established. Later, when strikers took over the mill in 1933, the first thing they did was to declare "free commerce" in Macabí.

Their struggle, in turn, influenced the young communist party in Cuba. At the founding congress in August 1925, Mella brought up the issue of free enterprise in the bateyes of Cuba. The young leader knew of the Banes workers' efforts to eliminate the company's monopoly in Macabí when he discussed the United Fruit Company, proposed a rural campaign, and called for bateyes to be considered state lands.[52] For half a decade, however, little was to come of this suggestion, or really any mobilizing effort regarding sugar workers. The PCC spent this time small, relatively isolated from other regional communist parties (CPs), struggling to survive, and not making a significant effort to organize workers in the island's most important industry.

Sugar Workers and the Partido Comunista de Cuba

In August of 1925, representatives from four Cuban *Agrupaciones Comunistas* met in Havana to found the Partido Comunista de Cuba. The party was internationally influenced from the start. Of the seventeen individuals present, six were foreign, including the Mexican revolutionary Enrique Flores Magón who chaired the congress, a Spaniard, and three Eastern European Jews.[53] Two Cubans present, Carlos Baliño and Julio Antonio Mella, are commonly recognized as the founding fathers of Cuban communism. Over three decades earlier, Baliño had worked with José Martí to found the Partido Revolucionario Cubano, which led Cuba's final independence war against Spain. During the republic's first decades, Baliño launched several socialist organizations and, after the Russian Revolution, became a dedicated communist.[54] As we have seen, the much-younger Mella was a student leader in the university-reform movement and a committed anti-imperialist.[55] This early iteration of Cuban communism thus fused the revolutionary nationalism espoused by Cuba's independence heroes, a younger generation active in the growing anti-imperialist movement, and the influence of radicals from abroad.

Despite Mella's remarks about the importance of the sugar proletariat at the founding conference and despite the theoretical importance of sugar in Cuba's revolutionary struggle, the party was slow to organize among sugar workers and generally declined to prioritize mill and field laborers before the 1930s. PCC leadership overlooked the sugar proletariat for several reasons. To some extent, racism persisted within the ranks of the party, and many sugar workers were Afro-Cuban or Afro-Antillean; in the sugar fields of the east, up to 90 percent of the workforce was Antillano.[56] Specifically, party militants believed that Haitian and British West Indians were part of the problem, not the solution; foreign workers were, as one organizer put it, "obstacles" to social revolution because of their language difference and a supposed willingness to work for low pay.[57] Additionally, as with organized labor, logistical factors impeded the party's ability to maneuver, including the geographical dispersion of sugar estates, company-controlled railways, and the presence of the Rural Guard and private armed forces. Instead, the PCC focused its initial energy on connecting with existing labor guilds and unions and on simply surviving.

In 1925, the same year that the party was founded, newly elected Cuban President Gerardo Machado launched a violent crackdown against labor activists and radicals of all stripes. Wearing the mantle of nationalism, he proclaimed that he would protect Cuba's independence by avoiding another US intervention. This, however, was to be achieved through protecting the interests of foreign capital. Two weeks after the party's founding conference, PCC Secretary General José Miguel Pérez was arrested and deported to Spain where he was later killed by *franquista* rebels during the Spanish Civil War.[58] On September 19, 1925, Enrique Varona, who led the railroad and sugar strike wave in eastern Cuba the year before, was gunned down in public view while heading to a union event with his wife and young daughter.[59] Soon Machado imprisoned or deported much of the PCC leadership.

Forced into clandestine operations, the PCC suffered from a dearth of financial resources and leadership in its early years. The party remained relatively small, struggling to survive rather than organizing broad swaths of workers, let alone sugar workers in remote company towns. In 1927, the PCC claimed fewer than two hundred members, concentrated primarily in Havana and the surrounding region, with some reach into the eastern port of Manzanillo and the central city of Cienfuegos. Repression against the party changed its demographics; while Europeans (Eastern European Jews and Spaniards) outnumbered Cubans upon the PCC's founding, by 1928 so many had been deported that Cubans made up 80 percent of the mere 149 members.[60] The

PCC struggled to accomplish basic tasks, such as securing a printing press and maintaining communication with remote cells, and spent its early years largely attempting to restructure in the aftermath of Machado's repression.[61]

Matters were made worse by Moscow's inattention to American Communist Parties. Founded in 1919 to spread communist revolution beyond Russia, the Communist International had mainly concentrated on Europe in its first decade. American CPs suffered from a lack of funds, tactical assistance, and leadership. Communication between Havana and Moscow was so poor that a fraudulent communist was able to carry on a brief correspondence with the Kremlin.[62] As Barry Carr has demonstrated, the PCC was a "Caribbean backwater" in global communist circles in its early years. He quotes one party official who recalled, "We had the sensation that the party was completely abandoned, dependent on its own resources and without international links with anyone."[63]

In 1928, things began to change for the Partido Comunista de Cuba, thanks to developments taking place on and off the island. Around this time, the global communist movement entered a new era characterized by closer collaboration with Moscow and among regional parties (though the PCC still would have appreciated more funding) and by a strong sense of international proletarian solidarity. At the same time, the PCC was regrouping its leadership and expanding its rank and file thanks to a changing political and economic climate in Cuba. With increased capacity at home and amid a period of greater international collaboration, the PCC began organizing hitherto neglected groups. By late 1932, Cuba's multinational, multiracial sugar workforce would be foremost among these newly prioritized constituencies.

The Communist International launched a new era of proletarian internationalism at its historic Sixth Congress in mid-1928. According to Soviet theorists, the Russian Revolution had ushered in successive stages of world capitalism's collapse: a first period of revolutionary struggle had been followed by a second period of capitalist stabilization. A "Third Period," known formally as such, was launched at the Sixth Congress and was said to be the final crisis of capitalism. Moscow put forth an ultra-leftist "class against class" approach and instructed CPs to reject cooperation with the noncommunist left and to assert leadership of the world's working classes.[64] The Comintern prioritized internationalism and criticized member parties for "provincialism."[65] With this focus on international proletarian solidarity, Moscow turned its attention to new groups overseas, two of whom would be pivotal to the PCC.

First, the Comintern "discovered" Latin America. Colonial subjects were mobilizing across the globe, especially in India, indicating a state of crisis for imperialist capitalism. The Sixth Congress declared that its "most important strategic tasks ... [were] concerned with the revolutionary battle in the colonies, semi-colonies, and dependent countries."[66] The Comintern and sister organizations, including Red Aid International (RAI) and the Red International of Labor Unions (Profitern), turned their attention to the Americas in order to confront the world's newest imperialist power, the United States, in its own backyard.[67] At the Sixth Congress, delegates from Latin American countries, including two from Cuba, represented the region in significant numbers for the first time, and the Partido Comunista de Cuba was formally admitted to the Communist International.[68]

Moscow hardly arrived at recognizing the revolutionary potential of the Americas in a vacuum; rather, the congress was responding to an upsurge of insurgency across the region. The Mexican Revolution of 1910 was the first great social revolution of the twentieth century (predating the Russian Revolution, for that matter). In Haiti, the Caco rebels had been waging a war of resistance against US occupation since 1915. Likewise, a guerrilla insurgency, often called *gavilleros* or bandits, made trouble for US Marines occupying the Dominican Republic from 1916 to 1924. A year before the Sixth Congress, Augusto César Sandino began a fierce insurrection against the US occupation of Nicaragua, and his was a cause célèbre for radicals across the Americas.[69] University-reform and anti-imperialist movements were also taking off in several Latin American countries, and labor strikes were on the rise. Protests against dictatorships in Cuba, Venezuela, and Peru were increasing. At the same time, violent suppression from the US Marines and regional dictators provided fodder for communist propaganda. With new attention on the Americas in light of this surge in popular resistance movements, the Comintern moved its South American Bureau from Moscow to Buenos Aires and established a Caribbean Bureau in New York shortly after the Sixth Congress.[70]

The second major Comintern priority that affected Cuban communism was the congress's forceful move on the "Negro Question," or the matter of how to approach the particular struggles of Black people globally.[71] The Sixth Congress declared that communists must make common cause with Black liberation struggles. Like the turn to Latin America, this position was developed in conversation with and in response to agitation already well under way. In 1913, Vladimir Lenin had expressed support for African Americans, a stance formalized in the Comintern's 1920 "Theses on the National and Colonial Question" which argued that communist parties must support "revolutionary movements among the dependent nations and those without equal rights (e.g. in Ireland, and among the American negroes), and in the colonies."[72] Several New Negro intellectuals joined regional communist parties and pushed for an aggressive approach to Black liberation. Suriname-born Otto Huiswoud and

Jamaican Claude McKay led a New York organization of Black communists called the African Blood Brotherhood (ABB) before joining the US communist party. They addressed the Communist International's Fourth Congress in 1922, which acknowledged the "awakened race consciousness" and "spirit of rebellion" of African-descended peoples worldwide and proclaimed that "the Negro problem has become a vital question of the world revolution."[73] African American PCC member leader Lovett Fort-Whiteman addressed the Fifth Congress in 1924, and his fellow African American Harry Haywood, known as the "Black Bolshevik," studied at Bolshevik schools in Moscow before attending the Sixth Congress. African American James Ford (who later attended the communist labor congress in Havana in 1934) represented the CPUSA at the Red International of Labor Unions (Profitern) and was heavily involved in 1928 Sixth-Congress debates. These diasporic intellectuals and activists pressured the Kremlin to address the specific needs of Black workers, a position that, in turn, reverberated across the Americas.[74]

Undergirding communist attention to the "Negro Question" was the widespread popularity of the Garvey movement and its success in mobilizing Black women and men around the world. Tens of thousands had joined the Universal Negro Improvement Association in the US and in the Caribbean, participated in its activities, and contributed their time, energy, and money to the cause, as communist leaders were well aware. In fact, the Black communist African Blood Brotherhood had caused an uproar at the 1921 UNIA Convention attended by Harold and Anita Collins of Banes. The ABB's delegation attempted to siphon supporters directly from the UNIA on the convention floor. ABB members publicly condemned Garvey and the Black Star Line and, when the convention proceedings did not include these remarks, disseminated an official-looking circular which included them. Garvey promptly had the delegation expelled.[75] According to Black communists like McKay and Huiswoud, Garvey's entrepreneurial program and, worse, his "Back to Africa" message had distracted Black workers from the essential work of class struggle.[76] This opinion was shared by Cuban communists who in 1929 and as late as 1932 were still discussing the dangers posed by Garveyism, which they claimed gave Black workers false hope and drove a wedge between the working classes.[77]

Even those who fundamentally disagreed with the tenets of Garveyism, however, understood Garvey's enormous appeal. Amid a vociferous critique of Garvey, McKay wrote in 1922, "No intelligent Negro dare deny the almost miraculous effect and the world-wide breadth and sweep of Garvey's propaganda methods."[78] He later argued that Garvey had "aroused the social consciousness of the Negro masses more than any leader ever did."[79] To observers, the Garvey movement signaled a renewed political awakening on the part of Black peoples worldwide and jolted many on the left into recognizing the mobilizing power of race.[80]

In short, Moscow's evolving thinking on national and colonial questions, engagement with diasporic figures, and awareness of a rise in Black activism—of all kinds, including Garveyism—all pushed the Comintern to forcefully proclaim its support for Black workers. Moscow directed local parties, like the PCC, to "struggle for the complete equality of rights for the Negroes," and urged organizing Black workers, largely through the International Trade Union Committee of Negro Workers (ITUCNW) and its paper, *The Negro Worker*.[81] The Comintern declared support for self-determination for African Americans in those parts of the US South where they were a majority of the population, a policy that was applied to eastern Cuba in 1932.[82]

Amid Moscow's Third Period directive for CPs to assume leadership of the global working masses, the "discovery" of Latin America, and the call to organize Black workers, American CPs began addressing hitherto neglected constituencies. In fact, doing so was a Third Period directive. In 1929, the Comintern's Political Secretariat instructed the PCC to agitate among Black workers.[83] The Cuban party's "big brother," the CPUSA, also charged the PCC to "energetically penetrate the masses" in a 1930 open letter.[84] Later, in 1932, Moscow told Red Aid International's Cuban arm, Defensa Obrera Internacional (DOI), to work with labor unions, the unemployed, and local peasantries in an effort to "grow extraordinarily" and "become a true organization of the masses."[85] The call to widen the party base, however, was actually much more specific; a geographically expansive and interconnected network of communists had their sights set on agricultural-export companies and explicitly called on the PCC to prioritize sugar workers.

The first serious discussion of the agricultural proletariat took place at the 1929 founding congress of the Confederación Sindical Latinoamericana (CSLA) in Montevideo. There, representatives of communist-affiliated labor unions debated, among other issues, how best to incorporate agricultural workers into the communist movement. The final resolution acknowledged that, although Latin America was largely a region of agricultural countries, rural wage earners were "completely disorganized in every country" and proclaimed that their unionization should be a top priority for local CPs.[86] The congress noted that "foreign capital has . . . converted Latin American agriculture into an economic appendage of the imperialist countries." Workers for foreign companies, then, "must be a strong focal point for all our labor actions and especially in our fight against imperialism."[87] The CSLA specifically condemned brutal conditions on United Fruit Company properties in Cuba,

Colombia, and Panama.[88] Its final resolution demanded measures such as an end to payment in company-store credit and criminalization of the practice of evicting workers who participate in strikes.[89]

At that congress, an Afro-Cuban communist named Sandalio Junco addressed the plight of Afro-Antillean workers for large US companies. Junco had been the leader of a bakers' union and had risen to prominence in the PCC, representing Cuba in the ITUCNW.[90] His CSLA paper "El problema de la raza negra y el movimiento proletario" detailed exploitation of Haitian, Jamaican, and other Antillano laborers on fruit, sugar, and other commodity-crop plantations. United Fruit and similar companies, he explained, carried out a "modern slave trade." Labor unions, he argued, must open their doors to foreign Black workers. Junco cited the Garvey movement as a reason local communist parties needed to be more aggressive in recruiting Black workers, arguing that Garveyism "divert[s] them from the path of anti-imperialism."[91] He suggested the formation of a union of immigrants, perhaps unaware of or ignoring the fact that the Unión de Obreros Antillanos had been active a few years prior. Junco's proposal made it into the final resolutions, which called on CPs to organize Afro-Caribbean immigrant workers.[92] While the theoretical importance of the region's agricultural proletariat was clear to figures like Junco, it would take the PCC two more years to make inroads among the sugar proletariat.

The Cuban Communist Party began to regroup at the end of the decade. Machado was doubling down on political repression, which actually increased support for the PCC. The traditional Conservative and Liberal parties were discredited after agreeing to extend the presidential term in 1927. In 1929, assassins gunned down Mella in Mexico City, where he had been living in exile since late 1925. He was killed in front of his girlfriend, the Italian American actress and photographer Tina Modotti. Modotti, the Mexican muralist Diego Rivera, and the US-based journalist Carleton Beals all stayed with his body for several hours after the autopsy, illustrating the range of cosmopolitan intellectuals and artists who supported the young revolutionary in exile.[93] While a smear campaign was launched against Modotti to shroud Mella's death in confusion, the murder was carried out by Machado's agents.[94] In 1930, the Cuban president outlawed rival political parties, closed the university, and expanded secret-police hit jobs.[95] In this repressive atmosphere, resistance to Machado's dictatorship grew, as did demonstrations, critical coverage (even in the conservative press), and protest culture.[96] Since its founding, the PCC had spoken out against Machado's "hand of terror" and the regime's "assassinations, illegal detentions and kidnappings."[97] In this repressive atmosphere, the party's longstanding record of opposition expanded its appeal.

Another factor contributing to the PCC's growing strength was its platform of economic redistribution. As several historians have pointed out, the worldwide Great Depression "came early" to Cuba.[98] In the mid-1920s, the US increased tariffs on sugar in order to protect domestic growers, and in 1926 Cuba's Verdeja Act restricted the cane crop in order to prevent oversupply. With Cuba's entire economy subject to the highs and lows of the sugar industry, the negative effects of crop restrictions were widespread. The PCC fought for measures such as unemployment pay, housing, and health insurance; debt relief for peasants and small farmers; rent reductions for workers and peasants; and an end to crop restrictions.[99] Economic grievances fused with anti-imperialism, which had been on the rise since the collapse of 1920–21. The PCC program entailed several anti-imperialist propositions, including "overthrow the foreign imperialist power and the domination of *latifundistas* and the great bourgeoisie; nationalization of the large companies . . . belonging to the imperialists; confiscation without indemnification of all land belonging to foreign companies . . . and redistribution among the peasantry; cancelation of all debts that the Cuban people owe to American banks."[100] The PCC platform, in other words, lent it political credence during difficult economic and political times.

In the late 1920s, the PCC's main goal was to penetrate Cuba's labor movement and, especially, to wrestle leadership of organized labor away from anarcho-syndicalists. Because tobacco and transportation workers were the most thoroughly organized and because there already existed guilds in the urban trades (such as bakers, bricklayers, carpenters, painters, and street sweepers), the party initially concentrated on making inroads into these sectors. Relying on a network of small, secret cells, organizers cooperated with friendly organizations and reached out to members of urban unions and guilds.[101] At the turn of the decade, the party finally succeeded in taking control of the Confederación Nacional de Obreros de Cuba (CNOC), which had over 16,000 members. CNOC, Cuba's first nationwide labor association was established just days before the PCC in August of 1925, when representatives from well over one hundred workers' organizations, including two from Banes, gathered to discuss uniting the labor movement across professional, regional, and national barriers. Anarcho-syndicalism dominated CNOC's early years, but Machado's repression of anarchists was so extensive that the PCC managed to assert control in 1929.[102] On May 20, 1930, marking the anniversary of the 1902 US withdrawal from Cuba, CNOC and the PCC organized a general strike. The strike paralyzed production and transportation in Havana and the "red" port city of Manzanillo in the east as well as some interior towns. Even though both the PCC and CNOC were operating illegally, the strike signaled the PCC's formal entry into mass politics.[103]

The strike was largely organized by the poet Rubén Martínez Villena of the PCC. Martínez Villena was from a well-off family, had worked as a secretary for Cuban anthropologist Fernando Ortiz, and had steadily moved to the left in his politics.[104] He had been active in Cuba's struggles against imperialism and for workers' rights since the early 1920s, having participated in the 1923 Veterans and Patriot's movement to Cubanize the state, the student movement, the Liga Antiimperialista de las Américas, and Mella's Universidad Popular José Martí.[105] He was close with Mella and accompanied the young leader to Banes in 1925. Martínez Villena joined the PCC in 1927, and rose within the ranks, eventually serving on its Central Committee. Upon Mella's death in 1929, Martínez Villena, despite suffering from tuberculosis, became the de facto leader and intellectual voice of the party. After the general strike of 1930, however, he fled the island and headed to New York, followed by the Soviet Union for medical treatment.[106]

With its popularity on the rise and with an invigorated base, the PCC expanded. In 1929, a cell was established at the Mabay mill near Bayamo in Oriente, though only one of the five militants was associated with the mill. By 1930, the party operated several cells in the central province of Santa Clara. That year, a cell was established in Banes, and one at the nearby Tacajó mill in 1931.[107] In Banes, young people led the way. Rafael Hernández, a former sugar worker, recalled that a student named Luis Felipe Fuente had been expelled from the University of Havana during Machado's crackdown and returned to his hometown to organize Oriente's northern coast. He made contact with those he expected to be sympathetic to party ideals, including young people and workers affiliated with existing unions. Fuente and a handful of Banes residents established a PCC cell after two secret meetings. A delegate from Banes attended the foundational conference of the Liga Juvenil Comunista (LJC) in 1931, and the league, in turn, aided the expansion of the PCC's work in Banes by writing slogans on walls, distributing pamphlets, and speaking with workers. Banes's early PCC leaders and members were by and large laborers for the company's repair shops, workshops, and transportation sectors, but not its sugar mills or cane fields.[108]

By 1931, the Partido Comunista de Cuba had successfully extended its reach from a small center of operations in Havana to a nationwide network of clandestine cells reaching the island's company towns. While formal numbers remained relatively small, the PCC's influence was felt across the island through its control of the CNOC, affiliated organizations (including the Liga Antiimperialista, DOI which defended political prisoners, and the LJC), and its and increasingly vocal leadership of the opposition movement.[109] Yet, despite this wide expansion and despite its status as one of the more prominent communist parties in the hemisphere, the PCC had yet to significantly reach into the nation's most important industry.

Certainly, leading Cuban communists believed in the theoretical and practical importance of mobilizing sugar workers. Most prominent among them was Martínez Villena himself, who had visited Banes in 1925. As early as 1926, he wrote that Cuba's economic problem was its dependence on US-run sugar and on the foreign market for that sugar.[110] By 1930, he saw organizing sugar workers as paramount to the island's revolutionary struggle, especially given the theoretical imperatives of the Third Period. In a letter to the CPUSA's Central Committee, he criticized the Comintern and the CPUSA for their inattention to Cuba and the PCC. "The Communist Party of Cuba has been criminally left out in the cold," he wrote, and complained that the PCC had not received promised funds from Moscow. He brought a careful study of Marxism to bear on the situation in Cuba and argued that inattention to Cuba was all the more criminal because the island represented the best chance for anti-imperialist revolution in the Americas. "Cuba is showing the characteristics of the third period perhaps more sharply than any other U.S. Caribbean colony," he wrote. The crisis of capitalism was at its worst there because Cuba had the largest US investment of all Latin American nations, and all of that investment rested on "the live axle of the economical life in Cuba: the sole basic industry, sugar." As with many export crops, the sugar industry created an agricultural proletariat. But what was unique about the Cuban situation, according to Martínez Villena, was that, because sugar is processed on site, it had also produced an *industrial* proletariat, "a remarkable characteristic of the imperialist investment in Cuba." Communist revolution required an industrial proletariat, and Cuba had one. In this sense, it was "the most advanced of the Caribbean countries." Martínez Villena condemned Moscow's inattention precisely because a lack of funds prevented organizers from traveling to the countryside. "The Communist party had not been able to . . . organize the interior of the country, farms, sugar mills, other cities besides Havana . . . because the party has no money for trips . . ." He asked for "economic support, MONEY," a printing press, and personnel so that they could begin this important work.[111] In short, the intellectual voice of the Communist Party of Cuba demanded funds from Moscow precisely so that the party could reach sugar mills and fields. Sugar was becoming the axle on which both the imperialist economy and oppositional organizing efforts pivoted.

While Martínez Villena and the CPUSA may have disagreed about financial matters, international communists would come to share Martínez Villena's commitment to harnessing the revolutionary potential of sugar workers. In March 1930, the Comintern's political secretariat wrote to the CPs of England, Holland, France, and the US about a revolutionary upsurge in the Caribbean; the letter urged these CPs to form "colonial committees." The directive pointed to a rise in demonstrations against regional dictatorships, as well as Sandino's insurgency in Nicaragua, the 1928 strike of banana workers in Colombia (which was brutally repressed and later became the subject of Gabriel García Márquez's novel, *One Hundred Years of Solitude*), and a 1929 incident in which exiled Venezuelans seized a Dutch arsenal in Curaçao. These events "signaled, once and for all the importance of the Caribbean region for the development of revolutionary struggle of workers and peasants against imperialism." Moscow explicitly urged attention to foreign workers on US-run fruit and sugar plantations. The letter noted that "United Fruit Co., Ford, [and] the sugar companies of Cuba import black laborers from Haiti, Santo Domingo, Jamaica, Martinique, etc. for their banana, rubber, and sugar plantations" and instructed CPs in the metropoles "to organize the agricultural working masses of large plantations."[112] Here, however, Moscow revealed its Eurocentrism. Leadership, in this model, came from the "mother countries"—not from local leaders like Martínez Villena who was urging exactly the same thing around the same time. A PCC member writing under the name "L. Miranda" criticized the Comintern on this front, writing "the CI has forgotten that it has in Cuba a communist party." He suggested wryly that such imperialist thinking would be rectified if the Comintern provided greater financial support to the PCC.[113] Indeed, as Margaret Stevens has pointed out, Caribbean communists often called out North American and European organizers for overlooking their work.[114]

The Caribbean Bureau of the Comintern also called for action among neglected constituencies in the Americas. Through this New York-based outfit, intellectuals, party members, and union organizers from the US and across the greater Caribbean used local knowledge to translate theoretical issues into political praxis. As Sandra Pujals explains, the bureau "added a more inclusive, local idiosyncrasy to an altogether Eurocentric and ideologically orthodox entity."[115] The bureau centered race and national oppression in its work and called upon local parties to address racism. In 1931, the bureau took the PCC to task for having "very few Negro workers, though a third of the [Cuban] population is Negro."[116] That same year, the Caribbean Bureau launched a weekly newspaper, *Mundo Obrero*, whose target audience was the "working masses and exploited peasants of the Caribbean." Its editors aimed to cover the region, including industrial centers and agricultural zones—especially the "banana plantations and sugar fiefdoms of yankee imperialism," where they made special appeals to organize workers on foreign-owned plantations.[117] Later, in 1933, Rubén Martínez Villena worked with the bureau and coedited the paper while sojourning in New York on his way back from the Soviet Union.

In short, by the early 1930s, communists on and off the island agreed that it was time to prioritize sugar workers, but the task was an uphill struggle. Moreover, even when focused on sugar, the PCC's institutional apparatuses only slowly came to recognize the revolutionary potential of Afro-Caribbean immigrants. In 1930, CNOC launched a sugar campaign, but only succeeded in organizing a few mills close to Havana.[118] To make matters worse, in the period between mid-1931 and the end of 1932, the party faced renewed persecution, with some leaders repeatedly detained and others spending their time and energy absconding into the countryside. In April 1932, the PCC's Political Bureau only had two members. Informers within the ranks and widespread censorship made the simple task of corresponding with interior cells nearly impossible.[119] Nevertheless, heeding calls from Moscow, the Caribbean Bureau in New York, fellow CPs, and its own leadership, the Partido launched a campaign to expand its base in 1931 and sent delegates to the provinces, especially eastern sugar regions. Organizers systematically collected information about working and living conditions in the Cuban countryside. Initially, these efforts remained largely focused on peasants and agrarian leagues—not necessarily on macheteros for foreign companies.

The year 1932 marked a major change in approach, however, as communist organizers moved from neglecting rural, foreign workers to demanding their full incorporation in the movement. At the beginning of the year, communist organizations in Cuba were still not thinking explicitly about the sugar proletariat in its entirety—that is, including foreign workers. In February, CNOC encouraged sugar workers to "prepare your fight" and distributed a manual for carrying out strikes. The authors carefully detailed the roles that distinct groups should have in the struggle; women and children, for instance, were to seek material support from nearby communities. The manual, however, included no specific demands or tasks for foreign workers.[120] This absence is particularly conspicuous in light of the fact that it did address macheteros and in the early 1930s Afro-Caribbean immigrants made up between 80 and 100 percent of cane cutters in most of Camagüey and Oriente.[121]

Over the course of 1932, the party's understanding of the sugar proletariat expanded. In January, the PCC had set up a planning commission for a national sugar workers' union and sent militants, especially Communist Youth League members, into the countryside to investigate labor and living conditions on the large sugar estates. Unsurprisingly, they found widespread exploitation and abuse, especially toward foreign workers. Some immigrants had been forcibly deported to their home islands, as in the case of twenty-three men from the Central Punta Alegre in Camagüey. Others had been violently compelled to work, as in the case of forty-eight Haitian workers forced by the Rural Guard to work at the Senado mill also in Camagüey. Others were murdered, as was Haitian Nicolás Simón near Santiago.[122] Confronted with the reality of abuse against foreign workers, the party and its sister organizations developed a much more inclusive and specific organizing agenda.

The Sindicato Nacional de Obreros de la Industria Azucarera (SNOIA) was founded in Santa Clara in December 1932.[123] Representatives from thirty-two mills and all provinces condemned working and living conditions in the sugar industry and called on all sugar workers to join. Sugar laborers, they claimed, "lived as though we were slaves with our bodies dying from work" in *barracones* without light and air and ridden with bedbugs, fleas, and lice. For as little as ten cents per day, the SNOIA complained, cane cutters and haulers suffered the persecution of the Rural Guard, company police, foremen, administrators, and Machado's security apparatus only to be compelled to work at gunpoint and denied pay. The SNOIA argued that the only way to prevent such suffering was to organize. Referencing the successful strikes of the mid-1920s, the founding manifesto exclaimed, "We have to fight next year. The only option we have is to go on strike like we did in 1925," and named Varona's inclusive union as a model to follow. "Yes, the company has a powerful Rural Guard," the SNOIA continued, "but we can be strong too if we create a united front." In contrast to the February strike manual, which made no mention of foreign workers, SNOIA founding documents included immigrants in both their plans and their demands: strike committees should be "elected and formed by all workers, by whites and blacks, by native and foreign, by Haitians, Jamaicans, and Chinese, by adults and young people, by men and women, by agricultural and mill workers." Because the SNOIA was "against all forms of discrimination, in salary and in treatment, toward *negros*, Jamaicans and Haitians," it demanded "equal pay for equal work and the right to all work positions for *negros*, Jamaicans, and Haitians."[124]

The SNOIA thus announced its firm commitment to labor internationalism not only in theory, but also in practice. The sugar workers' union quickly affiliated with the CSLA. It aimed to organize agricultural and industrial workers into a single sugar syndicate. The union served as a clearinghouse of information and surveyed workers at different centrales for details about wages, shift schedules, living conditions, and housing facilities. In response to its findings, the SNOIA formulated a set of nationwide demands, including task-specific minimum salaries, an eight-hour workday and the establishment of three distinct shifts (which would reduce unemployment as round-the-clock work would require three sets of laborers instead of two), abolition of payment in company-store credit, immediate back pay, housing and other support during the dead season, and the abolition of all forms of forced labor.[125]

The year 1932 also marked a sea change in the PCC approach to race. That year, two Cuban communists in Moscow, Aggeo Suárez Pérez and Ramón Nicolau (who would later organize Cubans in defense of the Spanish Republic), summarized the situation facing Afro-Cubans. As Tony Wood has detailed, they called Black Cubans an "oppressed national minority" and declared that they had the right to self-determination in the eastern regions of Oriente where they formed a numerical majority. The pair drew upon Oriente's history, highlighting the wars of independence and the Partido Independiente de Color's uprising as part of a larger tradition of Black struggle in the region.[126] Notably, the Garvey movement was never far from communist thinking on the race question, especially when it came to eastern Cuba; in that same report, Nicolau and Suárez Pérez were careful to distinguish the "right to self-determination" from "reactionary black separatism." They wrote, "petty bourgeoisie reformists have introduced to the black masses the 'Garveyist' theories," which, they claimed, called for "complete separation of black from white." Nicolau and Suárez Pérez urged the party to fight against and unmask the errors of the Garvey movement, which they claimed only harmed the struggle to liberate the Black masses.[127] As late as 1932, in other words, Cuban communists were still talking about the need to dissuade Black workers from Garveyism.

Their call for Black liberation through the right to self-determination was not initially met with enthusiasm in Cuba. As Wood puts it, "In late September 1932, an ocean—literally and figuratively—still separated the PCC's views on Black self-determination form those of Nicolau and Suárez Pérez. Yet, within three months, the gap closed."[128] It is no coincidence that the party moved away from a position, to use Wood's words, "constrained by [the] concept of racelessness" at the same time that it was wrapping up a major organizing campaign in the sugar industry. While Nicolau and Suárez Pérez were theorizing the Negro Question in Moscow and urging the PCC to do likewise in Cuba, the PCC was building the national sugar workers' union, collecting information on working conditions, and sending organizers into the field. Organizers on the ground were, albeit slowly, coming to terms with the essential nature of Cuba's sugar proletariat—not *in spite of* its largely Afro-Cuban and Afro-Antillano composition, but *because* of it—to revolutionary struggle on the island.

In mid-1933, the party-led SNOIA was up and running in Oriente and including foreign workers in its plans and goals. Organizers were instructed to "meet laborers in their places of work and in the language of the workers, distributing leaflets in English, French, and Chinese for the Jamaicans, Haitians, and Chinese, respectively." Revealing their own sense of intellectual superiority, party leaders planned to teach sugar workers about the connection between their "most basic demands" and the wider struggle against imperialism. Field organizers were instructed to "develop the voice" of workers and connect their demands to anti-imperialism.[129] The PCC told cells, especially near *ingenios*, to use the everyday demands of workers to "deepen the movement, demonstrate the political consequences of these demands and push for a wider struggle—not just economic, but also political." This would be accomplished through youth clubs, sporting clubs, libraries, and work with women and children.[130] The DOI also directed local organizers to connect immediate demands for better pay and conditions to anti-imperialism, emphasizing for distinct constituencies—women, Black workers, the youth, and so on—the connections between their daily battles and the "anti-imperialist character of our struggles and our role in developing solidarity among all groups exploited and oppressed by yankee imperialism and native exploiters."[131]

Such directives, of course, overlooked the fact that, as early as 1918, sugar workers were putting their daily struggles in wider anti-imperial context by demanding the removal of US Marines. The Unión de Obreros Antillanos was petitioning Great Britain's foreign office for better representation in 1924. And the Banes Unión Obrera had been calling for Cuban sovereignty in Macabí, on the grounds of the Hay-Quesada Treaty, since before the PCC was even formed in 1925. In short, though the PCC and its sister organizers presumed to bring international analyses of exploitation to sugar enclaves the 1930s, sugar workers had been thinking along these lines for over a decade.

By early 1933, the PCC and its sister organizations had achieved significant success in expanding their reach in sugar-producing regions, including the northern coast of Oriente. DOI, hoping to become "deeply entrenched . . . in plantations," had made a special effort to recruit sugar workers, and 16 percent of its members were in sugar the sugar industry that year, a larger portion than any other sector. DOI also succeeded in recruiting Black members; of its 500 members, 133 were "*negros nativos*" and another 42 were "*negros extranjeros.*"[132] The PCC itself claimed a membership of over 3,000 and a cell network in every city and large town. Additionally, affiliated organizations like the Anti-Imperialist League spread the party's influence while several thousand members of Cuba's Communist Youth League carried out organizing activities and propaganda efforts in company towns.[133]

In early 1933, a wave of dramatic sugar strikes began in Cuba. Most famously, agricultural workers at the Central Nazábal in Villa Clara struck in late February and were soon joined by mill workers. They demanded land during the dead season and union recognition. When the company refused to negotiate, strikers took control of the mill and imprisoned company management. They established a strike committee, a militia of peasants and workers, and an auxiliary committee that distributed food and provisions. Strikes erupted in Oriente and in Camagüey, where workers too established strike committees and militias. At Nazábal and at Jatibonico in Camagüey, worker militias repelled the Rural Guard.[134] Throughout these events, the communist party claimed responsibility for this revolutionary upsurge. Indeed, the early 1933 sugar strikes were strongest in regions most thoroughly organized by the PCC: Las Villas and near the "red" city of Manzanillo.[135]

Such was the state of affairs when Martínez Villena decided it was time to come home from exile. Having traveled to the USSR (a long trip that took him through Florida, New York, France, England, and Germany in 1930), he spent 1931 and 1932 receiving treatment for his tuberculosis in the Caucasus mountains and in Moscow as well as participating in the Latin American Secretariat of the Comintern. Upon hearing of Cuba's increasing mobilization against Machado in early 1933, however, he headed back. His first stop was New York, where he joined the anti-imperialist scene in Harlem and planned his clandestine return home. He contributed to radical newspapers and journals, including the *Mundo Obrero* and *The Communist*. Soon after his arrival in New York in March of 1933, Martínez Villena delivered a lecture at the Anti-Imperialist League headquarters on "The Problem of Cuba" and, shortly after, penned an essay on "The Rise of the Revolutionary Movement in Cuba."[136]

In his Marxist analysis, Martínez Villena argued that Cuba had tremendous revolutionary potential. His opening lines read, "In the Caribbean, we find nowhere at the present time a revolutionary movement at a higher level of development or of greater importance than that in Cuba . . ." He offered several explanations. First, a near-complete dependence on sugar resulted in a deep level of US imperialist penetration. Second, the global economic crisis was thus felt most acutely in Cuba where foreign interests and the state alike ensured economic burdens were passed onto workers. Finally, laborers, so burdened, increasingly resorted to revolutionary action. Cuba suffered even more than the monocrop republics of Central America because the economic crisis had led to the unique problem of production quotas, and thus even more widespread unemployment than the already-high norm. Unlike Central American bananas, Cuban cane competed with US cane and beet sugar, so powerful companies aimed to "force down their production costs practically to zero point." The situation was leading, at the time of his writing, to a breaking point: the working masses were becoming radicalized and rising up. According to Martínez Villena, the internal contradictions of capitalist imperialism in Cuba were doing exactly what they were supposed to do: generating revolution.[137]

The sugar proletariat, according to Martínez Villena, constituted Cuba's revolutionary vanguard. Their "revolutionary upsurge" was "without any kind of doubt the most important of the struggles of the Cuban masses against imperialism." Sugar workers in Cuba were paving the path forward for revolution at the heart of US imperialism, and thanks to their efforts, "It is possible to state categorically that Cuba at present constitutes the weakest link in the chain of Caribbean imperialism." Revolutionaries everywhere should emulate the salient features of their incipient insurgency. These features were: first, that it was "a mass struggle directed by the masses;" second, that industrial and agricultural workers had united; third, that there was "unity of black and white, of native and foreign-born;" and fifth, that peasants had joined. These were "prerequisites" for anti-imperialist revolution in the Third Period.[138] Sugar workers, in other words, were at the heart of the most significant struggle against US imperialism being waged in the Third Period. Little did Martínez Villena know when he wrote about the "revolutionary situation" in early 1933 just how revolutionary sugar workers would become by the end of the year.

Conclusion

In his 1944 novel *Masters of the Dew*, Haitian author Jacques Roumain's protagonist Manuel has returned home to Haiti after fifteen years harvesting cane in Cuba. He describes the sugar industry by explaining, "you could walk from here to town without seeing anything but sugar cane, sugar cane everywhere..." All of this is owned by "a white American, Mr. Wilson by name. The factory, too, everything all around is his." Workers, he says, "got nothing but the strength of their arms, not a handful of soil, not a drop of water—except their own sweat." Labor exploitation and pervasive contempt for field hands, especially Afro-Antilleans, Manuel tells us, were hallmarks of the sugar industry in Cuba, as was racism and abuse. He specifically mentions the *oriental* port city of Antilla near United Fruit's territory: "I left thousands and thousands of Haitians over there in Antilla. They live and die like dogs. *Matar a un Haitiano o a un perro:* to kill a Haitian or a dog is one and the same thing, say the rural police. They're just like wild beasts."[139]

But in Cuba, Manuel had also learned of labor solidarity. "At first, in Cuba, we had no defense and no way of resistance. One person thought himself white, another was a Negro, and there were plenty of misunderstandings among us. We were scattered like grains of sand, and the bosses walked on that sand. But when we realized that we were all alike, when we got together for the *huelga*—"Manuel was interrupted to explain what a strike is—"a NO uttered by a thousand voices speaking as one."[140] He had learned in Cuba that labor solidarity and work stoppages were the best ways to resist exploitation. In the story, Manuel's hometown of Fonds Rouges is suffering from a draught and the petty rivalries of its residents, but Manuel leads his neighbors in reviving a labor collective called *coumbite*. Though he does not live to see it, the coumbite eventually brings water to Fonds Rouges.

In Roumain's story, Manuel was not the only young person to have left home in search of work elsewhere. Some had gone to Haitian cities, and others had crossed the border into the Dominican Republic.[141] But it was Cuba—specifically northern Oriente—and the experiences of ubiquitous abuse and of cross-national labor organizing, that taught him the power of collective action and moved him to lead Fonds Rouges. By the time he wrote *Masters of the Dew*, Roumain had founded the Haitian Communist Party and was a member of an intellectual circle that included Black writers like African American poet Langston Hughes and Afro-Cuban poet and journalist Nicolás Guillén, Cuban Marxists like Leonardo Fernández Sánchez (who had accompanied Mella on his 1925 visit to Banes) and Juan Marinello (a PCC member who had worked closely with Martínez Villena), and other Latin American authors like the Chilean poet Pablo Neruda. For Roumain, Martínez Villena, and others who paid attention to the sugar proletariat in Cuba, it was not Havana or New York where one became politically educated; it was in the Cuban sugar fields near the port of Antilla where a character learned resistance, where a humble worker could become a traveled and experienced community leader.

Roumain's fictional Manuel has real-life counterparts, the most well-known of whom is Hugh Clifford Buchanan, "Jamaica's first Marxist." Buchanan spent several years in the 1920s laboring in the Cuban sugar industry before returning home in 1929. In Kingston, he was known to read communist literature by streetlight and to associate with fellow veterans of the Cuban sugar fields. Buchanan founded the Jamaican Workers and Tradesmen Union (JWTU) in 1936. He referred frequently to his time in Cuba in interviews and letters.[142] In 1938, the JWTU led a massive labor revolt on the island and joined in the wave of militancy sweeping the British West Indies in the late 1930s.[143]

In other words, the hubs of radical activism in the interwar period were not limited to major metropolises filled with well-known intellectuals, artists, and activists who traveled widely and contributed to newspapers with broad circulations. Certainly, Havana, New York, Mexico City, and Paris were unquestionably "nodal cities" in global radical networks.[144] But individuals like Mella, Martínez Villena, Junco, and Roumain also had their sights set on places such as northern Oriente—spaces that weighed heavy in their conceptualizations of imperialism, exploitation, and the path to revolution. In the early 1930s, the towns and sugar fields of companies like United Fruit, Cuba Cane, and the Cuban American Sugar Company figured prominently in communist approaches to these questions. As Anne Garland Mahler has written of Spanish Caribbean *novelas de la caña* (sugarcane novels), US-owned extraction zones functioned as a "microcosm" for wider analysis of capitalist imperialism and its possible opposition: the multilingual and multinational unity of workers.[145]

Indeed, for a moment in the history of the international left, Cuba's US-dominated sugar industry stood for all that was wrong with overlapping systems of capitalism, racial exploitation, and imperialism. The multinational workforce harvesting, hauling, grinding, and shipping Cuba's cane, however, also embodied the best possible response: cross-racial, cross-national labor unity. While the Comintern was calling for international proletarian unity and solidarity with Black workers during the Third Period, Cuba's diverse sugar workers were already there, launching strikes, fighting with the Rural Guard and private company guards, demanding better pay, and calling for Cuban sovereignty in the face of US imperialism. They would go on to show the world just how it was done in the fall of 1933, when they erupted into a cross-national, cross-racial insurgency. In that moment, communists looked on from near and far, watching as workers targeted the heart of US imperialism in Latin America.

4

"Hands Off Cuba"

The Sugar Insurgency of 1933 and International Responses

On August 30, 1933, Miguel Ángel Figueredo, a communist organizer who went by the name "Zapata," reported on strike activity in the United Fruit Company territory around Banes to Blas Roca, the Manzanillo district committee leader of the Partido Comunista de Cuba (PCC).[1] "The atmosphere here is completely revolutionary," he wrote. "Men and women of all nationalities fill the streets, and at any given moment, there are demonstrations in front of company offices." The day before, laborers had stopped work and taken control of the United Fruit properties, including the famous Boston sugar mill at Macabí and the surrounding cane fields. They had formed a strike committee, armed units known as *comités de estaca* for the wooden stakes they carried, a cooperative kitchen, and auxiliary groups. On August 31, Figueredo wrote, "To arrive at Macabí is to arrive in a soviet district."[2]

Figueredo was reporting from the frontlines of an insurgency that swept Cuba's sugar industry from August to November of 1933. In those months, workers struck across the island, seized thirty-six mills, and paralyzed almost a third of Cuba's sugar production.[3] The uprising began during a power vacuum formed in August when mounting opposition to President Gerardo Machado culminated a nationwide general strike and forced him from office. Sugar workers were among the first to strike that year, and they were not placated by Machado's removal. Instead, they continued striking through an interim administration and even through the short-lived administration of a reformist president, Dr. Ramón Grau San Martín. Only in February 1934 did the last of the strikes end. The insurgency was the culmination of decades of struggle in Cuban sugar fields and factories. Since the 1910s, workers had been forming increasingly inclusive labor unions and placing their local struggles in wider context, as chapter 3 details. By late 1932, the Communist Party was making inroads in Cuba's number one industry, and many (though not all) of the sugar strikers in 1933 were either led by the PCC or quickly affiliated with it.

While the revolution of 1933 is typically treated like a hallmark event in Cuba's national history (which it certainly was), it was also a transnational affair. For one, the workers who struck and seized sugar mills were themselves of diverse nationalities; Cubans joined Haitian, British West Indian, Chinese, and Spanish immigrants. In many cases Haitians and British West Indians were among the most militant. Throughout the insurrection, sugar workers and their allies connected the strikes to global events and wider systems of imperialism and exploitation, demonstrating a cosmopolitan sensibility. Insurgents deployed internationally recognizable symbols of revolution, such as the red flag and aliases like "Zapata" after the Mexican revolutionary icon. Most remarkably, strikers at several occupied mills formed "soviets," a reference to the councils of workers, peasants, and soldiers created during the Russian Revolution.

Also contributing to the revolution's transnational history is the fact that it reverberated well beyond Cuba. The world watched as sugar workers put international proletarian solidarity into practice and struck a blow to capitalist exploitation at the heart of US imperialism. From overseas, communists and other leftist figures corresponded with Cubans on the ground and launched a transnational defense of Cuba's workers. The 1933 revolution, and especially the sugar insurgency, figured prominently in an emerging landscape of radical, international resistance against racism, imperialism, and capitalist exploitation.

Rather than tell the national story of Cuba's 1933 revolution, which has been amply covered, this chapter takes a local-transnational approach.[4] First, I detail the sugar insurgency of 1933, focusing on events in the agricultural-export enclaves of northern Oriente. There, workers of diverse nationalities participated shoulder to shoulder, a fact which was not lost the international left, in a series of dramatic strikes and mill seizures that sent shockwaves through Cuba's most important industry. Although communists heralded the insurgency as a product of their leadership, sugar workers often organized spontaneously and disregarded party directives, seizing mills on their own and even defying the party line. In doing so, they radicalized the PCC, which had initially taken a more cautious position.

The chapter then moves on to address international responses to Cuba's revolution, especially the sugar insurgency. The global left heralded the workers' dramatic actions as a major strike against US imperialism and capitalist exploitation during a period of heightened repression in the Americas. Events in Cuba signaled the dawn of a new radicalism and promoted leftists to reconsider who constituted the revolutionary vanguard. Allies overseas rallied to protect the revolution under way against an expected US intervention, and "Hands Off Cuba" became a key item on the leftist agenda in the final third of 1933. Finally, the chapter explores the PCC's evolving approach to the plight of Afro-Antillean sugar workers. During and after the sugar insurgency, the party came to appreciate Antillano militancy and, by the end of the year, became Afro-Caribbean immigrants' biggest (and only) advocate in Cuba, vehemently defending immigrant workers against deportations and labor nationalization. This avid (and politically risky) position illustrates just how essential the island's multinational sugar workers had come to be in visions of anti-imperialist revolution in Cuba.

Cuba's 1933 Revolution and the Sugar Insurgency in Northern Oriente

In the early months of 1933, resistance against President Machado mounted and political violence overwhelmed the island. Even economic elites turned against the *machadato* as state forces, especially the secret police, interrogated, assassinated, and disappeared opponents of the regime in what became known as the "White Terror." The police killed thirty-two students between March 3 and May 7 alone, and the military regularly clashed with striking workers. Violent groups, including the right-wing ABC Revolutionary Society, used bombs and assassinations to destabilize the regime. In May and June, over 2,000 exiles of diverse political affiliations began returning home to play a part in the dictator's fall, including the young-but-ailing voice of the Cuban Communist Party, Rubén Martínez Villena.[5] Still suffering from tuberculosis, Martínez Villena boarded a United Fruit Company steamer called the SS *Platano* in New York on May 13 using a false US passport. Under the name José María Cintrón, a Puerto Rican, he disembarked uneventfully in Santiago de Cuba on May 17 and made his way to Havana with help from old friends.[6]

In May, US President Roosevelt sent Sumner Welles to replace Ambassador Harry F. Guggenheim and to mediate between Machado and opposition groups, including the ABC and the Unión Nacionalista composed of former Liberal and Conservative party leaders. The PCC, however, opposed the mediation process as yet another case of yankee interference and refused to participate. Mediation proved fruitless. In late July, bus drivers in Havana, angry about extortionary taxes, launched a strike that soon spread to taxi and truck drivers, then to other sectors across the country, including railway workers, printers, waiters, bakers, barbers, and shopkeepers. They paralyzed transportation in Cuba by August 1 and a general strike was under way by August 4. The movement spread across the island, with demonstrations in the streets of all Cuban provinces on August 8.[7]

That day, the communist-dominated Confederación Nacional de Obreros de Cuba (CNOC), which influenced most of the island's labor movement, met with Machado and agreed to end the strike in exchange for meeting the strikers' demands, as well as the release of political prisoners and legal recognition of the PCC and CNOC. Party leaders reasoned that a weakened Machado combined with greater room to maneuver for the party was preferable to a US intervention, which was sure to happen if the strikes continued. After accepting Machado's offer, party leaders instructed strikers to resume work. This deal, however, came to be known in communist circles as the "August mistake," as workers kept on striking—even after the fall of Machado.[8] On August 12, 1933, several army officers escorted the president to the airport, and he fled to Nassau. Jubilant crowded flooded the streets, and some took the opportunity to carry out violent reprisals against officials of the former regime. Crowds killed police officers in acts of retaliation against Machado's death squads. An interim government under President Carlos Manuel de Céspedes assumed power. Although (or perhaps because) it had Welles' support, the new administration could not contain the revolution taking hold in the country. The general strike ended on August 15 when transportation workers made a deal with the new government, but sporadic strikes and protests continued through August. Across the island, *antimachadista* political groups demonstrated and sacked the homes of prominent officials in the now-deposed government.[9]

On September 4, Fulgencio Batista, a Banes-born sergeant in the Cuban army, led a rebellion against the machadista officer corps. Born Rubén Fulgencio Batista Zaldívar, Batista grew up poor in the United Fruit region of Oriente and attended the Quaker school run by North American missionaries. As a young man, he cut cane and came to view companies like United Fruit as essential for Cuba's stability and prosperity.[10] His "Sergeants' Revolt" led to the overthrow of the Céspedes government. After five days of junta rule, Dr. Grau San Martín, a professor of medicine at the University of Havana, assumed the presidency. Grau and his left-leaning interior minister, Antonio Guiteras, launched a "Hundred Days" of reform, likening their project to Roosevelt's New Deal. The new government unilaterally abrogated the Platt Amendment, extended the franchise to women, lowered utility rates and rents, initiated a process of agrarian reform, established a Labor Ministry, and decreed labor reforms.[11] Predictably, the US refused to recognize Grau's government. Rather, by September 8, there were twenty-nine US warships in Cuban waters.[12]

The revolution spanned the island, including the northeastern sugar zone. A group of university students called the Directorio Estudiantil Universitario

(DEU) had joined the opposition movement against Machado—experiencing no shortage of deaths and imprisonments as a result—and formed Grau's principal base; the *New York Times* referred to Grau's administration as "the student government."[13] That September, the DEU's Antilla group traveled to the northeastern sugar district. As DEU member Octaviano Portuondo Moret later recalled, they were "hoping to bring the revolution to the farthest reaches of the country," suggesting (of course) that the centers of political action were located elsewhere. The young men were often confused with government representatives. As Portuondo explained, company administrators at United Fruit's Preston mill hosted the delegation—"nothing more than a group of *muchachos*"—at the exclusive American Club, provided a "luxurious" lunch, and offered a tour of the Nipe Bay on the administrator's yacht.[14] The group traveled through the towns of Antilla, Banes, Mayarí, and Sagua de Tánamo in this fashion, taking advantage of the general state of confusion to facilitate the removal of machadista officials from municipal posts.

For their part, multiethnic groups of sugar workers took matters into their own hands, often spontaneously and without instructions from student organizers, PCC leaders, or anyone else. Some strikes began at mills in August after Machado fled, while others began after the Sergeants' Revolt of September 4. By mid-September, a full-fledged insurgency was under way in the sugar industry.[15] Workers organized themselves into unions spanning labor sectors, and even small colonos participated.[16] Strikers demanded a return to 1930 wages, rent relief, housing support, and recognition of their new unions. They also demanded an eight-hour workday, which would improve labor conditions and would significantly reduce unemployment, as the twenty-four-hour work of sugar grinding would move from two shifts per day to three. By the end of the year, over 220,000 sugar laborers had struck since August.[17] Several dozen of these strikes turned into occupations, as laborers seized mills and company facilities. These workers formed militias, sometimes called "Red Militias," that defended the strikers against repression and prevented sabotage against the mills, indicating that they still believed their bread and butter was the sugar industry.[18] Women joined strike committees and auxiliary units, formed relief kitchens, collected supplies from peasants and shopkeepers, and distributed food among the long-hungry sugar workers' families. In all, workers seized thirty-six sugar mills that September. At some, strikers elected workers councils that they called "soviets." Two of the most famous were at Central Mabay near Manzanillo in southern Oriente and the Central Tacajó in northern Oriente.

The Tacajó mill was completed in 1916, founded with Cuban and Spanish capital on the coattails of US companies' great success in northern Oriente;

its lands were adjacent to United Fruit's territory and the mill was just fourteen miles west of Antilla.[19] By 1933, Tacajó and a nearby mill, Báguanos, were owned by the Antilla Sugar Estates, which was held by US investors. Tacajó workers established one of the most famous and longest-lasting soviets of 1933.[20] On August 12, they greeted news of Machado's flight with celebrations and announced a general strike. Rodolfo "Chepe" Díaz, a member of the PCC, presented the strikers' demands to the mill administrator, Manuel López Quintana, who claimed he had no authority to speak for the company; only the general administrator, Jorge A. Hernández, was authorized to do so, but he resided near Central Báguanos. The workers found this difficult to believe as Quintana had twice lowered their wages. Nevertheless, they seized a locomotive and several cars and headed to Báguanos armed with machetes and a few revolvers. Upon their arrival, a contingent of soldiers tried stop the workers from reaching the administrative offices. According to Ursinio Rojas, a Communist Youth League member at the time, a crowd of three or four thousand overwhelmed the soldiers shouting "Long live the strike!," "We're hungry!," and "Death to Sr. Quintana and Sr. Hernández!"[21] Like Quintana, Hernández demurred, claiming he needed time to travel to Havana and discuss the matter with company representatives. The workers' reply was "energetic." The Tacajó strike committee decided neither Quintana nor Hernández should be permitted to leave and put both administrators under the watch of armed guards.[22] During his imprisonment, Hernández's electricity was cut off and he was fed exclusively "cornmeal cooked without butter." They also used a loudspeaker outside his quarters through the night, mimicking the sleeplessness of overnight shifts at the mill.[23] The workers, it seems, wanted their boss to experience the hardships they endured.

Upon their return to Tacajó, the strike committee, which included representatives from the PCC, the Communist Youth League, and the union, held an all-night meeting and planned for the long haul. Over 4,000 people attended the assembly, which, according to a report by a party organizer writing under the name of "Emiliano," "had a clearly revolutionary character." Women and children waved red flags. He wrote, "The Partido Comunista de Cuba and CNOC are the leaders."[24] At the assembly, workers voted to continue the strike and to take over the mill. Few were actually employed at the time, so the strike itself was largely symbolic. Taking the mill, on the other hand, was very real. Communist Youth League members erected an eight-meter red flag on the mill tower so that all could see it was in the workers' hands. The strikers also took over the butcher's shop, dairy, bakery, and warehouses. They started a collective kitchen and distributed food. Strikers' wives solicited help from local peasants, who provided vegetables, tubers, milk, and other goods. Workers slaughtered company cows and requisitioned sacks of sugar. They also requisitioned horses and formed an armed militia to take custody of Quintana, patrol the company properties, and put down any outbursts of disorder. The PCC, Defensa Obrera Internacional (DOI), the Liga Juvenil Comunista, and Sindicato Nacional de Obreros de la Industria Azucarera (SNOIA) all set up offices at Tacajó, and each claimed strong memberships, including significant numbers of Black workers; the local PCC cell reported "we have in our ranks various black workers, good fighters."[25]

The Tacajó strike committee held control of the company properties for four months. As late as September 20, they had not released the administrator.[26] In the end, the Antilla Sugar Estates instituted Grau's new labor regulations, including an eight-hour workday, a minimum wage, and recognition of the union. As Rojas later recalled, "although the bosses didn't want to admit it, the workers had taken away all of the control they exercised over workers, salaries, schedules, etc."[27] The company agreed to involve the union in personnel matters, distribute parcels of land to families, repair employee housing, hire a nurse and a doctor to treat workers, and not to retaliate against strike leaders. The year 1934 began in a state of affairs largely victorious for Tacajó's workers.

Nearby in United Fruit territory, workers joined the stoppages of late July and early August. Led by the Unión Obrera, which had hosted Mella eight years earlier, laborers launched a forty-eight-hour strike on August 10. These early days of August were filled with demonstrations and fights between workers and local authorities, who arrested and beat several protestors. When news of Machado's flight reached town on August 12, however, the repressive forces were rendered ineffective. Crowds flooded the streets and disarmed police units. The Unión Obrera renewed the strike for two more days, hosted a general assembly, and formed a comprehensive labor association that included workers from both the Boston and Preston mills, as well as field and subsidiary workers. Banes's mayor and United Fruit lawyer, Rafael Díaz-Balart (Fidel Castro's future father-in-law), managed to remain in his post in the days immediately after Machado's fall. After a week of negotiations, however, the opposition secured his resignation on the condition that his replacement not be from the "revolutionary committee." A company man took over.[28]

Rural workers cleaning the cane fields were less concerned about political negotiations in town. On August 16, workers at two company cane farms again declared a strike. According to Figueredo (AKA "Zapata"), field workers, many of whom were Haitian and British West Indian, exhibited "great combativeness and resolution to fight."[29] Soon stoppage begun in the fields spread to the Boston mill, the Preston mill, the town of Banes, the port city of Antilla (where strikers raised a red flag over town hall), and other cane farms.[30] Unemployed workers joined the mobilization. By August 27, even transportation workers in Banes, known to be the least combative, had declared a strike. The next day, the newly constituted union drew up a list of demands, including an eight-hour workday, restitution of 1930 salaries, free homes with electricity for workers, compliance with the accident laws, and recognition of the union. In response, United Fruit requested fifteen days to correspond with headquarters in Boston, Massachusetts. In the meantime, the company claimed it would agree to limited demands but insisted that workers resume work immediately.[31]

In response to this stalling, the strike committee called a general assembly and voted to declare a general strike the next day at noon if all of their demands were not met. According to Figueredo, the decision was easy. At the Boston mill, some eager employees stopped work well before the appointed hour. At noon on August 29, workers announced a strike. "Five minutes later," Figueredo explained, "the whole *central* was in workers' hands." He wrote, "The stoppage was complete; the electrical plant was closed and in the custody of our brigades, as well as the offices and the ice factory. The boilers were turned off. The guards at the entrance to the batey were replaced by the red militias . . . A large group of dockworkers arrived [to support the strike]. Shortly after, the [entire vicinity] was surrounded by our men on horseback." United Fruit workers in Banes and at both mills formed strike committees, relief committees, and militia units. Some of the latter were armed with shotguns or revolvers, but most had wooden stakes or machetes. Even the company's private guards "made themselves available to the workers" and "declared they were under the command of the strike committee." Workers in Banes took control of company offices and facilities. At the Boston mill at Macabí, where the Union Obrera had fought in the mid-1920s to end the company's commercial monopoly, the strike committee's first action was to order the company's commissary sacked and to declare "free commerce" on the cay. According to Figueredo, by August 30, the atmosphere was "completely revolutionary" and United Fruit's territories were "under proletarian rule."[32]

Strikers held United Fruit properties for eight days, completely paralyzing productions. They occupied all major facilities and offices, and red militias tightly controlled access to the bateyes. Managers were confined to their homes and offices, not permitted to use electricity or the rail lines, and could only move about escorted by red militias. The local press was permitted to enter the properties only with a pass issued by the strike committee. Workers and their wives established a relief kitchen using company supplies and provided meals to strikers and their families. They also organized funds, auxiliary, and propaganda committees, as well as a disciplinary bureau. The auxiliary committee at Macabí distributed, meat, vegetables, and other necessities taken from the company's commissary.[33] Among the strikers at Preston was a young Afro-Cuban named Roberto Buzón Neira. He joined the SNOIA amid the strikes and, soon after, the local PCC cell. The experience was a formative moment for the young Buzón, who went on to volunteer to defend the Spanish Republic during the Spanish Civil War. He would later cite the insurgency as paramount in his political education.[34]

For Buzón and others, the days of the strike were filled with demonstrations, assemblies, and meetings, and the atmosphere was one of overwhelming support for United Fruit's workers. Women, young people, and children took to the streets to "defend the workers' power established at the mill."[35] In both Macabí and Banes, women gathered in public spaces and called on domestic workers to join the strike, which they did. A report from the PCC's district committee explained that even the barrio americano was controlled by workers, and "nannies, cooks, drivers, and laundresses" had stopped work.[36] Members of other local trade guilds also struck, including shoemakers, bakers, and tobacco rollers. Supporters contributed funds and supplies to auxiliary committees. According to one report, almost all shopkeepers contributed to auxiliary funds. Such was the state of affairs that United Fruit donated a cow to be butchered and distributed among workers.[37]

On September 1, the army dispatched to Banes a platoon of soldiers under a commander named Acosta. The soldiers were greeted with demonstrations and protests. When Acosta moved onto Macabí, the workers' militia briefly detained him.[38] In the end, the soldiers hardly served as a repressive force. Rather, they fraternized with the strikers like company guards had done before them. As a senior United Fruit administrator later recalled to his friend, Fulgencio Batista, "We had various army officials there, but since Machado's fall, there was no real head of government, and the [officials] didn't think they had to do anything."[39] This was consistent with soldiers' behavior elsewhere; at Santa Lucía, "the army is completely fraternizing with the workers," wrote one report, and soldiers had "placed red flags everywhere."[40] At Rio Cauto, "Emiliano" reported "the soldiers are fraternizing with the strikers and support their struggle." He explained, "In Oriente Province, there exists a magnificent situation in our favor among the soldiers; there are places where our compañeros penetrated the barracks and held meetings or where the soldiers openly fraternized with the workers."[41]

On September 4, the day of Batista's Sergeants' Revolt, United Fruit, likely fearing descent into anarchy, agreed to most workers' demands. One official wrote to headquarters, "Practically speaking, we are forced to accept some of these demands to avoid the possibility of damage to property, owing to the fact that there is no stable government and we do not have real protection."[42] The strikers held a mass meeting to address the offer, but disagreed about how to respond. Confusion abounded as rumors circulated (perhaps planted by company officials) that some workers had accepted the offer. While condemnations of exploitation continued, the tenor of events had changed. An army platoon was in town and meeting regularly with company officials and Rural Guard commanders at Díaz-Balart's house. Moreover, a US destroyer sat in the Bay of Banes. On September 5, the streets of Banes, which had been alive with demonstrations and mass meetings for weeks, were deserted. The strike committees at Banes, Preston, and Macabí accepted the company's offer, which included many of the workers' demands.[43] The company agreed to an eight-hour workday and to pay minimum wages in most sectors (including dock, cargo, mill, cane cutting, and warehouse work), provide overtime pay, post a doctor at Macabí, improve the hospital in Banes, improve sanitation facilities in the town centers, and add more water stations in the cane fields. The company also agreed to permit the "free entrance of street sellers with all types of merchandise available for workers and their families to purchase," per the longstanding call to end the company's commercial monopoly on the cay. United Fruit rejected some demands—it refused to eliminate piecework in the cane fields or to abolish contract work for painters—and it further stalled on others. But the company agreed to increase the number of schools in its territory, abide by the new Labor Ministry's regulations, and recognize the SNOIA.[44]

Shorter strikes continued at United Fruit properties through the remaining months of 1933. In late September, the company was publicly optimistic that things were under control, but as a precautionary measure gathered all US and British families in Preston for their "protection."[45] On October 9, workers at the Boston mill struck after company guards arrested three union leaders, and they only returned to work upon their release. On November 27, workers at Banes struck again to block a particularly abusive foreman from returning to work. A solidarity strike broke out in Preston, and soon most of the region's mills had declared solidarity stoppages. The conflict was mediated by Grau's administration, and the company withdrew the foreman.[46] In the end, workers had taken over the Cuban properties of the world-famous United Fruit Company for eight days, achieved most of their demands, and maintained an active strike committee through February of 1933.

Strikes and occupations took place across northern Oriente. At the Central Tamano twenty miles east of Preston, workers seized the mill and imprisoned ten US citizens and six Britons, including three women and five children. The Tamano mill was owned by the Atlantic Fruit and Sugar Company, in which

Vincent Astor and Percy Rockefeller were heavily invested. Adding to the newsworthy drama was the fact that the mill was only reachable by water or air. The United States promptly sent the destroyer *Hamilton* to nearby waters, and the workers negotiated safe passage for the women and children.[47] At the Manatí mill near the border with Camagüey, strikers held company properties from September 16 to September 23. Salvador Rionda explained that "after having spent twenty-two years in Cuba, [he had] never seen anything like these strikes." Management was prevented from using the telephone, walking or driving around the batey, and having their usual access to ice and electricity. It was, as he explained, "A complete SOVIET REPUBLIC!"[48]

The sugar workers of northern Oriente collaborated throughout the insurgency. Strikers sent delegates across the region to share news and coordinate meetings. Banes hosted a meeting of sugar workers from Boston, Preston, Marcané, Tacajó, and Báguanos. More than 5,000 workers of diverse nationalities and ethnicities attended and agreed to open PCC offices at each of the mills. Delegates formed a Buró Frente Unidos de los Centrales de la Costa Norte.[49] Figueredo (AKA "Zapata") was involved in the actions at Tacajó and helped organize "flying brigades" of unemployed men who traveled from mill to mill urging along the strikes.[50] Most dramatically, on September 4, a squadron of 3,000 men, many on horseback, from Tacajó and Báguanos, calling themselves a "red militia," invaded the nearby Santa Lucía sugar mill. A worker named Rafael de Hombre Mesa from Boston, a sergeant in the Banes red brigade, recalled joining the militias "liberating" Santa Lucía.[51] Santa Lucía was famous for repression; "The conditions of oppression are barbaric," wrote one report from the interior.[52] The Rural Guard had threatened to kill anyone organizing at the mill, and no one had even tried to open a branch of the SNOIA there. Yet when thousands of workers from Tacajó arrived, they "broke the symbolic [and physical] chains that blocked the fiefdom's entrance . . . and thus broke the terror" that had prevented the mill's workers from joining the insurgency.[53] When Santa Lucía workers began their strike, they seized the mill and the town theater, which they used for strike committee meetings. They formed a militia of over fifteen hundred members, and "four or five thousand workers" joined the strike.[54]

Events in the Cuban American Sugar Company (CASC)'s territory were no less dramatic. Although workers never took over Chaparra and Delicias, they were the only two mills that the government seized during the 1933 revolution.[55] Strike activity in CASC territory began in early September, when dockworkers at the private port, Juan Claro, stopped work and were joined by mill workers from Chaparra and Delicias. On September 5, strikers marched to the Rural Guard barracks, where a guard opened fire, killing two men.

According to a SNOIA report, in an act of retributive violence, "the revolutionary masses then demanded that the guard hand over the murderous soldier." The workers then "murdered him and burned [his body] to ashes."[56] The CASC manager and deputy manager fled to a British freighter. Workers formed a strike committee, a red guard, multiple auxiliary committees, and self-defense units.[57] Militias prevented strikebreakers from entering the properties. Despite the act of retributive violence that launched strike activities at CASC, the US Navy reported that the strike was well organized, that workers had efficiently orchestrated water deliveries and extended "courtesies" to citizens, such as allowing a funeral procession to use the railways.[58]

Strike activity in CASC territory continued through November. After the company stated flatly that it would grant no demands and raise no wages, workers renewed their general strike. In response, the company announced on December 19 that it would not grind in the 1933–1934 harvest and locked workers out of the hospital, food shops, and other services. In the face of company intransigence, Interior Minister Antonio Guiteras ordered Puerto Padre authorities to take control of and open the electric plant, hospital, and commercial departments. Local authorities—closely affiliated with the company—initially refused, but Guiteras pushed, and the departments opened.[59] McGillivray points out that, in this episode, "at least briefly, workers managed to pit the Cuban 'state' against one of the most powerful American companies."[60] The Grau administration believed that its continued governance depended on a successful sugar harvest and intervened to compel one of the island's largest producers to prepare for the grinding season. Another factor driving Grau to action was fear of what the approximately 100,000 local residents would do in the absence of essential services. Finally, the Grau administration likely understood the standoff as a test of its resolve. Several sugar companies were hostile to the leftist administration and assumed (correctly, as it turns out) that Grau's presidency would not last without US support; they had stopped paying taxes and were awaiting the counterrevolution.[61] Grau's determination to control the situation, protect workers, and oversee a successful harvest was tested at the CASC properties, and the intervention was clear evidence that the state had embraced a high degree of populist rule.[62]

Global events were never far from the minds of striking laborers, even as they were making history of their own; Tacajó workers affiliated with the DOI sent a telegram to the German embassy condemning "assassinations committed by Hitler."[63] Similarly, at the Central Punta Alegre, which had also been seized, striking workers and peasants spent time at a meeting discussing the 1927 executions of Italian American anarchists Nicola Sacco and Bartolomeo Vanzetti, whose detentions had galvanized a global defense campaign.[64] Local actors understood clearly the international symbols deployed in the insurgency. At Banes, a group opposed to the PCC waved the Cuban flag in response to the red flag, suggesting that the red flag was widely known to have internationalist significance.[65] When soldiers at Tacajó removed the eight-meter red flag from the mill tower, strikers retrieved it and marched it through the streets singing the Internationale.[66] Additionally, insurgent sugar workers across eastern Cuba were highly cognizant of the likely international ramification of their actions; everyone expected a US intervention. According to a report from Santa Lucía, the red militia asked local soldiers (with whom they were fraternizing) for military training so that they could fight the US Marines. At least one soldier agreed. When the district commander, however, suggested that they should be training to defend Cuba, not a particular labor union or strike, the militiamen balked. They argued "our brigades will fight for the defense of workers' interests and will fight fiercely against intervention" to defend "true revolution," but they would not defend Grau's government.[67]

It is no surprise that local workers were putting their grievances in international terms. As early as September 1932, Aggeo Suárez Pérez and Ramón Nicolau, commenting on the "Negro Question" from Moscow, wrote that Cubans in the east understood clearly and intimately the systemic pressures affecting their day-to-day lives. As they explained, "The expropriation of poor campesinos' lands by latifundia sugar companies, the denigration of their rights, the existence of thousands of hectares of uncultivated property owned by those same companies while poor peasants have no land to cultivate and maintain their existence, has created a situation in this region, where black people are the majority, [of] a strong anti-imperialist spirit, especially against the yanqui (North American) . . . [Their direct exploitation has caused] a popular hatred towards the Platt Amendment."[68] Similarly, in December 1933, a Polish organizer for the Red International of Labor Unions (Profitern) named Witold Lovsky, who went by the alias "Juan," remarked that comrades in the east were better read and more politically informed than their counterparts in the capital.[69]

Afro-Antillano immigrant workers participated widely at all levels of the sugar insurgency. Initially, foreign braceros' militancy took even party officials by surprise. As late as September 1933, some PCC leaders still believed that Antillanos hindered labor mobilizations and claimed that mills with a high proportion of foreign workers were the most difficult to organize. The slow start of the insurgency at Chaparra and Delicias, claimed one SNOIA report, was the result of the "many Haitians there, causing a difficult situation" for organized labor. Conversely, the report argued, a "greater number of white workers . . . facilitates the struggle."[70] Striking workers, too, could be skeptical about possibilities for cross-national solidarity due to sugar companies' long-standing practice of hiring foreign strikebreakers. On August 30, news that United Fruit was planning to bring in Jamaicans to replace strikers "ignited the spirits of all, and everyone prepared for battle," according to Figueredo. The strikebreakers, however, never arrived and, by the next day, "men and women of all nationalities were taking the streets."[71]

Later, the PCC admitted the folly of considering immigrant workers "unorganizable." As Lovsky (AKA "Juan") later explained, "[I]n past years when we discussed sugar work, we believed that this was difficult and that the main obstacles were the Haitian and Jamaican workers whom we could not reach because they spoke English or patois. But our assumption was built on complete ignorance.... Haitian and Jamaican workers demonstrated a high degree of combativeness in the recent labor struggle. They fought more like members of a slave rebellion who had nothing to lose. In many mills, they were in the front line of the struggle."[72] As Barry Carr has demonstrated, Haitians and British West Indians joined strikes, strike committees, armed guards, and soviets.[73] At Santa Lucía, Haitians and Jamaicans were among the four to five thousand striking workers. Similarly, at the United Fruit properties, Jamaican, Haitian, and Chinese workers joined the red militias and auxiliary committees.[74] Antillano participation in the strike committees in northeastern Cuba was so ubiquitous that a report in the communist paper *Bandera Roja* noted not their participation, but rather, the rare moments when Afro-Antillanos were excluded. Of the Santa Lucía mill, the paper reported that mill's strike committee "committed the error of not including Haitian and Jamaican representatives," but the author was reassured that immigrants "participated heavily in committees from different sugar colonies and plantations."[75]

Stories of cross-national cooperation during the insurgency abound. On at least one occasion, immigrant workers refused to act as strike breakers. According to the *Mundo Obrero*, when company managers at one mill brought in Haitians and Jamaicans to break a strike, the new workers accepted the machetes but then refused to scab. They "declared that they had taken the machetes to defend themselves and the strike."[76] When strikers at Tacajó traveled to Báguanos for a second time to press their demands, the manager Hernández escaped from militia custody and fled to nearby cane fields. Workers formed a search party and, soon a Haitian named José Luis and a Cuban known as "el Viudo" (the widower) emerged from the fields with Hernández, holding him at the point of José Luis's knife and el Viudo's revolver.[77]

As the PCC conducted its assessment of the strikes in early 1934, it repeatedly stressed the cross-national spirit of the insurgency. In all, CNOC and the SNOIA claimed, over 200,000 sugar workers had participated, "native and foreign, employed and unemployed."[78] In fact, they concluded that Afro-Caribbean workers had often been the most militant. At several mills, field workers (a majority of whom were Antillanos in Oriente) struck first. They would then march to the bateyes and demand that mill workers join. "In these marches and demonstrations," wrote one assessment, "as was the case throughout the strikes, Jamaicans and Haitians showed up with combative attitudes and fighting capacity, proving themselves always willing to struggle until the very end."[79] Company managers were annoyed that their British West Indian domestic servants struck. At a conference in mid-September, a SNOIA delegate from Banes noted merrily, "representative magnates of the company have had to go without cooks, laundresses, maids, drivers, etc."[80]

Employers singled out Caribbean immigrants for, in the words of a sugar trade journal, combativeness and a "tendency to join in extreme movements" in greater numbers than Cubans.[81] United Fruit went so far as to admit that, after years of importing Haitian and Jamaican workers, the company supported laws limiting foreign labor in Cuba because such laws would allow the company to weed out radicals.[82] Scapegoating foreigners for inciting political disturbances and labor insurgency was a time-honored tradition in Cuban political circles; in Oriente, Haitians had been blamed for the PIC uprising of 1912 and were targeted during the Liberal Revolt of 1917.[83] United Fruit officials, however, tended to support immigration to meet their labor needs and, as in the case of the Garvey movement, had a history of working with immigrant civic groups. That a company official went so far as to reverse course on immigration signaled that, indeed, the sugar insurgency was nourished by the cosmopolitan nature of enclaves—and that some administrators were figuring this out.

Leadership

Communists on and off the island credited the PCC and its sister organizations, especially CNOC and the SNOIA, for leading the insurrection. Based in Montevideo, the Confederación Sindical Latinoamericana (CSLA) wrote the "heroic communist party" had led the strike that led to Machado's fall without mentioning the fact that the PCC had made the distinctly unpopular decision to call strikers back to work in early August.[84] The *Communist International* newspaper in Moscow claimed that "on the whole, the leadership of these strikes is in the hands of the Cuban Communist Party."[85] And from New York, the *Mundo Obrero* contended, "The present strike movement was made possible thanks to the celebration of the National Conference of Sugar Industry Workers under the auspices of the Communist Party and the CNOC."[86] American CPs and the Comintern made similar statements.[87]

Ironically, these claims sounded a lot like those of the US State Department. Regarding Cuba's 1933 revolution, communists and imperialists agreed on one thing: the Partido Comunista de Cuba should be credited with—or blamed for—leading the insurrection, even when the situation on the ground was uncertain. The idea of communist leadership accorded well with the US State Department's long-held line that Kremlin agents were infiltrating Latin American political circles and stirring up labor trouble. Initially, diplomats in the field resisted this interpretation and offered a less conspiratorial picture of hardship and resistance in Cuba. In mid-1931, Ambassador Guggenheim wrote to Secretary of State Stimson acknowledging that the State Department was eager "to persuade foreign governments of the responsibility of 'Communists' for recurrent disorders," but he believed that the party lacked influence in Cuba. Rather, "The vast majority [of Cubans] are honest, hard-working individuals, only too anxious to acquire sufficient money to live comfortably." He criticized his remit to blame the reds, writing that many communist demands "in capitalistic countries, are considered legitimate, [such as] limitation of working hours, healthful conditions, workmen's insurance, etc."[88] As late as August 1933, Roosevelt's man in Havana, Sumner Welles, reported that although businessmen were fearful of communist agitation led by Moscow, he did not believe that communists had "support among the laboring classes." Rather, he claimed, the tense situation was due to starvation and dictatorship. Sugar companies had not been paying enough for workers to feed themselves or their families. He concluded, "I cannot see any indications of the 'red menace' . . . Immediate improvement of the economic situation in Cuba is a sure cure for the situation which now exists."[89]

A month into the insurgency, however, Welles and others changed their tune. Welles paid an informant at the telegraph agency to duplicate telegrams to and from Moscow, and he solicited reports from sugar companies about communist activities.[90] In late October, he concluded that "the strikes . . . declared on the sugar plantations are communistic in origin."[91] William L. Jackson, United Fruit Company's vice president and general counsel, also blamed communists for the uprising, claiming "the threat of communism is very real."[92] Blaming the reds, of course, helped Welles and sugar administrators deny any problem with the imperialist status quo. This wasn't the first time US officials red baited Latin American revolutionaries, nor would it be the last, but Welles's newfound attention to the communist menace has two additional explanations. First, the PCC and CNOC operated above ground after August

12, when Machado fled. Grau legalized the party and even supplied it with the houses of former machadistas to use as offices. Second, communist publications vocally took credit for the insurgency. That the party was operating in the open and consistently claiming to lead Cuba's insurgents gave weight to the idea that communists were, indeed, in command. Since the revolution of 1959, Cuban historiography has further emphasized communist leadership of events in 1933.[93]

While the PCC publicly claimed to be overseeing the strikes, the situation on the ground was less clear. As Carr has argued, "the sugar insurgency cannot adequately be explicated if the historian's point of reference is solely the world of organizations and ideologies."[94] In other words, over half a decade of worsening conditions (which at least two US ambassadors acknowledged) and a power vacuum in Havana caused the revolution—much more so than did Marxist-Leninism. Although the party influenced a majority of labor unions through CNOC, PCC leadership on the ground in 1933 was far from certain. For one, the party's authority over Cuba's labor movement was hardly uncontested after its "August mistake." Additionally, communication between the Central Committee and strikers deep in the countryside was uneven. In many cases, PCC organizers arrived at mills only to discover that multinational groups of workers had already begun a strike or seized the mill and raised a red flag.[95] "Emiliano's" report from Oriente criticized poor communication with the strikers, "in a majority of places, our compañeros and labor organizations are complaining that they haven't received CNOC communications giving then instructions or a sense of where they stand in relation to the situation of the whole country."[96] SNOIA officials indicated that workers had taken matters further than the party had planned, such as when workers at Santa Lucía formed a red militia "of a permanent character" and self-defense brigades preparing not only to defend the strike, but also to defend the island against a US intervention.[97]

Ultimately, party organization and leadership varied from mill to mill. Certainly, the party led several strikes. The SNOIA oversaw the soviet formed at the Central Mabay mill near the "red city" of Manzanillo in southern Oriente. There, workers' demands matched, almost word-for-word, those of the SNOIA, including a call for immigrant rights, a position unique to communists at the time.[98] The Mabay strike committee communicated regularly with party headquarters in Havana and declared itself a member of the SNOIA-CNOC network.[99] The party also led at Banes and Tacajó. The PCC had established local cells in these towns in 1930 and 1931, and PCC field organizers like Figueredo were heavily involved in the insurgency.[100] (Figueredo represented the Manzanillo district committee of the PCC, and would go on in 1934 to join the PCC Politburo, heading up the Agrarian Department.[101]) Banes' strikers successfully defended their PCC-led strike against outside influence; some noncommunist unions remained active, but party organizers hardly mentioned the presence of other groups, which was not the case elsewhere.[102]

Sometimes, however, PCC organizers simply got it wrong, an indication of how messy the situation was. In the early days of the strike at Banes, Figueredo considered the Tacajó and Báguanos mills lost causes because "a complete absence of employment in the mill and in the plantations" made it "impossible to foment a strike," yet Tacajó was home to one of the most famous soviets of 1933.[103] Communists had organized more successfully at Tacajó than at fellow Antilla Sugar Estates Central Báguanos; in October, the *Bandera Roja* reported that the PCC had a "weak influence" at Báguanos and explained that local party leaders still operated clandestinely while rival reformist groups operated in the open. The paper also blamed Báguanos mill workers for being "too easily" swayed by reformist leaders eager to collaborate with the Grau administration.[104]

PCC authority in the northeast was weakest at Cuban American's Chaparra and Delicias centrales, where the party vied with Trotskyists for leadership of the strikes.[105] Sandalio Junco, the Afro-Cuban PCC leader who had spoken about the plight of Afro-Antillean workers at the 1929 CSLA meeting in Montevideo, had been expelled from the party in late 1932 for Trotskyist activities and had formed the Partido Bolchevique-Leninista (PBL), which affiliated with the Federación Obrera de la Habana. The PBL led workers at the Chaparra mill and in the town of Puerto Padre, but communists challenged their leadership at every opportunity and complained of the "indifference" of the workers who failed to toe the PCC party line.[106] The *Bandera Roja* explained in October 1933 that others were leading the strikes in CASC territory and announced that its main task there was to replace noncommunist leaders.[107] In a postmortem broadside about "what could have been," Trotskyists in Puerto Padre accused the PCC of launching a smear campaign against the strikers, "calling us yellows and traitors." Rather than fighting the anti-imperialist revolution, the broadside declared, party militants and the youth league had "dedicated all of their revolutionary energy towards destroying our manifestos and violently tearing down our posters."[108] Unlike the PCC, the PBL was willing to work with President Grau; this may help explain why Grau's administration was willing to force the company's hand at Chaparra and Delicias.[109]

Hints about the uncertain state of leadership in the sugar insurgency even appeared in public-facing communist coverage of the insurgency. The *Mundo*

Obrero stated that the sugar strikes were "organized, in the majority, by the CNOC," but a parenthetical line conceded, "there have been some [strikes] of a spontaneous character, but they were *more or less influenced* by CNOC."[110] Internal conversations were more direct. In fact, the Caribbean Bureau explicitly criticized the Cuban party for failing to take control of events on the island. The Bureau wrote that "the party continues to remain in a dangerous state of backwardness in the face of the revolutionary movement of the masses."[111] Workers were taking matters into their own hands, the Bureau suggested, and the PCC needed to catch up.

The story of this criticism begins in August and early September, when Cuban and international communist leaders agreed to discourage workers from seizing foreign properties. They believed doing so would provoke another US military intervention and was therefore inadvisable. In August, the Political Bureau of the PCC met at Martínez Villena's sickbed to address the situation in sugar towns. They decided that they would support the formation of soviets, but only where conditions permitted.[112] Blas Roca, the district committee leader from Manzanillo, was tasked with delivering this message to the PCC Plenary in late August. The plenary adopted the position that workers should be encouraged to seize mills and form soviets, but not to do so at US-owned properties.[113] The August PCC platform called for the formation of "a soviet government of workers and peasants" in a general sense. Regarding mill seizures, PCC instructions specifically excluded foreign properties; workers should focus on "the expropriation of lands held by *native* landholders."[114] Field organizers were not to encourage the seizure of US-owned mills. The party "considere[d] it inadvisable for the workers to seize American enterprises." A Comintern report summarized, "the Communist Party of Cuba is striving to do everything possible to avert intervention."[115] The Caribbean Bureau agreed and "called on the party to not put open struggle against imperialism in the foreground, meaning that the main struggle should be against native landholders and the local bourgeoisie." It was this local struggle, the Bureau added, that would galvanize the masses and "deepen their class consciousness," assuming (again) that workers were not yet sufficiently educated to grasp the imperialist and class-based origins of their problems.[116]

Sugar workers, however, were unconcerned about whether or not organizers believed they had suitable class consciousness. As the insurgency unfolded, they disregarded party directives (if they even knew of them), jettisoned moderation, occupied sugar mills—even those belonging to US corporations, and expelled or imprisoned administrators, many of whom were US citizens. In the face of these dramatic actions, the Caribbean Bureau and the CPUSA then criticized the Cuban party for failing to take control of the situation and harness the popular revolution already under way toward the party agenda. Putting aside the irony of criticizing the PCC for heeding its own advice, the Bureau wrote, "The danger of intervention forces the party not to encourage the masses to occupy imperialist companies and plantations, but in the event that [workers for] imperialist companies proceed to occupy them, the party must take the lead and give it an offensive character. . . ."[117] With this somewhat confusing directive, the Caribbean Bureau revealed just how *not in control* the PCC was and that workers themselves had moved the party to the left.

In other words, many workers seized factories of their own accord, often without guidance from organizers and in defiance of the party line. In doing so, they pushed the party further than it was initially willing to go and vividly illustrated the revolutionary power of cross-racial, cross-national worker solidarity. Sugar workers in "remote" company towns had undermined the more cautious position of communist leaders in Havana and Harlem and had forced the hand of international movement. The Caribbean Bureau, the PCC, and other communists moved to get behind the revolution unfolding in Cuba's northeastern sugar fields and mill towns—not the other way around.

Repression

The sugar insurgency was largely repressed in January 1934. During Grau's presidency, the Cuban state was divided between three main factions. President Grau oversaw a populist government, which instituted reforms supported by Cuba's lower classes. Interior Minister Antonio Guiteras led the most radical, pro-labor, and anti-imperialist wing of Grau's administration. On the right, Army Chief Fulgencio Batista and the military represented US and Cuban corporate interests. While Grau and Guiteras embraced the revolution, Batista sought to suppress it and stabilize Cuba for international investment.[118] McGillivray writes of the situation, "Guiteras would set workers free from jail, but Batista would put them back."[119] By mid-October, Batista was openly operating in defiance of Grau's orders and suppressing labor mobilizations.[120]

Communists hardly helped matters for President Grau, continuously labeling his administration "counterrevolutionary," "fascist," and "proto-imperialist."[121] The PCC claimed that the "bloody Batista-Grau government" aimed to suppress revolution in Cuba and continue imperialist exploitation.[122] Later, in late 1934 and 1935, the party would admit that it had failed to recognize the revolutionary nature of Grau's administration, and historians have concurred. Angelina Rojas Blaquier writes, "the PCC's main error with respect to [the Grau government] was to consider it a single, homogenous body without distinguishing" between the factions led by Batista, Grau, and Guiteras.[123] Communist opposition to the government peaked on September 29, when Batista's army killed at least six people in Havana at a reburial of Mella's ashes, recently arrived from Mexico.[124] Rubén Martínez Villena spoke in public for the last time at the gathering. The massacre, according to Lionel Soto, who put the number of dead closer to thirty, marked a major turning point in Cuban history, as the army no longer operated under the command of the civilian government—whether that government was in the hands of army veterans (like Presidents Gómez, García Menocal, and Machado) or reformists (like President Grau).[125] Batista's defiance of the presidential administration also marks an early point in the long twentieth-century history of US authorities bypassing national governments to work directly with Latin American militaries.

The United States refused to recognize Grau's administration, but rather, sent warships to Cuban waters. Welles encouraged Batista to assume power. Not a week after the massacre at Mella's burial, on October 4, Welles invited Batista to his office and had "a protracted and a very frank discussion of the present situation in Cuba." Welles offered his advice: "I told him that in my judgement he himself was the only individual in Cuba today who represented authority." He emphasized that Grau's government did not have the support of the US or other Latin American republics (whom the US could influence), and that "the very great majority of the commercial and financial interest in Cuba who are looking for protection . . . could only find such protection in himself [Batista.]" At their meeting, Welles asked about the "intolerable conditions which had now existed for the last five weeks on the sugar plantations," and Batista assured the ambassador that the army would "guarantee the rights of the legitimate managers of such properties," imprison communist leaders, and expel foreign agitators.[126] (Batista's promise to expel foreign agitators suggests both the common scapegoating of foreigners but also that the sugar insurgency was associated with international agitation.) With encouragement from the US and in defiance of President Grau, Batista's army set about suppressing the strikes. In late October, Batista famously declared "there will be a zafra or there will be blood."[127] The army put down strikes at Jaronú in Camagüey, and massacred workers—including Haitians and Jamaicans—at the Senado mill in mid-November. By December, soldiers were breaking up meetings of the Liga Juvenil Comunista and other communist organizations and harassing strikers.[128]

On January 15, 1934, Batista led the army in overthrowing President Grau, who went into exile in Mexico. Colonel Carlos Mendieta, a prominent figure in the Liberal Party, replaced Grau as president with Batista as the de facto authority. The United States, with Jefferson Caffery as the new ambassador, quickly recognized the new government, and offered a trade deal and food aid. The Batista-Mendieta administration moved swiftly to squash the sugar insurgency. For their part, sugar companies were no longer inclined to engage with workers once Grau was gone and the sugar harvest was approaching. Sugar workers launched a new wave of strikes to protect the gains of the previous months, but the new government and sugar companies brooked little challenge to their authority. Many employers simply paused the zafra, threatening to end the harvest altogether, which would put laborers out of work during what was, for most, the only months of gainful employment during the entire year. Companies shared lists of union leaders, blackballed troublesome workers, evicted laborers and their families, and called in the Rural Guard. Mendieta, who donned the mantle of the previous administration's revolution, told workers that the United States would intervene if the strikes continued and that an intervention would undermine the gains of the previous year. Meanwhile, the Rural Guard and Batista's army violently crushed strikes.[129]

Batista sent three hundred infantry soldiers to Oriente province to ensure the zafra in late January. Unsurprisingly, given Batista's own origins in the region, their first stop was in United Fruit territory. At the Preston mill, an officer informed workers that they were to be "at their posts, ready to work" the next day or face the consequences.[130] Nevertheless, workers at Banes and Preston presented demands for improved pay to the company on February 5. At Preston, over 12,000 workers launched a strike, but the army responded with bullets, and several were injured and even killed.[131] Under such conditions, Preston's workers accepted the company's offer to raise salaries if and when the price of sugar improved. Banes remained on strike until February 22, but the workers there too were forced to accept the company's vague offer. With that settled, United Fruit, which had been keeping tabs on labor organizers and which had a network of spies reporting to the company since September, moved against prominent organizers. The company evicted labor leaders and their families, shared lists of organizers with other companies, and brought in workers to replace the lost manpower. Three hundred families were evicted from Preston alone. By the time milling began on February 23, the company reported having replaced 50 percent of its factory workers with new employees from "diverse parts of the island."[132]

At Tacajó, union leaders responded to the increased repression by planning a massive demonstration for February 28. That night in the town theater, army soldiers opened fire, killing a Spanish strike leader named Antonio

Nuñez and injuring others. Over the course of the following days, the Antilla Sugar Estates, with help from the Rural Guard, expelled over thirty strike and PCC leaders along with their families. The company deducted from salaries the costs of the cattle and parcels of land requisitioned during the insurgency. The two men who had found the Báguanos administrator hiding in the cane fields—the Haitian José Luis and the Cuban el Viudo—were accused of attempted homicide, tried, and sentenced to two years in prison.[133]

In the end, the Batista-Mendieta government crushed the early-1934 strike wave during what became known as the "bloody zafra." According to former sugar worker Rafael Hernández, families evicted from Preston, Tacajó, and elsewhere gathered near Báguanos and formed a cooperative, which shared food and information.[134] The government issued a series of decrees limiting labor mobilizations. Decree Number 3 on February 7 required workers to wait eight days before beginning a strike, outlawed solidarity strikes, and dissolved any labor union found breaking these rules. Decrees 51 and 52 in March outlawed communist agitation and empowered the government to expel "foreign agitators." By the end of March, sugar strikes were criminalized and endangering the sugar harvest was punishable by death.[135]

The years 1934 and 1935 were a low point for Cuba's labor movement thanks to Batista's repressive tactics. During the turbulent months of August through December 1933, however, no one knew how the revolution would end. For many leftists on and off the island, Cuba's revolution of 1933—and the sugar insurgency in particular—marked a high point in the global struggle against imperialism and capitalist exploitation. With their multinational rebellion, sugar workers had joined and dramatically fortified a brewing Americas-wide, anti-imperialist movement.

International Responses

During the final months of 1933, the Communist International and its affiliate organizations closely monitored events in Cuba, especially the sugar insurgency. As discussed in chapter 3, the Kremlin had declared at its Sixth Congress in 1928 that the world was entering a new era of class struggle. During this Third Period, Moscow jettisoned collaboration with the noncommunist left in favor of international proletarian solidarity under the red flag. The Comintern reached out to new constituencies, especially Black workers and Latin American victims of US imperialism. So, when Cuba exploded in revolution in 1933, communists across the globe paid attention. After all, multiracial, multinational groups of workers had paralyzed production in one of the most concentrated zones of US imperialism in the Americas, and many had formed workers councils that they actually called "soviets." The Comintern could not have imagined a better poster child for the Third Period party line.

From Moscow to Montevideo, the left celebrated the insurrection that toppled a dictatorship and that kept up momentum despite the threat of a US invasion. In both internal correspondence and press coverage, communists argued that the revolution was a significant blow to US imperialism in Latin America and a model for other Latin American countries to study and emulate. Sympathetic workers rallied not only to express solidarity but also to proactively protect the island against a US invasion. Throughout this international response, Cuba's multinational sugar workers figured prominently as their strikes, mill seizures, and soviets were widely considered the most radical expression of Cuba's revolution.

From the perspective of the global left, Cuba's 1933 revolution—and the sugar strikes in particular—formed a critical moment in the battle between increasingly radicalized Latin American masses and repressive US-backed political regimes. Cuba's revolution joined the Cacos in Haiti, the Gavilleros in the Dominican Republic, and Sandino's followers in Nicaragua all of whom fought against US Marine occupations; the 1928 banana workers' strike in Colombia, which was violently suppressed; and the peasant uprising in El Salvador in 1932 which ended with 30,000 massacred. With each event, the stakes of the anti-imperialist struggle rose. Communists argued that Cuba's working people were the latest and strongest iteration of the struggle against imperialism and exploitation in the Americas.

In September 1933, representatives from the communist parties of the US, Mexico, Panama, Colombia, Venezuela, Honduras, Guatemala, and El Salvador gathered in New York and issued a statement supporting the insurgency. They celebrated the fact that workers in Cuba had seized land and mills, which "places the private interests of the imperialists and bourgeoisie and land owners in great danger." The Cuban battle was bigger than one island, as the declaration explained. It was also "against the same enemy who yesterday drowned in blood the struggle for the liberation of the people of Nicaragua, Haiti and Santo Domingo, who murdered the Mexican people through their numerous interventions, who imposed military domination over the people of Panamá, and who under the pretext of fighting for freedom stole Puerto Rico and the Philippine islands from their people." Supporting the Cuban masses, the statement argued, amounted to struggling for the "liberation of the peoples of Central and South America."[136]

The Caribbean Bureau of the Comintern covered the revolution in its paper *Mundo Obrero*, dubbing it "a heroic and transcendental page in the revolutionary workers' movement history, and above all in the movement of South

America and the Caribbean." Readers were instructed to learn from the Cuban example; the events leading to Machado's fall "must be objects of intense study and widespread popularization" so that their lessons "might contribute to the development of the revolutionary struggle in other Caribbean and South American nations."[137] In an internal letter to Caribbean and Central American Communist Parties, the Bureau used Martínez Villena's language when it wrote, "Cuba right now is the weakest link in the chain of yankee imperialism in Latin America. The events that are taking place with such speed not only have a great significance for our movement—internationally and in the Caribbean—but their experiences also serve as a boost for all struggles against systems of exploitation and colonial oppression." The letter congratulated Cubans on their militancy and critiqued CPs elsewhere; in comparison to Cuba's workers, others were "alarmingly passive."[138]

According to supporters, working people everywhere, especially in Latin America, had an obligation to "support and express solidarity with the Cuban proletariat."[139] Earlier, during the initial strike wave of 1933, the *Mundo Obrero* had called for the "Latin American proletariat" to carry out a "dedicated solidarity campaign for the heroic Cuban proletariat," and demonstrations of solidarity with Cuba's workers took place in front of the Cuban consulate in New York that spring.[140] By the time Cuba exploded in rebellion in August and September, protecting the revolution and preventing US invasion was a top priority for the international left. From Moscow, the *Communist International* newspaper wrote, "It goes without saying that the Communist parties in other countries, and above all the Communist Party of the United States of America and the Communist Parties in Mexico and Caribbean America, are now confronted with the task of mobilizing the proletarian and the broad masses of toilers for active support of the revolutionary movement in Cuba."[141]

Fear of a US intervention, of course, was justified. The United States had invaded and occupied Cuba, Puerto Rico, and the Philippines at the turn of the century; and US Marines had remained in Nicaragua since 1912, Haiti since 1915, and the Dominican Republic from 1916 to 1924. Cuba experienced a second occupation from 1906 to 1909, and thousands of Marines were stationed in the east from 1917 to 1922 in the "sugar intervention" discussed in chapter 3. Few had reason to believe that US President Franklin D. Roosevelt was sincere when he announced his "good neighbor" policy of better relations with sovereign Latin American states earlier in 1933. Moreover, being a "good neighbor" was easy during sugar's dead season; just how long nonintervention would last, however, was far from clear as the harvest approached.

With almost thirty US warships in Cuban waters, a diverse range of actors in the US left urged readers to rally against an armed invasion. Grace

Hutchins, a white communist and labor-rights advocate, called for Hands Off Cuba in the International Labor Defense (ILD)'s paper *Labor Defender*. To protect bankers' investments, she wrote, and "the property of sugar capitalists, and to shoot down the sugar workers who ask for bread, the Wall Street government dispatches the battleship Mississippi, and surrounds the island of Cuba with a cordon of U.S. cruisers and destroyers, manned by Marines ready to land on Cuban soil. This is the beginning of the INTERVENTION, and it must be opposed with all the forces of the American working class. HANDS OFF CUBA."[142] Similarly, William Simons, a Jewish CPUSA member who had been at the founding CSLA conference in Montevideo and was a contributor to the *Mundo Obrero*, wrote a pamphlet called "Hands Off Cuba" urging readers to launch a campaign of farmers, students, professionals, and workers demanding "the immediate withdrawal of American warships from Cuban ports and waters." Simons asked readers, "Are the American warships in Cuban ports and waters for your sake?" The answer, of course, was no, they were there to protect markets for US goods, Wall Street, and a corrupt Cuban government.[143] James Ford, a prominent African American CPUSA member who ran three times to be the US vice president on the communist ticket and who later represented the party at Cuban labor conferences in 1934, covered Cuba for the communist paper *Harlem Liberator*. He saw the revolution as an opportunity to strengthen interracial unity and urged protests against US intervention. Roosevelt will intervene "unless the working class and the oppressed Negroes of that country use every possible means to prevent him, assisted by the American workers, Negro and white."[144]

In his book, *Crime of Cuba*, first published in 1933 and reissued in 1934 with an afterword about the Revolution, Carleton Beals wrote of the possibility of intervention, which "seemed definitely on the boards." He explained, "The reaction against such a step was prompt and strong in this country and throughout Latin America. Roosevelt got a nation-wide anti-interventionist press."[145] Supporters of insurgent Cubans collected funds for the PCC, organized demonstrations of support for Cuban workers, and wrote letters to US and Cuban officials urging nonintervention.[146] In late August, Harlem communists organized a demonstration to declare their support for "Cuban freedom." Attendees included Ford, Beals, and Congressman Vito Anthony Marcantonio.[147] In September, an unknown individual in New York raised a red flag in City Hall Park then had some fun phoning city offices, mentioning the new flag, and yelling, "Hands off Cuba! Good night, buddy" before hanging up.[148] As the general secretary of the PCC's Central Committee would later tell an audience in Moscow, "Our great brother Party of the United States has taken the task of the defense of the Cuban revolution as one of its major tasks."[149] Elsewhere, supporters protested US imperialism in Cuba outside of US consulates, including demonstrators in Guadalajara, Mexico, who chanted, "Death to the United States" before being arrested.[150] These celebrations of Cuba's insurgency and calls to protect the island against a US intervention amounted to a major turnaround from the "criminal neglect" that Martínez Villena condemned in 1930; the island had become a top priority for the international left.

To communists, sugar workers were the essence of Cuba's Revolution. After Machado fled in August, the *Mundo Obrero* explained, "We can directly trace [these events] to the influence of the sugar strikers."[151] Similarly, in early October, the Moscow newspaper *Pravda*, wrote that Cuba's "revolutionary movement . . . finds expression in the seizure of land by peasants and farm laborers [and] in the seizure of factories by the workers"[152] From Montevideo, the CSLA emphasized the importance of the sugar insurgency, writing that a key element of the strike movement was "the seizure of sugar *ingenios* by workers at the main imperialist companies." This attack on the "imperialist octopi that suck the blood of the Cuban people," including specifically United Fruit, constituted a strike against "one of the most important points of yankee domination in Latin America." CLSA suggested that sugar workers had dealt a serious blow to US imperialism and "elevated to a higher level the revolutionary upsurge of anti-imperialist and antifeudal struggle in Latin America."[153] In short, by disregarding instructions to avoid seizing foreign properties, sugar workers in Cuba had placed themselves front and center in a global struggle against imperialism—and international leftists celebrated.

Striking workers in Cuba were well aware that the world was watching, as international newspapers and pamphlets made their way to the island. Merchant mariners of diverse nationalities brought printed materials from overseas, often on sugar company ships. In late September, Cuban authorities intercepted a package of eighty communist pamphlets about the revolution from a Chilean printer named Oscar Kanter aboard the United Fruit steamer SS *Veragua*; he had asked for permission to bring the box ashore, but when that permission was denied, he threw it onto a lighter.[154] In a different incident, a seamen's messman named Harry Norman started arguing with a policeman aboard another United Fruit steamer, the SS *Quirigua*. Norman, who spoke Spanish and was trying to distribute clothing at the dock, claimed "that the poor abused Cuban people were his compañeros" and was found carrying the same pamphlets.[155] The pamphlets praised Cuban resistance, especially the sugar strikes, and called on workers to join the PCC—and not Junco's

Trotskyist group.[156] CPUSA organizers also visited the island regularly, including two women, Sonia Winette and Mary Perschonok, who were arrested in early 1934.[157] The circulation of information flowed both ways, as Cubans traveled overseas spreading news about the revolution; a PCC delegate spoke at an antiwar congress in the US in September of 1933.[158]

High hopes for the revolution unfolding in Cuba were not limited to communists. As Gerald Horne details, several African American newspapers closely followed events on the island and highlighted the fact that so many participants were Black. Periodicals such as the *Baltimore Afro-American* and the *Pittsburgh Courier* noted that Oriente had a significant Black population and, as one article explained, "most of the Communists who are seizing and operating sugar mills in Cuba are black men led by black men."[159] The Black press also addressed the threat of intervention, focusing on the hypocrisy of the US federal government's willingness to send warships to "protect the interests of Wall Street in Cuba" but not to protect the lives of African Americans lynched in the US South.[160] Pan-African activist and (just a few years later) Howard University historian Rayford Logan covered Cuba's turbulent 1933 for the *Baltimore Afro-American* and commented on Cuba's racial dynamics.[161] He noted the "camaraderie" of white and Black Cubans of Oriente, and he called Santiago "one of the most interesting experiments in race relations anywhere in the world."[162] During his time in Cuba, Logan relied upon British West Indian interpreters. English-speaking Black immigrants, in other words, not only participated in the turbulent events of 1933 as strikers, but they also helped disseminate information about these events to wider, international audiences.

Leftists of all stripes covered Cuba's 1933 revolution in pamphlets, broadsides, and books. Beals's famous book, *The Crime of Cuba*, covered the history of US imperialism and exploitation on the island and included photographs by Walker Evans. Republished in 1934 with an afterword penned on October 8, 1933, about the revolution, Beals explained that a new government could only succeed if it fulfilled the slogan of "Cuba for the Cubans!" He listed landlessness and absentee foreign capital as among the most pressing issues. John A. Gronbeck-Tedesco writes that the revolution became "part of the visual and textual pieces of humanitarian crises of the Depression decade, a stone in a topological mosaic of war, strikes, and fascist authoritarianism. It was a subject that lined left-wing literature along with reportage of breadlines, migrant workers, and peasant rebellion in China."[163] Cuba's sugar industry, in particular, represented the extremes of imperialist exploitation. That multinational groups of workers—called together by US sugar companies—collaborated in such dramatic acts of resistance suggested for many the arrival of a new era of radicalism. Sugar workers in Cuba had debunked, once and for all, the idea that they were hinderances to revolution; rather, they were the revolutionary vanguard.

Defending Antillano Workers

In 1933 and 1934, the very cross-national collaboration that made the sugar insurgency a forerunner in the global struggle against imperialism was challenged at home in Cuba by rising nativism and hostility toward foreigners. As part of his wider reform package, President Grau issued several decrees nationalizing labor and expelling foreign workers in the final months of 1933. For over a year, the PCC remained staunchly opposed to labor nationalization, even as the policy was widely popular among Cubans. Across the Americas, the PCC stood alone in defending foreign Black workers. This position was the outcome of both the PCC's steadfast ideological commitment to proletarian internationalism and the multinational revolutionary power demonstrated in Cuba's sugar fields and factories.

Calls for the nationalization of labor date back to the founding of the republic in 1902 with a cigar workers' strike. Since that time, restricting foreigners from the workplace had been a high priority among labor organizers.[164] In particular, Afro-Cubans supported labor nationalization, as they were often the last to be hired and the first to be fired. Many employers preferred Spaniards over Afro-Cubans, which the latter considered especially egregious in light of Black participation in Cuba's wars of independence against Spain. Accordingly, the Partido Independiente de Color included labor nationalization in its list of demands.[165] By the 1920s, with widespread bracero immigration, hostility toward Afro-Antillano immigration was on the rise. From right-wing fears of Cuba's racial degeneration to leftist critiques of foreign employers' reliance on imported labor, many Cubans saw the presence of poorly paid immigrants as a threat to national wellbeing. They believed that Antillanos drove down wages and took jobs from native Cubans. Organizations dedicated to promoting anti-immigrant legislation sprung up in 1933, including the "Association of National Reconquest" and the "Pro-80% Committee," both of which demanded Cuban majorities in workplaces.

Labor nationalization was also intended to diffuse racial tensions within Cuba. Anti-Black racism peaked in the aftermath of Machado's flight, as the power vacuum left open questions about political leadership and access to state resources. Right-wing and racist organizations like the ABC Revolutionary Society, the KKK Kubano, and the National White League used racial fearmongering to eliminate competition for state-positions.[166] Bombs exploded in buildings housing Afro-Cuban societies, including the Club Atenas, where Garvey met with Miguel Ángel Céspedes in 1921.[167] Harkening back to the rumors of a race war that took place on the eve of the 1912 massacre, white Cubans of all political stripes cast their opponents as Black in order to discredit their political ambitions. Exacerbating matters were rumors about newly empowered "Blacks in rebellion" in the east.[168] In this climate, Grau hoped anti-immigrant measures would calm intra-Cuban racial tensions, as Black foreigners (rather than Black Cubans) became the targets of "reclaiming" Cuba for Cubans. As Aviva Chomsky has written of the 1920s, white commentators opposed to Black immigration maintained "that Cuban blacks were somehow not really 'black' and that 'blackness' was a characteristic of foreign blacks."[169] Anti-immigrant campaigns, then, "attempted to reaffirm Cuban national solidarity and instill allegiance among Afro-Cubans."[170] Afro-Cuban intellectuals understood the racism inherent in this thinking, but many nevertheless opposed all immigration (Black and white) on the grounds that foreigners displaced, first and foremost, Black Cubans from the workplace.[171] Black journalist Alberto Arredondo argued that Afro-Cubans were the principal beneficiaries of nationalization and called the measures "an indisputable step advancing toward the elimination of prejudice and discrimination and toward jobs for thousands of unemployed individuals."[172]

In nationalizing labor, Cuba joined an Americas-wide movement in which state authorities sought to "improve" racial composition, reduce unemployment, and assert sovereignty. The United States' 1924 Johnson-Reed Act restricting immigration based on eugenic criteria was the most famous, but Honduras, Panama, Venezuela, and Costa Rica also enacted laws restricting the immigration of "undesirable" nonwhite persons during this period. A 1930 Cuban government report summarized other states' policies and recommended that the government prohibit the entrance of prostitutes, criminals, "the blind, idiots, lepers, epileptics, etc.," Chinese immigrants, and "Antilleans, except people from Puerto Rico and the Dominican Republic."[173] Bolivia, Brazil, Chile, Mexico, Panama, Peru, El Salvador, and Uruguay all required that employers hire a designated percentage of native workers, and Peru, Chile, and Mexico mandated that the portion of nationals be over 80 percent in some industries.[174] The Dominican Republic, which also received significant Haitian and British West Indian migration, taxed Asian and Black foreigners in 1932 and legislated that workplaces be 70 percent Dominican in 1933.[175] In many respects, such legislation represents the independent efforts of national governments to tackle common problems. As Lara Putnam explains, "International economic and political developments in the 1920s made nativism an irresistible campaign plank and border control a new hallmark of state sovereignty."[176] In the early 1930s, immigration restrictions were a means of asserting national sovereignty—especially in countries where imperialist companies had imported foreign workers—while also appealing to popular classes suffering during the Great Depression.

Amid widespread enthusiasm for immigration restrictions and labor nationalizations, President Grau issued a series of decrees aimed at protecting the Cuban laborer. On October 19, 1933, Decree 2232 ordered the obligatory repatriation of all unemployed foreigners without resources. On November 8, Decree 2583 or the Nationalization of Labor Law, stipulated that one half of all employees for any given industrial, commercial, and agricultural company must be native Cubans and that an additional 30 percent could be nationalized citizens. (The math here led to the confusing situation in which the legislation was sometimes called "the 50 percent law" and sometimes "the 80 percent law.") Finally, in December, additional regulation mandated the deportation of all foreign workers who failed to comply with earlier immigration-related laws.[177] Under the new rules, the "forceful repatriation of foreigners residing in the Republic, finding themselves without work and without any type of resources" was to be carried out by local municipal authorities under the supervision of the Ministry of the Interior and with army support.[178]

The legislation affected most dramatically Haitians in the east.[179] In 1933 and early 1934, thousands were forcibly deported, some of whom actually were employed. Haitians picked up by the Rural Guard—often violently—were not given the opportunity to collect belongings, settle affairs, or say goodbye to family. Cuban women who had formed families with Haitian men found themselves expelled from their homes with no recourse.[180] The first deportees were taken to Cayo Duán in Oriente, where they entered quarantine without food or medicine. The steamer *Julián Alonso*, where they awaited embarkation, had a maximum capacity of 70 but held 500 individuals; the captain purchased crackers and sardines for his otherwise-starved passengers.[181] Even after Grau was removed from office in early 1934, deportations continued under Mendieta. In all, 4,943 Haitians were deported between November 1933 and July 1934.[182]

As Giovannetti-Torres and others have detailed, British West Indians largely escaped the violent deportations to which Haitians were subjected.[183] For one, there were simply more individuals from Haiti than from any other single island, so they suffered the worst of the deportations. Additionally, British migrants' persistent efforts to secure representation from the Crown had resulted in a "cumulative effect"—whether or not individuals were actually supported by consular officials—and a history of "British-Cuba diplomatic travails" that mitigated against the worst abuse from Cuban authorities.

Additionally, British West Indians' relative skills and literacy had resulted in different work possibilities and settlement patterns from those of Haitians, who tended to remain in field work. Specifically regarding Jamaicans, another factor limiting their forcible repatriation was that the colony had (for a time, at least) a "secretary of immigration" in Cuba whose office "had managed to repatriate over 10,000 Jamaican migrants before the Ley del 50% was implemented," as Giovannetti-Torres explains.[184] There were simply fewer Jamaicans to deport by 1933. As for individuals from the eastern Caribbean, who had less representation than their Jamaican counterparts, the distance (and thus cost) for repatriation was significant when compared to that of nearby Haiti and probably curbed Cuban enthusiasm for deportations.[185]

Throughout this period of nationalist legislation and violent deportations of Haitians, the Communist Party and its sister organizations stood alone in defending Black immigrant workers. For the PCC, protesting deportations was a matter of putting internationalist solidarity into local practice. Nationalist legislation, the party maintained, was "intended to divide the working classes" and to "increase racial tensions."[186] The party centered its defense of immigrant workers on eastern Cuba and urged workers, "ABOVE ALL IN ORIENTE" to organize "meetings, demonstrations, strikes, [and] protest resolutions" against the new laws.[187] Amid the sugar strikes, CNOC and SNOIA proclamations called for working people to stand together regardless of race or nationality. Organizers warned of the divisive threat represented by nativism.[188] They argued that strikers should be careful not to listen to "words of 'Cuban chauvinism' and other hollow messages about 'our patria' because we are all workers, native and foreign. We do not see differences of race, nationality, or gender."[189] The SNOIA also condemned the 50 percent law as a "criminal maneuver" attempting to "deceive the masses of workers and to break the unified front."[190] Communist publications called for solidarity and urged strikers to do likewise. The *Bandera Roja* singled out strike committees that had "errored" by not fully incorporating foreigners.[191] Having viewed the extent of Afro-Caribbean militancy and having come to understand them as essential in the insurgency, one of the SNOIA's key tasks for its January 1934, conference was "drawing up specific demands for Antillean workers (Jamaicans, Haitians, etc.)."[192]

In contrast to the anti-immigrant sentiment undergirding deportations, which downplayed Afro-Cubans' racial identities in favor of emphasizing their *cubanidad*, the PCC called on Afro-Cubans to oppose deportations specifically on the grounds of racial solidarity. The party explicitly emphasized the importance of Black Cubans in the struggle against the 50 percent law and deportations of Antillanos, connecting defense of immigrants with international Black liberation more widely.[193] The *Bandera Roja* condemned the "pogroms" of immigrant workers and urged readers to "respond by strengthening the fighting front of all workers, black and white, native and foreign, against the racist campaign, against the beginnings of pogroms!" The paper even wrote that supporters should "organize the armed resistance of blacks, and intensify the fight for their absolute equality."[194] Given Cuba's long history of racist backlashes against "Blacks in rebellion"—including, the Guerra Chiquita of 1879, the 1912 PIC uprising, and the turbulence after Machado's fall—it is striking that the PCC openly called for armed resistance in its defense of foreign and Cuban Black workers.[195]

In late 1933, the DOI launched an aggressive "campaign against anti-black terror" and called on supporters to defend the rights of Black workers of all nationalities. A proclamation explained, "Grau's bloody government, that calls itself a friend of the negroes for having promulgated an 80% law" is only using them "as support for the government and as instruments for attacking the foreign workers."[196] According to *Defensa*, "black masses are terrorized so that they may be better exploited," a practice that was particularly "savage" toward Antillanos. The group called on members to "fight against every incidence of violence and against the deportations of Haitians and the stripping of their lands." DOI proclaimed, "In Oriente there should be a massive mobilization using all the troops to stop the dispossession and deportation of Haitians. We should have meetings, demonstrations, etc. in every place where they have taken a Haitian . . . we should have protest resolutions sent to the consul of Haiti, the Secretary of State and the President of the Republic." *Defensa* added a suggestion: "also [send protests] to the yankee consuls and to President Roosevelt demanding the freedom of the Scottsboro *negros*," referring to nine young African Americans imprisoned on false rape charges in Scottsboro, Alabama.[197] Their defense campaign had reached global proportions—with demonstrations reaching as far as Japan, Buenos Aires, and South Africa, and the PCC leading the Cuban effort.[198] In this understanding of international Black liberation, the forced deportations of Haitians were part and parcel of the same system of racist, imperialist capitalism that generated lynch justice in the US South.

Although the PCC had a strong ideological justification for defense of Antillano workers, this position stands out in both Cuba's political landscape and that of the Americas. Ideological support for Third Period ideals rarely translated into individual CPs sticking their necks out in defense of foreign workers. As Jacob Zumoff points out, Costa Rica and Panama both had communist parties *and* significant populations of Afro-Caribbean workers, yet neither CP tried to recruit these foreigners nor did they "stress fighting for Antillano rights as part of the struggle for national liberation and workers' power."[199] In Cuba, the 50 percent law was widely popular. In fact, it was especially well received among the very groups that the PCC hoped to bring into its ranks, including unemployed workers and Afro-Cubans.

The PCC's defense of Antillano workers against labor nationalization, then, emerges as, at least in part, the product of the multinational sugar insurgency. PCC officials were impressed—and perhaps surprised—by Haitian and British West Indian militancy; field organizers (like Figueredo and "Emiliano"), countless Communist Youth League members (like Rojas), and SNOIA delegates had personally witnessed Antillano militancy in action and sent reports to the party's Central Committee. Their participation in the insurgency demonstrated the revolutionary power of Antillano workers and undermined the idea that Haitians and British West Indians were hinderances to organized labor. If there was ever a time and place to take seriously the Third Period call for cross-racial, cross-national proletarian solidarity, it was in Cuba's sugar fields in late 1933. Viewed from the perspective of the sugar insurgency, the PCC's hostility to Grau's administration emerges less as a short-sighted allegiance to Moscow's Third-Period sectarianism and more as consistent with calls for labor internationalism. After all, Grau's "so-called authentic revolution" was behind the "bloody" and "savage" deportations of Afro-Antillanos.[200]

Nevertheless, restrictions against foreign labor were widely popular across Cuba. Junco's Trotsktyist party supported the measures and worked with the FOH to support implementation.[201] In Cuban cities, the 50 percent law principally affected Spanish-owned shops and restaurants, where Spaniards privileged their own countrymen, and was especially popular among unemployed Afro-Cubans. Communist opposition to anti-immigrant legislation pitted the party against the very people it was trying to recruit and, ironically, put the party in the same camp as powerful sugar companies who also opposed labor nationalization.[202] In December 1933, the party attempted to organize a general strike against labor nationalization, but the strike failed as most rank and file favored the laws. That same month, over 20,000 people marched to the presidential palace in a show of support for nationalization, and crowds in Havana led by Afro-Cubans confronted shopkeepers who had failed to comply with the 50 percent law. Supporters of the legislation clashed with communist protestors and threatened to seize businesses that did not nationalize. The party, which had expanded considerably from a few hundred people in 1929 to over three thousand by the end of 1932 and peaked at 10,000 after Machado's fall, was again struggling to survive by the time of its second congress in April 1934. In the face of anti-immigrant nationalism and repression from the Batista-Mendieta government, the PCC's support for foreign workers hindered its own desperately needed efforts to widen its rank and file.[203] Nevertheless, in mid-1934, the PCC still opposed nationalizations and supported immigrant workers, running headlines such as, "Fight against the Haitian Hunt!"[204]

By the end of the 1934, however, communists knew they had a political problem and began to slowly reverse course as part of wider changing tides. In March 1935, the PCC organized a general strike, which Batista violently suppressed. Margaret Stevens dubbed it "the final hurrah of the working-class-oriented Third Period."[205] Soon after, the PCC found itself isolated and many of its unions illegal. The party moved toward moderation.[206] Moscow too was moving out of the sectarianism of the Third Period and into a new era of "Popular Front" collaboration against fascism, de-emphasizing proletarian internationalism in favor of national coalition building.

In early 1934, Blas Roca (né Francisco Calderío), the mixed-race leader of the shoemakers' union in Manzanillo, had been appointed general secretary of the PCC, replacing Martínez Villena, who died of tuberculosis one day after Batista removed Grau from office. Roca had overseen the PCC's *oriental* district committee during the sugar insurgency and was reluctant to disavow support for foreign workers. The Cuban Party's Politburo debated its position on the 50 percent law in July 1935, with some continuing to oppose the legislation and others admitting that restricting foreign labor was widely popular, especially among Afro-Cubans.[207] In July and August, Moscow formally launched the Popular Front at the Seventh World Congress of the Communist International. There, Roca emphasized the need for collaboration with "national reformist and national revolutionary parties" and criticized his own party for having underestimated potential allies on the left, especially Grau and Guiteras. He remained tactically and ideologically committed to anti-imperialism but conceded that the matter of labor nationalization and solidarity with foreign workers was tricky. Roca acknowledged that the PCC's opposition to nationalization measures diminished the party's appeal on the island, yet he still hoped to "struggle against" labor nationalization. "As a last resort," he suggested, the PCC could settle for the "maintenance of the Grau law 'status quo,'" which had "great popularity."[208] In other words, Roca, who had led an eastern district committee during the sugar insurgency and understood Antillano militancy firsthand, only reluctantly gave up on defense of Afro-Caribbean immigrants; he hoped to avoid supporting the 50 percent law but openly feared the political risks of opposition.

In October 1935, Roca announced a reversal on labor nationalizations; the party would now support the 50 percent law.[209] The deportations had slowed down, and the PCC was moving toward collaboration with other leftist groups. In 1936, CNOC explained its reversal in a *carta abierta,* which acknowledged the "erroneous" nature of its previous position and that the party had not understood how popular the legislation was with its a "deep national content." CNOC now demanded "comprehensive compliance" with laws requiring a Cuban majority in the workplace and called for an end to exemptions.[210] Whereas the party's previous opposition to labor nationalization had been expressed in terms of proletarian solidarity with exploited Antillano workers, the new position in favor of nationalization was articulated as a means of ridding the country of the vestiges of Spanish privilege. This rhetorical shift allowed the PCC to reverse position while never formally disavowing Antillanos or internationalist anti-imperialism.

Even though Antillano-defense was displaced from the party platform, the PCC's commitment to interracial proletarian solidarity had lasting consequences. As Wood and others have argued, the contours of communist antiracism shifted over the course of the 1930s, but the party's commitment to Black equality held fast.[211] Far from a hollow or opportunistic maneuver to recruit Black workers, the PCC's belief in interracial solidarity as the best defense against imperialism was the product of several factors. For one, the organizing campaign of 1932 and the 1933 revolution catapulted Afro-Cubans into key leadership positions, as individuals such as Blas Roca and his brother Remigio Calderío as well as Lazaro Peña, Martín Castellanos, and the sugar organizer Jesús Menéndez rose to prominence in the PCC.[212] Additionally, field organizers had personally witnessed the revolutionary strength of interracial collaboration during the sugar insurgency. In the second half of the 1930s, their commitment to racial justice was redirected in a Popular Front context toward national liberation with lasting effects. Wood and Kaitlyn Henderson both point to the lasting consequences of Cuban communists' anti-racist agenda, including the 1940 constitution. The communist party, legal since 1938, helped draft the constitution, which criminalized racial discrimination and prohibited discriminatory hiring.[213]

Conclusion

The story of Cuba's revolution of 1933 is often told as a national one. In Cuban historiography, it was a "precursor" revolution that created a generation ("la generación del 30") whose experience of a frustrated uprising accounted for their enthusiasm for Fidel Castro two-and-a-half decades later. This is no doubt true. Additionally, the revolution catalyzed lasting shifts in Cuban politics. The labor ministry remained intact, and many of Grau's reforms stayed in place even under future administrations. The idea that the state must be responsive to the popular will (or at least appear to be) was firmly entrenched after the upheavals of 1933.[214] The state had become a mediator between employers and laborers, and it did not always side with capital.[215] Events that year—especially the sugar insurgency—also radicalized a generation of young communist activists who believed that multinational, multiracial proletarian solidarity was the best defense against imperialism and became lasting champions of Black liberation.

But the outside world also paid attention to the revolution of 1933, a point easy to overlook in light of the 1959 revolution's overshadowing effect on Cuban history. Leftists in Moscow, New York, Mexico City, Montevideo, and beyond celebrated Cuba's international proletarian solidarity in action. The island's sugar fields and factories, in particular, represented the worst of US imperialism, but workers' multinational collaboration represented the most radical form of resistance. The global left heralded insurgent sugar workers as harbingers of a new era of anti-capitalist, anti-imperialist resistance and rallied to defend Cuba against a probable US intervention. Theirs was a struggle shared by peasants in El Salvador, oil workers in Venezuela, and African Americans in the US South. In turning global attention to Cuba, sugar workers and other participants in the revolution of 1933 placed themselves in the vanguard of anti-imperialism struggle in the Americas.

The wider significance of their revolution was not lost on sugar workers themselves, who sang the Internationale, prepared for an intervention, and established DOI offices from which they set off telegrams condemning Hitler's crimes. Organizers found workers in the east better read than their comrades in the capital and were impressed by the strikers who flew red flags over sugar mills even before party officials arrived. Their example was the model to follow, not that of the party officials who made the "mistake" of calling strikers back to work in August and who advised caution in the face of US intervention. Insurgent sugar workers did not have to travel widely to join what Gronbeck-Tesco has called a "cartography of dissident cosmopolitanism."[216] Though the insurgency was put down in early 1934, eastern Cuba's internationalist spirit did not die. Rather, it took off again in the late-1930s when local and exile networks formed in the aftermath of '33 mobilized in defense of the Spanish Republic and men like Roberto Buzón Neira took up arms against Francisco Franco.

5

In Defense of the Spanish Republic

Oriental Antifascism at Home and Abroad

On February 5, 1938, the SS *Oropesa* set sail from Havana to La Rochelle, France. On board were seventy-three Cuban volunteers for the 59th Battalion of the XV International Brigades, an international unit defending Republican forces during the Spanish Civil War. Two such men prepared to risk life and limb for this cause far from home were Ángel López Estévez and Roberto Buzón Neira, both hailing from the sugar towns of northeastern Cuba. López was twenty-three years old at the time—a white Cuban with close-cut curly hair, high cheekbones, and a faint, youthful mustache. He was born in Camagüey and had spent the previous few years at the Central Palma in Oriente, where he was unemployed more often than not, as were most sugar workers. López largely avoided labor unions and radical politics, only joining the International Red Aid in 1938 when he and a friend from Camagüey, Armando Torres, decided to volunteer in Spain. In Spain, López supported the Popular Front because it was the best means of "crushing fascism" and fighting for "independence."[1] López's shipmate Roberto Buzón Neira had been active in the labor movement since Cuba's 1933 revolution, when he was just nineteen years old. Buzón, a Black Cuban and twenty-four years old when he set sail for Spain, had a small, tidily trimmed mustache and grinning eyes. From paperwork he filled out a year later, we can tell that he was lighthearted and a bit irreverent, poking fun at authority. (His commanders were not amused; one described him as a "regular" communist—neither good nor bad—who "has ability, but lacks seriousness."[2]) Born at Mayarí, near the United Fruit Company's Central Preston, Buzón was a construction worker on the mill, but like López, often found himself unemployed due to the seasonality of sugar work. He joined the Sindicato Nacional de Obreros de la Industria Azucarera (SNOIA) during the sugar strikes of 1933 and the Partido Comunista de Cuba (PCC) in 1934. He rose in the ranks and was arrested several times. By the time he set sail on the *Oropesa*, Buzón was well versed in the history of the labor movement and Marxist theory. He would go on to become a political commissionaire in Spain, tasked with educating Spaniards and international volunteers about the importance of their Republican cause.[3] For these two young men from humble backgrounds in northeastern Cuba's sugar fields and factories, men whose lives were marked by the routine hardships of low pay and underemployment, the Cuban opposition was on hold, its leaders underground or in exile. But in Spain, *brigadistas* could put words into action and political ideology into practice. Spain was the new front in the interconnected global struggles against exploitation, imperialism, and fascism.

On July 17, 1936, a rebellion against the democratically elected government of Spain had broken out among Spanish colonial army officers in Morocco.[4] One day later, the rebellion spread to mainland Spain, supported by a confederation of right-wing organizations, especially the Falange Española. Within a week Spain was territorially and politically divided between the fascist rebels and the Spanish Republic. The Popular Front government of Spain, which had been in power since February with the electoral victory of a coalition of left and center-left parties, remained in control of Spain's industrial urban centers with strong worker movements, the southern countryside with high concentrations of landless peasants, and the Basque Country. Meanwhile, the military rebels led by General Francisco Franco seized control of and crushed working-class resistance in the northern rural areas and Catholic strongholds. The Republic held Madrid where government officials, unsure of army loyalty, distributed arms to workers and authorized the formation of popular militias. Adolf Hitler and Benito Mussolini aided the military rebels in transporting Spanish troops over the Strait of Gibraltar and, later, with munitions, tanks, airplanes, and other military assistance. The UK, France, and the US, however, agreed upon a policy of nonintervention in August 1936 and turned a blind eye to Italian and German interference. For its part, the Soviet Union began giving the Republic material assistance that September, and the Communist International (Comintern) organized International Brigades of volunteers to defend the besieged Republic. Thus, the war was transformed from an internal Spanish fight, which had been waged between the Spanish right and the left since the formation of the Second Republic in 1931, into an international struggle between forces allied with fascism and those opposed to it.[5]

Other causes of the interwar period spanned borders and moved diverse groups to action. The execution of Italian American anarchists Nicola Sacco and Bartolomeo Vanzetti in 1927 had become a touchpoint for international struggles against political repression. Cuban sugar workers were still discussing Sacco and Vanzetti when they erupted into insurgency in 1933. Similarly, global communists rallied in defense of the nine African American boys and young men arrested on false rape charges in Scottsboro, Alabama, tying the struggle against "lynch justice" in the US to larger battles against imperialism and economic exploitation. The PCC called on workers to defend the Scottsboro Nine in the same breath as it called on them to defend Haitians against deportation in 1933 and 1934.

Perhaps most significantly, in 1935, the Italian invasion of Ethiopia captured the attention of the global left and the African diaspora (many of whom, of course, were one and the same), and many rallied in defense of the African state. Ethiopia had been a powerful symbol of African independence and resistance in the international Black imagination since 1896 when Emperor Menelik fought back an Italian invasion, and the territory was the only African state never ruled by Europeans. As Ariel Mae Lambe has demonstrated, outrage over the Italian invasion mobilized communists, Afro-Cubans, and many others in Cuba, ultimately serving "to build up Cuban antifascism in 1935."[6] Indeed, an antifascist Ethiopian-defense campaign took off across the African diaspora.[7] For several reasons, defense of Ethiopia, however, did not galvanize global antifascists to the same extent that Spain did. For one, Ethiopia was ruled by an elite class of monarchists.[8] Moreover, dominant Eurocentrism simply did not render Ethiopia essential to the global geopolitical landscape in the same way as it did Spain. Finally, no internationally organized effort to recruit volunteers for the Ethiopian front ever came to fruition.

Spain was different. There, a democratically elected government was besieged by a foreign-backed military rebellion. The Spanish Republic had been a profound experiment in representative, leftist governance. In 1931, the Spanish people had overturned the centuries-old monarchy and abolished church dominance. With the support of women, workers, peasants, and intellectuals, the Republic instituted land reforms, secular education, a program of workers' rights, and regional autonomy. Franco's rebellion and fascist intervention threatened to annihilate this democratic project. Women and men across the globe came to the Republic's defense with expressions of support and material contributions. They viewed Spain's civil war as a world-historical turning point. In Spain, men and women could actually fight fascism not with words alone but with their physical selves in arms and service. Over 35,000 volunteers from fifty-three countries defended the Republic in the International Brigades, while another 5,000 foreigners joined the medical service, local unions, and left-wing parties to support the Popular Front government.[9]

Cubans rallied around the Spanish cause.[10] After the failed general strike in March of 1935, opposition activists went underground and into exile; but all was not lost. Activists for a New Cuba, as Lambe explains, "continued in the face of defeat by refusing to view their political goals as confined to the island."[11] Diverse Cubans came to view international antifascism an extension of their own local struggles. Black Cubans articulated a vision of antifascism rooted in anti-racism. In the midst of the war at a 1937 international writers' conference in Madrid, the Afro-Cuban poet Nicolás Guillén proclaimed, "No one is as antifascist as the *negro*, especially the Cuban *negro*, because he knows that the roots of fascism lie in a land sewn with racial hatred . . ."[12] Spaniards, the largest immigrant group in Cuba, paid close attention to events in their homeland and mobilized around defense of the Republic. Women across the island, of diverse backgrounds, organized to aid Spanish children.[13] Communists condemned Italian and German support for Franco and reminded supporters that Cuba too had experienced foreign domination—first by Spain and then by the United States. For them, fighting fascism was a matter of struggling against imperialism. In short, with the Spanish-solidarity campaign, Cubans of a variety of political stripes finally achieved the unity that had eluded them during the 1933 revolution. Denise Urcelay-Maragnès explains that solidarity in the struggle against Machado and Batista had been "impossible on internal issues," but "solidarity with republican Spain gradually regrouped the opposition . . . bringing together different associations and, more than anything, thousands of Spaniards and Cubans across the country."[14] Defending the Spanish Republic appealed to anyone who believed in democracy or identified with the poor, marginalized, or oppressed. Cuba's first and most famous martyr in Spain, Pablo de la Torriente Brau, wrote, Spain "is where today the hopes of the world's oppressed pulsate."[15]

Cuba's major newspapers gave the war front-page coverage, and readers paid close attention. Women and men formed support committees; raised money for the Spanish government; sewed clothing for Spanish orphans; hosted informative meetings and rallies; and collected cash, sugar, and tobacco to be sent directly to the front. In addition to this mobilization on the island, over 1,200 Cubans traveled to Spain and took up arms, with over a third losing their lives on Spanish soil. Among those who died fighting Franco was José Miguel Pérez, who had helped found the Cuban Communist Party with Julio Antonio Mella in 1925. With approximately 1,200 brigadistas, Cuba sent more volunteers to Spain per capita than any other country and likely more than the rest of Latin America combined.[16] Several Cuban authors have emphasized the PCC's leading role in the Spanish-solidarity campaign, but historians should approach claims of PCC leadership with a degree of skepticism, given the credit that the post-'59 revolutionary state ascribed retrospectively to the party's role leading leftist organizing.[17] While the PCC certainly led in recruiting volunteers for the front, a broad coalition of groups working across the center-left political spectrum organized the popular Spanish-defense campaign.

Just as they were during the peak of Garveyite Pan-Africanism and rise of communist-led international labor solidarity during the Third Period, Cuban northeastern sugar towns were steeped in popular internationalism during the Spanish Civil War. Many agreed that Spain was the next front in an international struggle against imperialism, exploitation, racism, and fascism. A journalist covering the campaign in the east wrote that Cuba felt that "humanity is living in a transcendental moment hanging on the Spanish contest."[18] A vibrant pro-Republican mobilization was under way in northeastern Cuba by early 1937. Layered on top of these efforts were interconnected exile networks formed during the struggles against Machado and Batista that bridged the region with New York, Paris, Madrid, and Barcelona. Several sugar workers with experience in northeastern Cuba mobilized within these networks and voyaged to Spain.

This chapter focuses on the men and women politicized in northeastern Cuba during the 1920s and 1930s who saw Spain as the next front in a global struggle they had been waging in Cuba for years. After an overview of the island-wide mobilization, the chapter details the pro-Republican scene in northeastern sugar towns. Several organizations explicitly cited the Spanish government's redistributive programs, especially agrarian reform and unemployment assistance, as reasons for their support, a fair argument in a region dominated by monopolistic companies offering only seasonal employment. The final section focuses on those Cubans who volunteered for the front from company towns. To willingly enlist in an overseas war and be prepared to sacrifice one's life in battle is no small gesture but is, rather, the ultimate commitment to one's political ideals. Like Buzón, many recalled the sugar insurgency of 1933 as a formative moment for their political consciousness and drew connections between the experience of US imperialism and their decision to support the Spanish Republic.

Defending the Spanish Republic in Cuba

Overseas, popular opinion on the situation in Spain was divided. The Republic's anticlericalism was deeply unpopular with Catholics, and anarchist attacks on churches and priests provided fodder for Franco's propaganda. Large landholders viewed Spanish land reform with deep fear and supported the right-wing rebellion. These factors contributed to a particularly divisive climate in Latin America.[19] Cuba, however, was largely a stronghold of Republican sympathy for several reasons.[20] First, as historian Alistair Hennessy points out, the Catholic Church was less influential in Cuba, where it remained mainly an urban institution, than in other parts of Latin America. Therefore, Republican anticlericalism and attacks on religion were a less effective propaganda weapon in Cuba than they were elsewhere.[21] Perhaps more importantly, Cuba had a significant and recently arrived Spanish population, the majority of whom were pro-Republican. At the dawn of the twentieth century, US occupying authorities encouraged immigration from the former colonizer, a policy that continued through the first decades of the Cuban Republic. From 1902 to 1933, more immigrants came from Spain than from any other country. The Spanish presence reached its peak at almost 16 percent of Cuba's population in 1931, yet this sizable *peninsular* community was not a major source of falangist support.[22] Many were active within the Cuban labor movement and thus unlikely to support Franco's nationalists. In fact, some unions were so dominated by Spaniards that one of the laws enacted during the 1933 revolution was an ordinance preventing Spanish-born workers from holding leadership positions in unions.[23] Even Spaniards working in commerce were often products of the *sobrinismo* system of sending for nephews with few prospects in Spain to apprentice in Cuban shops, and these young men, living under difficult conditions and working long hours, were sympathetic to the Republican cause.[24]

Finally, while landholders in Latin America tended to be *profranquista*, Cuba's own experience of US imperialism mitigated against the possibility that the island's landed elites would support Franco. For one, Cuba's native landholders had been significantly wiped out in the nineteenth-century wars for independence and by debt to US banks in the aftermath. US companies bought out Cuban properties at the dawn of the century, and foreign penetration of the economy deepened with the economic crashes of 1921 and 1929. Those who remained by the late 1930s were more concerned with reducing Wall Street's control of Cuban resources than with supporting Franco's defense of property rights.[25] Cuban nationalism and resentment of foreign companies was particularly strong among the middle and upper-class landholding colonos, who were indebted to US banks and locked into selling their product to monopolistic sugar companies.[26] That Franco was backed by the Italian and German governments opened him up to criticisms about foreign meddling, an experience only too familiar to Cuba's cane growers. In fact, while landholder sympathy may have initially laid with Franco, by the end of the war, colonos and hacendados were donating sugar to the Republican government.[27]

Of course, not all of Cuba was pro-Republican. Franco and the nationalists did garner support, especially among well-to-do Spanish merchants and businessmen. Falangists in Cuba marched through the streets of Havana wearing their blue-shirt uniforms.[28] They established the "plato unico" (single course), in which diners in restaurants ate only one course but paid for three, a system that was essentially a restaurant tax for Franco's insurrection.[29] In Havana, plato unico events included a fundraiser held at the Casino Nacional, a social club for wealthy Spaniards, in May 1938. According to the communist newspaper *Hoy*, the event was cosponsored by the Italian and German embassies and covered in the society pages of Havana's daily newspapers without criticism.[30]

Opinion on the war was particularly divided within the Spanish cultural centers, especially the Centro Gallego and the Centro Asturiano.[31] These institutions were historically dominated by wealthy merchants and began the 1936–1939 period as bases of support for Franco. Quickly, however, rank-and-file members and a new generation of leaders lodged protests about their organizations' pro-nationalist positions. For instance, upon the outbreak of war, the Centro Gallego in Havana removed the Spanish Republican flag from its headquarters only to find several internal groups complaining.[32] The Centro was embroiled in controversy about flags, insignias on school uniforms, and other symbols of Spain's political division throughout the war years. Opposition organizations, such as the Hermandad Asturiania and the Hermandad Gallega, formed within the main centros to offer an alternative leadership and, by 1938, had won elections in both centros.[33] Despite these pockets of rebel sympathy, Cuban support for the Republican government grew throughout the war.

The December 1936 death on a Spanish battlefield of journalist Pablo de la Torriente Brau did more than any other event to mobilize Cuban support for the Republican cause. The Puerto Rican–born writer was a quintessential member of Cuba's Generación del '30s. He had been a student leader against Machado and was forced into exile by Batista in 1935, when he found himself in New York.[34] So many of Cuba's opposition leaders from the 1930s were in the city that Cuban organizations proliferated. De la Torriente Brau cofounded the Organización Revolucionaria Cubana Antiimperialista (ORCA).[35] ORCA's central objective was to "bring about the establishment of indispensable unity of action among forces of the Cuban left."[36] He was also involved in the Club Cubano Julio Antonio Mella, which had been established in 1931 by a group of students expelled from the University of Havana during Machado's crackdown. Located in Spanish Harlem, the Club Mella was a gathering place for Cubans and other Latin Americans of leftist political tendencies—even those who used to battle one another, including communists, Auténticos who supported Ramón Grau San Martín, and Joven Cuba members who supported Antonio Guiteras, the latter groups having been vilified by the PCC in 1933. A host of other leading intellectuals affiliated with the club, including prominent leaders in the Cuban Communist Party such as Juan Marinello, Rubén Martínez Villena, Blas Roca, and Fabio Grobart; North American journalist Carleton Beals; African American CPUSA leader James Ford; and the secretaries general of the Mexican and US communist parties.[37] The Club Mella would later become a fertile recruiting ground for the pro-Republican mobilization and a center of brigadista preparations. In 1935, de la Torriente Brau helped establish a similar organization, the Club Cubano José Martí. The Club Martí was frequented by Latin American radicals but catered to a more recent wave of political exiles from Batista's dictatorship.[38]

To make ends meet in New York, de la Torriente Brau waited tables and worked as a correspondent for the Mexican daily *El Machete* and the American journal *New Masses*. After the outbreak of war in July 1936, he pitched the idea of reporting on New York's pro-Republican mobilization to the editor of Cuba's *Bohemia* magazine but, while covering a Spanish-solidarity demonstration in Union Square on August 22 and hearing the chants of "Long Live the Popular Front," he decided that he must go to Spain. "The idea exploded in my head," he later wrote, and, fed up with washing dishes in New York, he had to join the "ultimate battle between oppressors and the oppressed."[39] After a month of securing credentials through *New Masses* and gathering funds for his voyage, de la Torriente Brau departed for Spain. He quickly abandoned journalism and joined the armed struggle, becoming political commissar serving under the command of Commander Valentín Gonzáles or El Campesino.[40] He died just three months later on December 19 marching on Majadahonda to defend Madrid.[41] De la Torriente Brau left for Spain and died in defense of the Republic long before an international mobilization and formal recruitment effort was under way.[42] Simply scraping together funds for the voyage was more difficult for him than it would be for later volunteers. De la Torriente Brau served as an example and martyr for pro-Republican Cubans, and his early death helped launch the pro-Republican campaign in Cuba.

The pro-Republican mobilization was so widely popular that it eventually pushed Cuba's dictator to change positions on the war in Spain. Initially, Fulgencio Batista—who had been the de-facto leader of the country since 1934—joined the United States and declared Cuba's neutrality. Presidential decree No. 3411 banned material and moral support for belligerents in overseas conflicts, rendering fundraising and volunteer recruiting for Spain illegal.[43] In November 1936, Cuban authorities impounded the Spanish vessel *Manuel Arnús* on its way to load arms in Mexico. The case became so heated that the Spanish government recalled its ambassador from Cuba in early 1937, though an interim official continued to support the Cuban mobilization. It was not until the spring of 1938 that the ship finally set sail.[44] By then, Batista had relaxed his anti-Republican obstructionism. He was simply unable to suppress popular expressions of support for the republic. Facing increasing pressure from the Cuban people and in the midst of an ideological shift of his own toward populist democracy, Batista welcomed Spanish Ambassador to Cuba and Mexico Félix Gordón Ordás in mid-1938 and, after publicly expressing support for the Spanish Republic, authorized collections for the front in October.[45] Batista's change of heart was part of his effort to gain political support. As Lambe has explained, "Cuba's widespread grassroots antifascist movement" made defense of the Spanish Republic popular, and "Batista cared about being elected and gaining political legitimacy."[46]

Around the same time that he unfroze relations with Republican Spain, Batista forged an alliance with the communist party. In early January 1938, he met with party officials and hinted at the possibility of cooperation. In May, he permitted the communist newspaper *Noticias de Hoy* to publish. And finally, in September, he legalized the party.[47] For its part, the PCC had changed tactics in 1935 and 1936, shifting away from its sectarian Third-Period hostility to noncommunist groups. Fighting for survival in the mid-1930s, and under directions from Moscow to build a Popular Front coalition, the PCC pursued avenues of legalization and entrance into mainstream politics in the second half of the 1930s, which it finally achieved with legalization in 1938.[48] Communists, however, hardly had a monopoly on pro-Republican organizing.

By early 1937, Cuba's mobilization in defense of Republican Spain was well under way even though material contributions were technically illegal. In late 1936 and early 1937, pro-Republican organizations had sprung up across the island, including most prominently the Círculo Republicano Español, the Círuclo Español Socialista, and Izquierda Republicana Española. Many Republican organizations, such as the Republican and Socialist circles, were initiated by the Spanish community but widened over time to incorporate Cubans. These groups, in addition to the Centro Catalán, which was loyalist in light of the Spanish Republic's support of regional autonomy, eventually united in the Frente Democrático Español to cohere their efforts. They raised funds to help supply Republican troops with clothing, food, medicine, coffee, and cigarettes. Republican associations also organized collection drives on paydays and sales of pro-Republican stamps, buttons, and leaflets.[49] In February 1937, de la Torriente Brau's widow, Teté Casuso established in Cuba the Asociación de Auxilio al Niño del Pueblo Español (AANPE or Auxilio al Nino).[50] The organization maintained a children's shelter and school near

Barcelona at Sitges and sent regular food and clothing contributions. Within a short period of its founding, the association claimed membership of 300,000 across the towns and cities of Cuba.[51] Auxilio al Niño was the recipient of frequent donations from other organizations and from massive rallies in Cuba supporting the Republican war effort.[52] Although Auxilio al Niño claimed to be nonpartisan in its aid to Spanish children, its mouthpiece *Ayuda* clearly demonstrated its Republican sympathies.

Massive rallies in support of the Republic were held in parks and theaters across the country. The first took place in Havana in April 1937. On the 5th, the Círculo Republicano Español organized an event in the Gran Teatro Nacional in which over 5,000 people paid homage to the slain Spanish poet Federico García Lorca; on the 14th, the Frente Democrático Español hosted an educational rally in the Havana's Hatuey Park, attended by over 12,000 people, commemorating the sixth anniversary of the Spanish Republic. On the 19th, several groups gathered to honor Pablo de la Torriente Brau in the Auditorium Theater. Among the speakers featured were anthropologist Fernando Ortiz, historian Emilio Roig de Leuchsenring, and de la Torriente Brau's close friend and prominent communist Raúl Roa.[53] These gatherings educated the public on the achievements of the Spanish Republic, reported news from the front, and raised funds for the war effort.[54]

Collections and expressions of support for the Republican cause were so numerous that, by the spring of 1938, the Spanish ambassador boasted that he had received thousands of letters and telegrams all wishing successes to the embattled Spanish government. Of the "very emotional" messages the ambassador said, "they come from the whole island" and were authored by both individuals and groups. He was particularly touched by a group of fifty workers who wrote that they would happily go without food for a day in order to help send coffee and sugar to the front.[55] The embassy coordinated money and supply collection drives and dispatched its consular offices to organize donations on a local level.[56]

In the context of changing state attitudes toward the Spanish Civil War, pro-Republican organizations initially operated in secret, as with the communist party, or under the pretense of neutrality, as with Auxilio al Niño. This approach to civic organizing within the constraints of restrictive Cuban laws is reminiscent of the Universal Negro Improvement Association simply removing the word "Negro" from its name in compliance with the Morúa law. To skirt the issue of political partisanship, the Casa de la Cultura y Asistencia Social was founded as a cultural and charitable organization yet became an important base of support for the Spanish Republic. Over time and with increased freedom to operate, these organizations dropped their pretenses of being apolitical. The Casa published its own journal, *Nosotros,* which covered events at the front, offered profiles of Republican leaders, and updated readers on the Cuban mobilization. The Casa de Cultura spread throughout the towns and cities of eastern Cuba and claimed a membership of over 10,000 by 1938 when it openly and freely supported the Republican cause.[57] Additionally, the PCC had been actively engaged in supporting the Republican war effort, albeit illegally, since late 1936.[58] On November 18, 1936, the party had declared its support for the Spanish Republic, explaining that supporting Spain was the PCC's "first international responsibility."[59]

Afro-Cubans were included among the many who looked to Spain as a continuation of the global antifascist struggle begun in Ethiopia, and they saw the Spanish battlefield as an opportunity to fight some of the same oppressive forces that affected them at home in Cuba. The Black Cuban press had largely rallied against the Italian invasion of Ethiopia and decried the fascist threat to Africa.[60] The island-wide mobilization in defense of the Spanish Republic often fused the struggles against foreign invasion in Ethiopia, China, and Spain.[61] Afro-Cuban writer Nicolás Guillén traveled to Spain as a journalist and interviewed his fellow Cubans on the front. His accounts suggest that many Black Cubans saw fascism as a grave threat to racial harmony at home and abroad.

In July 1937, Guillén joined several dozen of the world's most famous writers in Spain and Paris at the Segundo Congreso Internacional de Escritores para la Defensa de la Cultura. The conference was an opportunity for a global network of intellectuals to express solidarity with the Spanish Republic and was cosponsored by the Republic's Ministry of Public Instruction and Fine Arts. Cuban representatives included Guillén, Alejo Carpentier, Juan Marinello, Félix Pita Rodríguez, and Leonardo Fernández Sánchez (who accompanied Mella on his 1925 visit to Banes), together forming the largest Latin American delegation. Other prominent attendees included Mexico's Octavio Paz, African American Langston Hughes, German Bertolt Brecht, Chilean Pablo Neruda (whose 1950 poem "United Fruit Company" directly condemned the company's actions across the Americas), and the Haitian Jacques Roumain, whose novel *Masters of the Dew* depicted Antilla in northern Oriente as a space where workers were subjugated but also where they could come together, learn to strike, and resist.

The Madrid gathering of intellectuals marked a crucial moment in transnational literary history, as dozens of writers made contact with one another, debated important literary questions as well as political events, and initiated longstanding conversations that would in turn shape cultural and intellectual processes within individual states.[62] Guillén told the congress that his solidarity with the Spanish people had a triple nature; it was based in his identity as a writer, as a Cuban, and as a *negro*. As a writer, he believed that fascism was "suffocating free expression of thought." As a Cuban, Guillén claimed that his home island also faced a "dictatorship of the military fascist kind," and likened Batista to Franco. He argued that all of Cuba supported the Spanish Republic because the island "could not ignore that both [Cuba and Spain] have identical enemies, identical destinies, and identical heroic solutions." According to Guillén, Cuban solidarity with Spain was also rooted in anti-imperialism. He referred to Cuba as "semicolonial society, looted by North American imperialism."[63] Elsewhere he claimed that, like China against the Japanese, like Venezuela against English and German petroleum companies, like Spain against German and Italian interference, the Antillas "battled against the sugar greed, the banana and mining avarice, of the United States of America."[64] In short, Guillén saw antifascism and Cuban anti-imperialism as closely related.

Finally, Guillén told the congress that Cubans, and especially Black Cubans, avidly supported the Spanish Republic: "*El negro* suffers the Republican tragedy," he said, and "the black Cuban is united with the Spanish people."[65] He argued that his support for Republican Spain was based in fascism's "most dangerous" threat: racial prejudice.[66] In his address to the writers' congress, Guillén argued, "No one is as antifascist as the *negro*, especially the Cuban *negro*, because he knows that the root of fascism lies in a land sewn with racial hatred and division among men into inferiors and superiors, and the *negro* belongs to the inferior." Fascism's ultimate danger, according to Guillén lay in its move to "block the universalization of the human spirit."[67] For Guillén, then, Afro-Cuban support for Republican Cuba was rooted simultaneously in Cuba's experience of foreign exploitation and in fascism's move to exacerbate anti-Black racism and threaten human brotherhood. The links forged in Guillén's analysis, especially between anti-imperialism and antifascism, were reoccurring themes in the narratives of Cubans who mobilized around the Spanish Civil War, including many brigadistas who fought on Spanish battlefields.

Mobilizing Eastern Cuba

Rafael Hernández, who worked in the United Fruit town of Banes in the 1920s and 1930s, recalled in an interview decades later that there was a vibrant pro-Republican mobilization in town during the era of the Spanish Civil War: "The fact is," he said, "we participated heavily in the fight for the Spanish people." Hernández and his fellow workers collected sugar and medicine for the front, and they attended rallies, concerts, public lectures, educational evenings, and other *actas* in the Teatro Heredia and Parque Cárdenas. He recalled three kinds of individuals traveling through Banes to rally support for the Republic. First, communist organizers, such as the *compañero* known as "Trigo," collected funds and organized meetings.[68] Second, Spanish officials also "visited us to give lectures, ask for help, and bring us the latest news about the revolutionary process in Spain." Finally, Cuban volunteers on their way to the front came through Banes "looking for financial support" to buy provisions and passage "so they could leave and fight for Spanish liberty." In addition to these activists who circulated through the region, most of Cuba's major pro-Republican organizations had active chapters in Banes, including the Casa de Cultura, Círculo Republicano Español, and Auxilio al Niño Español. The Banes mobilization was so successful, according to Hernández, that the nearby towns of Bayamo, Palma Soriano, and Holguín held a friendly competition to see "who could emulate us and. . . . raise the most money for the Spanish people," much like UNIA divisions used a spirit of competition with Banes Division #52 to raise funds a decade and a half earlier.[69]

Banes was hardly an exception. In 1937, *Facetas de la Actualidad Española*, a Havana-based monthly bulletin of news about the war in Spain and Cuba's mobilization, sent Jorge Almeyda Montaña to eastern Cuba to report on the *oriental* campaign. He wrote of his experience in the east, "No one can put in doubt international solidarity with the Spanish Republic. Not just in the big cities, the industrial centers, and in the larger towns [, but all the way] to the most isolated corners of the earth, the Spanish people have obtained admiration."[70] Almeyda found pro-Republican clubs everywhere he went, from cities like Guantánamo and Santiago to small mining towns to the sugar zone on the northern coast. Antonio Jiménez, the twenty-seven-year-old Spanish consul in Santiago de Cuba, coordinated much of the region's mobilization. He oversaw the founding of Santiago's Casa de la República Española, which by the summer of 1937 had over 500 members. Thanks to their size, cities like Santiago could host impressive events in support of the Republic, such as a July 19, 1937, soirée benefiting children's hospitals in Spain. Consul Jiménez also worked closely with the local branch of the Círculo Español Socialista, which by July 1937 claimed over 400 diverse members, including both Spaniards and Cubans of varied economic backgrounds.[71]

Eastern Cuba's pro-Republican campaign extended well beyond major cities. Individuals with little money from company towns contributed to the cause. Women and men in small pueblos organized their own pro-Republican activities—typically collecting funds and supplies for the front—and connected with nationwide organizations. Workers in the towns run by the US-owned Cuban Mining Company collected funds and set up pro-Republican associations. The company had established iron mines at Cristo and Ponupo—

both near Santiago de Cuba—at the turn of the century to feed the new railroads, and many of the workers were *asturianos*. At Cristo, workers collected money for the Republic. The Ponupo miners, men of modest means who lived in shacks and barracones, established a Comité de Ayuda al Frente Popular Español and used their only day off for meetings and discussions of politics, the war in Spain, and strategies for continued aid. They set aside a portion of their earnings for contributions to the "Spanish people."[72] The Ponupo miners sent checks to several causes, including a committee to aid the release of the *Arnús* and a fund for Spanish orphans.[73] According to Almeyda, workers from both mines had written to the Spanish government volunteering for service immediately after hearing of the military rebellion but the Republic was not yet accepting volunteer soldiers.[74]

As was the case during the heyday of Garveyism, officials and dignitaries traveling through the region helped drum up support for the Republican cause. Ambassador Gordón Ordás traveled through eastern Cuba in August and September of 1938 and was the guest of honor at *actas* and rallies numbering as many as 5,000 attendees. Diverse organizations co-hosted his events and shared in ceremonies, including familiar pro-Republican groups like Casa de Cultura and Auxilio al Niño, but also seemingly unrelated associations like a women's tennis organization in Camagüey and a police association in Holguín, illustrating the widespread popularity of the Republican cause. Well aware of Cuban patriotism and of how formative the wars of Independence against Spain were in Cuba's national consciousness, the ambassador distinguished between the colonial Spain of years past and the Republican Spain of today. In his speech in Holguín, Gordón Ordás emphasized the idea that when the Spain of colonialism, militarism, and monarchy fell, a new Spain was born—one "surer of itself and more certain that it has nothing to gain [from conquest] abroad." For any possible skeptics in the audience, he reminded readers that churches had stayed open in Spain; that the government wished to persecute no one; and that agrarian reform meant "peace in the countryside." The redistributive measures, he claimed, had amounted to "allowing a few young men to enjoy modestly the fruits of their labor . . . and an end to starvation wages."[75] The Spanish cause, in other words, was one everyone could support.

The sugar towns of northeastern Cuba were steeped in this mobilization. Sugar workers, like Hernández, later remembered participating extensively in the campaign in ways similar to those of the miners. They collected money, sugar, and tobacco for the front, organized drives for Spanish orphans, disseminated propaganda, and held public events. They often articulated their communities' enthusiasm in terms of antifascism, claiming the region had a tremendous sense of solidarity with "Europe's antifascist struggle."[76] At the Central Santa Lucía near Gibara, east of Banes on Oriente's northern coast, which had been dramatically "liberated" by workers from nearby mills in 1933, Ramón Vidal Zaldivar joined local Spaniards collecting money for the front. He explained that, while the effort began in the Spanish community, it soon was a popular cause among all of the area's residents. According to Vidal's compañero, Mario Ortíz Drigg, the war was a chief topic of conversation among workers who kept abreast of developments in Spain through several local papers as well as the national dailies. Ortíz recalled that men and women collected sugar as well as cash.[77]

Indeed, sugar collection was a key mechanism of Cuban support for Republican Spain. When the famous Galician nationalist, Alfonso Daniel Manuel Rodríguez Castelao, known simply as Castelao, traveled through Cuba raising awareness and funds for the Republican cause, he collected sugar in the towns of the northeastern coast.[78] The newspaper *Hoy* regularly reported on thousands of pounds of sugar donated to the front. Far from isolated backwater then, the sugar towns of northern Oriente were keeping abreast of overseas news and, more importantly, doing something about it. Collecting sugar for the front inverted the dominant economic arrangement of the day; rather than heading off to refineries in the United States, sugar was diverted to the support the Republican cause of antifascism and anti-imperialism.

The Casa de Cultura was the most politically inclusive pro-Republican organization and was widely popular in northeastern Cuba. While the Casa de Cultura was strongest in Cuba's largest cities (with 4,249 registered members in Havana and 550 in Santiago de Cuba), it was also an important element of civic life in sugar towns like Banes (where it claimed 86 members), the Central Chaparra (79 members), and several other company towns.[79] Hernández in Banes recalled that the Casa de Cultura served to bridge the Spanish and Cuban communities: "We established the Casa de Cultura [so that] we could we could work together in this period [with] various Spaniards sympathetic to the Republic and, with them, we did good work."[80]

In the fall of 1937, Banes's Republican sympathizers convened to establish another association, a local branch of the Círculo Republicano Español. They aimed to "reinforce the Spanish Republic, defend and disseminate [information about] its progress and prestige; endeavor to incorporate all Cubans . . . who want to help in this goal of exaltation of the fatherland." The Círculo Republicano unified people across political difference and, according to its guidelines, hoped to encourage a spirit of cooperation.[81] The Círculo supported the Spanish Republic for many reasons, including admiration for the government's positions on "absolute equality and equal opportunity for all

Spaniards," prohibition of religious interference in education, elimination of subsidies to religious institutions and priests, and abolishment of the death penalty for political crimes. Residents of Banes also supported the Spanish government's "ample legislation providing subsidies for all unemployed workers" and its "expropriation—free or without indemnification—of all *latifundios* or similar properties that are being poorly exploited." That unemployment relief and agrarian reform had such support in Banes makes sense; after all, United Fruit owned 283,000 acres of land in 1937 and unemployment was rampant.[82] Intense struggles with the company over workers' rights were hardly a distant memory, and men who had participated in the 1933 insurgency in United Fruit towns were among those who volunteered for the Spanish battlefields.

Other organizations in eastern Cuba, such as the Círculo Español Socialista founded in August 1937 in Victoria de las Tunas, a municipality dominated by the Cuban American Sugar Company, were more partisan than the Círculo Republicano. Also headquartered in Havana, this club was distinct from the Círculo Republicano in that individuals had to be "pure marxists" in order to join and the club intended to only affiliate with other "Marxist-Leninist Organizations." This goal, however, was not to limit its spirit of collaboration; the Círculo Socialista eventually joined in the Frente Democrático Español, a coalition that included non-Marxist organizations. The editors of *Facetas de Actualidad Española* considered the Círculo Español Socialista in Las Tunas, south of Puerto Padre, to be the local "vanguard of the movement in solidarity with the Spanish Government and the Popular Front." With a largely Spanish-born leadership, the Círculo Socialista had its own "spacious" meeting place and met weekly, claiming over 300 members within its first months of operation. Two of its major achievements included a cash collection drive and campaign to sell leaflets titled "Horrores del Fascismo" and "Verdades sobre la Guerra de España."[83] Like other pro-Republican organizations, the Círculo Socialista aimed to disseminate information on the Spanish government by organizing festivals, lectures, and commentaries. Additionally, the socialist group would help with members' needs, such as unemployment relief or repatriation.[84] Although technically prohibited from "interfering in what we can call 'domestic or internal' Cuban politics," the Círculo Socialista, used Spain as an opportunity to address "questions about universal political doctrine." Examples from Spain would educate members and help develop "a collective consciousness that aims towards to victory for socialist ideals." In other words, while they were preventing from engaging in Cuban politics, the Círculo would use "problems that have developed in Spain" to advance the socialist consciousness of its members. For the Círculo Socialista, support for the Spanish government was a means of political consciousness raising, an endeavor they suggested would have long-term effects for Cuba.[85]

Finally, in northeastern Cuba, the Partido Comunista de Cuba mobilized a Spanish Republican defense. Women often played a significant role in the party effort, traveling from house to house collecting cash and goods for the front.[86] Like other pro-Republican groups, the party sent individual organizers across the region raising awareness about the war and collecting goods and funds. Several sugar workers remembered a communist *compañero* nicknamed "Trigo" who traveled from town to town.[87] Defensa Obrera Internacional, CNOC, and its affiliate unions, all remained active in northeastern Cuba and led organizing efforts around the Spanish Civil War. Many brigadistas would later cite their experiences with these organizations as contributing to their political radicalization. The PCC's most famous contribution to the war effort, however, was in recruiting volunteers for the front and in getting them there.

"To Fight Fascism": Brigadistas from Northeastern Cuba

The most dramatic and historically celebrated way Cubans contributed to the war effort was by taking up arms against Franco. Men from northeastern sugar towns were represented in all three waves of Cuban combatants who fought in Spain: those already living in Spain, those arriving from New York with the Abraham Lincoln Brigade, and those recruited directly from Cuba.[88] Thanks to forms required of all individuals affiliating with the Partido Comunista de España (PCE), which ultimately facilitated repatriation when the volunteers were sent home, we have written records of how brigadistas described their own political formation.[89] Like the pro-Republican associations, they expressed a range of political beliefs but most cited antifascism as the main explanation for their service. Many had been involved in the sugar insurgency just four years earlier, with some fleeing into exile as a result, and explicitly cited the 1933 revolution as a politically formative moment. In this way, the political turbulence of 1933 generated yet another mode of inside-outside connections for the sugar towns of northeastern Cuba, as Cubans at home and in exile organized to defend the Spanish Republic.

The first Cubans to volunteer for the front were those already living in Spain, mainly Madrid and Barcelona, at the outbreak of war. Many were political exiles, students, or children of Spanish emigrants to Cuba. They participated in organizations such as Madrid's anti-Batista Círculo Antonio Guiteras, the anti-imperialist Federación Universitaria Hispanoamericana, the Comité Antiimperialista de Revolucionarios Cubanos, the Asociación Amigos de América Latina, Red Aid International, and the Partido Comunista de España.[90] Through their involvement with left-wing organizations, Cubans were among the thousands of civilians who defended Madrid after Franco's uprising and were among the first to mobilize in the Republican war effort. They joined the militias formed in the wake of the insurrection and, for the most part, were incorporated into the Fifth Regiment of Popular Militias, organized by the PCE.[91]

Cuban women were among these early defenders of the Republic. María Luisa Lafita de Juan was born in Spain but raised in Cuba. Having participated in the insurgency of the 1933 and the failed general strike of 1935, she was living exile in Spain when the war broke out. She quickly volunteered as a hospital nurse treating and feeding wounded Republicans. In Madrid, she worked alongside Tina Modotti, the Italian American photographer who had been with Mella when he was killed in Mexico.[92] Lafita supported the 1959 Revolution and went on to publish profiles of Cuban brigadistas.

Luis Rubiales Martínez from Puerto Padre in CASC territory also mobilized quickly to defend Madrid. Rubiales was not a member of either the Cuban or the Spanish Communist Party, yet he joined in the Spanish defense, indicating a diversity of political affiliations among the early defenders of Madrid. According to his superiors, Rubiales was a soldier with "good conduct" and strong "antifascist" tendencies.[93] Fellow *oriental* Benjamín Lafarga Fernández, a working-class political exile from el Cobre, was another early defender of the Spanish government. As a young man, Lafarga had moved to United Fruit's Central Preston and became involved in the labor movement. Having been exiled, he was living in Barcelona in 1936. Early on, Lafarga quickly made his way to the Spanish capital and joined the militias. During the war, he served as a bodyguard and driver for PCE officials and, after an injury, helped deliver basic goods to Madrid. After the war, Lafarga found himself trapped in Franco's Spain, and once again, forced overseas—this time, back to Cuba. Fellow *oriental* Sixto Cordero Nicot helped Lafarga escape and, in return, tasked him with informing Cordero's family in Baracoa, near the eastern tip of the island, that his brother, Pelayo, was sentenced to death in a nationalist prison.[94] That these two men from Oriente knew each other in Spain was not surprising. The Cordero brothers had also been active in Madrid's left-wing Latin American community and were both members of the Federación Universitaria Hispanoamericana.[95] Such overseas activist clubs of exiled Cubans were essential in the network building that facilitated the mobilization of brigadistas.

The second wave of Cuban volunteers in Spain came from New York, where they had already been involved in the Spanish-defense campaign through the

Club Cubano Julio Antonio Mella.[96] After the July rebellion in Spain, the club was converted into New York's center of Latin American antifascist activity. Working with the CPUSA, Club Mella members hosted a full schedule of events, including a mass rally in Madison Square Garden supporting the Spanish Republic and condemning the United States' nonintervention policy. The club worked in conjunction with over one hundred other associations in the Sociedades Hispanas Confederadas de Ayuda a España, which took up collections for the front—enough to send an ambulance to the Republic—and distributed news about Spain. Quickly, the Club Mella became a recruitment center for volunteers who also prepared for their journey there.[97] The club served not just Latin American volunteers but also English speakers, including John Tisa. Tisa later wrote that he was sent from the Sloan YMCA on West 34th Street, the center of CPUSA recruitment, to the Club Mella for briefings before his journey. There he joined others planning their voyages and made necessary preparations, such as a visit to the Army-Navy store. Tisa fondly described the Cuban recruits with whom he spent time while in New York, en route to Europe, and in Spain. He wrote, "Cubans loved to sing anti-Batista and revolutionary songs and did so at the club in Harlem." At sea, the Cuban brigadistas "invaded the upper, first-class decks and often were ordered back to our third-class holes" whereas the non-Cubans "were more reserved" and stuck to their third-class quarters.[98]

While individual volunteers had been leaving for Spain from the United States since the summer of 1936, including Pablo de la Torriente Brau, it was not until December 1936 that formal recruitment efforts were under way and early 1937 that Cubans joined the International Brigades. On January 5, 1937, the French vessel *Champlain* sailed from New York to France with between 70 and 150 Cubans aboard. Prominent among them was Rodolfo de Armas y Soto, who had been involved in the anti-Machado student movement and was exiled from Cuba shortly after the strike of March 1935. De Armas later died on a Spanish battlefield and was "transformed into a martyr," according to Lafita, thanks to his charisma and leadership skills.[99]

The Cuban volunteers voted to form the Centuria Cubana Antonio Guiteras, named for President Grau's interior minister who was killed in 1935 fighting Batista's army. The Centuria Guiteras, the James Connolly Column of Irish volunteers, and a US section joined the First Infantry Company of the Abraham Lincoln Battalion of the XV International Brigade.[100] (In nationalist spirit, the James Connolly Column voted not to join the 16th British Battalion but instead to stick with the Lincoln Battalion.[101]) The Centuria Guiteras facilitated smooth relations between US volunteers and the locals at Villanueva de la Jara, near Albacete, in light of their Spanish language skills.[102]

Ricardo Gómez Oliva, a white son of poor peasants in Pinar del Rio, was among the Cubans who participated in this second wave of brigadistas. Having attended his local public school only intermittently, Gómez had moved throughout Cuba working different jobs, from a general store in Las Villas to the sugar fields of Morón, Camagüey. In 1926, he moved to the United States where he worked, among other places, in quarries and copper mines. He was a founding member of the Club Mella and was club treasurer, secretary general, and director of propaganda.[103] Gómez joined the CPUSA in 1933, held leadership positions within the party, and was active in New York's anti-Machado and anti-Batista movement before signing up to join the International Brigades in December 1936 and setting sail on the *Champlain* with the Centuria Guiteras.[104] He was wounded at Jarama and at Brunete, rendered unfit for service, and repatriated in October 1938.

Gómez had personal experiences with *el pulpo*, the United Fruit Company. He had worked in the United Fruit Company's merchant marine and sailed throughout the Caribbean, Central America, South America, and Europe visiting nodes in the company's imperialist operations, likely stopping through his homeland Cuba on those trips.[105] In 1931, he joined the merchant mariner's strike, alongside de Armas y Soto, who was on the strike committee.[106] Gómez explicitly mentioned the conditions of sugar labor in Cuba, employer abuse, and anti-imperialism as motivating his decision to join the labor struggle. In June 1938, he described his "political history" on a PCE form. When asked when and why he became involved in the labor movement, he answered, "Since 1926, under the oppressive conditions in which sugar workers lived in Cuba; after, in the US, because of the mistreatment that workers received from the boss; contact with the unemployed and fighters against imperialism in Cuba." Such experiences moved him to study further. Gómez enrolled in a three-week course on Marxism and Leninism through the Club Mella. When asked, "With what objective did you come to Spain?" he replied, "To fight fascism."[107] He suggests a direct relationship between his experience in Cuba, his decision to join New York's left-wing community, and, ultimately, volunteer to fight in Spain.

Gómez's political trajectory is indicative of a wider pattern playing out in New York, as young radicals harnessed exile networks built through the struggles against Machado and Batista to join the fight in Spain. When asked for the names of responsible people who could vouch for him, Gómez listed Cuban communist Joaquín Ordoqui, the Afro-Cuban baseball player and fellow Club Mella member Basilio Cueria, and another Club Mella leader Leonardo Fernández Sánchez who had visited Banes in 1925.[108] Gómez was one of the many peripatetic workers and activists who, laboring in a zone of US hegemony and dispersed by political repression, were volunteering together to fight in Spain.

Volunteers who left directly from the island formed a third wave of Cuban brigadistas. Most were recruited through the PCC even if they were not themselves members of the communist party. They came from a variety of political affiliations, including the PCC and Liga Comunista de Cuba but also groups emerging from the 1933 revolution, including Auténticos and Joven Cuba. After the Spanish government authorized the formation of international units in late 1936, the PCC began a campaign to find volunteers. The white Cuban communist Ramón Nicolau González was charged with heading a recruitment commission. Nicolau had been writing about the "Negro Question" from Moscow in 1932 and would later collect testimonies on the Spanish Civil War for a 1981 volume. He explained that, although recruitment efforts were carried out clandestinely in light of the party's illegal status and the prohibition on organizing for the war, the campaign "extended its branches far and wide through the national territory."[109] Organizers would identify potential recruits and initiate conversations. With sympathy for the Spanish Republic so high, talk in the street was common and, according to Víctor Pina Cardoso, a fellow PCC member and recruiter, "it was not unusual for us to encounter on a bus [or in the street] someone of a disposition to be recruited."[110] Serious candidates would be sent to a meeting space in interior of the country where they underwent medical examination, were provided with uniforms from friendly Spanish merchants, and prepared their documentation for travel.[111] On April 15, 1937, the first contingent of Cubans left from the island for France.[112] As Spanish speakers, volunteers arriving directly from Cuba were often integrated into the People's Republican Army. A large portion, however, joined fellow Cubans from New York in the Abraham Lincoln Brigade and served in the Spanish-speaking 24th Battalion, which later became the 59th Battalion.[113] In December 1937, Nicolau traveled to Spain, and Víctor Pina Cardoso took over recruitment efforts. He later described the job as taking him to clandestine meetings across the country where, with the help of friendly locals he carried out secret information sessions on volunteering in Spain, such as a meeting in Santiago de Cuba with four workers from Palma Soriano during which he was arrested.[114]

Roberto Buzón Neira, introduced at the beginning of this chapter, was one of those recruited directly from Cuba. Born in 1912 in Mayarí, the home of United Fruit's Preston mill, Neira was a construction worker in the mill. In a familiar pattern, the young Afro-Cuban was radicalized in the United Fruit Company's sugar mills, joined the sugar insurgency in 1933, and went on to become a dedicated labor organizer before traveling to Spain. Swept up in the revolutionary enthusiasm that permeated the country after the overthrow of General Machado, the nineteen-year-old participated in sugar strikes at Preston in 1933 and 1934. It was around this time that a fellow mill worker and Secretary General of the local Sindicato Nacional de Obreros de la Industria Azucarera branch encouraged him to join the union. Buzón rose within the SNOIA ranks and participated in the division's central committee, serving in multiple leadership positions, including secretary of record keeping. In early 1934, he joined the Cuban Communist Party's cell at Preston. Because of his involvement with the illegal party, Buzón was arrested on five occasions, tried twice, and served prison time in Havana. He was a leader in his local action committee during the general strike of March 1935. He was also a member of Joven Cuba, the DOI, and other smaller organizations including a local youth group. In 1936, Buzón served as the Organizational Secretary of his local section of the Liga Juvenil Comunista and, in that capacity, attended the league's second national conference. Buzón accumulated diverse work experiences before traveling overseas. Construction had been his principal employment but also had experience working as cigar roller. His peripatetic roots began in eastern Cuba; he was familiar with several towns in eastern Cuba, including Holguín, Baracoa, Banes, and Sagua de Tánamo, as well as Havana. He wrote, "In all the factories that I have worked in, I have had the role of union representative" and claimed that he regularly represented his local union in labor conflicts and in "other communications with the boss." By the outbreak of war in Spain, he was living in Havana and possibly working full time for the construction workers' union. In short, the well-traveled Buzón had become a committed labor organizer. He reported having contributed "a few" articles on the labor question to Preston's SNOIA publication and to another local Mayarí paper.[115]

In early 1938, Buzón decided to join the International Brigades. Because he had been arrested on several occasions, he used his brother's name to obtain a passport and, with help from the party, signed up to set sail on the *Oropesa* on February 5. Together with seventy-three other Cubans, Buzón disembarked in La Pallice, France. There, members of the French Communist Party, charged with coordinating international volunteers' arrival in Spain, arranged the Cubans' customs forms and paperwork for the move into Spain. Before the group could cross the Pyrenees, they traveled to Paris, where Buzón was detained longer than his compatriots due to a foot injury.[116] There, he spent time with Cuban authors Nicolás Guillén, whom he claimed to have known before the war, and Félix Pita Rodríguez, both of whom were covering the war for Cuban periodicals. The writers loaded Buzón with cigarettes, toothbrushes, toothpaste, soap, shaving cream, and other supplies that he and his compañeros would need. Pita Rodríguez arranged for him to travel by rail, a rare luxury for brigadistas, across the Pyrenees as a journalist for *Mediodía*.[117]

In Paris Buzón met a young woman named Ivette Curiel at a workers' organization and fell in love, as he wrote in a letter discovered by the French CP. While the letter is engaging for its effusive language ("the divine splendor of your eyes") and his Marxist vocabulary (romance, apparently, is part of the "dialectical evolution" of human sentiment), it also reveals Buzón's motivation for volunteering in Spain, as he emphasizes interracial, international solidarity and defense of democracy. As he explained, "the Spanish Problem has the virtue of uniting destinies; it is linked with the fate of all peoples of the world. [All peoples] and all races agree and [are giving] the greatest quantity of energy to support the Spanish Republic because to say 'Spanish Republic' is to say 'World Democracy.'"[118]

After crossing into Spain, and brief stays at Portbou and Figueras, Buzón finally arrived in Tarazona, a small town in Catalonia where his fellow Cubans were training. He wrote to Curiel, "The Cubans that came through Paris are all together here," and described their state of mind: "We are, apart from the nostalgia that is produced in isolation from our families and our people, sustained by a great enthusiasm."[119] Buzón served in the second company of the 24th Battalion in the XV Brigade.[120] Having stood out for his intellectual abilities and experience as a strong propagandist and party leader, he was selected by the political commissioner of his division for a training course to study Spain's political situation, the history of the worldwide workers' movement, and the Popular Front government. The young volunteers were to serve as political commissars for their units. As part of their training, the students hosted talks in hospitals and schools, detailing the progress of the Republican struggle, military strategies, and Popular Front goals. After he was wounded, Buzón was sent to the local hospital, where he was placed in charge of organizing lectures and distributing newspapers to fellow patients. He was appointed political commissioner of the 4th Company of the 24th Battalion, the same rank that Pablo de la Torriente Brau held in 1936.[121] Battalion Political Commissar of the XV Brigade, John Gates, ordered Buzón to head to Barcelona and meet with Afro-Cuban socialist Salvador García Agüero. García was in Spain organizing a group of pro-Republican Cuban intellectuals and who would later represent the communist party at the 1940 Constitutional Convention.[122] Buzón took the opportunity to deliver García a petition asking that organizations in Cuba, including the Comité Nacional de Ayuda al Pueblo Español, send their tobacco donations directly to the XV Brigade.[123] In other words, the antifascist network that sent Buzón from Preston to Spain now tasked him with delivering messages home.

When the tides of the war turned in Franco's favor and International Brigades were recalled, the 24th Battalion began its retreat. Buzón later remembered that all of the men voted to return to the front but were never able to do so. (Several Cubans, however, did manage to stay after the *internacionales* retreated by integrating into the Spanish army.) Returning to France, the unit stopped at Pont-Bou before joining the French camp for Republican Army veterans at Argelès Sur Mer. As a Cuban at Argelès, Buzón probably read or, more likely given his extensive communications experience, contributed to *Orientación* a bulletin put out by the "grupo cubano" in the camp. Indeed, so many Cuban brigadistas found themselves at Argelès after the war that they printed their own weekly organ which was dedicated to taking care of internal issues (such as the unsanitary state of the facilities), organizing leisure activities (mainly baseball), disseminating international news, and detailing the ongoing efforts in Cuba to repatriate the veterans. The March 31, 1939, edition described Cuba's newly formed Comité Pro Ex-Combatientes y Presos de España, which had begun working through the printed press, radio, and popular meetings to repatriate Cuban brigadistas stranded in France.[124]

Along with his fellow Cubans, Buzón moved to another camp at Gurs, from where the volunteers departed for Cuba in May 1939. Aboard the SS *Orduña* on their return trip, the Cuban Communist Party organized a "solemn *velada*" commemorating the anniversary of José Martí's death. Buzón was selected to give the panegyric. He later remembered having used the opportunity to detail the similarities between the Spanish Republican Army and the *mambises* who fought for Cuban independence; between Cuba's independence struggle and Spain's antifascist struggle; between the brutal Spanish General Weyler, responsible for death and destruction in the Cuban countryside during the War of 1895, and Franco; and the continued role of the United States throughout as "collector of fruits wrought from the sacrifices of others."[125] His comparison of the Spanish Republic with colonial Cuba was a common rhetorical tool used in by Cubans in their pro-Republican campaign.[126] Buzón, however, also included references to US exploitation. In short, in this story of a mobile and adventurous worker-activist, we find an Afro-Cuban labor organizer from United Fruit territory who was politicized during the sugar insurgency of 1933, delivering lectures and organizing educational events for Spaniards and their comrades in the midst of a make-or-break war against fascism.

Buzón surely knew Ángel López Estévez, who also set sail for France from Cuba aboard the *Oropesa* on February 5, 1938. While both men came from backgrounds in the sugar industry, their trajectories were quite different. López had been a field hand for the Central Palma, a mill owned by the US-incorporated Altagracia Sugar Company but was not a member of the PCC, Joven Cuba, any other left-wing organization, or even a labor union. He, however, did claim to have participated in the sugar insurgency of 1933 and in the general strike of 1935. Like Buzón, López was incorporated into the 24th Battalion of the XV International Brigade, although they served in different companies. Unlike Buzón, however, López was considered by Spanish party officials to have exhibited "bad conduct." A handwritten note on an evaluation signed by John Gates reads, "Weak. Good conduct at the beginning. Later he left himself influenced by bad elements . . ." The evaluation concluded, "He is unaware of the [workers'] struggle and even less [aware] of political questions." PCE and Comintern personnel files exhibit a strong concern with determining which brigadistas toed the party line and which were potentially subversive. So, while one cannot read much into Gates's negative review other than Lopez's standing in the party, that he claimed no union or party membership indicates diversity among the *oriental* brigadistas in Spain. The party, in other words, did not recruit exclusively from its own rank and file. López used the PCC mainly as a mechanism for travel to Spain. We should not discount the possibility that some brigadistas were simply politically unengaged adventurers. (Several men were written up for faking their antifascist credentials or their formal induction into the services.) López could have been encouraged to join the brigades by friends steeped in communist politics, including Manuel Alonso and Armando Torres, both of whom he listed as party contacts who would vouch for him.[127]

Alejandro Laurell Olivera's story offers another path from Cuba's sugar towns to Spain. Laurell, like López and Buzón, was in the 59th Battalion of the XV Brigade and had traveled to Spain in early 1938, but he came from a more privileged background. In Cuba, he had been a chemistry student who worked as an assistant chemist in various sugar mills but mainly the Canadian-owned Ingenio Rio Cueto, ten miles southwest of Antilla, where de los Reyes Castillo Bueno had recruited Cubans to the UNIA in the early 1920s. Laurell joined the communist party in 1930, and like the others, he participated in the sugar insurgency of 1933. It was during this time that he, having found himself working in a Matanzas mill, joined a newly formed sugar workers' union at the Central España. Laurell had been propaganda organizer for the party from 1930 to 1935, wrote several organizational flyers, and attended the 1935 PCC plenum. When asked why he came to Spain, he answered, "to help liberate Spain from international fascism." When asked if he had ever disagreed with the party he did not write "no," as did most brigadistas, but "only during the revolution of 1933 when the party refused to take power." This was not only a smart reply on a form designed to ascertain one's dedication to the party, but it was also a reminder that the PCC was seen as needing to catch up with the workers, who led the 1933 revolution, not the other way around. Laurell credited an early visit to the Central España and seeing "need for [an organized program of] demands among those sugar mill workers there and the influence of certain Spanish elements" for his decision to join the proletarian movement. His personal work experience may have influenced his leftist politics; like unskilled laborers for the mills, he was unemployed for several months every year after the sugar harvest because "the *ingenio* only works more or less three or four months per year." In other words, like his fellow brigadistas, Laurell knew firsthand the inequities and failures of Cuba's dependence exporting sugar, a knowledge that brought him to Spain.[128]

Whether volunteering from Spain, New York, or Cuba, Cuban brigadistas used networks established in the early days of the struggle against Machado and later against Batista to undertake their journey. For the young men from Cuba's sugar territories, the battle in Spain was, in many ways, a continuation of the fight they had been waging since the early part of the decade— against sugar companies, Machado, and Batista. Several volunteers, including Ricardo Gómez and Carlos Laurell Olivera, explicitly cited exploitation in Cuba's sugar fields and factories as an important factor in their politicization. They, like the Banes locals who saw land expropriation and unemployment benefits as central to their support for the Spanish Republic, were engaged in a global struggle that reached from the sugar towns of Cuba to the battle theater in Spain.

Conclusion

Sugar workers on the northern coast of Oriente understood clearly their role in Cuba's imperialist-dominated economy of the 1930s: individuals like Ángel López Estévez harvested cane, which was processed in US-owned factories maintained by men like Roberto Buzón Neira and sent aboard ships staffed by people like Ricardo Gómez Oliva to be refined in the US and consumed by others. Loading sacks of raw sugar and watching them leave the port at Antilla, to be enjoyed elsewhere, was a normal feature of life on the *oriental* coast. In collecting sugar for the Spanish front, however, women and men subverted this imperial, capitalist order. The product that had so shaped their corner of the world was being diverted to an important cause. Instead of thinking of themselves as laboring away on the sidelines of history, sugar workers knew they produced an essential commodity, one they could use to support the

Spanish Republic and, by extension, struggles for political freedom, for land reform, for unemployment rights, and, above all, against fascism.

As Lambe has demonstrated, activists for "a New Cuba" did not give up after the defeated general strike of 1935. Rather, they expanded their vision and rallied around defense of the Spanish Republic in the name of antifascism. The sugar towns of northeastern Cuba—never actually isolated to begin with—certainly joined in the effort, and connected their own struggles against unemployment and underemployment, landlessness, and dictatorship to antifascism. The women and men in eastern Cuba who sewed clothing, collected money and goods, organized informational lectures and fundraising parties, and who took up arms came from all walks of life and from different political orientations, yet they found common cause in defending the Spanish Republic.

The global fight against fascism, of course, was just beginning. The same ship, SS *Orduña*, which sailed into the port of Havana on May 27, 1939, bringing Buzón and other Cuban veterans home from Spain, was also carrying 120 Jewish Refugees from Austria, Germany, and Poland, 72 of whom were denied permission to disembark in Cuba.[129] The ship traveled through South and Central America, searching for a port where the refugees would be admitted. Almost a year later, the *Orduña* passengers were able to immigrate to the United States by way of the Canal Zone, but another, more infamous ship scheduled to bring Jewish refugees to the United States via Havana along with the *Orduña*, the SS *St. Louis*, was forced back to Europe, where many perished. That Buzón and his comrades were fêted with homecoming celebrations in Havana while Jewish refugees on the same ship were just beginning their long journey to safety reminds us of the difficulties of heroic narratives of Cuban antifascism.

Nevertheless, subaltern actors in northeastern Cuba made Spain's cause their own and forcefully proclaimed their role in this global struggle against fascism. Cuba's company towns were once again engaged in internationalist struggle, as men and women organized spontaneously and joined in nationwide efforts to offer aid to the Spanish Republic. The specific conditions of eastern Cuba's development—economic dependency, highly concentrated land ownership in the hands of foreign monopolistic companies, rampant unemployment—ensured that Oriente's working classes continued to see themselves as forefront of a global battle that united Cuba and Spain.

Conclusion

This book charts the many paths by which the sugar towns along the northern coast of Cuba's Oriente province became hubs of internationalist organizing over the course of the early-to-mid-twentieth century. Certainly, northern Oriente's connections with the outside world did not begin with the arrival of foreign capital; the region was never isolated to begin with. At the risk of taking things a bit too far, it is worth remembering that Christopher Columbus's first stop on the island of Cuba was in the harbor of Nipe Bay. By the dawn of the twentieth century, northeastern Cuba was home to a sizable banana-export company and a robust, mixed-race peasantry that soon would be displaced entirely. The idea that sugar enclaves were carved out of untouched jungle was a construct of companies like United Fruit promoting themselves as harbingers of modernity.

Nevertheless, the establishment of vast sugar enclaves ushered in a new era—and a long list of unintended consequences. With the spread of foreign-dominated export agriculture, the northern coast of Oriente came to be a quintessential zone of company control. Banes was run by the world-famous United Fruit Company, which, in the history of US-Latin America relations, is the archetype of economic imperialism, labor subjugation, and company dominance.[1] Yet at the same time, the business model of sugar companies relied on constant exchange with the outside world, on shipping goods in and out, and on the mobility of its workers. Sugar corporations thus inadvertently facilitated the creation of internally diverse, transnationally connected local societies. Company power and labor exploitation certainly characterized the region, but subaltern subjects managed to carve out room to maneuver, interact regularly with men and women of a variety of nationalities, and connect with their counterparts in far-flung parts of the globe—all in the service of internationalist causes. Residents were nothing short of cosmopolitan.

What emerges from the collective stories told here is a very different picture of eastern Cuba's sugar region than the one we might expect. Far from being one-sided spaces of company dominance, northeastern Cuba's sugar towns were hubs of transnational race, class, and political solidarity movements. This history challenges how we think about the geographies of radicalism and about where the centers of oppositional politics lay in the early twentieth century. In the 1920s, British West Indian immigrants in Banes not only *joined* the global Garvey movement, but they also *led* it. Banes was a key base of operations for the largest Black organization in world history, as individuals like Harold and Anita Collins and Arnold Cummings traveled widely in service of the organization and as countless others contributed to the *Negro World*. The women and men of northern Oriente helped build a vision of Black uplift that has had a long-lasting and far-reaching impact on Black liberation struggles globally.[2]

By the time communists mobilized to reach Cuba's sugar enclaves and "educate" laborers about class consciousness and imperialism in the early 1930s, the region's multinational sugar workers had already been combining into inclusive labor unions and fighting for Cuban sovereignty in the face of monopolistic foreign power for half a decade. These two forces—organized labor and the Partido Comunista de Cuba (PCC)—coalesced in the early 1930s, as international conversations spanning Moscow, New York, Montevideo, and Havana theorized the role of Cuba's sugar workforce in anti-imperialist revolution. This work was just getting under way when sugar workers thrust themselves into the international spotlight with the insurgency of 1933. In doing so, they pushed the PCC out of its nonconfrontational policy with respect to US-owned properties and moved the Americas-wide communist movement to the left. Later in the decade, women and men who were politicized in company towns, especially during the insurgency, collected funds and supplies to fight fascism in Spain, and some risked life and limb to join the International Brigades. Exile networks, formed during Batista's crackdown, helped get those volunteers overseas. Individuals whose political education took place in cane fields and on United Fruit Company ships argued that Spain was the next front in the global struggle against racism, exploitation, and imperialism. Their cause was widely popular and helped push Fulgencio Batista himself to recognize the communist party in 1938 as part of his own (temporary) move toward constitutional democracy.

From the perspective of interwar internationalism, the US-dominated north coast resembles the whole of Oriente Province—famous as the cradle of Cuba's revolutionary tradition—more than it does a remote backwater of worker subjugation. It is not a coincidence, then, that battles playing out in northern Oriente during the interwar period contributed significantly to populist visions for Cuba crystalizing in the 1940s. On the right, figures like United Fruit lawyer and local mayor, Rafael Díaz-Balart and Fulgencio Batista (who was from Banes) demanded order, stability, and protection for foreign capital. Díaz-Balart's son, Rafael Jr., went on to be the founding president of Batista's youth league in 1949, to serve in Cuba's House of Representatives, and to become first minister of governance after Batista's 1952 coup.[3] Rafael Jr.'s sons, Lincoln Díaz-Balart and Mario Díaz-Balart, extended the family's conservativism to the halls of the US Congress, where both have represented the state of Florida. Their name is widely recognized as a force with which to be reckoned in Cuban American politics.

On the left, multinational groups of insurgent laborers fought for workers' rights and Cuban sovereignty during the interwar years. The biracial, fellow *oriental* Blas Roca was the PCC eastern district leader in the early 1930s, communicating closely with sugar workers in the north during the insurgency of 1933 before he went on to lead the party for over a quarter of a century. Sugar workers' demand for a corporatist state, one that mediated between labor and capital and that recognized their unions, remained entrenched in Cuban politics through the 1930s and 1940s. In 1947, Fidel Castro, who was also from the area and who was briefly married to Mirta Díaz-Balart, Rafael Jr.'s sister, joined Eduardo Chibás's Orthodoxo Party, which called for economic independence and vowed to sweep out corruption.[4] As Lillian Guerra explains, Castro later modeled his own populist appeal on Chibás's movement, right down to his denunciatory catchphrase "Yo acuso" (I accuse). Moreover, Chibás's tremendous popularity primed Cubans—an "*already* prepared, *already* revolutionary citizenry"—to embrace Castro's 1959 anti-imperialist revolution.[5] Castro, in other words, didn't come out of nowhere; he emerged from a decades-old, popular, anti-imperialist tradition that saw its greatest standoff against the right in Cuba's sugar field and factories in 1933.

Cuba's 1959 Revolution fundamentally altered the island's relationship with the outside world. As Castro co-opted earlier forms of populism into a one-party state, transnational solidarity did not fade. Rather, internationalism was an important element of state rhetoric and became the lynchpin of Cuban foreign policy during the Cold War. Cuba led the Tricontinental Movement of African, Asian, and Latin American solidarity against Western imperialism. Havana hosted the 1966 Tricontinental Conference attended by hundreds of delegates from recently decolonized countries and from various national liberation organizations. The Cuban model of revolution had proven successful, and delegates vowed to support armed struggles across the globe. The Cuban state put its money where its mouth was, "exporting revolution" to far-flung corners of the globe, most famously the decolonizing countries of Africa.[6] United States officials were so focused on what Europe, China, and the Soviet Union would do in newly independent Africa that they were taken completely by surprise when thousands of Cubans showed up in Angola in

1975.[7] In short, just as the island's northeastern sugar towns punched above their weight in interwar internationalism, Revolutionary Cuba's engagements overseas exceeded what one might expect from a small, poor, and supposedly isolated island.

But Castro's internationalism was different. For one, it was (and remains) top-down, a far cry from the diverse, organically formed, popular solidarity movements of northern Oriente's sugar towns in the 1920s and 1930s. By the late 1970s, Cubans, who had grown accustomed to state-sponsored mass rallies, were told to care about their brothers and sisters overseas—not the other way around. The Angola example is most famous because of its size; Christine Hatzky estimates that 400,000 Cubans soldiers and 50,000 Cuban civilians served in Angola between 1975 and 1991.[8] These soldiers were often conscripted, and many civilians served in a form of compulsory volunteerism. More than a few resented their time overseas.[9] Today, Cuba is no longer sending soldiers and advisors to national liberation struggles overseas. Instead, the island sends doctors, nurses, and aid workers to developing nations and disaster sites in a robust program of medical internationalism. More than 135,000 Cuban medical personnel have participated in missions abroad since 1960, and a remarkable 69 percent of all Cuban doctors have traveled overseas as *internacionalistas*.[10] As with the soldiers in Angola, this south-south cooperation is not optional for most, and the conditions for medical professionals range from grueling to downright dangerous.[11] Nevertheless, medical diplomacy remains a hallmark of Cuban foreign policy.

Another key distinction between Cuba's interwar internationalism and more recent iterations lies in the very framing of what transnational solidarity looks like. The Cold War and single-party state have recast the way Cuba understands its own history of internationalism. Cubans are familiar with the standard (and teleological) narrative. As the story goes, one hundred years of thwarted revolutionary ambitions were finally fulfilled in 1959. Whereas the nineteenth-century wars for independence from Spain ended with the island under the thumb of the United States and the frustrated 1933 revolution catapulted the dictator Fulgencio Batista to power, the Revolution of 1959 ushered in actual independence and revolutionary socialism. Within this historiography, the meaning of previous internationalisms shifted, most clearly regarding Cuba's substantial contribution to defending the Spanish Republic. What was on the ground in 1937–1939 a politically diverse and messy coalition of antifascists is now remembered as a communist-led move to join the Soviet Union in coming to Spain's aid in the name of proletarian internationalism. As Ariel Mae Lamb writes, "as the Cuban Communists became increasingly powerful and influential in the months and years following the triumph of the revolution, so, too, did the Communist narrative of antifascism."[12] Lamb points to Cuban historiography that has all but erased the legacy of Teté Casuso, the anti-communist widow of Cuba's first martyr in Spain, Pablo de la Torriente Brau. Casuso organized and ran the impressive, island-wide Asociación de Auxilio al Niño del Pueblo Español. Later, she even helped the idealistic, young Fidel Castro during his time in Mexico, but she was disillusioned after 1959, and like so many others, left for the United States.[13] Casuso barely makes an appearance in Cuban studies of the Spanish Civil War.

The reconfiguring of Spain's legacy also appears in the personal narratives of lesser-known antifascists. In 1938, Roberto Buzón Neira, the Afro-Cuban brigadista profiled in chapter 5 who had taken part in the sugar insurgency of 1933, wrote to his French girlfriend Ivette Curiel about why Spain mattered. "All races agree," he explained, and are giving "the greatest quantity of energy to support the Spanish Republic because to say 'Spanish Republic' is to say 'World Democracy.'"[14] Decades later, Buzón was interviewed by former member of Castro's Revolutionary Armed Forces, Ramón Nicolau González, for his book on the Spanish Civil War. The thrust of Buzón's antifascism had changed, as he declared, "Spain was the epic battle, the political message, the unknown destiny, and the heart and soul of the revolutionary movement of the great popular masses of the whole world!"[15] Democracy was out, and the revolutionary masses were in.

Banes today is, once again, off the beaten path. The vibrant civil society of the 1920s and 1930s is a thing of the past. The very revolution that responded to and harnessed decades of workers' struggles ended up dismantling the labor movement. The change is ironic. Famous for its ability to mobilize the masses, the revolutionary state all but eliminated the rich, autonomous associational life of 1920s and 1930s. The process began early. A file in the Archivo Histórico Provincial Santiago de Cuba containing records pertaining to the Universal Negro Improvement Association's Division #52 in Banes has a plain cover sheet with very little written, save a one-sentence note saying that the organization closed in 1960 due to the triumph of the Revolution. Evidently, the revolution's success had eliminated the need for a Black-uplift association.[16]

In northeastern Cuba today, exchange with the outside world is limited, as Cubans cannot travel freely and have only limited, expensive internet access. According to Carmelo Mesa-Lago and Jorge Pérez-López, since Raúl Castro took over in 2006, citizens have longed for a socialist society with open debate and room to criticize the state, and where citizen participation goes beyond mass mobilization.[17] State policies, however, are driven in large part by fear of "losing political control," a fear that prevails "even if it resulted in deterioration of economic living standards."[18] And the economic situation is bad.

The commodity that made Banes a key node in global trade networks in the interwar years is disappearing and with it, the bustling towns deeply engaged with the outside world. During the Cold War, the United States, which had so dominated the island's economy, embargoed trade with Cuba; the country's new trading partner was no longer its neighbor to the north, but the USSR. Cuba nationalized the properties of foreign companies, and the Boston, Preston, Chaparra, Delicias, and dozens of other mills all operated under new names (Nicaragua, Guatemala, Jesús Menéndez, and Antonio Guiteras, respectively). After a brief and unsuccessful attempt to dethrone king sugar and diversify Cuban agriculture, Cuba returned to sugar for survival in the late 1960s. Fidel Castro announced plans to harvest 10 million tons of sugar in 1970. The feat, he argued, would facilitate industrialization and end Cuban underdevelopment. Despite mobilizing the whole of the island and dedicating a year to the effort, Cuba fell short, producing 8.5 million tons. The economic-policy pendulum swinging between the idealism of Che Guevara's "New Man" (motivated by moral incentives rather than material incentives) and market-based pragmatism swung back toward the market.[19] In a series of favorable trade deals, the Soviet Union agreed to purchase Cuban sugar above market rates and sell the island oil below rate. Producing sugar, in other words, continued to keep the island afloat.

When the Soviet Union collapsed and Cuba lost its patron state, however, sugar-for-oil was over. Cuba downsized its sugar industry, reduced its output, and decommissioned old mills. In 2002, the state announced the Tarea Álvaro Reynoso, a plan to restructure the sugar industry, closing 71 mills out of the 156 that were still operating. Production has since declined rapidly. Only 25 mills ground cane in the 2023–24 harvest, only one of which is in northeastern Cuba.[20] Recently, in May 2024, the state announced that Cuba was unlikely to meet the island's needs; Cuba is set to import sugar for the first time since cane cultivation began on the island.[21] The old sugar mills have largely been dismantled and abandoned, and the visuals are fodder for ruins photography.[22]

Revisiting the popular internationalism of the 1920s and 1930s in Cuba's eastern sugar towns reminds us that struggles for uplift and solidarity can emerge in surprising places. The centers of oppositional politics are always moving, as are their targets. The outward-facing visions that took hold in Banes and other company towns in the interwar period ushered in an era of new possibilities that reverberated through the generations and across space. In the global north today, we carry the world in our pockets, but we lose sight of the commodity chains connecting our everyday conveniences to the rest of the world. Even our activist efforts too often assume that radicalism flows outward from the north, not the other way around. We might take a cue, however, from the subjects of this book, who understood clearly how their struggles were related to wider systems of racial subordination, labor exploitation, and imperialism and who fought tirelessly to do something about it.

NOTES

In citing works in the notes, texts frequently cited have been identified by the following abbreviations:

ANC	Archivo Nacional de Cuba
AHPH	Archivo Histórico Provincial de Holguín
AHPSC	Archivo Histórico Provincial de Santiago de Cuba
AHPLT	Archivo Histórico Provincial de Las Tunas
Baker Library	Harvard University, Harvard Business School, Baker Library
Braga Brothers	University of Florida, George A. Smathers Libraries Braga Brothers Collection
CSLA	Confederación Sindical Latinoamericana
HAHR	*Hispanic American Historical Review*
IHC	Instituto de Historia de Cuba
MG and UNIA Papers	*The Marcus Garvey and Universal Negro Improvement Association Papers*
MO	*Mundo Obrero*
NW	*Negro World*
UKNA	United Kingdom National Archives
USNA	United States National Archives
RGASPI	Russian State Archives of Socio-Political History
Tamiment	New York University, Tamiment Library and Robert F. Wagner labor Archives
Schomberg	New York Public Library, Schomburg Center for Research in Black Culture

Introduction

1 The names of Cuba's provinces have changed over the years. The easternmost province covered in this book was called Santiago de Cuba until 1905, after which it was called Oriente Province. In 1976, Oriente was divided into Las Tunas, Granma, Holguín, Santiago de Cuba, and Guantánamo Provinces.
2 Adams, *Conquest of the Tropics*, 297.
3 Portuondo Moret, *Tacajó*, 19.
4 Argote-Freyre, *Fulgencio Batista*, 17.
5 I am unabashedly using here, almost *verbatim*, the wise words of UFP Caribbean Crossroads series editor, Lillian Guerra, who wrote this in her report on my manuscript. She said it better than I can.
6 Castro and Ramonet, *My Life*, 28.
7 Quirk, *Fidel Castro*, 27; Castro and Ramonet, *My Life*; Argote-Freyre, *Fulgencio Batista*.

8 Ferrer, "History and the Idea of Hispanic Caribbean Studies," 63. See also Lara Putnam's superb essay on the connections between microhistory and Atlantic history. Putnam, "To Study the Fragments/Whole," 621.
9 Neptune, "At Sea: The Caribbean in Black Empire," 272.
10 Lindner, *A City Against Empire*, 3.
11 Lindner, 6.
12 McNamara, *Ybor City*, 3.
13 Joseph, LeGrand, and Salvatore, *Close Encounters of Empires*.
14 Soto, *La Revolución precursora*, 59–64. See also, Guerra y Sánchez, *Azúcar y población en las Antillas*; Soto, *La revolución del 33*; IHC, *Movimiento obrero*, 1: 179–80. For *dependista* studies which emphasize enclaves as cut off from national processes, see Cardoso and Faletto, *Dependency and Development*; Andre Gunder Frank, "The Development of Underdevelopment"; Levin, *Export Economies*.
15 LeGrand, "Living in Macondo"; Putnam, *The Company They Kept*; Chomsky, *West Indian Worker*; Harpelle, *West Indians of Costa Rica*; Corinealdi, "Envisioning Multiple Citizenships: West Indian Panamanians and Creating Community in the Canal Zone Neocolony"; Flores-Villalobos, *The Silver Women*.
16 Grandin, "Your Americanism and Mine"; McPherson, *Anti-Americanism*; Dalleo, *American Imperialism's Undead*; Gobat, *Confronting the American Dream*.
17 See Guerra y Sánchez, *Azúcar y población en las Antillas*; José Martí, Ana Dopico, and Fred Fornoff, *José Martí: Revolution, Politics and Letters* Vol. 1 Cuba: The Struggle for Independence (Oxford: Oxford University Press, 2007); Guerra, *The Myth of José Martí*.
18 For just a few texts from the on US imperialism at the dawn of the twentieth century, see LaFeber, *The New Empire*; Foner, *Spanish-Cuban-American War*; Benítez, *Las Antillas*; McPherson, *The Invaded*.
19 On the business of empire, see Ayala, *American Sugar Kingdom*; Hudson, *Bankers and Empire*; Colby, *The Business of Empire*.
20 Carr, "Across Seas"; Carr, "Pioneering Transnational Solidarity"; Shaffer, *Anarchists of the Caribbean*; Stevens, *Red International and Black Caribbean*; Hernández, *Bad Mexicans*; Heatherton, *Arise!*
21 Guridy, *Forging Diaspora*, 7–9.
22 In this book, "Antillano," a term commonly used at the time under consideration, refers to Afro-Caribbean migrants and immigrants in Cuba. Individuals from Haiti and the British West Indies were also called "Haitianos" and "Jamaicanos" (or more pejoratively "Jamaiquinos"). I do not replicate that language because it is both clunky and incorrect (many British West Indians were not Jamaican, and some Afro-Caribbean migrants were from French-held islands, for example). "Antillean" in English could also work, but I have chosen to use the Spanish word "Antillano" and capitalize according to English practice.
23 For more on the "third country labor system," in which the United States government or US private companies imported workers from abroad, see Conniff, *Black Labor on a White Canal*, 5, 176–78. For companies' strategic reasons for importing third country laborers, see Langley and Schoonover, *Banana Men*, 24.
24 Putnam, *Radical Moves*; Giovannetti-Torres, "The Elusive Organization of Identity"; Giovannetti-Torres, *Black British Migrants*; Corinealdi, "Envisioning Multiple Citizen-

ships"; Flores-Villalobos, *The Silver Women*; Pérez Nakao, "The Jamaican Community in Banes"; Garnes, "Memory of West Indians."

25 Trouillot, "Theorizing a Global Perspective," 5. I am grateful to Jorge Giovannetti-Torres for pointing me to this excellent article.
26 Mintz, "The Caribbean as a Socio-Cultural Area"; Mintz, "Localization of Anthropological Practice."
27 Carr, "Across Seas," 233.
28 Sergio Guerra Vilaboy accessed the Managers Letters Books housed in the Archivo de Banes. Vilaboy, "La United Fruit Company."
29 Zanetti and García, *United Fruit*. Additionally, Philippe Bourgois published a helpful collection of United Fruit documents he stumbled across in a Costa Rican warehouse. Bourgois, "One Hundred Years of United Fruit Company Letters."
30 Putnam, "The Transnational and the Text-Searchable," 377, 396.
31 French, "Another World History," 6.
32 Laqua, "Preface," xii.
33 Glenda Sluga and Patricia Clavin write, "At the turn of the twenty-first century, historical interest in internationalism—as anything but the call to the workers of the world to unite—is gradually becoming the norm in a relatively short space of time." Sluga and Clavin, "Rethinking the History of Internationalism," 4.
34 I take a cue here from Linebaugh and Rediker, who write that the "sailors and slaves" at the heart of their book on the revolutionary Atlantic were "the real citizens of the world . . . This multiethnic proletariat was 'cosmopolitan' in the original meaning of the world." Linebaugh and Rediker, *The Many-Headed Hydra*, 246.
35 Bender, "The Cosmopolitan Experience and Its Uses," 116.
36 Guridy, *Forging Diaspora*, 5-6. This book is very much indebted to scholars of the African diaspora who, for decades, have implicitly and explicitly debunked recent concerns about cosmopolitanism as a framework for historical analysis of subaltern subjects, namely that it diminishes the importance of power discrepancies, states, and ethnic and racial allegiances. Diaspora scholars have demonstrated that subalterns can be cosmopolitan while at the same time operating in variegated fields of power, that states have been and remain relevant, and that there is a long history of cross-pollination between visions for Black liberation and other anti-racist, anti-imperialist struggles. For just the tip of the iceberg, see Berlin, "From Creole to African;" Matory, *Black Atlantic Religion*; Nwankwo, *Black Cosmopolitanism*; Patterson and Kelley, "Unfinished Migrations;" Scott, *Common Wind*.

Chapter 1. Constructing Oriente's Cosmopolitan Coast

1 Wright, *Cuba*, 464–66.
2 Wright, 484.
3 Adams, *Conquest of the Tropics*, 243, 252–54.
4 United Fruit Company, *Some Facts*, 16, 5.
5 Lasso, *Erased*, 13.
6 In 1939, Carey McWilliams used this term to describes the expansion of agrobusiness (as opposed to farming) in California. McWilliams, *Factories in the Field*.

7   For the interconnected British West Indian diaspora, maintaining contact through letters and print journalism, see Putnam, *Radical Moves;* Giovannetti-Torres, *Black British Migrants.*
8   Dye, *Cuban Sugar,* 15; Hoernel, "Sugar and Social Change," 217; Giusti-Cordero, "Beyond Sugar Revolutions."
9   Perez, "The Pursuit of Pacification"; Pérez, "Insurrection, Intervention," 245–46; Cárdenas Tauler, "La ruta del Nororiente cubano hacia el capitalism," 126–28. For *haciendas comuneras,* see Cárdenas Tauler, *La ruta holguinera.*
10 Hoernel, "Sugar and Social Change," 219–220, 223.
11 United States War Department, Report on the Census of Cuba, 1899, 555–56; Hoernel, 219–23; de la Fuente, *Nation for All,* 106.
12 United Fruit Company, *Some Facts,* 5.
13 Zanetti and García, *United Fruit,* 47; Dumois, *A Name,* 42. The numbers for the Dumois holdings vary. Zanetti and García estimate Dumois properties totaled approximately 1,000 caballerías (33,000 acres) in 1895. James puts the number at 3,000 caballerías (over 99,000 acres) by 1899 but concedes that a precise total is difficult to calculate. Afred Dumois, a descendant of the Dumois brothers, has the highest estimate, claiming the family held 8,000 caballerías (over 265,000 acres) by the turn of the century. Zanetti and García, *United Fruit,* 47; James, *Banes,* 59, 67; Dumois, *A Name,* 48.
14 Dumois, *A Name,* 33–47; Varona Pupo, *Banes, Crónicas,* 45–47; "Hipólito Dumois," in *Prominent and Progressive Americans: An Encyclopoedia of Contemporaneous Biography,* 1:107–8, *New York Tribune,* 1902; Zanetti and García, *United Fruit,* 46–49; James, *Banes,* 58–61.
15 James, *Banes,* 60, 68.
16 Dumois, *A Name,* 67; Zanetti and García, *United Fruit,* 48–49.
17 Pérez, "Toward Dependency and Revolution," 134,136.
18 Cuba: Oficina del Censo, *Cuba: Population, History and Resources 1907,* 131–32; Pérez, *Cuba: Between Reform and Revolution,* 127, 145–48; McGillivray, *Blazing Cane,* chapter 2; Smith, "Political Economy," 32; Zanetti and García, *Sugar and Railroads,* 197–99; Foner, *Spanish-Cuban-American War,* 2: 379–80.
19 Varona Pupo, *Banes, Crónicas,* 46; Zanetti and García, *United Fruit,* 48; Dumois, *A Name,* 60.
20 Pérez, *Cuba Between Empires,* 230–67; Ferrer, *Insurgent Cuba,* 195–202; Foner, *Spanish-Cuban-American War,* 2: 388–421; Tone, *War and Genocide;* Ferrer, *Cuba,* chapter 13.
21 Pérez, *Ties of Singular Intimacy,* 29–54; Neagle, *America's Forgotten Colony,* chapter 1; Granding, *The End of the Myth,* 127.
22 Louis Pérez argues that the whole of Cuba represented "a new frontier at about the time that Frederick Jackson Turner was lamenting the passing of the old one." Cuba was described alternatively as "virgin land," "another California," and "a brand new country." Pérez, *Ties of Singular Intimacy,* 123. I would add that this was especially true of eastern Cuba.

23 United States Tariff Commission, *The Effects of the Cuban Reciprocity Treaty of 1902*, 168.
24 "New Sugar Factories in Cuba," *Louisiana Planter and Sugar Manufacturer*, November 10, 1900.
25 Foner, *Spanish-Cuban-American War*, 2: 2, 70, 468.
26 An often-repeated story is William Van Horne's railroad venture. When workers reached public property, such as a stream or road, he abruptly fired them and made a big show of not having proper authorization. Wood's office, in turn, was flooded with telegrams demanding that the work continue in a demonstration of the people's will. Wood then granted the project a "revocable permit." Jenks, *Our Cuban Colony*, 1970, 151–52; McGillivray, *Blazing Cane*, 73; Zanetti and García, *Sugar and Railroads*, 221.
27 Adams, *Conquest of the Tropics*, 252–53.
28 Pérez, *Cuba Between Empires*, 334–44; Pérez, *Army Politics*, 14–16; Hernández, *Cuba and the United States*, 94–95, 107–15; Casey, "The Paramilitarism of Politics and Production in Early Republican Cuba"; Uralde Cancio, "Orígenes de la Guardia Rural."
29 The text of the Platt Amendment is available in Pérez, *Cuba Between Empires*, 323–24. For histories of the Constitutional Convention and the Platt Amendment, see Foner, *Spanish-Cuban-American War*, 2: 534–58; Pérez, *Cuba Between Empires*, 284–313, 23–25; Ferrer, *Insurgent Cuba*, 199–200.
30 Zanetti and García, *United Fruit*, 53–56. Exacerbating matters for Cuban landholders, the hacienda comunera system had fostered messy record keeping.
31 Smith, "Political Economy," 35; Hoernel, "Sugar and Social Change," 223–26.
32 Neagle, *America's Forgotten Colony*, 64–98.
33 The Isle of Pines south of Cuba came to be almost-entirely dominated by North American colonizers. Foner, *Spanish-Cuban-American War*, 2: 481; Jenks, *Our Cuban Colony*, 1928, 144; Neagle, *America's Forgotten Colony*; Deere, "Here Come the Yankees!" 740.
34 Jenks, *Our Cuban Colony*, 1928, 141–42, 44.
35 George Reno, "Oriente, The California of Cuba," *The Cuba Review* (August 1927): 14–20.
36 United States Department of Commerce and Labor et al., *Report on Trade Conditions in Cuba*, 38. See also, Munson Steamship Line, "Suggestions to the Homeseeker," *The Cuba Review* XV, no. 17 (June 1917): 13–19.
37 Deere describes the confluence of events that caused most American colonists to leave Camagüey and Oriente. These included the Liberal Revolt of 1917 when many American properties in the east were burned; a sense that the United States Marines were more interested in protecting large American sugar estates than small farms; World War I when many Americans were drafted to serve in the military; and rising wartime prices for sugar, which made selling land to sugar interests attractive to settlers. Deere, "Here Come the Yankees!," 752–56.
38 US Tariff Commission, "Effects of the Cuban Reciprocity Treaty," 1–2, 65; Zanetti, *Los cautivos de la reciprocidad*.
39 American Vice Consul at Antilla, Cuba to George P. Geinler, June 25, 1919, USNA, Record Group 84: Foreign Service Posts of the Department of State (hereafter RG 84), Antilla: Vol. 43, File 861.5.
40 Ayala, *American Sugar Kingdom*, chapter 4.

41 Smith, "Political Economy," 39.
42 Zanetti and García, *Sugar and Railroads*, 214–31; Santamarina, "The Cuba Company," 62–66.
43 Santamaría García, *Sin azucar no hay país*, 440.
44 Zanetti and García, *Sugar and Railroads*, 231.
45 Munson Steamship Line, "Active Sugar Plantations of the Island of Cuba," 1918, American Geographical Society Library Digital Map Collection accessed through Digital Library of the Caribbean.
46 Adams, *Conquest of the Tropics*, 296.
47 Cuba Importadora y Industrial, *Anuario Azucarero de Cuba, 1937*, 28–31; James, *Banes*, 90, 107, 142; Zanetti and García, *United Fruit*, 46–51, 53–56; Adams, *Conquest of the Tropics*, 297; Santamaría García, *Sin azucar no hay país*, 426.
48 Hoernel, "Sugar and Social Change," 229; McGillivray, *Blazing Cane*, 77, 102.
49 "Giant Sugar Enterprise in Cuba," *Louisiana Planter and Sugar Manufacturer*, December 8, 1900, 363.
50 Hawley, "Cuban-American Sugar Company, Annual Report for the Fiscal Year Ending September 30, 1910," 5, 6; Hawley, "Cuban-American Sugar Company, Annual Report for the Fiscal Year Ending September 30, 1911," 3.
51 "Chaparra" and "Delicias" *Manual Azucarero de Cuba* (La Habana, 1927), 135–6E, 138E. For the *colonato*, see Ayala, *American Sugar Kingdom*, chapter 5; McGillivray, *Blazing Cane*, 157–66.
52 A special edition of *Agricultura y Zootecnica* in July of 1924 was devoted to coverage of these massive mills as symbols of Cuba's progress.
53 By 1910, CASC owned a total of 276,000 acres of land, a refinery in Cuba (in addition to one in Louisiana), four sugar factories in addition to Chaparra and Delicias, almost 195 miles of private railroad, a cattle processing plant, seven electric plants, ice plants, brick yards, lime kilns, machine and carpenter shops, roads, bridges and fences, water supply plants, 411 miles of telephone lines, fuel plants, fire protection plants, four wharves, three steam tugs and seven barges. Hawley, "Cuban-American Sugar Company, Annual Report for the Fiscal Year Ending September 30, 1910."
54 Cuba Importadora y Industrial, *Anuario Azucarero de Cuba*, 1937, 28–29.
55 Ayala, *American Sugar Kingdom*, 79–85.
56 Ayala, 100.
57 Ayala, "Sugar Production in Cuba," 122.
58 Sullivan and Cromwell was a major player in the Latin American investment scene, and would later become famous for the firm's relationship with United Fruit and involvement, through Allen and John Foster Dulles, with the 1954 coup that overthrew the democratically elected president of Guatemala, Jacobo Arbez.
59 Ayala, *American Sugar Kingdom*, 87–89; McGillivray, *Blazing Cane*, 77, 114; McAvoy, *Sugar Baron*.
60 Ayala, *American Sugar Kingdom*, 92; González and Luis, "Los enclaves azucareros," 399–401. Cárdenas Tauler, *La ruta holguinera*.
61 Ayala, *American Sugar Kingdom*, 211; Dye, *Cuban Sugar*, 175.
62 James, *Banes*, 113.

63 Together, United Fruit and CASC were responsible for about 10 percent of the entire sugar harvest in 1919. Santamaría García, *Sin azucar no hay país*, 146.
64 Wiles, *Cuban Cane Sugar*.
65 Hoernel, "Sugar and Social Change," 228.
66 Varona Pupo, *Banes, Crónicas*, 120–22.
67 McGillivray, *Blazing Cane*, 162–172.
68 Hoernel, "Sugar and Social Change," 230.
69 De la Fuente, *Nation for All*, 106.
70 Wiles, *Cuban Cane Sugar*, 83–84.
71 National City Company, *Sugar*, 23.
72 Reynolds, *The Story of Cuban Sugar*, 15. For ideas about "taming the tropics," see Lasso, *Erased*; Colby, *The Business of Empire*.
73 Reynolds, *The Story of Cuban Sugar*, 18.
74 Zanetti and García, *United Fruit*, anexo estadistico, np.
75 "Fifteenth Census of the United States, 1930, Agriculture, Volume II, Part 3, the Western States, Reports by States," Census, Census of the United States, 24–25.
76 Annual Reports available for a subsidiary of the United Fruit Company, the Nipe Bay Company. Nipe Bay Company Annual Reports, 1909–1916, Baker Library, Records of Companies Acquired by the United Fruit Company, vol. 6. See also, Smith, "Political Economy," 37–40.
77 Casey, *Empire's Guestworkers*, 49; James, *Banes*, 174–75; Zanetti and García, *United Fruit*, 211.
78 Giovannetti-Torres, *Black British Migrants*, 47.
79 FitzGerald and Cook-Martín, *Culling the Masses*, 192; Pérez de la Riva, "Cuba y la migración antillana," 28.
80 Giovannetti-Torres, *Black British Migrants*, 47; Pérez Nakao, "Inmigración Españoa, Jamaicana, y Árabe," 14.
81 United Fruit Company, *Some Facts*, 17.
82 Pérez de la Riva, "Cuba y la migración antillana," 28; Zanetti and García, *United Fruit*, 212; Petras, *Jamaican Labor Migration*, 232; Gómez Navia, "Lo haitiano en lo cubano," 10.
83 Álvarez Estévez, *Azúcar e inmigración*, 86–87; Casey, *Empire's Guestworkers*, 57.
84 Álvarez Estévez, *Azúcar e inmigración*, 268–69.
85 Álvarez Estévez, 270.
86 For comprehensive immigration statistics over time, see Benítez, *Las Antillas*; Giovannetti-Torres, *Black British Migrants*, 51; Pérez de la Riva, "Cuba y la migración antillana," 38–43.
87 McLeod, "Undesirable Aliens," 599. Cuban historian Pérez de la Riva places the figure specifically at 636,532 by 1931. Pérez de la Riva, "Cuba y la migración antillana," 38–39.
88 Zanetti and García, *Sugar and Railroads*, 231.
89 Dr. Rolegio Pina y Estrada, "Informe sobre la inmigración haitiana y jamaicana," June 29, 1934, ANC, Fondo Sec. de la Presidencia, Box 181, No. 84.

90 "Repatriation of Haitians by Cuban Government from Santiago de Cuba, November 22, 1933," prepared by Edwin Schoenrich, November 28, 1933, USNA, RG 84: Vol. 340, File 850.4.
91 Conniff, *Black Labor on a White Canal*, 15, 176–78; Langley and Schoonover, *Banana Men*, 24.
92 Colby, *The Business of Empire*; Bourgois, *Ethnicity at Work*.
93 Gómez Navia, "Lo haitiano en lo cubano," 10; Álvarez Estévez, *Azúcar e inmigración*, 39, 44, 51; Matthew Casey, "Haitians' Labor and Leisure," 6.
94 Cuba Dirección general del Censo, *Census of the Republic of Cuba 1919*, 284–86, 328.
95 "Población por provincías, 1953," in *Censos de población, viviendas y electoral, enero 28 de 1953* (1955), 182.
96 "Diez millones de pesos han sacando de Cuba los jamaicanos en dos años de trabajo," *El Cubano Libre*, July 9, 1921, 1.
97 E. Molinet to the Secretaria de Agricultura, Comercio, y Trabajo, November 12, 1924, ANC, Fondo Secretaria de Agricultura, Comercio, y Trabajo (hereafter Secretaria de Agricultura): Leg. 4, Exp. 45.
98 G. De Aranguren, Jefe de la Sección de Inmigración, Colonización, y Trabajo, to Eugenio Molinet, Administrator General to the Chaparra Sugar Company, November 19, 1924, ANC Fondo Secretaria de Agricultura: Leg. 4, Exp. 45. (Emphasis in original.) For concerns about migrants becoming public wards, see the file, "Documents relating to the solicitation of aauthorization by the administration of the *centrales* 'Chapara' and 'Delicias' in order to bring to this Republic through Puerto Padre 2000 immigrants from the British islands for the 1923–4 zafra" ANC, Fondo Secretaria de Agricultura: Leg. 4, Exp. 45.
99 Decree Number 1611 of Sec. of Agriculture, Comercio y Trabajo, November 1924, ANC Fondo Secretaria de Agricultura: Leg. 4, Exp. 45.
100 E. Molinet to the Sec of Agriculture, Comercio, y Trabajo, November 4, 1924, ANC Fondo Secretaria de Agricultura: Leg. 4, Exp. 45.
101 Giovannetti-Torres, *Black British Migrants*, 250; Casey, *Empire's Guestworkers*, 160–61; McLeod, "Undesirable Aliens," 608.
102 Gómez Navia, "Lo haitiano en lo cubano," 10–11; Giovannetti-Torres, *Black British Migrants*, 60–61; Casey, *Empire's Guestworkers*, 94.
103 "Documents relating to the solicitation of authorization by the administration of the centrals 'Chaparra' and 'Delicias' in order to bring to this republic through Puetro Padre 2000 immigrants from the British islands for the 1923–4 zafra" December 10, 1923–July 6, 1926, ANC, Secretaria de Agricultura, Comercio, Y Trabajo; Leg. 4, Exp. 45; Giovannetti-Torres, *Black British Migrants*, 60.
104 See AHPSC, Fondo Gobierno Provincial (hereafter GP) Leg. 309, Exp 11. for a thick pile of such authorizations, many of which are from *colonos* on CASC lands.
105 R. B. Wood to Bartlett, November 24, 1928; Godoy to Wood, November 22, 1928; and Godoy to Wood, November 19, 1928; Letter to Bartlett, November 15, 1928, AHPLT, Fondo: Cuban American Sugar Mills Company (hereafter, CASC): Signatura 0444/43.
106 Giovannetti-Torres, *Black British Migrants*, 51–64; Casey, *Empire's Guestworkers*, 58. H. Shackleton to His Majesty's Minister, Havana, April 1, 1924, UKNA, Foreign Office

371, Identifier 2903/13/14; Palma Sugar Company to Hon Sr. Guillermo F. Mascaro, Gobernador de Oriente, March 5, 1919, AHPSC, GP, Leg. 307, Exp. 21.
107 Giovannetti-Torres, *Black British Migrants*, 57–62; Pérez de la Riva, "Cuba y la migración antillana," 40–41.
108 Cuban historian Juan Pérez de la Riva was the first scholar to suggest a link, claiming that the stream of migrants from Jamaica to Cuba was maintained in part because United Fruit had holdings in both locations. Pérez de la Riva, "Cuba y la migración antillana," 13. See also, Pérez Nakao, "Inmigración jamaicana a Banes," 70; James, *Banes*, 174. Similarly, Álvarez Estévez claimed that United Fruit established encampments in Haiti where recruited workers prepared for their journey. Álvarez Estévez, *Azúcar e inmigración*, 59. In Central America, United Fruit arranged to recruit laborers directly from the Canal Zone upon the canal's completion to work in its Costa Rican plantations. Petras, *Jamaican Labor Migration*, 209–10, 32.
109 Illegible sender (likely CASC General Manager Wood) to Walter S. Bartlett, November 15, 1928, AHPLT, CASC, Signatura 0444/43, p. 201. See also "Sociales de Chaparra," *Diario de Cuba*, March 2, 1927, announcing the return of Edilberto Rodríguez from Barbados where he had just completed a successful bracero recruitment campaign.
110 McGillivray, *Blazing Cane*, 113.
111 Chailloux Laffita and Whitney, "British Subjects y Pichones En Cuba," 57.
112 "Petition of the Natives of All the West Indian Islands Residing in Cuba, Prepared and Forwarded Under the Auspices of the West Indian Workers Union," Undated, but likely April 23, 1924, UKNA, Foreign Office 371, Identifier 2903/13/14.
113 Rojas, *Luchas obreras*, 30–33.
114 Uralde Cancio, "Orígenes de la Guardia Rural."
115 Secretariado de Justicia to Tribunal Supremo, July 3, 1923, ANC, Fondo Secretaria de la Presidencia: Leg. 86, Exp. 7; Giovannetti-Torres, *Black British Migrants*, 142–44. For additional examples of Rural Guard violence, see Whitney, *State and Revolution*, 94–95; McGillivray, *Blazing Cane*, 92, 102–3, 52–55.
116 "Havana Correspondence," *Cuba Review* XIX, no. 11 (October 1921): 13. J. W. Sheridan of the British Consulate, Santiago de Cuba, to Colonial Secretary, Kingston, "Report in connection with the work of repatriation of distressed Jamaican labourers in Cuba and the endeavor to assist these labourers in obtaining payment of promissory notes, etc.," November 17, 1921, AHC, Fondo Secretaria de Estado: Leg. 532, Exp. 12473.
117 Administrador General RB Wood to Dr. Francisco Cháves Milanés, February 17, 1928, AHPH, Fondo Gobierno Municipal de Holguín, Ayuntamiento Neocolonía (hereafter GM): Leg. 88, No. 4806, pp. 20–22.
118 Wright, *Cuba*, 467–469; Skelly, *I Remember Cuba*, 74.
119 McGillivray, *Blazing Cane*, 102.
120 McGillivray, 104–7, 19–21; James, *Banes*, 114–16; Pérez Nakao, "Inmigración Españoa, Jamaicana, y Árabe," 36–38; Pérez de la Riva, "Cuba y la migración antillana," 37; Casey, *Empire's Guestworkers*, 108.
121 Pérez, *On Becoming Cuban*, 224.
122 Carlos Forment, "En Banes se polarizan dos civilizaciones," *Bohemia*, November 6, 1938; James, *Banes*, 151–54; Wright, *Cuba*, 473.

123 Pérez, *On Becoming Cuban*, 221–24.
124 Forment, "En Banes se polarizan."
125 Frank Stockdale, comptroller for development and welfare in the West Indies, "Report on the Present Conditions of the British West Indian Community in Cuba," July 21, 1943, UKNA, FO 371/33832, p. 13. Jorge Giovannetti-Torres generously shared this source.
126 Pérez, *On Becoming Cuban*, 222, 224, 226–29; Zanetti and García, *United Fruit*, 302–5.
127 "Dry Goods department," "Hat and Boot Department," "Grocery Department," and "Hardware Department." Baker Library, United Fruit Photography Collection, Box 42, Folder 8.
128 Baker Library, United Fruit Photography Collection, see Box 44B, Folder 8 for instance.
129 William Joseph Showalter, "Cuba—The Sugar Mill of the Antilles," *The National Geographic Magazine*, December 1920, 30, Haiti Trust.
130 Terry, *Terry's Guide to Cuba*, 383.
131 LeGrand, "Living in Macondo"; Putnam, *The Company They Kept*; Casey, *Empire's Guestworkers*.
132 Neagle, *America's Forgotten Colony*.
133 Jenks, *Our Cuban Colony*, 1928, 142.
134 Wright, Cuba, chapter 21, *Cuba*. Bartle was developed by railroad magnate Van Horne and his Cuba Company before he turned his attention to sugar. Zanetti and García, *Sugar and Railroads*, 229.
135 Pérez Nakao, "Inmigración española, jamaicana, y árabe"; Pérez de la Riva, "Los recursos humanos"; Naranjo Orovio, "Emigracion española a Cuba."
136 Pérez Nakao, "Inmigración española, jamaicana, y árabe," 14.
137 Pérez Nakao, 13–16; Naranjo Orovio, "Emigracion española a Cuba," 510–11; McGillivray, *Blazing Cane*, 105–6.
138 For a listing of foreigners' occupations at Chaparra and Delicias, see "Declaraciones juradas elaboradas por los obreros del central para dar cumplimiento a la dispuesto en el decreto presidencial #2583 sobre nacionalización de trabajo" February 1937, AH-PLT, CASC Signatura 0457/45.
139 Pérez, "Protestant Missionaries in Cuba," 105–8.
140 Leimdorfer, *Cultural Imperialism*
141 Hilty, "Zenas L. Martin," 82; Leimdorfer, *Cultural Imperialism*, 82.
142 Leimdorfer, *Cultural Imperialism*, 62–65,73,81–85; Jason M. Yaremko, *U.S. Protestant Missions in Cuba*, 1–12,49–50, 52–53; Hilty, "Zenas L. Martin, Quaker Pioneer in Cuba," 82,87–88.
143 Pérez, "Protestant Missionaries in Cuba," 119; Leimdorfer, *Cultural Imperialism*, 62–63,65; Yaremko, *U.S. Protestant Missions in Cuba*, 11.
144 Yaremko, 97–98.
145 Yaremko, 53, 71,74, 109, 119.
146 Pérez, *On Becoming Cuban*, 320–21.
147 Leimdorfer, *Cultural Imperialism*, 78–79.
148 Yaremko, *U.S. Protestant Missions in Cuba*, 75–76.
149 Sylvester Jones, "The Outlook for College Men and Women in Spanish-Speaking

150 Pérez, *On Becoming Cuban*, 231.
151 Eldon B. Lehman, "My Visit to Cuba," *The Whitened Harvest* vol. 4, no. 1 (May 1939); Enclosure to L. E. Thompson to Manager of the Chaparra Sugar Company, June 29, 1939, AHPLT, CASC: Exp 198, Exp 2694.
152 "Petición Para Inscripción," April 15, 1924, Unión Antillana de los Adventistas del Séptimo Día, ANC, Registro De Asociaciones: Leg. 342, Exp. 10170.
153 L. E. Thompson, Representative of the West Indies Mission, to the Manager of the Chaparra Sugar Mill. June 29, 1939. AHPLT, CASC, Signatura 2964/198.
154 Lehman, "My Visit to Cuba"; Leimdorfer, *Cultural Imperialism*, 79.
155 Jacobson, *Barbarian Virtues*, 50.
156 Jacobson, 17.
157 E. V. Thompson, Director West Indies Mission, to General Manager Wood of Chaparra Sugar Company, June 29, 1939, AHPLT, CASC: Signatura 2964/198.
158 Wright, *Cuba*, 483.
159 Paris to Walter S. Bartlett, January 16, 1929, AHPLT, CASC: Signatura 0444/43, pp. 20–25.
160 Martin, *Banana Cowboys*. These men's experiences are similar to those of the "engineering migrants" Jonathan Curry-Machado describes as having spread sugar technology to Cuba in the nineteenth century. Curry-Machado, *Cuban Sugar Industry*.
161 Giovannetti-Torres, *Black British Migrants*, 60.
162 Joseph N. Richards to Horace J. Dickinson, American Consul to Antilla, Cuba, April 10, 1932; Joseph N. Richards to US Consul at Santiago de Cuba, Redirected to American Consul at Antilla, April 28, 1932; From Joseph N. Richards, Received by Horace J. Dickinson, American Consul to Antilla, Cuba, April 23, 1933; and Manuel Rodriguez to American Consul at Antilla, Cuba, Received May 16, 1932, all in USNA, RG 84: Vol. 112; File 310.
163 "Francisco Chiong to the Administrator General de la Chaparra Sugar Company," April 4, 1936, AHPLT, CASC: Signatura 0456/45.
164 American Vice Consul at Antilla, Cuba to US Secretary of State, June 24, 1919, USNA, RG 84: Vol. 46, File 800.
165 Enrique Torres Santanera to American Consul at Antilla, Cuba, July 7, 1932, USNA, RG 84: Vol. 112, File 310.
166 Skelly, *I Remember Cuba*, 34, 48, 158, 60.
167 McGillivray, *Blazing Cane*, 175; Álvarez Estévez, *Azúcar e inmigración*, 22–23.
168 "Inmigración y movimiento de pasajeros, año de 1930 y comparaciones con el año de 1929" ANC, Fondo Donaciones y Remisiones, Leg. 403, Exp. 11; Petras, *Jamaican Labor Migration*, 209–13, 232–34; Garnes, "Memory of West Indians," 139; Giovannetti-Torres, *Black British Migrants*, 54.
169 Giovannetti-Torres, *Black British Migrants*, 191.
170 Casey, "Haitians' Labor and Leisure"; Casey, *Empire's Guestworkers*.
171 McLeod, "Undesirable Aliens"; Pérez de la Riva, "Cuba y la migración antillana," 11–13, 17–21, 27–29; Wright, *Cuba*, 477. For further information on the relative ad-

vantages British West Indians had within the Cuban economy see McLeod, "Undesirable Aliens," 607–13; Knight, "Jamaican Migrants," 104.
172 Skelly, *I Remember Cuba*.
173 Carr, "Omnipotent," 265; Matthew Casey, "Haitians' Labor and Leisure," 18–19.
174 Knight, "Jamaican Migrants," 104.
175 Pérez Nakao, "Inmigración jamaicana a Banes," 70; Skelly, *I Remember Cuba*, 4.
176 Sociedad de instrucción y cultura "Asociación Universal para el Adelanto de la Raza Negra División No 52 de Banes" April 1, 1926, and October 14, 1927, AHPSC, GP; Leg. 2452, Exp. 2.
177 Dumois, *A Name*; Osorio, *Banes (1513–1958)*; Skelly, *I Remember Cuba*; Kushner, *Telex from Cuba*.
178 United Fruit Photography Collection, Baker Library. Box 42A, Folder 9.
179 "Possible Return to the United States of Miss Elise M. Forbes" American Vice Consul at Antilla, Cuba to US Secretary of State, July 18, 1919, USNA, RG 84: Vol. 43, File 855.
180 See, Putnam, *Radical Moves*.
181 Ober, *A Guide to the West Indies and Bermudas*, 113. See also, *The Cuba Review*, a periodical put out by Munson with regular schedules, which ran from 1907 to 1931.
182 "Review of Shipping for the Quarter Ended March 31, 1931." Prepared by Horace J. Dickenson, American Consul to Antilla, Cuba, April 9, 1931, USNA, RG 84: Vol. 110, File 885.
183 Advertisement in the *Diario de Cuba*, March 2, 1927.
184 "Review of Shipping for the Quarter Ended June 30, 1931." Prepared by Horace J. Dickenson, American Consul to Antilla, Cuba, July 6, 1931, USNA, RG 84: Vol. 110, File 885, p. 6.
185 Dumont, American Consul General, to Sec. State, September 26, 1933, USNA, RG 59, Folder 4, 837.00B/76, with enclosures.
186 M. Franklyn to American Consul at Antilla, Cuba, April 5, 1932; "Whereabouts of Donald Bairon MacArmour, Alias Sylvester Donald Armour" October 16, 1933; W.L.S. Gordon, Postmaster, New Orleans to US Secretary of State, July 31, 1933; American Consulate General, Havana to US Secretary of State, November 20, 1933; "Dispatch of the American Vice Consul at Tegucigalpa, Honduras" Enclosure in Horace Dickenson to Mrs. Gloria Cabrera de MacArmour, August 30, 1933; "Report of Investigation" enclosure to Horace Dickenson to Mrs. Gloria Cabrera de MacArmour December 14, 1933; "Report of Investigation" enclosure to Horace Dickenson to Mrs. Gloria Cabrera de MacArmour December 14, 1933, USNA, RG 84: Vol. 118, File 310.
187 O. W. Clark, Veterans Administration, to U.S Secretary of State, April 20, 1935, USNA, RG 84: Vol. 128, File 310-R. Other documents in the same file include: "Request of Mr. Fred Roberts to be Repatriated," Horace J. Dickinson, American Consul to Antilla, Cuba, to US Secretary of State, March 8, 1935; "QM: Fred Roberts, report prepared by Quartermaster General," April 25, 1935; R. P. Cockshott, C/O United Fruit Company, to H. J. Dickinson, American Consul to Antilla, Cuba, June 8, 1935.
188 Scott, *Degrees of Freedom*, 61–62; Gatewood, *Smoked Yankees*; Gatewood, *Black Americans and the White Man's Burden*.
189 For racial lines hardening at the war's end in the shadow of US empire, see Ferrer,

"Rustic Men." For Cuban race relations in the early twentieth century, de la Fuente, *Nation for All*; Helg, *Our Rightful Share*; Bronfman, *Measures of Equality*.

190 Julio Ramos Rivera to American Consul at Santiago de Cuba, Redirected to American Consul at Antilla, Cuba; January 10, 1932, and Horace Dickinson, American Consul at Antilla, Cuba to Edwin Schoenrich, American Consul at Santiago de Cuba, January 16, 1932, USNA, RG 84: Vol. 112, File 310.

191 Amanda Isaroon to Edwin Schoenrich, American Consul at Santiago de Cuba, Referred to American Consul at Antilla; July 18, 1932, USNA, RG 84: Vol. 112, File 310. Yurisay Pérez Nakao, however, contends that, for the most part, the Jamaican community in Banes was endogamous. Pérez Nakao, "Inmigración jamaicana a Banes," 39–40.

192 "Wedding Bells in San Manuel, Oriente," *NW*, February 24, 1923.

193 Wright, *Cuba*, 486–91.

194 Irwin D. Arter to Horace J. Dickinson, American Consul at Antilla, Cuba, February 12, 1935, USNA, RG 84: File 330.

195 Putnam, *Radical Moves*; Corinealdi, *Panama in Black*; Maddox, *A Home Away from Home*.

196 Leimdorfer, *Cultural Imperialism*, 76.

197 Petición Para Inscripción, April 15, 1924, Unión Antillana de los Adventistas del Séptimo Día, ANC, Registro De Asociaciones: Leg. 342, Exp. 10170.

198 See, for example, listings in the AHPSC, GP under "Sociedades" 1922.

199 Zebadiah Myrie, Iglesia Unión de Banes President, to Governor, Oriente, Cuba. April 4, 1924, Banes Union Church Relief Association, AHPSC, GP Sociedades: Leg. 2747, Exp. 4, p. 3.

200 Gobierno de la Provincia to Gobernador Provincial, July 20, 1926, Banes Union Church Relief Association, AHPSC, GP Sociedades: Leg. 2747, Exp. 4, p.9.

201 Kane Lodge Secretary to Gobernador Provincial, November 10, 1923, and Kane Lodge, Bye Laws. AHPSC, GP: Leg. 915, Exp 8.

202 Resp. Logia 'Kane,' AHPSC, GP: Leg. 915, Exp. 8, p. 19.

203 Juan G. Suarez to Emilio Soto Barranco, Luz Unida, October 25, 1926, AHPSC, GP: Leg. 916, Exp. 2, p. 3.

204 Reglamento de la Logia Luz Unida, No 10, 975, "Gran Orden Unida de Oddfellows," November 7, 1925, AHPSC, GP: Leg. 916, Exp. 2, p. 5

205 Putnam points out that many organizations at the time printed "Traveling Cards" or "Clearance Cards," which responded to and facilitated members' travel between locales. Putnam, "Nothing Matters but Color," 112.

206 American Vice-Consul at Antilla to US Secretary of State, June 24, 1919, USNA, RG 84: Box 46, File 800. Alan McPherson also writes about the Pro-Santo Domingo campaign. McPherson, *The Invaded*, 160–62.

207 American Vice-Consul at Antilla to US Secretary of State, June 24, 1919.

208 US Vice-Consul at Antilla to US Sec. of State, June 24, 1919; Gobernado, Prov. Oriente to Alcaldes Municipales, February 22, 1919; AHPSC, GP, Leg. 786, Exp. 10.

209 Gobernador to the Secretaría de Gobernacion, February 22, 1919, AHPSC, GP Leg. 786, Exp. 10. See whole expediente for additional telegrams.

210 McPherson, "Yankee No!"; Power, *Solidarity across the Americas*; Gobat, "The Invention of Latin America"; Shaffer, *Anarchists of the Caribbean*.

211 US Vice-Consul at Antilla to US Sec. of State, June 24, 1919; Gobernado, Prov. Oriente to Alcaldes Municipales, February 22, 1919.
212 LeGrand, "Living in Macondo," 352–352.
213 Soto, *La Revolución precursora*, 63.

Chapter 2. Garveyism, Community Building, and Forging Diaspora in Company Towns

1. "List or Manifest of Alien Passengers for the United States" SS *Munamar*, Sailing from Antilla, Cuba, July 23, 1921 (Microfilm Serial: T715, 1897–1957), reproduced as "New York, U.S., Arriving Passenger and Crew Lists (including Castle Garden and Ellis Island), 1820–1957" on Ancestry.com, accessed 25 February 2021, https://www.ancestrylibrary.com/imageviewer/collections/7488/images/NYT715_3000-0289
2. "The Black Star Line Parade," *New York Age*, August 6, 1921; "Editorial Letter by Marcus Garvey," *NW*, August 3, 1921, reprinted in Hill, *MG and UNIA Papers*, 3: 610–12.
3. "Second International Convention of Negroes, Summary of Report for Fourth Week," *NW*, September 3, 1921.
4. "First UNIA Court Reception," *NW*, September 3, 1921, "Convention Reports" August 22–26, 1921, and "Convention Reports" August 29–31, 1921, reprinted in Hill, *MG and UNIA Papers*, 3: 683–711.
5. "Speech by Marcus Garvey," *NW*, September 10, 1921, reprinted in Hill, *MG and UNIA Papers*, 3: 734–39.
6. Plunkett, "Banes, Oriente, Cuba," *NW*, October 9, 1921, in Hill, *MG and UNIA Papers*, 13: 104–6.
7. Benjamin Dean, "U.N.I.A. News of Banes, Cuba"; "Banes Division U.N.I.A. and A.C.L Making Progress," *NW*, February 1921, reprinted in *MG and UNIA Papers*, 12: 144–45.
8. The SS *Munamar*'s manifest states that Ethel hosted her brother and sister-in-law. "List or Manifest of Alien Passengers." For the Collins family, see "Ivan J. Collins Dies in Harlem Hospital," *New York Age*, November 19, 1938, and "Many Helped to Sponsor . . . ," *New York Age*, December 10, 1949.
9. "First UNIA Court Reception."
10. Bair, "True Women; Real Men," 165.
11. Putnam, "Unspoken Exclusions," chapter 4.
12. Around the time Harold and Anita Collins set sail, Frank Munson of the Munson steamship line was making a name for himself as a segregationist in Caribbean tourism. Saunders, *Race and Class in the Colonial Bahamas*, 112.
13. "List of United States Citizens," SS *Munamar*, Sailing from Antilla, Cuba, July 23, 1921 (Microfilm Serial: T715, 1897–1957), reproduced as "New York, U.S., Arriving Passenger and Crew Lists (including Castle Garden and Ellis Island), 1820–1957" on Ancestry.com, accessed February 25, 2021.
14. "Hard Treatment to the Preston Division in Cuba by the United Fruit Company," *NW*, October 8, 1921, reprinted in Hill, *MG and UNIA Papers*, 13: 99–100.
15. G. R. Christian, "A Staunch Member Tells His Experience," *NW*, August 4, 1928.
16. Kohler, "Chesapeake-Built and Caribbean-Bound: U.S.M.S. *Munamar*."
17. Mintz, "The Caribbean as a Socio-Cultural Area," 38.

18 García Domínguez, "Garvey and Cuba," 303.
19 Tolbert, "Outpost Garveyism."
20 Castillo Bueno and Rubiera Castillo, *Reyita*, 26–29.
21 Howard, *Changing History*, xiv–xv; Pappademos, *Black Political Activism*, 113–14.
22 Martí, "Nuestra America," *El Partido Liberal*, January 20, 1891, reprinted in Martí, *Selected Writings*, 288–96, 295.
23 Ferrer, *Insurgent Cuba*, 9–10; Guerra, *The Myth of José Martí*, 25–29.
24 Brunson, *Black Women*, 62–63; de la Fuente, *Nation for All*, 26–39; Pappademos, *Black Political Activism*, 9–11.
25 For the history of the PIC and the massacre of 1912, see Helg, *Our Rightful Share*; Castro Fernández, *La masacre de los Independientes de Color en 1912*; Meriño Fuentes, *Una vuelta necesaria*; Guerra, *The Myth of José Martí*, 226–42; de la Fuente, *Nation for All*, 66–91; Fernández Robaina, *El negro en Cuba*; Scott, *Degrees of Freedom*, 226–52; Pérez, "Politics, Peasants, and People of Color." The narrative here draws from these excellent sources.
26 Guerra, *The Myth of José Martí*, 237–39.
27 García Domínguez has pointed to these two events as shadowing Garvey's work in Cuba, as has Sandra Estévez Rivero more recently. García Domínguez, "Garvey and Cuba"; Estévez Rivero, *La sombra de Marcus Garvey*.
28 Giovannetti-Torres, *Black British Migrants*, 92–96.
29 Guridy, *Forging Diaspora*, 63.
30 McLeod, "Garveyism in Cuba"; McLeod, "Cuba, Historical Commentaries," in *MG and UNIA Papers*, 11: clxxxix–cxcv; Giovannetti-Torres, "The Elusive Organization of Identity."
31 Gaines, *Uplifting the Race*; Putnam, *Radical Moves*.
32 In an article from Banes, mothers were encouraged to educate children so that *they* may see Africa free and redeemed. R.G. Murray, "Big Day at Banes, Oriente, Cuba," *NW*, March 24, 1923. Garnes writes, "The return was not physically realized; it was about the mind, the spirit," "Memory of West Indians," 142.
33 James R. Cato, "Division 194 of Santiago de Cuba," *NW*, March 17, 1923. "Capt. Joshua Cockburn to Marcus Garvey," Sagua la Grande, December 2, 1919, in Hill, *MG and UNIA Papers*, 2: 161–62; "Report of UNIA Meeting," *NW*, March 6, 1920, reprinted in in Hill, 2: 233.
34 "Divisions of the UNIA, 1925–1927," Schomburg, UNIA, CD: reel 1, box 2, A16; Martin, *Race First*, 17.
35 Hill, "General Introduction" 11: lxxxvi; James, "Culture, Labor, and Race in the Shadow of US Capital," 450–51; Putnam, *Radical Moves*, 17.
36 Hill, "General Introduction," 11: lxxxvi.
37 Sullivan, "'No Surrender.'"
38 Putnam, *Radical Moves*, 131–32.
39 "Cuba Sends Message of Sympathy to Tulsa Negroes," *NW*, August 20, 1921.
40 Norman J. Douglas, "Second Sunday Night's Mass Meeting at Antilla," *NW*, September 2, 1921.
41 Garland Murray, "Prominent Member Passes Away," *NW*, August 27, 1921; Robert S. F. Blake, "Banes Division, UNIA & ACL," *NW*, March 26, 1921; "Speech by Marcus

Garvey, Liberty Hall, New York, July 20, 1921" in Hill, *MG and UNIA Papers*, 3: 532–45, 533.
42. R. A. Bennett, "Impressions of Banes Division," *NW*, July 15, 1922.
43. Jemima Kelso, "UNIA in Banes, Cuba Forging Ahead," *NW*, February 26, 1921; Banes Division UNIA and ACL Making Progress reprinted in Hill, 12: 144–45.
44. Bennett, "Impressions of Banes Division."
45. Robert S.F. Blake, "All's Well in Banes, Oriente, Cuba," *NW*, May 26, 1923; D.H. Stennett, "Camaguey, Cuba Elia No. 754," *NW*, January 10, 1925; "The Camaguey Division Holds Inspiring Meeting," *NW*, August 25, 1923.
46. "His Grace, The Right. Hon. Chaplain General, The Rev. Dr. George Alexander M'Guire, Given Great Ovation on His Return from Cuba," *NW*, March 19, 1921.
47. "Chaplain General's Visit to Cuba-His Grace the Most Rev. George Alexander McGuire, MD," *NW*, May 7, 1921.
48. Unreadable, "The Chaplain General Bids Farewell to Antilla, Oriente, Cuba," *NW*, August 13, 1921.
49. Blake, "Banes Division, UNIA & ACL."
50. "Banes Division Welcomes Hon. Marcus Garvey," *NW*, April 30, 1921; "Speech by Marcus Garvey," July 20, 1921, 533–534.
51. Jemima Kelso, "An Encouraging Report from the Banes, Cuba, UNIA," *NW*, December 17, 1921; Eduardo Morales, "Commissioner Morales Gives Brilliant Description of Geographical Positions of Cuban Divisions," *NW*, July 29, 1922; Morales, "Hour of Africa's Triumph Is Near, Says High Com. Morales," *NW*, May 6, 1922; Eduardo Morales, "Thanks Division for Their Tribute to Him," *NW*, March 25, 1922; J.W.D. Fuller, "Com. Morales Settles Disputes Arising out of Insular Prejudices," *NW*, April 1, 1922.
52. "Commissioner Morales Going Strong in Cuba," *NW*, March 25, 1922; Morales, "Thanks Division for Their Tribute to Him"; Fuller, "Com. Morales Settles Disputes Arising"; Morales, "Hour of Africa's Triumph"; A.C. Cain, "U.N.I.A and A.C.L. Marcane Division, No. 267, Marcane, Oriente, Visited by the High Commissioner," *NW*, July 29, 1922. The old province of Oriente was actually just over 2.5 times the size of Jamaica.
53. Morales, "Commissioner Morales Gives Brilliant Description"; Jemima Kelso, "The UNIA in Banes, Cuba," *NW*, January 28, 1922.
54. "Branch of the UNIA and ACL Formed at Port Pastellio," *NW*, March 19, 1921.
55. E. H. Hope Williams, "The UNIA Almost Encircles Island of Cuba," *NW*, March 26, 1921.
56. Hope Williams, "The UNIA Almost Encircles."
57. "Marcus Garvey to William H. Ferris, Literary Editor," *NW*, reprinted in Hill, *MG and UNIA Papers*, 3: 423–25, n6; S. P. Radway, "Report of Conditions Existing in the Cuban Republic," *NW*, August 27, 1921; McLeod, "Los Braceros Antillanos," 143.
58. "UNIA Declaration of Rights," August 13, 1920, reprinted in Hill, *MG and UNIA Papers*, 2: 571–80.
59. "The Chaplain General Bids Farewell to Antilla, Oriente, Cuba."
60. "His Grace . . . Given Great Ovation."; Sec. Ejecutivo to Gob. Prov, April 1, 1928, AHP-SC, GP: Leg. 2452, Exp. 2, p. 49. Arnold S. Cummings's name is spelled differently in

local UNIA documents and in Hill's volume ("Cunning") than in the *NW*'s article on McGuire's speech ("Cummings"), though we have every reason to believe that he is one and the same person. "The Chaplain General Bids Farewell to Antilla, Oriente, Cuba"; "UNIA, Marcane," *NW*, August 13, 1921; "Visit by Chaplain General to Guaro, Oriente, Cuba," *NW,* March 12, 1921.

61 "The U.N.I.A in Cuba," *NW*, April 23, 1921, reprinted in Hill, *MG and UNIA Papers,* 12: 181–83.
62 O. Louis Sherwood, "Further Distinguished Visit Paid to Several Branches of U.N.I.A in Cuba by His Excellency, the Hon. Marcus Garvey, Provisional President of African and President General of the U.N.I.A.," *NW,* April 16, 1921, reprinted in Hill, 12: 207–21.
63 "His Grace . . . Given Great Ovation"; "Visit by Chaplain General to Guaro, Oriente, Cuba."
64 Rev. J. J. Mumford, "News from Winston-Salem Div., U.N.I.A," *NW*, February 4, 1922; Harold, *Rise and Fall of the Garvey Movement*, 21.
65 "Reglamento," AHPSC, GP: Leg. 2452, Exp. 2.
66 "Asociación Universal Para el Adelanto De la Raza Negra, División #326, Antilla Oriente-Reglamento" AHPSC, GP, Leg. 2452, Exp. 10.
67 William Holmes, "Manati Division, Oriente de Cuba, Secretary's Report," *NW*, September 3, 1921.
68 Bennett, "Impressions of Banes Division."
69 Burkett, *Garveyism as a Religious Movement*, 7; Giovannetti-Torres, "The Elusive Organization of Identity," 14.
70 "Speech by Marcus Garvey," July 20, 1921, 533.
71 Murray, "Prominent Member Passes Away."
72 Whitney and Chailloux, *Subjects or Citizens*, 148.
73 Murray, "Prominent Member Passes Away."
74 Joseph E. Thompson, "Pleasant Times in Preston, Cuba: His Grace, Dr. McGuire, the Chaplain General, Sweeps Cuba on a Triumphant Tour," *NW*, February 19, 1921; Arthur M Sutton, "Preston Division, U.N.I.A. and A.C.L.," *NW*, March 19, 1921.
75 Prince R. Simon, "Death of a Faithful Member in Cuba," *NW*, January 10, 1925; Murray, "Prominent Member Passes Away"; Con Adj Howlitt, "Florida, Cam, Cuba," *NW*, September 11, 1926.
76 "Reglamento de La Asociación Universal Para el Adelanto de la Raza Negro División No. 52 de Banes," (hereafter UNIA Division 52) July 3, 1922, GP, AHPSC, Leg. 2452, Exp. 2, pp. 11–24; "Asoc. Univ. para el Adelanto de la raza negra to Provincial Governor," July 28, 1924, AHPSC, GP: Leg. 2452, Exp. 2; Blake, "All's Well in Banes, Oriente, Cuba"; Robert S.F. Blake, "A Ringing Message from Banes, Oriente, Cuba," *NW*, April 14, 1923; Universal Negro Improvement Association and African Communities' League, *UNIA Constitution and Book of Laws*.
77 "U.N.I.A. in Moron, Camaguey, Cuba," *NW,* September 17, 1921.
78 "Speech by Marcus Garvey," July 20, 1921, 533.
79 McLeod, "Garveyism in Cuba," 147.
80 Colin A. Wilson, "Banes, Cuba," *NW,* July 10, 1926.

81 Christian Alexander Frederick, "Racial Experience," *NW*, July 9, 1921, reprinted in Hill, *MG and UNIA Papers*, 12: 345–47.
82 R. H. Bachelor, "Garvey Relief Cantata Is Staged by Division #164, at Guantanamo," *NW*, September 8, 1923; Dora Stennett, "Elia, Cam. Cuba," *NW*, August 21, 1926.
83 Kelso, "An Encouraging Report"; Harold A. Collins, "Banes Division U.N.I.A. and A.C.L. Making Progress," *NW*, February 5, 1921.
84 Kelso, "Encouraging Report"; Kelso, "The UNIA in Banes, Cuba"; Kelso, "UNIA in Banes, Cuba Forging Ahead"; "Reglamento, UNIA Division 52."
85 Morales, "Hour of Africa's Triumph."
86 Similarly, Claudrena Harold has written that the UNIA in the US South offered authority roles not limited to men with college degrees. Harold, *Rise and Fall of the Garvey Movement*, 37, 44.
87 Bair, "True Women; Real Men," 156.
88 Ford-Smith, "Women and the Garvey Movement," 78.
89 Bair, "True Women; Real Men," 165–66.
90 "His Grace . . . Given Great Ovation."
91 George Clarke, "Red Letter Day in Rio Canto Division of the U.N.I.A," *NW*, August 27, 1921.
92 McLeod, "Undesirable Aliens," 600-602; McLeod, "'We Cubans Are Obligated Like Cats,'" 57.
93 "Un haitiano salvaje asesinó a un niño, y se comió su cuerpo," *El Cubano Libre*, October 20, 1921; "Varios hatianos fueron sorprendidos en grotescas prácticas de brujería," *Diario de Cuba*, May 5, 1927. A Garveyite from Sagua La Grande in central Cuba reported that such newspaper coverage fanned the flames of anti-immigrant hostility, and that West Indians walking down the street were subject to harassment and "such vile names as cannibal, anthropophagus, etc., and if you attempt to deny the story[,] a copy of the paper is held up to your view to confirm the insults." J. A. Thorpe, "Propaganda in Cuba to Divide Cuban and West Indian Negroes," *NW*, August 20, 1921, reprinted in Hill, *MG and UNIA Papers*, 13: 30–31.
94 "Reglamento, UNIA Division 52."
95 Kelso, "Encouraging Report."
96 Blake, "Banes Division, UNIA & ACL." See also Blake, "A Ringing Message"; Murray, "Big Day at Banes, Oriente, Cuba."
97 "UNIA in Cuba Celebrates Mothers' Day," *NW*, April 14, 1923.
98 "His Grace . . . Given Great Ovation"; Secretario-Ejecutivo to Gobernador de Oriente, April 1, 1926, AHPSC, GP: Leg. 2452, Exp. 2, p. 49.
99 Blake, "A Ringing Message"; Robert S.F. Blake, "A Message from Banes, Oriente, Cuba," *NW*, April 16, 1921.
100 See "Sociedad de instrucción y cultura 'Asociación Universal para el Adelanto de la Raza Negra División No 52 de Banes" AHPSC, GP: Leg. 2452, Exp. 2 for several documents listing the officers, their names, and their professions in Banes.
101 Hope Williams, "The UNIA Almost Encircles"; Blake, "A Ringing Message."
102 "His Grace . . . Given Great Ovation."
103 Helg, *Our Rightful Share*, 228, 241–42.
104 Estévez Rivero, *La sombra de Marcus Garvey*, 53-54.

105 "Marcus Garvey, Moises de la raza negra expone al *Heraldo* sus amplios planes sobre la futura República del África," *Heraldo de Cuba*, March 4, 1921, cited in McLeod, "'Sin Dejar Ser Cubanos,'" 79.
106 Estévez Rivero, *La sombra de Marcus Garvey*, 53-57; García Domínguez, "Garvey and Cuba"; Lewis, *Marcus Garvey: Anti-Colonial Champion*, 99-103; Rodríguez, "Marcus Garvey En Cuba."
107 Pappademos, *Black Political Activism*, 7-11; de la Fuente, *Nation for All*, 8-9; Brunson, *Black Women*, 11; Guridy, *Forging Diaspora*, 74-77.
108 Guridy, *Forging Diaspora*, 64.
109 Helg, *Our Rightful Share*, 165.
110 For instance, see Sec. Beausoleil to Gobernador Provincial de la Habana from July 4, 1921, ANC, Fondo: Registro de Asociaciones, Leg. 388, Exp. 11640.
111 "Brotherhood of Man," *NW*, October 22, 1921, reprinted in Hill, *MG and UNIA Papers*, 13: 36-38.
112 Sherwood, "Further Distinguished Visit."
113 Morales, "Thanks Division for Their Tribute to Him."
114 Guridy, *Forging Diaspora*, 100.
115 "UARN Capitulo Cubano 7i, División del Habla Española, Santiago de Cuba" Mach 17, 1927, AHPSC, GP: Leg. 2452, Exp. 9, p. 3; Lewis, *Marcus Garvey: Anti-Colonial Champion*, 108.
116 "Remedios Division 150 Holds Grand Meeting on Behalf of the Convention and Emancipation," *NW*, August 27, 1921.
117 Douglas, "Second Sunday Night's Mass Meeting at Antilla."
118 Williams, "The UNIA Almost Encircles"; Douglas; "Gala Day in San Manuel-Unveiling of Charter," *NW*, May 7, 1921.
119 Clarke, "Red Letter Day."
120 "Commissioner Morales Going Strong in Cuba"; Kelso, "Encouraging Report."
121 R. G. Murray, "Another Big Hit by the Commissioner for Cuba," *NW*, January 7, 1922.
122 Castillo Bueno and Rubiera Castillo, *Reyita*, 26-29.
123 Santamaría García, *Sin azucar no hay país*, 413.
124 "Havana Correspondence," *The Cuba Review* XIX, no. 1 (December 1920): 12. The "Havana Correspondence" and "Sugar Review" sections of this journal cover the crisis in detail. See all of vol. XIX. See also, Ayala, *American Sugar Kingdom*, 233-34; Zanetti and García, *Sugar and Railroads*, 275-76; Thomas, *Cuba or the Pursuit of Freedom*, 543-53; Grogan, "Cuba's Dance of the Millions"; Santamaría García, *Sin azucar no hay país*, 55-60.
125 Dye, *Cuban Sugar*, 161; Commission on Cuban Affairs and Buell, *Problems of the New Cuba*, 287.
126 "The Economic Situation" reports for June 24, July 8, and July 22, 1921, 2655-Q-27; Q-28; Q-30, USNA, Microfilm RG 165: War Department. General and Special Staffs; M1507 Correspondences & Record Cards of the MI Div. Relating to General Political, Economic, Military Conditions in Cuba and the West Indies, 1918-1941, reel 5. See also, "Sugar Review," *Cuba Review* XIX, no. 9 (August 1921): 31.
127 "Iconoclast" to the *Workman*, August 27, 1921, reprinted in Hill, *MG and UNIA Papers*, 13: 34-36.

128 Giovannetti-Torres, *Black British Migrants*, 130.
129 Junco, "El problema de la raza negra y el movimiento proletario," 160–76.
130 "News from Cuba," *Louisiana Planter and Sugar Manufacturer*, September 1921.
131 "News of the Cuban Sugar Industry" section of *Facts about Sugar*, October 1, 1921, and October 22, 1921.
132 Ewing, *Age of Garvey*, 6. Similarly, McLeod writes that the movement was "not monolithic, but in fact adopted different forms in different countries." McLeod, "'Sin Dejar Ser Cubanos,'" 135.
133 Hulme, "Wilfred Domingo under Investigation," 61–62.
134 Ewing, "Caribbean Labour Politics," 29–31; Howison, "Let Us Guide," 37–38.
135 Zumoff, "Black Caribbean Labor Radicalism"; Burnett, "'Unity Is Strength.'"
136 GP Chittenden to VM Cutter, December 21, 1919, in Bourgois, "One Hundred Years," 120–121.
137 Blair, Division Manager, UFC, to George P. Chittenden, December 19, 1919, reproduced in Hill, *MG and UNIA Papers*, 11: 477–78.
138 Chittenden to Cutter, December 21, 1919.
139 Harpelle, "Cross Currents," 55–56.
140 "Speech by Marcus Garvey" July 20, 1921, 361.
141 GP Chittenden to AA Catterall, [illegible] April 1921, reproduced in Bourgois, "One Hundred Years," 124–25.
142 Hill, "General Introduction," 1: lxxviii–lxxx.
143 Hill, "General Introduction," 1: lxxx.
144 "Miss H. Vinton Davis Speaks at Big Meeting," *Workman*, January 3, 1920, reproduced in Hill, "General Introduction," 11: 500–502, 502.
145 Burnett, "'Unity Is Strength,'" 60; Zumoff, "Black Caribbean Labor Radicalism," 443–445.
146 "Commissioner Morales Going Strong in Cuba."
147 Clarice G. Walters, "Gov. Coronel Alfredo Lora of Oriente, Cuba, Visits U.N.I.A. Amidst Tremendous Enthusiasm," *NW*, July 30, 1921.
148 Walters.
149 R. Theo Webley, "Troubles That Were Overcome in Marcane," *NW*, August 20, 1921.
150 Harold D. Clum, US Consul, Santiago de Cuba, to John. R. Putnam, US Consul, Havana, September 23, 1921, reprinted in Hill, *MG and UNIA Papers*, 13: 70–72.
151 Walters, "Gov. Coronel Alfredo Lora of Oriente, Cuba, Visits U.N.I.A."
152 Guridy, *Forging Diaspora*, 102–4.
153 "Reglamento, UNIA Division 52."
154 McLeod explains the association was often viewed as an "immigrant protection society." McLeod, "Garveyism in Cuba," 134.
155 Pappademos, *Black Political Activism*, 28.
156 "Mr. Edward Green Speaks," *NW*, May 1, 1920, reprinted in Hill, *MG and UNIA Papers*, 11: 646–52; Guridy, *Forging Diaspora*, 81.
157 Ada Ferrer, *Cuba*, 214; de la Fuente, *Nation for All*, 88; Scott, *Degrees of Freedom*, 250–51.
158 Webley, "Troubles That Were Overcome in Marcane."

159 "Marcane, Cuba, U.N.I.A. Presents Address to Commissioner Morales," *NW*, October 1, 1921; Webley, "Troubles That Were Overcome in Marcane."
160 Kelso, "Encouraging Report."
161 McGillivray, *Blazing Cane*, 137.
162 Clarke, "Red Letter Day."
163 "Banes Division Welcomes Hon. Marcus Garvey."
164 For example, see Williams, "The UNIA Almost Encircles."
165 McGillivray, *Blazing Cane*, 119, 122; McAvoy, *Sugar Baron*.
166 Holmes, "Manati Division."
167 "The UNIA Progressing in Manatí, Cuba," *NW*, November 5, 1921.
168 "Report of UNIA Mass Meeting held in Florida, Cuba," *NW*, 10 Sept. 1921 reprinted in Hill, *MG and UNIA Papers*, 13: 7–10.
169 Hill, 13: lxx.
170 "Commissioner Morales Going Strong in Cuba."
171 "Hard Treatment to the Preston."
172 Christian, "A Staunch Member."
173 R. G. Murray, "Enthusiastic Meeting Held at Banes, Oriente, Cuba," *NW*, March 25, 1922. R. Hytton, "Faithful Followers [Unreadable] U.N.I.A. Success," *NW*, March 30, 1927.
174 Radway, "Report of Conditions Existing in the Cuban Republic."
175 McKenzie, "Africa Our Hope," *NW*, October 29, 1921, reprinted in Hill, *MG and UNIA Papers*, 13: 121–22.
176 A.M.G Procope, "[Unreadable] . . . Reports from Cuba," *NW*, September 19, 1921.
177 Thorpe, "Propaganda in Cuba to Divide Cuban and West Indian Negroes."
178 Radway, "Report of Conditions Existing in the Cuban Republic."
179 McLeod, "Los Braceros Antillanos," 148; McLeod, "Garveyism in Cuba." E. Brice, British Consul, Santiago de Cuba, to the Municipal Mayro, Santiago de Cuba, September 18, 1921, reprinted in Hill, *MG and UNIA Papers*, 13: 66–67; Harold D. Clum to John R. Putnam, September 23, 1921, reprinted in Hill, 13: 70–72.
180 Harold D. Clum to John R. Putnam, September 23, 1921, in Hill, *MG and UNIA Papers*, 13: 70–72.
181 Their determination to seek redress through British imperial channels would eventually result in a 1924 "White Paper" in which consular officials condemned the ill-treatment of British subjects in Cuba. Giovannetti-Torres, *Black British Migrants*, 149–50.
182 McLeod, "Garveyism in Cuba," 142; Ewing, "Caribbean Labour Politics," 28–29.
183 Giovannetti-Torres, *Black British Migrants*, 136.
184 Giovannetti-Torres, 115–16.
185 Estévez Rivero, *La sombra de Marcus Garvey*, 34; McLeod, "Garveyism in Cuba," 138.
186 J. A. Kelso, "Greetings to Hon. E. V. Morales, High Commissioner for Cuba," *NW*, March 4, 1922.
187 McLeod, "Garveyism in Cuba," 141.
188 McKenzie, "Africa Our Hope."
189 R. A. Martin, "Florida Division," *NW*, May 5, 1923.

190 Aubrey Jones, "The UNIA in Camaguey, Cuba, Surmounts Difficulties," *NW,* May 26, 1923.
191 Sydney F. Hugh Miller, "Memorial Day for Banner Division, 323," *NW,* April 28, 1923.
192 Blake, "A Ringing Message."
193 "UNIA Marcane, Oriente, Cuba on the Upward March," *NW,* March 19, 1921.
194 Putnam, "Nothing Matters but Color," 113.
195 S.E.E. Grant, "Spirit of Garveyism," *NW,* January 10, 1931.
196 Murray, "Enthusiastic Meeting"; Stennett, "Elia, Cam. Cuba"; Blanche M Thomas, "Miranda, Cuba, Division 608, Unveils Its Charter-Event Very Impressive," *NW,* February 14, 1923; A. E. Bridgeman, "Sola Division," *NW,* January 17, 1931; Grant, "Spirit of Garveyism."
197 Murray, "Another Big Hit."
198 Lemelle and Kelley, "Introduction—Imagining Home: Pan-Africanism Revisited," 7.
199 Putnam, *Radical Moves,* 126.
200 Egbert C. Squires, "Warning Against Priest," *NW,* January 24, 1931.
201 *NW,* January 10, 1922, and *NW,* July 29, 1922.
202 "Troubles of the Haitian President," *NW,* July 10, 1926. See also "160,000 Demand Borno to Quit Haitian Presidency" and "Ciento sesenta mil emigrados haitianos en Cuba protestan contra Luis [sic] Borno" of the same issue.
203 "Speech by Marcus Garvey," July 20, 1921; See also, "Hon. Rev. McGuire Speaks in Guantanamo," *NW,* March 19, 1921.
204 "Convention Reports," New York, August 14, 1922, reprinted in Hill, *MG and UNIA Papers,* 4: 868.
205 Adams, *Pioneering in Cuba,* 35–38.
206 Sherwood, "Further Distinguished Visit."
207 Mulzac, *A Star to Steer By,* 86, as cited in Martin, *Race First,* 155.
208 In Panama, Garveyites complained that United Fruit would not let them sail on company ships. "Reports of the Convention," New York, August 1920, in Hill, *MG and UNIA Papers,* 2: 512.
209 Martin, *Race First,* 157.
210 Hill, "Introduction," *MG and UNIA Papers,* vol. 13.; Hill, "Chronology," in *MG and UNIA Papers,*13: lxix, lxviii; Bandele, *Black Star,* 113–17; Martin, *Race First,* 157–59.
211 "Convention reports" Afternoon Session, August 15, 1922, in Hill, *MG and UNIA Papers,* 4: 876–77.
212 See especially, Cronon, *Black Moses.*
213 Howison, "Let Us Guide," 33–34.
214 Howison, 30; Carnegie, "Politics of Transterritorial Solidarity," 152–56.
215 Mulzac, 79 as cited in Howison, "Let Us Guide," 39.
216 Richards to King of England, enclosure in Grindle, Assistant Under Secretary of State, Colonial Office, to the Under Secretary of State, Foreign Office, August 26, 1921, reprinted in Hill, *MG and UNIA Papers,* 13: 32–34.
217 Joseph A. Todd, "British Rule Bad for Black People," *NW,* April 21, 1923.
218 Giovannetti-Torres, *Black British Migrants,* 51.
219 McLeod, "Undesirable Aliens," 602.
220 Post, *Arise Ye Starvelings,* 417.

221 Guridy, "'Enemies of the White Race.'"
222 Isaac S. Hall to Provincial Governor of Oriente, April 7, 1927, AHPSC, GP, Leg. 2697, Exp. 4, p. 2.
223 "Lista de la Directiva, Asoc. Univ. Para el Adelanto de la Raza Negra, Div #52 Banes," November. 1930, AHPSC, GP, Leg. 2452, Exp. 2, p. 67.
224 Putnam, "Provincializing Harlem," 249.

Chapter 3. "The Weakest Link of Imperialism's Chain in the Caribbean"

1 Mariblanca Sabas Alomá, "Julio Antonio Mella: La Acción Antiimperialista de Banes," *Bohemia*, December 4, 1964; James, *Banes*, 249–52; Varona Pupo, *Banes, Crónicas*, 252.
2 Santo Domingo was occupied by Haiti from 1822 to 1844, when it became an independent state. In 1861, however, the country was reconverted to a Spanish colony. The country fought a "War of Restoration" against Spain from 1863 to 1865, when it again secured independence. It was in this war that Don Nicanor's father, Matías Ramón Mella, had fought. Eller, *We Dream Together*, 182, 186.
3 For Mella's biography, see Hatzky, *Julio Antonio Mella*, 25–33. Quote is from p. 33.
4 "Convocatoria y actas del Congreso de fundación del primer partido marxista-leninista de Cuba, Acta de la cuarta sesión" in IHC, *El movimiento obrero cubano, documentos*, 1975, 1:453; Rojas Blaquier, *El primer Partido*, 1:35.
5 Delfín E. Mercade Pupo, "Mella en el feudo de la United Fruit Co de Banes," *Bohemia*, January 17, 1969.
6 Ramiro Guerra's book exemplifies this argument. Guerra y Sánchez, *Azúcar y población en las Antillas*.
7 Later, the PCC-led Defensa Obrera Internacional put this clearly in many of its manifestos, including DOI-Comité Ejecutivo Nacional "Frente al aparato militar criminal que funciona regularmente asesinado, atropellando, descargando, implacable entre sobre las masas trabajadores las medidas represivas mas duras y salvajes del terror blanco" Date NA, IHC, Fondo 1: Organizaciones de Trajabadores (hereafter Fondo 1), Signatura 1/8:223/5.1/1–109.
8 Sidney Mintz points out that scholars too have overlooked the fundamentally industrial nature of sugar production. Mintz, "The Caribbean as a Socio-Cultural Area," 36.
9 "Circular sobre la reunión y preparación del Primer Congreso Nacional de 'Defensa Obrera Internacional'" [NA but 1933] IHC, fondo 1, sig. 1/8:223/2.1/1–42.
10 Carr, "Mill Occupations," 134–35; Whitney, *State and Revolution*, 74–76; Zanetti and García, *United Fruit*, 237–39; Dumoulin, *Azúcar y lucha*, 54–57.
11 For a collection on company towns, see Dinius and Vergara, *Company Towns in the Americas*.
12 Gerard Smith to Leandro Rionda, Francisco, February 15, 1917, Braga Brothers Collection, RG 10, Series 10a, Box 8 quoted in de la Fuente, "Two Dangers," 40.
13 [illegible] To Manuel Rionda, Manatí Sugar Company October 9, 1924; To Manuel Rionda, October 18, 1924, in Braga Brothers, Record Group 2, Microfilm "Latin American History and Culture, Series 8: Cuba and the American Sugar Trade: The Braga Brothers Collection," Thomson Gale, 2006, Reel 45.
14 In 1912, Gómez had overseen the Cuban state's violent massacre in response to the Partido Independiente de Color's political rebellion, yet he apparently saw no contra-

diction between his violent overreaction to the PIC uprising and leading a political revolt himself.
15 McGillivray, *Blazing Cane*, 84–85; Pérez, *Cuba Under the Platt Amendment*, 61–67, 160–61.
16 Jenks, *Our Cuban Colony*, 194–95; Pérez, *Intervention, Revolution*, chapter 6.
17 IHC, *Movimiento obrero*, 1: 181–82; Zanetti and García, *Sugar and Railroads*, 303–4.
18 Dumoulin, *Azúcar y lucha*, 13, 57, 96; IHC, *Movimiento obrero*, 1: 182–85.
19 Dumoulin, *Azúcar y lucha*, 114–15.
20 Carr, "Mill Occupations," 134–35; de la Fuente, "Two Dangers," 42–44; Alexander, 24–25; IHC, *Movimiento obrero*, 1: 182–85.
21 Dumoulin, *Azúcar y lucha*, 183-184.
22 IHC, *Movimiento obrero*, 1: 200–201.
23 "News Letter from Our Havana Office," *Louisiana Planter and Sugar Manufacturer*, December 18, 1918, 359
24 IHC, *Movimiento obrero*, 1: 200; Zanetti and García, *Sugar and Railroads*, 304–5.
25 "Entrevista efectuada a Rafael Hernández," May 28, 1986, conducted as part of the project Historia del Movimiento Comunista en la actual provincia Holguín, AHPH, Colección Movimiento Obrero (hereafter MO) No. 122; Zanetti and García, *United Fruit*, 237.
26 Shaffer, *Anarchist Cuba*, 83; Zanetti and García, *United Fruit*, 243–45.
27 Grobart, "Cuban Working Class," 76; Zanetti and García, *Sugar and Railroads*, 310–11; IHC, *Movimiento obrero*, 1: 219.
28 Zanetti and García, *Sugar and Railroads*, 311–13; IHC, *Movimiento obrero*, 1: 219–20.
29 Howard, *Black Labor, White Sugar*, 157–58. For an excellent account of the anarchist movement across the island and especially into the countryside, see Shaffer, "Havana Hub."
30 McGillivray, *Blazing Cane*, 155; Zanetti and García, *Sugar and Railroads*, 313–15.
31 McGillivray, *Blazing Cane*, 155–56; Zanetti and García, *Sugar and Railroads*, 315–16.
32 [illegible] To Manuel Rionda, Manatí Sugar Company, October 8, 1924, and To Manuel Rionda, October 18, 1924, LAHC Series 8, Reel 45.
33 McGillivray, *Blazing Cane*, 172–78.
34 "Ill Treatment of British West Indians in Cuba" Gainer to British Legation, Havana, July 20, 1924 (Registry No. A 4290/13/14) and "Ill Treatment of British West Indians in Cuba" Gainer to British Legation, Havana, May 17, 1924 (Registry No. 3391/13/14). See also, Henry Hayden to HBM Charge d'Affaires, Havana, June 7, 1924 (No. A 4567/13/14) and "Ill Treatment of British West Indians in Cuba" Gainer to British Legation, Havana, May 8, 1924 (Registry No. 3385/13/14) all in UKNA, Foreign Office Records (hereafter FO) 371.
35 Henry Hayden to HBM Charge d'Affaires, Havana, June 7, 1924, UKNA, FO 371 Registry No.A 4567/13/14. See also "Ill Treatment of British West Indians in Cuba" Gainer to British Legation, Havana, May 8, 1924, UKNA.
36 Howard, *Black Labor, White Sugar*, 163–64.
37 "Ill Treatment of British West Indians in Cuba" Gainer to British Legation, Havana, April 26, 1924, UKNA, FO 371, Registry No. 3385/13/14.
38 Alexander, *Organized Labor in Cuba*, 29; Howard, *Black Labor, White Sugar*, 159; Whitney, *State and Revolution*, 28.

39 For British West Indians' organizing tradition, see Giovannetti-Torres, "The Elusive Organization of Identity."
40 McLeod, "Los Braceros Antillanos," 145–46; McLeod, "Undesirable Aliens," 611–12.
41 Casey, *Empire's Guestworkers*, 145.
42 H. Shackleton to His Majesty's Minister, Havana, April 1, 1924, UKNA, FO 371, Registry No. 2903/13/14.
43 "Petition of the Natives of All the West Indian Islands Residing in Cuba, Prepared and Forwarded Under the Auspices of the West Indian Workers Union," April 23, 1924, UKNA, FO 371, Registry No. 2903/13/14.
44 Giovannetti-Torres, *Black British Migrants*, 128–29.
45 "Entrevista efectuada a Rafael Hernandez."
46 James, *Banes*, 245–51; Zanetti and García, *United Fruit*, 249–51.
47 Pupo, "Mella en el feudo"; Sabas Alomá, "Julio Antonio Mella."
48 James, *Banes*, 246–49; Zanetti and García, *United Fruit*, 250–52.
49 Zanetti and García, *United Fruit*, 68–70.
50 Pérez, *Ties of Singular Intimacy*, 126.
51 Zanetti and García, *United Fruit*, 68–70.
52 Muñiz, "Mella," 124. "Convocatoria y actas del congreso del fundación, Acta de la cuarta sesión," 1: 453.
53 Córdova, *Clase trabajadora*, 1: 130.
54 IHC, *Movimiento obrero*, 1: 230.
55 Benjamin, "The Machadato and Cuban Nationalism,"; Caballero, *Latin America and the Comintern*, 48–49; Rojas Blaquier, *El primer Partido*, 1:23–37.
56 For racism within the ranks of the PCC, see Tony Wood, "Another Country," 650; Carr, "Identity, Class, and Nation," 101. For percentages of Antillano workers, Schoenrich to Sec. State, "Desired repatriation . . ." July 18, 1931, USNA RG 59, Box 5945, No. 837.504/336.
57 "Juan" to "estimados compañeros," December 2, 1933, RGASPI, Fondo 495, Opis 105, Delo 68, cited in Carr, "Identity, Class, and Nation," 110. For the difficulty organizing workers, see Whitney, *State and Revolution*, 73–76; Carr, "Mill Occupations," 136–37; Soto, *La Revolución precursora*, 335–49; Zanetti and García, *United Fruit*, 237–39.
58 Hennessy, "Cuba," 107; Rojas Blaquier, *El primer Partido*, 1: 41.
59 Zanetti and García, *Sugar and Railroads*, 319.
60 Rojas Blaquier, *El primer Partido*, 1: 64, 71–73.
61 Rojas Blaquier, *El primer Partido*, 1: 58–69, 108.
62 Carr, "From Caribbean Backwater"; Erik Ching, "In Search of the Party"; Rojas Blaquier, *El primer Partido*, 1: 91–106.
63 Unsigned letter from Havana, May 19, 1929, "Informe sobre el Primero de mayo y el Congreso de Montevideo," RGASPI, Fondo 354, Opis 7, Delo 380, as cited in Carr, "From Caribbean Backwater," 238. Carr's translation.
64 Worley, "Courting Disaster," 4; Sixth Comintern Congress, "Extracts from the Theses of the Sixth Comintern Congress on the International Situation and the Tasks of the Communist International, August 29, 1928," in Degras, *Communist International*, 2: 455–56.

65 Sixth Comintern Congress, "Extracts from the Theses . . ." in Degras, *Communist International*, 2: 461.
66 Communist International, "Program of the Communist International Adopted at the Sixth Congress, September 1, 1928," in Degras, *Communist International*, 2: 521.
67 For the Comintern's "discovery" of Latin America, see Aguilar, "Introduction," 16–18; Becker, *Mariátegui and Latin American Marxist Theory*, chapter 1; Caballero, *Latin America and the Comintern*, 24; Carr, "Identity, Class, and Nation," 97; Rojas Blaquier, *El primer Partido*, 1: 93. For a summary of the evolving historiography of this discovery see footnotes 4 and 5 of Ching and Pakkasvirta, "Latin American Materials in the Comintern Archive," 140–41.
68 Aguilar, "Introduction," 17.
69 For an account of resistance efforts against US Marine occupations in the Americas, see McPherson, *The Invaded*. For the rising tide of Latin American anti-imperialism, see Carr, "Across Seas." For transnational support of Sandino, see Carr, "Pioneering Transnational Solidarity."
70 Ching, "In Search of the Party," 9, 12; Smith, *The Russians Aren't Coming*, 3.
71 Adi, *Pan-Africanism and Communism*, 47–85.
72 "Thesis on the National and Colonial Question Adopted by the Second Comintern Congress," July 28, 1920, reproduced in Degras, *Communist International*, 1: 138–44, 142.
73 "Thesis of the Fourth Comintern Congress on the Negro Question," November 30, 1922, in Degras, *Communist International*, 1: 399–401.
74 For the influence of Black diasporic figures on Moscow's position, see Kelley, *Freedom Dreams: The Black Radical Imagination*, 38.
75 Hill, "General Introduction" 3: xxxvi–xxxvii; Zumoff, "The African Blood Brotherhood," 213–17.
76 Post, *Arise Ye Starvelings*, 2–3.
77 Sandalio Junco, "El problema de la raza negra y el movimiento proletario," 160–76; Rios and Ávarez, "Los negros en Cuba como nacionalidad oprimida," September 26, 1932, RGASPI. Fondo 495, Opis 105, Delo 64, pp. 5–26,
78 McKay, "Garvey as a Negro Moses," *The Liberator*, April 1922.
79 McKay, *A Long Way from Home*, 354.
80 James, *Holding Aloft the Banner of Ethiopia*, 171; Martin, *Race First*, 238–41; Adi, "The Negro Question," 159.
81 Comintern, "Extracts from the Theses on the Revolutionary Movement in Colonial and Semicolonial Countries Adopted by the Sixth Comintern Congress" in Degras, *Communist International*, 2: 526–48, 46.
82 Adi, "The Negro Question"; Wood, "Another Country," 2022.
83 Wood, "Another Country," 649.
84 "Letter of the Central Committee of the CPUSA to the Central Committee of the CP of Cuba," *The Communist*, October 1930, 66.
85 Alberto Sánchez, "El Congreso Mundial del S.R.I. y las Secciones de los Países del Caribe," *MO*, February 1, 1933, 7, 18.
86 CSLA, "Resoluciones," 64–74.

87 CSLA, "Informe General Sobre La Situación Del Proletariado Latinoamericano y Los Trabajos Realizados Por El C.P.C.S.L.A." in CSLA, *CSL, Bajo de La Bandera*, 15–43, 26.
88 CSLA, "Informe General," 21, 27.
89 CSLA, "Programa de Reivindicaciones Inmediatas Para La Acción Del Proletariado Continental" in CSLA, *CSL, Bajo de La Bandera*, 75–86, 84.
90 Adi, *Pan-Africanism and Communism*, 296; Mahler, "The Red and the Black in Latin America," 3–4.
91 Junco, "El problema de la raza negra y el movimiento proletario," 160–76, 172–173.
92 Junco, "El problema de la raza negra," 165, 175; Melgar Bao, "Rearmando La Memoria," 156–58.
93 Lindner details the rich history of Mexico City as a space of anti-imperialist agitation hosting political exiles from across the Americas. Lindner, *A City Against Empire*.
94 Hatzky, *Julio Antonio Mella*, 265–300.
95 Rojas Blaquier, *El primer Partido*, 1: 108; Whitney, *State and Revolution*, 58, 67–68.
96 Moore, *Nationalizing Blackness*, 120–23.
97 "Manifesto del Partido Comunista de Cuba" originally published in *El machete* (no. 50, September 16, 1926) and reprinted in Pichardo Viñals, *Documentos para la historia*, 3: 352–53.
98 Hoernel, "Sugar and Social Change," 238; Pérez, *Cuba Under the Platt Amendment*, 265.
99 "Plataforma electoral del Partido Comunista de Cuba," in IHC, *El movimiento obrero cubano, documentos*, 2: 288–93.
100 "Editorial de *El Trabajador* exponiendo el programa de lucha del Partido Comunista de Cuba," in IHC, 2: 253–54. Originally published as "Por qué luchamos" *El Trabajador*, órgano del Comité Central del Partido Comunista de Cuba, July 1931, p. 1.
101 Córdova, *Clase trabajadora*, 1: 133; IHC, *Movimiento obrero*, 1: 225.
102 "Entrevista efectuada a Rafael Hernández;" Benjamin, "The Machadato and Cuban Nationalism," 70, 80–83; Rojas Blaquier, *El primer Partido*, 1: 106–10.
103 "Manifesto del Partido Comunista de Cuba con motivo del Día Continental del Desocupado," March 1930, reproduced in Rosell, *Luchas obreras contra Machado*, 163–64.
104 Fernando Martínez Heredia, "El héroe romántico," 196–97; Soto, *La revolución del 33*, 1: 172–73, footnote 24; Núñez Machín, *Rubén Martínez Villena*.
105 Roa, "Una semilla en un surco de fuego."
106 Núñez Machín, *Rubén Martínez Villena*, 199–200, 213.
107 García Domínguez and Rovira González, "Los 'Soviets'"; Carr, "Mill Occupations," 136.
108 James, *Banes*, 264–65; Zanetti and García, *United Fruit*, 255. "Entrevista efectuada a Rafael Hernandez."
109 Rojas Blaquier, *El primer Partido*, 1: 136–38.
110 "Un aspect del problema económico de Cuba" *Venezuela Libre*, Año V, I de junio de 1926, republished in Martinez Villena, *Rubén Martínez Villena: Poesía y prosa*, 76–82.
111 "To the Political Bureau of the C.C. of the Communist Party of the U.S. from Martínez Villena" [Undated, but not long after March 1930] RGASPI, Fondo 495, Opis 105, Delo 33, pp. 47–50. Original is in English.

112 "Aux Partis Communistes des Etats Unis, de France, d'Angleterre et de Hollande de le Secrétariat politique," March 27, 1930, RGASPI, Fondo 495, Opis 3 Political Secretariat of the EECCI, Delo 161, pp. 12–16.
113 L. Miranda to Harrison George, May 19, 1930, RGASPI, Fondo 495, Opis 105, Delo 33, pp. 47–50.
114 Stevens, *Red International and Black Caribbean*, 2.
115 Pujals, "A 'Soviet Caribbean,'" 260.
116 O. Rodriguez, "Our Present Tasks in Cuba," *The Communist*, June 1931, 516–524, 524.
117 "Mundo Obrero," *MO*, July 1931.
118 "Huelgas de Masas en los Centrales Azucareros de Cuba," *MO,* March–April 1933, 22.
119 Rojas Blaquier, *El primer Partido*, 1:137–39, 150–59.
120 CNOC, "¡Obreros Azucareros, preparan vuestras luchas!" February 8, 1932, IHC Fondo 1: Signatura 1/8:7/17.1
121 Pérez de la Riva, "Cuba y la migración antillana," 70.
122 "Manifesto de la Primera Confederación de Obreros de la Industria Azucarera, Celebrado bajo de las Auspicios de la CNOC y de la Confederación Sindical Latino-Americana" [Date NA, but must be December 1932] IHC Fondo 1, Signatura 1/8:87/2.1/1–8.
123 Carr, "Mill Occupations," 136–37; Soto, *La Revolución precursora*, 335–49.
124 "Manifesto de la Primera Confederación de Obreros de la Industria Azucarera."
125 Albert Granda, Sec. De Educación y Propaganda, SNOIA Comité Ejecutivo Nacional "Circular: A Todos los Comités de Delegaciones de Ingenio, Colonia, Plantación, Etc.," August 10, 1933, IHC, Fondo 1; Signatura 1/8:87/6.1/1–21(.2).
126 Wood, "Another Country." Wood's archival research revealed that the authors of the report, which I have also reviewed, were Ramón Nicolau and Aggeo Suárez Pérez, although the report is signed "Rios" and "Álvarez," p. 643.
127 Rios and Ávarez, "Los negros en Cuba," 24.
128 Wood, "Another Country," 652.
129 SNOIA, "Proyecto de resoluciones para la segunda conferencia nacional" June 16, 1933, IHC, Fondo 1: Signatura 1/8:87/3.1/1.6.
130 "PCC, Carta orgánica de las células comunistas," [Date, NA] RGASPI, Fondo 495, Opis 105, Delo 25.
131 "Circular sobre la reunión y preparación del Primer Congreso Nacional de 'DOI.'"
132 DOI, "Composición de DOI" [1933] IHC, Fondo 1: Signatura 1/8:223/5.1/1–109 p. 108; "Circular sobre la reunión y preparación del Primer Congreso Nacional de 'DOI.'"
133 Benjamin, "The Machadato and Cuban Nationalism," 72, 85. The PCC and its sister organizations did not simply recruit the same individuals to multiple associations; rather only 10 of the DOI's members were also PCC members, and only 40 belonged to a CNOC-affiliated union, but 70 belong to noncommunist "reformist" organizations, signifying a diversity of members and indicating that the DOI achieved its goal of reaching out to potential members across political tendencies. "Composición de DOI."
134 García Domínguez and Rovira González, "Los 'Soviets'"; García and Mironchuk, *Los soviets obreros y campesinos en Cuba*; Soto, *La Revolución precursora*, 340–42.
135 Carr, "Mill Occupations," 137.

136 Rubén Martínez Villena, "Las contradicciones internas del imperialismo yanqui en Cuba y el alza del movimiento revolucionario," *MO*, May 1, 1933. The essay was translated into English and printed in *The Communist* the following month. The quotes in the following analysis are from the English essay. Rubén Martínez Villena, "The Rise of the Revolutionary Movement in Cuba," *The Communist*, June 1933.
137 Martínez Villena, "Rise of the Revolutionary Movement," 559, 561.
138 Martínez Villena, "Rise of the Revolutionary Movement," 560, 563, 566, 567.
139 Roumain, *Masters of the Dew*, 49–50.
140 Roumain, 89–90.
141 Roumain, 47,103.
142 Post, *Arise Ye Starvelings*, 5, 133, 146.
143 Bolland, *On the March*; Bolland, *The Politics of Labour*, chapter 5.
144 Shaffer, *Anarchists of the Caribbean*, 22.
145 Mahler, "South–South Organizing."

Chapter 4. "Hands Off Cuba"

1 For "Zapata's" identity, see Rojas Blaquier, *El primer Partido*, 1: 221, n.b. 426.
2 "Zapata," "Informe No. 8 to Comité Distrital #2," September 8, 1933, RGASPI, Fondo 495, Opis 105, Delo 77, pp. 45–50.
3 Carr, "Mill Occupations"; García Domínguez and Rovira González, "Los 'Soviets'"; Whitney, *State and Revolution*, 110.
4 Aguilar, *Cuba 1933*; Carrillo, *Cuba 1933*; Whitney, *State and Revolution*; Soto, *La Revolución precursora*.
5 Whitney, *State and Revolution*, 82–85; Benjamin, *The United States and Cuba*, 86; Soto, *La Revolución precursora*, 320–33.
6 Reig Romero, "Cronología," 284–85; Núñez Machín, *Rubén Martínez Villena*, 240–41.
7 Commission on Cuban Affairs and Buell, *Problems of the New Cuba*, 11; Soto, *La Revolución precursora*, 362–401; Whitney, *State and Revolution*, 83–93; Carr, "From Caribbean Backwater," 241–42.
8 For the "August mistake" see, Soto, *La Revolución precursora*, 444–55.
9 For a first-hand account of *antimachadista* violence in Santiago de Cuba, see Cuban American actor and bandleader Desi Arnaz' autobiography. His father, Desiderio Alberto Arnaz, had been mayor of Santiago and a congressman under Machado. Arnaz, *A Book*, 23–32.
10 For a biography of Batista, see Argote-Freyre, *Fulgencio Batista*.
11 Whitney, *State and Revolution*, 102–6; McGillivray, *Blazing Cane*, 207–10; IHC, *Movimiento obrero*, 1: 298–300; Soto, *La Revolución precursora*, 547–58.
12 "Intervention is Put Off," *New York Times*, September 8, 1933, 1.
13 "Fascists of Cuba Plan War on Reds," *New York Times*, September 20, 1933, 1.
14 Portuondo Moret, *Tacajó*, 56–57.
15 The most comprehensive descriptions of the sugar insurgency are Carr, "Mill Occupations"; García Domínguez and Rovira González, "Los 'Soviets'"; García and Mironchuk, *Los soviets obreros*; Portuondo Moret, *Tacajó*; Soto, *La Revolución precursora*, 335–54.
16 Commission on Cuban Affairs and Buell, *Problems of the New Cuba*, 183–84.

17 Rojas Blaquier, *El primer Partido*, 1: 205.
18 SNOIA "Datos sobre huelgas azucareras en el interior . . ." September 16, 1933, IHC Fondo 1: Signatura 1/8:87/9.1/1–3.
19 González and Luis, "Los enclaves azucareros."
20 The most thorough accounts of the soviet at Tacajó are Rojas, *Luchas obreras*, 67–90; Portuondo Moret, *Tacajó*, 63–76.
21 Rojas, *Luchas obreras*, 73–74.
22 Russell Porter, "6 American Mills in Cubans' Hands," *New York Times*, September 9, 1933; Rojas, 74.
23 Portuondo Moret, *Tacajó*, 69; Rojas, *Luchas obreras*, 83. See also, McGillivray, *Blazing Cane*, 211, 215; Carr, "Mill Occupations," 135.
24 Emiliano, "Informe de la situación del movimiento revolucionario en las provincias de Oriente y Camagüey," September 18, 1933, RGASPI, Fondo 495, Opis 105, Delo 82 pp. 29–35.
25 "La revolución agraria-antiimperialista en marcha," *Bandera Roja*, October 1933.
26 Ambassador Welles to Sec. State, September 20, 1933, USNA, RG 59, Folder 1, 837.00B/72.
27 Rojas, *Luchas obreras*, 85.
28 "Entrevista efectuada a Rafael Hernández"; James, *Banes*, 265–67.
29 "Zapata," "Informe No. 8."
30 Commission on Cuban Affairs and Buell, *Problems of the New Cuba*, 183.
31 "Zapata," "Informe No. 8"; James, *Banes*, 266–71; Zanetti and García, *United Fruit*, 257.
32 "Zapata," "Informe No. 8," 46.
33 "Zapata," "Informe No. 8," 46–47; James, *Banes*, 273–74.
34 "Biographía de Militantes," Roberto Buzón Neira, April 11, 1938, RGASPI, IBR, Opis 6, Subseries III, File 587, pp. 68–69.
35 "Zapata," "Informe No. 8," 46.
36 "Comité distrital de Oriente a Comité Central del PCC," September 11, 1933, RGASPI, Fondo 495, Opis 105, delo 82, pp. 27–29. See also, Emiliano, "Informe de la situación."
37 A. Granda, Delegado del Buró Nacional Del SNOIA "Conferencia Provincial de Oriente de Obreros de la Industria Azucarera" September 18, 1933, IHC, Fondo 1: Signatura 1/8:87/15.1/1–10; James, *Banes*, 271–74; Zanetti and García, *United Fruit*, 257–58.
38 "Zapata," "Informe No. 8," p. 48.
39 Archivo United Fruit Company, División Banes "Administración General" as cited in James, *Banes*, 272.
40 "La revolución agraria-antiimperialista en marcha."
41 Emiliano, "Informe de la situación."
42 Walker to Worcester, [Date unclear] AUFC, DB, "File Confidential," as cited in Zanetti and García, *United Fruit*, 258.
43 "Informe No. 8," 48–49; James, *Banes*, 272–75; Zanetti and García, *United Fruit*, 258.
44 SNOIA Delegación Regional del Central Boston, "Untitled," [September 1933], IHC, Fondo 1: 1/8:87/18.1/1–2.
45 Ambassador Welles to Sec. State, September 26, 1933, USNA, RG 59, Box 5924, folder 1. 837.00B/78.

46 James, *Banes*, 276–81; Zanetti and García, *United Fruit*, 259–60.
47 Russell B. Porter, "U.S. Warship is Rushed to Rescue 16 Americans and Britons in Cuba," *New York Times*, September 24, 1933; "U.S. Sends Marines as Cuba Masses Seize More Factories," *Western Worker*, October 2, 1933.
48 "General Strike at Manatí," September 25, 1933, Braga Brother's collection, as cited in Whitney, *State and Revolution*, 109.
49 "Zapata," "Informe No. 8," 46; Rojas, *Luchas obreras*, 81–83.
50 "Zapata," "Informe No. 8," 46; Rojas, *Luchas obreras*, 81–83. For the "flying brigades," see Carr, "Mill Occupations," 149; McGillivray, *Blazing Cane*, 212.
51 Núñez Machín, "Rafael de Hombre Mesa."
52 Granda, "Conferencia Provincial de Oriente."
53 "La revolución agraria-antiimperialista en marcha."
54 "Comité distrital de Oriente a Comité Central del PCC," September 11, 1933, RGASPI, Fondo 495, Opis 105, delo 82, pp. 27–29; Granda, "Conferencia Provincial."
55 See McGillivray's superb account, McGillivray, *Blazing Cane*, 217–25.
56 Quote is from Granda, "Conferencia Provincial de Oriente." See also, Emiliano, "Informe de la situación."
57 Granda, "Conferencia Provincial."
58 Carr, "Mill Occupations," 140, 156; McGillivray, *Blazing Cane*, 217.
59 Partido Bolchevique-Leninista, "Lo que pudo haber sido" enclosure to Dispatch #617, June 11, 1934, Ambassador to Sec. State, USNA, RG 59m Box 5924, folder 2, 837.00B/150.
60 McGillivray, *Blazing Cane*, 220.
61 For nonpayment of taxes see, "Cuba: Passive Anarchy," *Time*, October 2, 1933.
62 McGillivray, *Blazing Cane*, 220–22.
63 "La revolución agraria-antiimperialista en marcha."
64 Soto, *La revolución del 33*, 1977, 1:157. For the global campaign in defense of Sacco and Vanzetti, see Lindner, "Standing with Sacco and Sandino"; McGirr, "The Passion of Sacco and Vanzett."
65 Emiliano, "Informe de la situación del movimiento revolucionario."
66 Rojas, *Luchas obreras*, 82–83.
67 "La revolución agraria-antiimperialista en marcha."
68 Rios and Ávarez, "Los negros en Cuba como nacionalidad oprimida," September 26, 1932, RGASPI, Fondo 495, Opis 105, Delo 64, pp. 5–26.
69 Wood, "Another Country," 655–56.
70 SNOIA, "Datos sobre huelgas azucareras en el interior . . ."
71 "Zapata," "Informe No. 8."
72 "Juan" to "estimados compañeros," December 2, 1933, RGASPI, Fondo 495, Opis, 105, Delo 68 as cited in Carr, "Identity, Class, and Nation," 110.
73 Carr, *Identity, Class, and Nation,* 108–14; Carr, "Mill Occupations," 150–51; McLeod, "Undesirable Aliens," 604.
74 Granda, "Conferencia Provincial."
75 "La revolución agraria-antiimperialista en marcha."
76 "Revolucionario de las Masas Termina con la Dictadura Machadista," *MO*, August–September 1933.

77 Rojas, *Luchas obreras*, 76.
78 CNOC and SNOIA, "La zafra actual y las tareas de los obreros azucareros," January 1934, IHC Fondo 1: Signatura 1/8:87/1.1/2–11.
79 "Resoluciones de la III Conferencia Nacional Del Sindicato Nacional de Obreros de la Industria Azucarera," January 15–16, 1934, reprinted in IHC, *El movimiento obrero cubano, documentos*, pp. 2: 624–652.
80 Granda, "Conferencia Provincial."
81 *Facts about Sugar*, November 1933 as cited in Carr, "Identity, Class, and Nation," 111.
82 Carr, "Identity, Class, and Nation," 111–12. The company would later be careful to explain that it supported laws restricting foreigners to 50 percent of the workplace, but that it had no intention of applying 50 percent laws to each sector of its operations individually, but rather to its workforce as a whole. This position would allow the company to maintain a foreign majority in certain sectors, mainly cane cutting and hauling. See, "Labor difficulties of the United Fruit Company due to previsions of the fifty-percent Nationalization Labor Law." December 22, 1933, USNA, RG 59, Box 5945, 837.504/440.
83 Helg, *Our Rightful Share*, 176–77, 197.
84 "Llamado de la Confederación Sindical Latinoamericana en apoyo a Cuba" September 7, 1933, reprinted in IHC, *El movimiento obrero cubano, documentos*, 2: 420–24.
85 Translation of excerpt: Gomez, "Revolutionary Events in Cuba, and the Tasks of the Communist Party," *Communist International*, no. 25, p. 44, Moscow, September 1, 1933, Enclosure #1 in Felix Cole to Sec. State "Communist Leadership in Cuba," October 13, 1933, USNA, RG 59 Box 5924, Folder 1, 837.00B/95.
86 "Huelgas de masas en los centrales azucareros de Cuba," *MO*, April 1933.
87 Gray to Sec. State, October 9, 1933, USNA, RG 59, Box 5924, folder 1,837.00B/86; "A todos los pueblos explotados y oprimidos de Centro y Sur América," CPs of Mex, US, Panama, et. al., enclosure in Welles to Sec. State, September 22, 1933, USNA, RG59, Box 5924, Folder 3, 837.00B/75.
88 Harry F. Guggenheim to Sec. of State. December 31, 1931, USNA, RG 59, Box 5945, Folder 1, 837.00B/34. Lest the reader concludes that Guggenheim was a moderate figure and a defender of Cuba's working men and women, I point to his own account of US-Cuban relations, which opens with a racist depiction of the Cuban people, and the fact that Beals devoted an entire section of *The Crime of Cuba* to Guggenheim's complicity with US businesses. Guggenheim, *The United States and Cuba*; Beals, *The Crime of Cuba*, 223–54.
89 Welles to Sec. State, August 30, 1933, USNA, RG 59, Box 5924, Folder 1. 837.00B/54.
90 Welles to Sec. State, September 15, 1933.
91 Welles to Sec. State, October 24, 1933, USNA, RG 59, Box 5924, folder 1.
92 *Havana Post*, December 3, 1933, p. 1 as cited in Whitney, *State and Revolution*, 119.
93 See, for example, Soto, *La Revolución precursora*, 738.
94 Carr, "Mill Occupations," 130.
95 Carr, 130, 142–43; Whitney, *State and Revolution*, 97–99.
96 Emiliano, "Informe de la situación."
97 Guarda, F.C. del Buro Nacional del SNOIA (Santiago), "Informes sobre los puntos

salientes del problema azucarero en Oriente," September 17, 1933, IHC, Fondo 1, 1/8:87/7.1/1.
98 To the Administrator of the *Central Mabay* from the Comité de Huelga de Mabay, August 1933, IHC, Fondo 1: Signatura 1/8:87/21.1/1–9 and letter to Administrator of *Central Mabay* from Comité de Huelga de Mabay [Date NA but August 1933], IHC, Fondo 1: Signatura 1/8:87/21.1/2–3.
99 See a series of bulletins issued by the Mabay strike committee. ("Boletín de Huelga No 2. A los obreros de Mabay y masas explotados en genera," IHC, Fondo 1: Signatura 1/8:87/21.1/5; "Boletín Num. 4—A todos los trabajadores del central y las colonias" [Date NA], 1/8:87/21.1/6–8; "Boletín Num. 5, del CNOC Sección Sindical de Mabay del SNOI, Comité de Huelga," 1/8:87/21.1/109.)
100 A report from Tacajó mentions the "great influence" of the party at Macabí, home to the Boston Mill. "La revolución agraria-antiimperialista en marcha."
101 Rojas Blaquier, *El primer Partido*, 1:221.
102 "La revolución agraria-antiimperialista en marcha"; Emiliano, "Informe de la situación."
103 "Zapata," Informe No. 8.
104 "La revolución agraria-antiimperialista en marcha."
105 Partido Bolchevique-Leninista, "Lo que pudo haber sido (Ay... ¡y no fué!)" enclosure to dispatch from US Embassy at Havana to Sec. State, June 11, 1934, USNA, RG 59, Box 5924, Folder 2; "La revolución agraria-antiimperialista en marcha;" McGillivray, *Blazing Cane*, 217.
106 Emiliano, "Informe de la situación."
107 "La revolución agraria-antiimperialista en marcha."
108 PBL, "Lo que puder haber sido."
109 Soto, *La revolución del 33*, 1977, 3: 155.
110 Luis Ortíz, "El Empuje Revolucionario de las masas termina con la dictadura machadista," *MO*, August-September 1933, 12–13.
111 Caribbean Bureau to Central Committee of the PCC, October 31, 1933, RGASPI, Fondo 500, Opis 1, Delo 12.
112 García Domínguez and Rovira González, "Los 'Soviets,'" 224; Soto, *La revolución del 33*, 1977, 3: 142.
113 Soto, *La revolución del 33*, 1977, 3: 142.
114 For instructions regarding soviets, see "¿Que son los soviets?," *Bandera Roja*, October 1933. For the early August PCC platform, see "Communist Program of Action" as reproduced in Martin Kaye, Louise Perry, and Anti-Imperialist League of the United States, "Who Fights for a Free Cuba" (Workers Library Publishers, PRISM: Political & Rights Issues & Social Movements, 1933), 34, UCF Libraries Special Collections, http://purl.flvc.org/FCLA/DT/363430. See also, IHC, *Movimiento obrero*, 1: 289–91.
115 G. Sinani, "The New Phase in the Revolutionary Events in Cuba," *The Communist*, December 1933, 1221–1230.
116 Caribbean Bureau to Central Committee of the PCC, October 31, 1933.
117 Caribbean Bureau to CC of the PCC, October 31, 1933.
118 For a summary, see IHC, *El movimiento obrero cubano, documentos*, 2: 393–94.

119 McGillivray, *Blazing Cane*, 220. See also, IHC, *Movimiento obrero*, 1: 300–301. Similarly, Robert Whitney writes that the problem for the Grau coalition was that "while the left hand of the government (Guiteras) tried to build bridges with the working class and the poor, the government's right (Batista) was knocking them down." Whitney, *State and Revolution*, 115.
120 Whitney, *State and Revolution*, 107.
121 For example, see CNOC and SNOIA, "La zafra actual"; "IV Congreso Obrero de Unidad Sindical convocado por la CNOC" reprinted in Pichardo Viñals, *Documentos para la historia*, IV: 194–232, 208.
122 For example, see "La revolución agraria-antiimperialista en marcha."
123 Rojas Blaquier, *El primer Partido*, 1:201. This critique is repeated often in the historiography. See also, IHC, *Movimiento obrero*, 1: 301–2; Soto, *La Revolución precursora*, 583.
124 IHC, *Movimiento obrero*, 1: 299; Soto, *La Revolución precursora*, 596–99; Commission on Cuban Affairs and Buell, *Problems of the New Cuba*, 185.
125 Soto, *La revolución del 33*, 1977, 3: 172–73.
126 Welles to Sec. State, October 4, 1933, USNA, RG 59, Box 5924, folder 1. 837.00/41.31.
127 IHC, *Movimiento obrero*, 1: 695.
128 Carr, "Mill Occupations," 140–41; McLeod, "Undesirable Aliens," 604; Whitney, *State and Revolution*, 107; Carr, "From Caribbean Backwater," 247.
129 McGillivray, *Blazing Cane*, 222–23; Benjamin, *The United States and Cuba*, 181; Ferrer, *Cuba*, 247–247.
130 Rojas, *Luchas obreras*, 89–90.
131 IHC, *Movimiento obrero*, 1: 317.
132 "Entrevista efectuada a Rafael Hernández"; IHC, *Historia del movimiento obrero cubano* 1: 317–18; James, *Banes*, 275–81; Zanetti and García, *United Fruit*, 261–62.
133 Rojas, *Luchas obreras*, 91–101.
134 "Entrevista efectuada a Rafael Hernández."
135 Rojas, *Luchas obreras*, 159; Whitney, *State and Revolution*, 125; Commission on Cuban Affairs and Buell, *Problems of the New Cuba*, 16.
136 "A todos los pueblos explotados . . ."
137 Ortiz, "El empuje revolucionario," *MO*, August–September, 1933.
138 Caribbean Bureau to CPs of the Caribbean, November 14, 1933, RGASPI, Fondo 500, Opis 1, Delo 12, pp. 66–68.
139 Ortiz, "El empuje revolucionario."
140 "Huelgas de masas en los centrales azucareros de Cuba." See also, "Cuban Consul Ousts Reds," April 16, 1933, *New York Times*, 26.
141 Translation of Excerpt: Gomez, "Revolutionary Events in Cuba, and the Tasks of the Communist Party," *Communist International*, no. 25, p. 44, Moscow, September 1, 1933, Enclosure #1 in Cole to Sec. State "Communist Leadership in Cuba," October 13, 1933, USNA, RG 59 Box 5924, Folder 1, 837.00B/95.
142 Grace Hutchins, "Hands Off Cuba!," *Labor Defender*, October 1933, 51. The Anti-Imperialist League wrote along the same lines: "Wall Street says Cuba must be quiet. The American toilers must smash these war plans. Let our answer to Wall Street be,

'Cuba must be free!'" Kaye, Perry, and Anti-Imperialist League of the United States, "Who Fights for a Free Cuba."
143 Simons, "Hands Off Cuba."
144 James Ford, "Next Steps in the Struggles of the Cuban Masses," *Harlem Liberator*, August 26, 1933.
145 Beals, *Crime of Cuba*, Fourth Printing, 457.
146 "Desde los Estados Unidos: La solidaridad del proletariado norteamericano," *Bandera Roja*, October 20, 1933.
147 Gronbeck-Tedesco, *Cuba, the United States*, 59.
148 "Red Flag at City Hall Orders 'Hands Off Cuba,'" *New York Times*, September 13, 1933.
149 Blas Roca, "Forward to the Cuban Anti-Imperialist Popular Front," *The Communist*, October 1935, 966.
150 Special cable to the *New York Times*, "Reds at Our Consulate Routed," *New York Times*, September 15, 1933.
151 Ortiz, "El empuje revolucionario."
152 "The Communist Party at the Head of the Revolutionary Movement of the Toilers of Cuba," *Pravda*, No. 276, October 6, 1933, Moscow, translated and enclosed in Cole to Sec. State "Communist Leadership in Cuba" October 13, 1933, USNA, RG 59 Box 5924, Folder 1, 837.00B/95.
153 "Llamado de la Confederación Sindical Latinoamericana en apoyo a Cuba," September 7, 1933.
154 V. Molanphy to F.T.F. Dumont, American Consul General, September 22, 1933, USNA, RG 59, Box 5924, Folder 4, 837.00B/76.
155 Dumont, American Consul General, to Sec. State, September 26, 1933, USNA, RG 59, Box 5924, Folder 4, 837.00B/76, with enclosures.
156 "El Partido Comunista y los problemas de la revolución en Cuba," enclosure to Dumont to Sec. State, September 26, 1933.
157 H. Freeman Matthews, Chargé d'Affaires ad interim, to Sec. State, February 26, 1934, USNA, RG 59, Box 5924, Folder 2, 837.00B/118
158 "Discurso del Delegado del Partido Comunista de Cuba al Congreso Antiguerrero de Los E.U.," *Bandera Roja*, October 20, 1933.
159 *Pittsburgh Courier*, September 30, 1933, as cited in Horne, *Race to Revolution*, 230.
160 Horne, 224.
161 Horne, 228–30. See also, Guridy, "'War on the Negro,'" 53.
162 *Baltimore Afro-American*, September 9, 1933, as cited in Horne, *Race to Revolution*, 229.
163 Gronbeck-Tedesco, *Cuba, the United States*, 64.
164 Pérez, "Aspects of Hegemony," 61.
165 IHC, *Movimiento obrero*, 1: 165.
166 Guridy, "'War on the Negro,'" 50.
167 Defensa Obrera Internacional-Comité Ejecutivo Nacional "Circular—Asunto: 3 de Enero, culminación de la campaña contra el terror a los negros y embarque de Haitianos," December 21, 1933, IHC, Fondo 1: Signatura, 1/8:223:5.1/1–109.
168 Porter, "U.S. Warship is Rushed to Rescue"; Porter, "No Intervention in Cuba Now"; Guridy, "'War on the Negro,'" 55; Horne, *Race to Revolution*, 230.

169 Chomsky, "Barbados or Candada?," 436.
170 Chomsky, 443.
171 Arredondo, *El Negro En Cuba: Ensayo*.
172 Arredondo, 146–47.
173 Juan Maspons Franco "Informe," March 7, 1930, ANC, Fondo Sec. de la Presidencia, Leg. 48, Exp. 42.
174 Putnam, "Eventually Alien," 288–96; Commission on Cuban Affairs and Buell, *Problems of the New Cuba*, 212–13, footnote 31; Casey, *Empire's Guestworkers*, 236–37.
175 Giovannetti-Torres, "Before the Windrush," 67.
176 Putnam, "Eventually Alien," 278.
177 Commission on Cuban Affairs and Buell, *Problems of the New Cuba*, 211–17; Pérez de la Riva, "Cuba y la migración antillana," 70–71.
178 "Repatriación forzosa de extranjeros sin trabajo ni recursos; Decreto no. 2232 de 18 de octubre de 1933," reprinted in Pichardo Viñals, *Documentos para la historía*, IV: 80–82.
179 De la Fuente, *Nation for All*, 104; Casey, *Empire's Guestworkers*, 138–42; McLeod, "Undesirable Aliens."
180 Carr, "Identity, Class, and Nation," 106–7; McLeod, "Undesirable Aliens," 605; Giovannetti-Torres, *Black British Migrants*, 197–98.
181 Schoenrich, "Repatriation of Haitians by Cuban Government Officials" November 22, 1933; USNA, RG 59, Box 5945, 837.504/427; SNOIA, December 21, 1933, manifesto, "Contra el terror a los negros," IHC, Fondo 1: Signatura 1/8:223:5.1/1–109; "En Oriente cazan haitianos," *Bandera Roja*, January 5, 1934, 1–5, reprinted in IHC, *El movimiento obrero cubano, documentos*, 2: 653–54.
182 McLeod, "Undesirable Aliens," 604–5.
183 McLeod, 604–5; Giovannetti-Torres, *Black British Migrants*, 197–204; de la Fuente, *Nation for All*, 104.
184 Giovannetti-Torres, *Black British Migrants*, 200.
185 Giovannetti-Torres, 197–203.
186 CNOC, César Vilar, Secretario General del Pleno del Comité Ejecutivo Confederal a Central Mabay, November 2, 1933, IHC Fondo 1, Signatura, 1/8:7/4.1/1–3 p. 1; DOI-Comité Ejecutivo Nacional "Circular—Asunto: 3 de Enero."
187 "En Oriente cazan haitianos."
188 CNOC, "A Central Mabay."
189 CNOC and SNOIA, "A las masas," September 1933, IHC Fondo 1, Signatura1/8:87/22.1/1.
190 "La zafra actual."
191 "La revolución agraria-antiimperialista en marcha."
192 "La zafra actual."
193 "En Oriente cazan haitianos."
194 "Inicios de pogromos contra los negros en Camagüey," *Bandera Roja*, October 20, 1933.
195 For the Guerra Chiquita, see Ferrer, *Insurgent Cuba*, chapter 3.
196 DOI, "Circular—Asunto: 3 de Enero, culminacion de la campania contra el terror a los negros y embarque de Haitianos." December 21, 1933, IHC, Fondo 1: Signature 1/8:223:5.1/1–109.

197 DOI, "Culminación de la campaña contra el terror..."
198 Sullivan, "For the Liberty"; Miller, Pennybacker, and Rosenhaft, "Mother Ada Wright."
199 Zumoff, "Black Caribbean Migrants," 33, 44.
200 DOI, "Circular—Asunto: 3 Enero."
201 Rojas Blaquier, *El primer Partido*, 1: 206.
202 De la Fuente, *Nation for All*, 195; Whitney, *State and Revolution*, 116; Carr, "Identity, Class, and Nation," 109; Horne, *Race to Revolution*, 227–28; Wood, "Another Country," 655.
203 Whitney, *State and Revolution*, 117; de la Fuente, *Nation for All*, 195–98; Carr, "Identity, Class, and Nation," 103, 109; IHC, *Movimiento obrero*, 1: 324.
204 "¡Luchemos contra la cacería de haitianos! / Bajo Mendieta siguen embarcando haitianos igual que cuando Grau," *Bandera Roja*, June 16, 1934. See also, Blas Roca, Sec. Gen. to Comité Conjunto de Acción de Manzanillo, July 4, 1934, reprinted in IHC, *El movimiento obrero cubano, documentos*, 2: 779–80.
205 Stevens, *Red International and Black Caribbean*, 220.
206 Roca, "Forward to the Cuban Anti-Imperialist Popular Front," 957.
207 Tony Wood was kind enough to share a chapter of his dissertation with me. Wood, "The Problem of the Nation," 52–53 of chapter 5.
208 Roca, "Forward to the Cuban-Anti-Imperialist..."
209 Wood, "Another Country," 663.
210 CNOC-Mesa Ejecutiva "La nacionalización del trabajo: Una reivindicación imperiosa del pueblo cubano—Carta Abierta, May 1936," IHC Fondo 1, Signatura 1/8:7/11.1/1–8.
211 Wood, "Another Country"; Henderson, "Race, Discrimination." I have also contributed to this discussion. Sullivan, "Negro Question in Cuba."
212 Pappademos, *Black Political Activism*, 217; de la Fuente, *Nation for All*, 190–93; Wood, "Another Country," 662–63; Carr, "Pioneering Transnational Solidarity," 101.
213 Henderson, "Race, Discrimination," 259.
214 Whitney, *State and Revolution*, 182, 304. See also, Wood, who writes "Yet, across its short span, Grau's administration unleashed a political ferment that continued for much of the decade, placing key questions of sovereignty, democracy, and national liberation firmly on the agenda." Wood, "Another Country," 653–54.
215 McGillivray, *Blazing Cane*, 225.
216 Gronbeck-Tedesco, *Cuba, the United States*, 45.

Chapter 5. In Defense of the Spanish Republic

1 "Biografía de militantes: Ángel López Estévez," RGASPI, Fondo 545, Fondo 545: International Brigades of the Republican Army of Spain; Opis 6: Lists, Personal Files of fighters and commanders of International Brigades (herafter IBR-6), File 596, pp. 71–79. (I initially accessed these records at the New York University's Tamiment Library and Robert F. Wagner Labor Archives on microfilm. Subsequentially, they were digitized and available through the RGASPI website.) See also Nicolau González and IHC, *Cuba y la defensa*, 162.
2 "Relación de los Comunistas Cubanos," Date NA, but probably November 1938. RGASPI, IBR, Opis 5: Statistical data on the national composition of the International Brigades, File 585, p. 32.

3 "Biografía de Militantes: Roberto Buzón Neira" RGASPI, IBR, File 586, pp. 68–79.
4 The literature on the Spanish Civil War is exhaustive. For the tip of the iceberg in English, see Preston, *Revolution and War in Spain, 1931–1939*; Thomas, *The Spanish Civil War*.
5 Alpert, *A New International History of the Spanish Civil War*; Falcoff and Pike, *The Spanish Civil War*; Landis, *The Abraham Lincoln Brigade*; Requena Gallego and Sepúlveda Losa, *Las Brigadas Internacionales*; Hochschild, *Spain in Our Hearts*; Tremlett, *The International Brigades*.
6 Lambe, *No Barrier*, 74. For Cuban response to the Italian invasion of Ethiopia, see Lambe's chapter 2.
7 Fronczak, "Local People's Global Politics"; McDuffie, *Sojourning for Freedom*, 96–103; Yelvington, "Dislocando la diáspora"; Buelli, "The Hands Off Ethiopia Campaign"; Makalani, *In the Cause of Freedom*, chapter 7; Shadle, "The Unity of Black People."
8 Kelley, "Introduction: This Ain't Ethiopia But It'll Do," 20.
9 For estimates about the number of international brigadistas, see Jackson, *Fallen Sparrows*, 60–72; Graham, *The Spanish Civil War: A Very Short Introduction*, 123,42; Tremlett, *The International Brigades*. Castells puts the number of international volunteers much higher, at over 59,000. Castells Peig, *Las Brigadas Internacionales de La Guerra de España*, 443.
10 Lambe, *No Barrier*; Naranjo Orovio, *Cuba, otro escenario*; Urcelay-Maragnès, *La leyenda roja*; Alfonso Bello and Pérez Díaz, *Cuba en España*. We await with enthusiasm Kirsten Weld's forthcoming book on the Spanish Civil War's reverberations in Latin America, *Ruins and Glory: The Long Spanish Civil War in Latin America*.
11 Lambe, *No Barrier*, 2.
12 Nicólas Guillén, speech given at the closing session of the Congreso Internacional de Escritores en Defensa de la Cultura, Paris, July 16, 1937, reprinted in Guillén, *Prosa de prisa, 1929–1972*, 1: 83–85.
13 Lambe, *No Barrier*, 104, 123.
14 Urcelay-Maragnès, *La leyenda roja*, 48.
15 "New York, 6-8-1936," in de la Torriente Brau, *Cartas y crónicas de España*, 21–22.
16 Figures of Cuban volunteers in the war are hard to pin down for a variety of reasons, not the least of which is the fact that many Cubans integrated directly into the Spanish Popular Army. Institut mezhdunarodnogo rabochego dvizheníià (Akademiíà nauk SSSR) and Sovetskii komitet veteranov voiny, *International Solidarity with the Spanish Republic, 1936–1939*, 103; Nicolau González and IHC, *Cuba y la defensa*, 293–301; Vera Jiménez, "Cubanos en la Guerra Civil Española," 318; Urcelay-Maragnès, *La leyenda roja*, 82. María Mercedes Sánchez Dotres and Enrique Cirules place the number at 1,225. Luis Hernández Serrano, "Valioso aporte de Cuba en la lucha antifascista," *Juventude Rebelde*, abril 2011; Hernández Serrano, "Expedientes cubanos de gloria en Guerra Civil Española (entrevista a Enrique Circules y Maria Mercedes Sánchez),"*Juventude Rebelde*, abril 2011. Baumann offers numbers on all Latin American volunteers. Baumann, *Los volunarios latinoamericanos*, 39.
17 Nicolau González and IHC, *Cuba y la defensa*; Lafita, *Dos héroes cubanos en el 5to regimento*.

18 Jorge Almeyda Montaña, "Como se labora en Oriente para ayudar a la República Española," *Facetas de Actualidad Española*, September 1937, 33.
19 Falcoff and Pike, *The Spanish Civil War*.
20 González Martínez and Sánchez Baena, "El apoyo," 381.
21 Hennessy, "Cuba," 108–11.
22 Hennessy, 105, 110.
23 De la Fuente, *Nation for All*, 195.
24 Naranjo Orovio, *Cuba vista por el emigrante español*, 37; Pérez, *Cuba: Between Reform and Revolution*, 101.
25 Hennessy, "Cuba," 108–11.
26 McGillivray, *Blazing Cane*, 159–72.
27 Gordón Ordás, *Mi política fuera de España*, 2: 119.
28 Alfonso Bello and Pérez Díaz, *Cuba en España*, 144; Naranjo Orovio, *Cuba, otro escenario*, 1–57; Figueredo Cabrera, *Cuba y la Guerra Civil Española*.
29 Thomas, *The Spanish Civil War*, 503.
30 "Información Social," *Hoy*, May 17, 1938, 9; "Información Social" *Hoy*, May 18, 1938, 9.
31 Hennessy, "Cuba," 128.
32 Edwardo P. Marzoa, "Quijotadas," *Hoy*, May 17, 1938, 4; "La prensa dice," *Hoy*, May 17, 1938, 2.
33 Naranjo Orovio, *Cuba, otro escenario*, 94–105.
34 For an excellent English summary of de la Torriente's life, see Lambe, *No Barrier*, chapter 1.
35 Baumann, *Los volunarios latinoamericanos*, 184–86; Suárez Díaz, *Escape de Cuba*, 25–28; Gronbeck-Tedesco, *Cuba, the United States*, 57–61; Lambe, *No Barrier*, 77.
36 See R. Roa's speech at the April 1937 Havana commemoration of de la Torriente's life and work in Roa, *Pablo*, 16.
37 Alfonso Bello and Pérez Díaz, *Cuba en España*, 149–50; Gronbeck-Tedesco, *Cuba, the United States*, 39–42, 58–59; Lambe, *No Barrier*, 40–41.
38 Roa, *Pablo*, 17.
39 De la Torriente Brau, "New York, 6-8-1936."
40 Urcelay-Maragnès, *La leyenda roja*, 65; Lambe, *No Barrier*, 1.
41 Baumann, *Los volunarios latinoamericanos*, 185.
42 For de la Torriente Brau's writing from the Spanish Front, see de la Torriente Brau, *Peleando con los milicianos*.
43 Lambe, *No Barrier*, 91.
44 Alfonso Bello and Pérez Díaz, *Cuba en España*, 142; Hennessy, "Cuba," 123–27; Urcelay-Maragnès, *La leyenda roja*, 58–61.
45 Hennessy, "Cuba," 124–26.
46 Lambe, *No Barrier*, 189–90.
47 Lambe, 190; Whitney, *State and Revolution*, 169.
48 González Martínez and Sánchez Baena, "El apoyo," 380–82; Whitney, *State and Revolution*, 165–70.
49 Domingo, *El Exilio Republicano Español En Cuba*, 24; Institut mezhdunarodnogo rabochego dvizheniíà (Akademiíà nauk SSSR) and Sovetskii komitet veteranov voiny,

International Solidarity with the Spanish Republic, 1936–1939, 102; Urcelay-Maragnès, *La leyenda roja*, 47–48.
50 Urcelay-Maragnès, *La leyenda roja*, 48; Lambe, *No Barrier*, chapter 4; Naranjo Orovio, *Cuba, otro escenario*, 87–94.
51 Hennessy, "Cuba," 129.
52 Almeyda Montaña "Como se labora en Oriente," 33–46.
53 "Tres Actos de Adhesión al Pueblo Español," *Facetas de Actualidad Española*. 1:6, May 1937, 19–20. The many lectures delivered at the *Homenaje a Torriente Brau* are reprinted in this same issue of *Facetas*.
54 Spanish Ambassador to Cuba and Mexico, Gordón Ordás, describes many such events in his autobiographical work. See vol. 2 of Gordón Ordás, *Mi política fuera de España*, 1965.
55 "Como en 1808, hemos regresado al pueblo y estamos viviendo de nuevo los episodios de Galdós," *Noticias de Hoy,* May 19, 1938, 1, 10.
56 "Azúcar y tabaco para los leales," *Noticias de Hoy*, May 18, 1938, 1, 10. See also, Ambassador Gordón's account of donations to the Republic, Gordón Ordás, *Mi política fuera de España*, 2: 117–21.
57 "Organización," *Nosotros*, 1:10, November 1938, 26–27.
58 As Urcelay-Maragnès explains, it is unclear whether the PCC began its Spanish campaign in August, with the creation of a Solidarity Committee in Paris, or in November, after Georgi Dimitrov, Secretary General of the Communist International, called for the recruitment of volunteers and thus facilitated the creation of the International Brigades. Urcelay-Maragnès, *La leyenda roja*, 51–52.
59 "Buró Político, Blas Roca, Sec. General Resolución del Buró Político del Primer Partido Comunista de Cuba," November 18, 1936, reprinted in Nicolau González and IHC, *Cuba y la defensa*, 205–7.
60 See, for example "El Conflicto Italo-Abisinio," *Adelante* 1, no. 5 (October 1933): 8–9,18; "Cuba y Abisinia," *Adelante* 11, no. 6 (November 1935): 3. See also, Pappademos, *Black Political Activism*, 180.
61 Lambe, *No Barrier*, chapter 2.
62 The 1930s dialogue between Harlem intellectuals and the *negritude/afro-Cubanismo* movements in the Caribbean is just one example of these conversations. Nicolás Guillén and Langston Hughes, already in contact with one another through their respective travels, spent significant time together in Spain, while forging new contact with Haitian writer Jacques Roumain. See Fowler, "The Shared Vision of Langston Hughes and Jacques Roumain."
63 Nicólas Guillén, speech given at the closing session of the Congreso Internacional de Escritores en Defensa de la Cultura, Paris, July 16, 1937, reprinted in Guillén, 83–85.
64 Nicolás Guillén's "Un pelotero," *Mediodía,* December 6, 1937, reprinted in Guillén, 107–110.
65 Guillén, Speech given to the Congreso Internacional de Escritores en Defensa de la Cultura in Madrid, July 6, 1937, printed in *Mediodia*, August 17, 1937, and published in Guillén, 80–82.
66 Guillén, July 6, 1937, Speech given to the Congreso Internacional.

67 Guillén, Closing Speech, July 16, 1937, in Guillén , 83–85.
68 For additional references to "Trigo," see "Entrevista realizada a Mario Ortiz Drigg," October 21, 1986, AHPH, Colección Movimiento Obrero (MO): No 4.
69 Transcript of "Entrevista efectuada a Rafael Hernández." May 28, 1986, AHPH, MO: No. 122. See also, "Directorio Nacional de la A.A.N.P.E.," reprinted in Naranjo Orovio, *Cuba, otro escenario*, Appendix II.
70 Almeyda Montaña, "Como se labora en Oriente," 33.
71 Almeyda Montaña, 37.
72 Almeyda Montaña, 36–39.
73 Naranjo Orovio, *Cuba, otro escenario*, 86.
74 Almeyda Montaña, "Como se labora en Oriente," 36–39.
75 Gordón Ordás, "*Mi política fuera de España*," 1: 165–68.
76 Quote is taken from "Entrevista con Ramón Vidal Zaldivar," April 8, 1988, AHPH, MO: No. 255. See also, "Entrevista realizada a Mario Ortiz Drigg"; Sonia Sanfiel, "Alfredo Sánchez," April 8, 1988, AHPH, MO: No 259.
77 "Entrevista realizada a Mario Ortiz Drigg."
78 Naranjo Orovio, *Cuba, otro escenario*, 68–69.
79 "Organización," 26–27.
80 "Entrevista efectuada a Rafael Hernández."
81 "Bases Estatutarias, Circulo Republicano Español," November 14, 1937, AHPSC, GP: Legajo 2567, Expediente 2.
82 Cuba Importadora y Industrial, *Anuario Azucarero de Cuba, 1937*, 28–31.
83 Almeyda Montaña, "Como se labora en Oriente," 45–46.
84 "Faustino Fraile, Secretario del Circulo Español Socialista, a Antonio Pimentel Herrera, Gobenador," September 5, 1937, and "Bases Estatutarias, Circulo Español Socialista," September 5, 1937, AHPSC, GP, Leg. 2567, Exp. 7.
85 "Bases Estatutarias, Circulo Español Socialista."
86 "Entrevista realizada a Mario Ortiz Drigg"; "Alfredo Sánchez."
87 "Entrevista realizada a Mario Ortiz Drigg"; "Entrevista efectuada a Rafael Hernández."
88 Vera Jiménez, "Cubanos en la Guerra Civil Española," 296–97.
89 These same forms do not ask about racial background, so information about the racial identity of Cuban volunteers has to be discerned from other sources and the rare photos attached to PCE files.
90 Vera Jiménez, "Cubanos en la Guerra Civil española," 297–98.
91 Castells Peig, *Las Brigadas Internacionales de La Guerra de España*, 38–41. Their early incorporation into the ERP means that archival documentation on their activities is harder to pin down than that of members of the International Brigades, who had to fill out membership applications to the PCE in order to be repatriated.
92 Lola Jiménez, "Maria Luisa Lafita: Una cubana en la guerra civil," *¡Unidad y Lucha!*, February 22, 2015; Nydia Sarabia and María Luisa Lafita, "Cubanas antifascistas en la Guerra Civil Española," *Granma*, March 8, 2005; Argenteri, *Tina Modotti*, 164.
93 Nicolau González and IHC, *Cuba y la defensa*, 138–137; "Personnel File for Luis Rubiales Martínez," January 8, 1939, RGASPI, IBR, File 600, p. 148.
94 Nicolau González and IHC, 82–85; Alfonso Bello and Pérez Díaz, *Cuba en España*, 260. Unfortunately, no personnel file exists for Lafarga. Pelayo was only released con-

ditionally from prison in 1945 and, with help from Cuban diplomats, departed from Spain later that year. Nicolau González and IHC, *Cuba y la defensa*, 48–49; Vera Jiménez, "Cubanos en la Guerra Civil española," 297.
95 Vera Jiménez, "Cubanos en la Guerra Civil española," 297–98.
96 Lambe, *No Barrier*, 137–38.
97 Alfonso Bello and Pérez Díaz, *Cuba en España*, 149–50; Urcelay-Maragnès, *La leyenda roja*, 63–64.
98 Tisa, *Recalling the Good Fight*, 16,17.
99 Lafita, *Rodolfo Ricardo Ramón de Armas y Soto*; Lambe, *No Barrier*, 100.
100 Alfonso Bello and Pérez Díaz, *Cuba en España*, 150–51; Vera Jiménez, "Cubanos en la Guerra Civil española," 305–11.
101 Tisa, *Recalling the Good Fight*, 24.
102 Castells Peig, *Las Brigadas Internacionales de La Guerra de España*, 155; Thomas, *The Spanish Civil War*, 557, note 2.
103 Alfonso Bello and Pérez, Nicolau, and Urcelay-Maragnès mention that Gómez was a founding member and treasurer of the Club Mella. Alfonso Bello and Pérez Díaz, *Cuba en España*, 149; Nicolau González and IHC, *Cuba y la defensa*, 189; Urcelay-Maragnès, *La leyenda roja*, 66. Gómez himself, however, didn't list founder-but rather "secretary general," "agitprop," and "treasurer" when detailing his Club Mella leadership roles in his "Biografia de Militantes." See, "Personnel File for Ricardo Gómez Oliva."
104 Personnel File for Ricardo Gómez Oliva, June 23, 1938, RGASPI, IBR, File 594, p. 5.
105 Nicolau writes that he "saw directly the terror and exploitation imposed upon the banana workers in Central America." Nicolau González and IHC, *Cuba y la defensa*, 188–89.
106 "Personnel File for Ricardo Gómez Oliva;" Nicolau González and IHC, 188–89. For de Armas y Soto in the merchant marine strike, see Lafita, *Rodolfo Ricardo Ramón de Armas y Soto*, 65–66.
107 "Personnel File for Ricardo Gómez Oliva."
108 "Personnel File for Ricardo Gómez Oliva."
109 Nicolau González and IHC, *Cuba y la defensa*, 8.
110 Alfonso Bello and Pérez Díaz, *Cuba en España*, 147.
111 Nicolau González and IHC, *Cuba y la defensa*, 9–10; Urcelay-Maragnès, *La leyenda roja*, 54–55.
112 Nicolau González and IHC, *Cuba y la defensa*, 9; Vera Jiménez, "Cubanos en la Guerra Civil española," 311–12.
113 The XV Brigade's 24th Battalion, the "Spanish Battalion," was later assigned the number 59, but continued to be known as the 24th division. Vera Jiménez, "Cubanos en la Guerra Civil española," 313. Thanks to an excellent publicity campaign by the CPUSA, the XV Brigade, which was composed of several battalions including the British and French Battalions in addition to the Abraham Lincoln Battalion, became popularly, albeit incorrectly, known as the "Lincoln Brigade."
114 Alfonso Bello and Pérez Díaz, *Cuba en España*, 147.
115 "Biographía de Militantes," Roberto Buzón Neira.

116 "Biographía de Militantes," Roberto Buzón Neira; Nicolau González and IHC, *Cuba y la defensa*, 39; Vera Jiménez, "Cubanos en la Guerra Civil española," 313.
117 Hennessy, "Cuba," 139; Nicolau González and IHC, *Cuba y la defensa*, 37.
118 Roberto Buzón to Y. Curiel.
119 Roberto Buzón to Y. Curiel.
120 Nicolau González and IHC, *Cuba y la defensa*, 37–39.
121 Nicolau González and IHC, 36–45.
122 De la Fuente, *Nation for All*, 216.
123 Nicolau González and IHC, *Cuba y la defensa*, 38–41.
124 "Información de Cuba" *Orientacion*, March 31, 1939, RGASPI, Opis 4: Documents of the former volunteers of the international brigades of the Republican Army Interned in the Concentration Camps of France and North Africa, File 20: Bulletin of the Cuban Group. Unfortunately, this bulletin contains almost no bylines.
125 Nicolau González and IHC, *Cuba y la defensa*, 45. We can only speculate about whether mention of the United States was actually in his 1939 lecture or whether his memory was influenced by the 1959 revolution.
126 Lambe, *No Barrier*, 15. Juan Marinello made a similar comparison, echoing José Martí's notion of "good" and "bad" Spaniards, Hennessy, "Cuba," 142–43.
127 Personnel file for "López Estévez, Angel," December 30, 1938, RGASPI, Opis 6, File 596, pp. 73-79.
128 "Carlos Manuel Alejandro Laurell Olivera," Date NA, 1938 Tamiment, RGASPI, International Brigade Records, Opis 6, Subseries III, File 596, pp. 10–17.
129 Thomas and Morgan-Witts, *Voyage of the Damned*, 66, 154–70.

Conclusion

1 Dosal, *Doing Business with the Dictators*; Striffler, *In The Shadows of State and Capital*; Zanetti and García, *United Fruit*. For a literary take, see García, *One Hundred Years of Solitude*.
2 West, "Decolonization, Desegregation, and Black Power."
3 Guerra, *Heroes, Martyrs, and Political Messiahs*, 82–83.
4 For Chibás, see Ehrlich, *Eduardo Chibás*.
5 Guerra, *Heroes, Martyrs, and Political Messiahs*, 14.
6 Randall, *Exporting Revolution*; Brown, *Cuba's Revolutionary World*; Hatzky, *Cubans in Angola*.
7 Gleijeses, *Conflicting Missions*, 8.
8 Hatzky, *Cubans in Angola*, 4-5.
9 Hatzky, Part III.
10 Kirk, *Healthcare Without Borders*, 3.
11 "The Hidden World of the Doctors Cuba Sends Overseas," BBC, May 14, 2019, https://www.bbc.com/news/uk-48214513
12 Lambe, *No Barrier*, 211–12.
13 Lambe, 212; Casuso, *Cuba and Castro*, 50–84.

14 Roberto Buzón to Y. Curiel, April 15, 1938, "Personnel File for Roberto Buzón Neira," April 11, 1938, RGASPI, IBR, File 587, pp. 75–79.
15 Nicolau González and IHC, *Cuba y la defensa*, 37.
16 Alejandro de la Fuente addresses this contradiction in *Nation for All*, 300–302.
17 Mesa-Lago and Pérez-López, *Cuba Under Raul Castro*, 180.
18 Mesa-Lago and Pérez-López, 25.
19 Mesa-Lago and Pérez-López, 8–9.
20 "Operarán 25 centrales azucareros durante la próxima zafra," *Cubadebate*, October 24, 2023, sec. Economía, http://www.cubadebate.cu/noticias/2023/10/23/operaran-25-centrales-azucareros-durante-la-proxima-zafra-en-el-pais/.
21 Mark Frank, "Cuba May Import Sugar, Rum Industry Pressed amid Disastrous Harvest," *Reuters*, May 9, 2024.
22 Grethel Morell, "Preston, caligrafía del silencio," *Rialta Magazine*, November 9, 2020, https://rialta.org/preston-caligrafia-del-silencio/

BIBLIOGRAPHY

Archival Collections

Cuba

Archivo Nacional de Cuba
    Audiencia de Santiago
    Fondo Especial
    Registro de Asociaciones
    Secretaria de Estado
    Secretaria de la Presidencia
    Secretaría de Trabajo, Agricultura, y Comercio
Archivo Histórico Provincial de Holguín
    Gobierno Municipal de Holguín
    Colección Movimiento Obrero
Archivo Histórico Provincial de Santiago de Cuba
    Gobierno Provincial
Archivo Histórico Provincial de Las Tunas
    Cuban American Sugar Mills Company
Archivo Histórico Provincial de Villa Clara
    Registro de Asociaciones
Archivo del Instituto de Historia de Cuba, Havana
    1: Organizaciones de Trabajadores
    8: Museo Obrero
Biblioteca del Instituto Cubano de Historia
Biblioteca Provincial Elvira Cape, Santiago de Cuba
Biblioteca Nacional José Martí

United States

National Archives and Records Administration, College Park, Maryland
    Records of the Foreign Service Posts of the Department of State
    Military Intelligence Division
Baker Library, Harvard University School of Business
    Nipe Bay Company, Annual Reports
    Records of Companies Acquired by the United Fruit Company
    United Fruit Company Photograph Collection
New York University
    Bobst Library, Research Institute for the Study of Man
    Tamiment Library and Robert F. Wagner Labor Archives

New York Public Library
  Schomburg Center for Research in Black Culture
    UNIA Central Division Records
  Science, Industry, and Business Library
    United Fruit Company, Annual Reports
    Cuban American Sugar Company, Annual Reports
University of Florida
  Braga Brothers Collection

United Kingdom

United Kingdom National Archives, London
  Foreign Office Records

Russia

Russian State Archives of Socio-Political History
  Organizations and Institutions
    Executive Committee of the Comintern
    The Caribbean Bureau
    International Brigades in Spain

Newspapers and Periodicals

Adelante
Bandera Roja
Bohemia
The Communist
El Cubano Libre
The Cuba Review
Diario de Cuba
Diario de la Marina
Facetas de Actualidad Española
Facts about Sugar
Harlem Liberator
Hoy/Noticias de Hoy
Labor Defender
Louisiana Planter and Sugar Manufacturer
Mundo Obrero
Negro World
New York Times
Nosotros

Published Primary Sources

Adams, Frederick Upham. *Conquest of the Tropics: The Story of the Creative Enterprises Conducted by the United Fruit Company.* Garden City, NY: Doubleday, Page & Company, 1914.
Adams, J. M. *Pioneering in Cuba: A Narrative of the Settlement of La Gloria, The First American Colony in Cuba, and the Early Experiences of the Pioneers.* Concord, NH: The Rumford Press, 1901.
Arnaz, Desi. *A Book.* Cutchogue, NY: Buccaneer Books, 1994.
Arredondo, Alberto. *El Negro En Cuba: Ensayo.* Havana: Editorial "Alfa," 1939.
Beals, Carleton. *The Crime of Cuba.* Philadelphia, PA: J. B. Lippincott Company, 1933.
Bourgois, Philippe I. "One Hundred Years of United Fruit Company Letters." In *Banana Wars: Power, Production, and History in the Americas,* edited by Steve Striffler and Mark Moberg, 103–44. Durham, NC: Duke University Press, 2003.
Castillo Bueno, Maria de los Reyes, and Daisy Rubiera Castillo. *Reyita: The Life of a Black Cuban Woman in the Twentieth Century.* Durham, NC: Duke University Press, 2000.
Castro, Fidel, and Ignacio Ramonet. *Fidel Castro: My Life, A Spoken Autobiography.* New York: Scribner, 2009.
Casuso, Teresa. *Cuba and Castro.* Translated by Elmer Grossberg. New York: Random House, 1961.
Commission on Cuban Affairs, and Raymond Leslie Buell. *Problems of the New Cuba: Report of the Commission on Cuban Affairs.* New York: Foreign Policy Association, Inc., 1935.
Confederación Sindical Latino Americana. *Bajo de La Bandera de La C.S.L.A.: Resoluciones y documentos varios del congreso constituyente de la Confederacion Sindical Latino Americana afectuado en Montevideo en Mayo de 1929.* Montevideo: Imprenta la Linotipo, 1929.
Cuba Dirección general del Censo. *Census of the Republic of Cuba 1919.* Havana: Maza, Arroyo y Caso, S. en C., printers, 1922.
Cuba Importadora y Industrial. *Anuario azucarero de Cuba, 1937.* Censo de la Industria Azucarera de Cuba y Manual Estadístico Internacional. Havana: Editorial Mercantil Cubana, 1937.
Cuba: Oficina del Censo. *Cuba: Population, History and Resources 1907.* Washington DC: United States Bureau of the Census, 1909.
Cuba Oficina Nacional de los Censos Demográfico y Electoral. *Censos de población, viviendas y electoral, enero 28 de 1953.* P. Fernández, 1955.
De la Torriente Brau, Pablo. *Cartas y crónicas de España.* La Memoria. Havana: Centro Cultural Pablo de la Torriente Brau, 2002.
De la Torriente Brau, Pablo. *Peleando con los milicianos.* Mexico City: Editorial México Nuevo, 1938.
Degras, Jane. *The Communist International: 1919–1943, Documents.* 3 vols. London: Frank Cass & Co. Ldt., 1971.
Dumois, Alfred. *A Name, a Family, and a Town.* Bountiful, UT: Family History Publishers, 1999.

Gordón Ordás, Félix. *Mi política fuera de España,* vols. 1 and 2 of 4. Mexico D.F.: Victoria, 1965.

Guillén, Nicolás. *Prosa de prisa, 1929–1972.* Vol. 1 of Letras cubanas. Havana: Editorial Arte y Literatura, 1975.

Hawley, R. B. "Cuban-American Sugar Company, Annual Report for the Fiscal Year Ending September 30, 1910." New York: Cuban-American Sugar Company, 1910.

Hawley, R. B. "Cuban-American Sugar Company, Annual Report for the Fiscal Year Ending September 30, 1911." New York: Cuban-American Sugar Company, 1911.

Hill, Robert, ed. *The Marcus Garvey and Universal Negro Improvement Association Papers.* Vols. 1, 2, 3, and 4. Berkeley: University of California Press, 1985.

Hill, Robert, ed. *The Marcus Garvey and Universal Negro Improvement Association Papers.* Vols. 11, 12, and 13. Durham, NC: Duke University Press, 2016.

Instituto de Historia de Cuba. *El Movimiento obrero cubano: Documentos y articulos.* Havana: Editorial de Ciencias Sociales, Instituto Cubano del Libro, 1975. Tomos 1 y 2.

Jenks, Leland Hamilton. *Our Cuban Colony: A Study in Sugar.* Studies in American Imperialism. New York: Vanguard Press, 1928.

Junco, Sandalio. "El problema de la raza negra y el movimiento proletario." 160–180 Congreso de Constitución de la CSLA, Montevideo: Imprenta la Linotipo, 1929.

Kushner, Rachel. *Telex from Cuba.* New York: Scribner, 2008.

Martí, José. *Selected Writings.* Edited by Esther Allen. New York: Penguin Books, 2002.

Martínez Villena, Rubén. *Rubén Martínez Villena: Poesía y prosa.* Vol. 2. Havana: Editorial Letras Cubanas, 1978.

McKay, Claude. *A Long Way from Home.* Harcourt, Brace & World, 1970.

Mulzac, Hugh. *A Star to Steer By.* 1st ed. International Publishers, 1963.

National City Company. *Sugar.* New York: The Company, 1922.

Ober, Frederick Albion. *A Guide to the West Indies and Bermudas.* Dodd, Mead & Company, 1908.

Osorio, Victor Amat. *Banes (1513–1958): Estampas de mi tierra y de mi sol.* Miami, FL: V. Amat Osorio, 1981.

Pichardo Viñals, Hortensia. *Documentos para la historia de Cuba.* Vols. 3 and 4 of *Nuestra Historia.* Havana: Editorial de Ciencias Sociales, 1973.

Reynolds, Philip Keep. *The Story of Cuban Sugar.* Boston, MA: United Fruit Company, 1924.

Roumain, Jacques. *Masters of the Dew.* Translated by Langston Hughes and Mercer Cook. Oxford: Heinemann, 2001.

Skelly, Jack. *I Remember Cuba: Growing Up American-Cuban, A Memoir of a Town Called Banes.* Houston, TX: Jack Skelly (Bookstand Publishing), 2006.

Terry, Thomas Philip. *Terry's Guide to Cuba.* Havana: Houghton Mifflin Company, 1926.

Tisa, John. *Recalling the Good Fight: An Autobiography of the Spanish Civil War.* South Hadley, MA: Bergin & Garvey, 1985.

United Fruit Company. *Some Facts Regarding the Development and Operation of the United Fruit Company Sugar Properties in the Republic of Cuba.* Preston, Oriente, Cuba: United Fruit Company, 1944.

United States Department of Commerce and Labor et al. *Report on Trade Conditions in Cuba.* Washington DC: US Government Printing Office, 1906.

United States Tariff Commission. *The Effects of the Cuban Reciprocity Treaty of 1902*. Washington DC: US Government Printing Office, 1929.
United States War Department. *Report on the Census of Cuba, 1899*. Washington DC: US Government Printing Office, 1900.
Universal Negro Improvement Association, and African Communities' League. *UNIA Constitution and Book of Laws: Made for the Government of the Universal Negro Improvement Association, Inc., and African Communities' League, Inc., of the World: In Effect July 1918: Revised and Amended Aug. 1920: Revised and Amended Aug. 1921*. 80 pages. New York: Universal Negro Improvement Association and African Communities' League, 1921.
Varona Pupo, Ricardo. *Banes, crónicas*. Santiago de Cuba: Imprenta Ros. Masó, 1930.
Wiles, Robert. *Cuban Cane Sugar: A Sketch of the Industry, From Soil to Sack, Together with a Survey of the Circumstances Which Combine to Make Cuba the Sugar Bowl of the World*. Indianapolis, IN: Bobbs-Merrill, 1916.
Wright, Irene Aloha. *Cuba*. New York: Macmillan, 1910.

Secondary Sources

Adi, Hakim. "The Negro Question: The Communist International and Black Liberation in the Interwar Years." In *From Toussaint to Tupac: The Black International since the Age of Revolution*, edited by Michael O. West, William G. Martin, and Fanon Che Wilkins, 155–75. Chapel Hill: University of North Carolina Press, 2009.
Adi, Hakim. *Pan-Africanism and Communism: The Communist International, Africa and the Diaspora, 1919–1939*. The Harriet Tubman Series on the African Diaspora. Trenton, NJ: Africa World Press, 2013.
Aguilar, Luis E. "Introduction." In *Marxism in Latin America*, edited by Luis E. Aguilar, 3–59. New York: Alfred A. Knopf, 1968.
Alexander, Robert. *A History of Organized Labor in Cuba*. Westport, CT: Praeger, 2002.
Alfonso Bello, Alberto, and Juan Pérez Díaz. *Cuba en España: Una gloriosa pagina de internacionalismo*. Havana: Editorial de Ciencias Sociales, 1990.
Alpert, Michael. *A New International History of the Spanish Civil War*. New York: Palgrave Macmillan, 2004.
Álvarez Estévez, Rolando. *Azúcar e inmigración*. Historia de Cuba. Havana: Editorial de Ciencias Sociales, 1988.
Argenteri, Letizia. *Tina Modotti: Between Art and Revolution*. New Haven, CT: Yale University Press, 2003.
Argote-Freyre, Frank. *Fulgencio Batista: The Making of a Dictator*. New Brunswick, NJ: Rutgers University Press, 2006.
Argote-Freyre, Frank. *Cuba en el Caribe y el Caribe en Cuba*. Colección La fuente viva 30. Havana: Fundación Fernando Ortiz, 2008.
Ayala, César J. *American Sugar Kingdom: The Plantation Economy of the Spanish Caribbean, 1898–1934*. Chapel Hill: University of North Carolina Press, 1999.
Ayala, César J. "Social and Economic Aspects of Sugar Production in Cuba, 1880–1930." *Latin American Research Review* 30, no. 1 (1995): 95–124.

Bair, Barbara. "True Women; Real Men: Gender Ideology and Social Roles in the Garvey Movement." In *Gendered Domains: Rethinking the Public and the Private in Women's History, Essays from the 7th Berkshire Conference on the History of Women*, edited by Susan Reverby and Dorothy O. Helly. Ithaca, NY: Cornell University Press, 1990.

Bandele, Ramla M. *Black Star: African American Activism in the International Political Economy.* Urbana: University of Illinois Press, 2008.

Baumann, Gerold Gino. *Los volunarios latinoamericanos en la Guerra Civil Española: En las Brigadas Internacionales, las milicias, la retaguardia y en el Ejército Popular.* San José, Costa Rica: Editorial Guayacán Cenroamericana, S.A., 1997.

Becker, Marc. *Mariátegui and Latin American Marxist Theory.* Monographs in International Studies, Latin America Series 20. Athens: Ohio University Center for International Studies, 1993.

Bender, Thomas. "The Cosmopolitan Experience and Its Uses." In *Cosmopolitanisms*, edited by Bruce Robbins and Paulo Lemos Horta, 116–26. New York: New York University Press, 2017.

Benítez, José Antonio. *Las Antillas: Colonización, azúcar e imperialismo.* Havana: Casa de las Américas, 1976.

Benjamin, Jules R. "The Machadato and Cuban Nationalism, 1928–1932." *The Hispanic American Historical Review* 55, no. 1 (February 1975): 66–91.

Benjamin, Jules R. *The United States and Cuba: Hegemony and Dependent Development, 1880–1934.* Pittsburgh, PA: University of Pittsburgh Press, 1974.

Berlin, Ira. "From Creole to African: Atlantic Creoles and the Origins of African-American Society in Mainland North America." *The William and Mary Quarterly* 53, no. 2 (1996): 251–88.

Bolland, O. Nigel. *On the March: Labour Rebellions in the British Caribbean, 1934–39.* Kingston: Ian Randle Publishers, 1995.

Bolland, O. Nigel. *The Politics of Labour in the British Caribbean: The Social Origins of Authoritarianism and Democracy in the Labour Movement.* Princeton, NJ: Markus Wiener Publishers, 2001.

Bourgois, Philippe I. *Ethnicity at Work: Divided Labor on a Central American Banana Plantation.* Johns Hopkins Studies in Atlantic History and Culture. Baltimore, MA: Johns Hopkins University Press, 1989.

Bronfman, Alejandra Marina. *Measures of Equality: Social Science, Citizenship, and Race in Cuba, 1902–1940.* Envisioning Cuba. Chapel Hill: University of North Carolina Press, 2004.

Brown, Jonathan C. *Cuba's Revolutionary World.* Cambridge, MA: Harvard University Press, 2017.

Brunson, Takkara K. *Black Women, Citizenship, and the Making of Modern Cuba.* Gainesville: University of Florida Press, 2021.

Buelli, Arlena. "The Hands Off Ethiopia Campaign, Racial Solidarities and Intercolonial Antifascism in South Asia (1935–36)." *Journal of Global History* 18, no. 1 (March 2023): 47–67.

Burkett, Randall K. *Garveyism as a Religious Movement: The Institutionalization of a Black Civil Religion.* ATLA Monograph Series 13. Metuchen, NJ: The Scarecrow Press, Inc. and the American Theological Library Association, 1978.

Burnett, Carla. "'Unity Is Strength': Labor, Race, Garveyism, and the 1920 Panama Canal Strike." *The Global South* 6, no. 2 (2012): 39–64.

Caballero, Manuel. *Latin America and the Comintern 1919–1943.* Cambridge: Cambridge University Press, 1987.
Cárdenas Tauler, Rafael Ángel. "La ruta del nororiente cubano hacia el capitalismo agrario: El deslinde y la división de las haciendas comuneras (1902–1958)." *História e Economia Revista Interdisciplinar* 16, no. 1 (2016): 125–46.
Cárdenas Tauler, Rafael Ángel. *La ruta holguinera hacia el capitalismo.* Holguín: Editorial La Mezquita, 2014.
Cardoso, Fernando Henrique, and Enzo Faletto. *Dependency and Development in Latin America.* Berkeley: University of California Press, 1979.
Carnegie, Charles V. "A Politics of Transterritorial Solidarity: The Garvey Movement and Imperialism." In *Postnationalisms Prefigured: Caribbean Borderlands.* New Brunswick, NJ: Rutgers University Press, 2002.
Carr, Barry. "'Across Seas and Borders': Charting the Webs of Radical Internationalism in the Circum Caribbean, 1910–1940." In *Exile and the Politics of Exclusion in the Americas,* edited by Luis Roniger, Pablo Yankelevich, and James Green, 217–40. Brighton: University of Sussex Press, 2012.
Carr, Barry. "From Caribbean Backwater to Revolutionary Opportunity: Cuba's Evolving Relationship with the Comintern, 1925–1934." In *International Communism and the Communist International, 1919–43,* edited by Tim Rees and Andrew Thorpe, 234–53. Manchester: Manchester University Press, 1998.
Carr, Barry. "Identity, Class, and Nation: Black Immigrant Workers, Cuban Communism, and the Sugar Industry, 1925–1943." *Hispanic American Historical Review* 78, no. 1 (February 1998): 83–116.
Carr, Barry. "Mill Occupations and Soviets: The Mobilization of Sugar Workers in Cuba 1917–1933." *Journal of Latin American Studies* 28, no. 1 (February 1996): 129–58.
Carr, Barry. "'Omnipotent and Omnipresent'? Labor Shortages, Worker Mobility, and Employer Control in the Cuban Sugar Industry, 1910–1934." In *Identity and Struggle at the Margins of the Nation-State: The Laboring Peoples of Central America and the Hispanic Caribbean,* edited by Aviva Chomsky and Aldo Lauria-Santiago, 260–91. Durham, NC: Duke University Press, 1998.
Carr, Barry. "Pioneering Transnational Solidarity in the Americas: The Movement in Support of Augusto C. Sandino 1927–1934." *Journal of Iberian and Latin American Research* 20, no. 2 (May 4, 2014): 141–52.
Casey, Matthew. *Empire's Guestworkers: Haitian Migrants in Cuba during the Age of US Occupation.* Cambridge: Cambridge University Press, 2019.
Casey, Matthew. "Haitians' Labor and Leisure on Cuban Sugar Plantations: The Limits of Company Control." *New West Indian Guide* 85, no. 1–2 (2011): 5–30.
Casey, Matthew. "The Paramilitarism of Politics and Production in Early Republican Cuba." *The Global South* 12, no. 2 (2018): 64–89.
Castells Peig, Andreu. *Las Brigadas Internacionales de la guerra de España.* Horas de España. Esplugues de Llobregat: Editorial Ariel, 1974.
Castro Fernández, Silvio. *La masacre de los Independientes de Color en 1912.* Havana: Editorial de Ciencias Sociales, 2002.
Chailloux Laffita, Graciela, and Robert Whitney. "British Subjects y Pichones En Cuba."

In *De Dónde Son Los Cubanos,* edited by Graciela Chailloux Laffita, 53–115. Havana: Editorial de Ciencias Sociales, 2007.

Ching, Erik. "In Search of the Party: The Communist Party, the Comintern, and the Peasant Rebellion of 1932 in El Salvador." *The Americas* 55, no. 2 (October 1998): 204–39.

Ching, Erik and Jussi Pakkasvirta. "Latin American Materials in the Comintern Archive." *Latin American Research Review* 31, no. 1 (2000): 138–49.

Chomsky, Aviva. "'Barbados or Canada?': Race, Immigration, and Nation in Early Twentieth-Century Cuba." *Hispanic American Historical Review* 8, no. 3 (August 2000): 415–62.

Chomsky, Aviva. *West Indian Workers and the United Fruit Company in Costa Rica, 1870–1940.* Baton Rouge: Louisiana State University Press, 1996.

Colby, Jason M. *The Business of Empire: United Fruit, Race, and U.S. Expansion in Central America.* The United States in the World. Ithaca, NY: Cornell University Press, 2011.

Conniff, Michael L. *Black Labor on a White Canal: Panama, 1904–1981.* Pitt Latin American Series. Pittsburgh, PA: University of Pittsburgh Press, 1985.

Corinealdi, Kaysha. "Envisioning Multiple Citizenships: West Indian Panamanians and Creating Community in the Canal Zone Neocolony." *The Global South* 6, no. 2 (2013): 87–106.

Corinealdi, Kaysha. *Panama in Black: Afro-Caribbean World Making in the Twentieth Century.* Durham, NC: Duke University Press, 2022.

Cronon, E. David. *Black Moses: The Story of Marcus Garvey and the Universal Negro Improvement Association.* Madison: University of Wisconsin Press, 1960.

Curry-Machado, J. *Cuban Sugar Industry: Transnational Networks and Engineering Migrants in Mid-Nineteenth Century Cuba.* New York: Palgrave Macmillan, 2011.

Dalleo, Raphael. *American Imperialism's Undead: The Occupation of Haiti and the Rise of Caribbean Anticolonialism.* Charlottesville: University of Virginia Press, 2016.

De la Fuente, Alejandro. *A Nation for All: Race, Inequality, and Politics in Twentieth-Century Cuba.* Envisioning Cuba. Chapel Hill: University of North Carolina Press, 2001.

De la Fuente, Alejandro. "Two Dangers, One Solution: Immigration, Race, and Labor in Cuba, 1900–1930." *International Labor and Working Class History,* no. 51 (Spring 1997): 30–49.

Deere, Carmen. "Here Come the Yankees! The Rise and Decline of United States Colonies in Cuba, 1898–1930." *Hispanic American Historical Review* 78, no. 4 (1998): 729–65.

Dinius, Oliver J., and Angela Vergara. "Company Towns in the Americas, an Introduction." In *Company Towns in the Americas: Landscape, Power, and Working-Class Communities.* Athens: University of Georgia Press, 2011.

Domingo, Jorge. *El exilio republicano español en Cuba.* Madrid: Siglo XXI de España Editores, 2009.

Dosal, Paul J. *Doing Business with the Dictators: A Political History of United Fruit in Guatemala, 1899–1944.* Latin American Silhouettes. Wilmington, DE: Rowman & Littlefield, 1993.

Dumoulin, John. *Azúcar y lucha de clases, 1917.* Nuestra Historia. Havana: Editorial de Ciencias Sociales, 1980.

Dye, Alan. *Cuban Sugar in the Age of Mass Production: Technology and the Economics of the Sugar Central, 1899–1929.* Stanford, CA: Stanford University Press, 1998.

Ehrlich, Ilan. *Eduardo Chibás: The Incorrigible Man of Cuban Politics*. Lanham, MD: Rowman & Littlefield, 2015.
Eller, Anne. *We Dream Together: Dominican Independence, Haiti, and the Fight for Caribbean Freedom*. Durham, NC: Duke University Press, 2016.
Estévez Rivero, Sandra. *La sombra de Marcus Garvey sobre el oriente cubano*. Santiago de Cuba: Ediciones Santiago, 2005.
Ewing, Adam. *The Age of Garvey: How a Jamaican Activist Created a Mass Movement and Changed Global Black Politics*. America in the World. Princeton, NJ: Princeton University Press, 2014.
Ewing, Adam. "Caribbean Labour Politics in the Age of Garvey, 1918–1938." *Race & Class* 55, no. 1 (2013): 23–45.
Falcoff, Mark, and Fredrick B. Pike. *The Spanish Civil War, 1936–39: American Hemispheric Perspectives*. Lincoln: University of Nebraska Press, 1982.
Fernández Robaina, Tomás. *El negro en Cuba, 1902–1958: apuntes para la historia de la lucha contra la discriminación racial*. Havana: Editorial de Ciencias Sociales, 1990.
Ferrer, Ada. *Cuba: An American History*. New York: Scribner, 2021.
Ferrer, Ada. "History and the Idea of Hispanic Caribbean Studies." *Small Axe* 20, no. 3 (November 2016): 49–64.
Ferrer, Ada. *Insurgent Cuba: Race, Nation, and Revolution, 1868–1898*. Chapel Hill: University of North Carolina Press, 1999.
Ferrer, Ada. "Rustic Men, Civilized Nation: Race, Culture, and Contention on the Eve of Cuban Independence." *Hispanic American Historical Review* 78, no. 4 (November 1998): 663–86.
Figueredo Cabrera, Katia. *Cuba y la Guerra Civil Española: Mitos y realidades de la derecha hispano-cubana (1936–1942)*. Havana: UH Editorial, 2014.
FitzGerald, David, and David Cook-Martín. *Culling the Masses: The Democratic Origins of Racist Immigration Policy in the Americas*. Cambridge, MA: Harvard University Press, 2014.
Flores-Villalobos, Joan. *The Silver Women: How Black Women's Labor Made the Panama Canal*. Politics and Culture in Modern America. Philadelphia: University of Pennsylvania Press, 2023.
Foner, Philip. *The Spanish-Cuban-American War and the Birth of American Imperialism, 1895–1902*. Vol. 2. Modern Reader. New York: Monthly Review Press, 1972.
Ford-Smith, Honor. "Women and the Garvey Movement in Jamaica." In *Garvey: His Work and Impact*, edited by Rupert Lewis and Patrick Bryan, 73–83. Mona, Jamaica: Institute of Social and Economic Research, University of the West Indies, 1988.
Fowler, Carolyn. "The Shared Vision of Langston Hughes and Jacques Roumain." *Black American Literature Forum* 15, no. 3 (1981): 84–88.
Frank, Andre Gunder. "The Development of Underdevelopment." In *Promise of Development: Theories of Change in Latin America*, edited by Peter F. Klarén and Thomas J. Bossert, 111–23. Boulder, CO: Westview Press, 1986.
French, John D. "Another World History Is Possible: Reflections on the Translocal, Transnational, and Global." In *Workers Across the Americas: The Transnational Turn in Labor History*, edited by Leon Fink, 3–11. New York: Oxford University Press, 2011.

Fronczak, J. "Local People's Global Politics: A Transnational History of the Hands Off Ethiopia Movement of 1935." *Diplomatic History* 39, no. 2 (April 1, 2015): 245–74.
Gaines, Kevin Kelly. *Uplifting the Race: Black Leadership, Politics, and Culture in the Twentieth Century.* Chapel Hill: University of North Carolina Press, 1996.
García, Angel, and Piotr Mironchuk. *Los soviets obreros y campesinos en Cuba.* Historia de Cuba. Havana: Editorial de Ciencias Sociales, 1987.
García Domínguez, Bernardo. "Garvey and Cuba." In *Garvey: His Work and Impact,* edited by Rupert Lewis and Patrick Bryan, 299–308. Trenton, NJ: Africa World Press, 1991.
García Domínguez, Sthel, and Violeta Rovira González. "Los 'Soviets' de Nazábal, Hormiguero y Parque Alto de La Provincia de Las Villas." *Islas* 18 (October 1968): 221–53.
Garnes, Walterio Lord. "Marcus Garvey and the UNIA in the Memory of West Indian Residents in Cuba." *76 King Street, The Journal of Liberty Hall: The Legacy of Marcus Garvey* 1 (2009): 130–44.
Gatewood, Willard B. *Black Americans and the White Man's Burden, 1898–1903.* Blacks in the New World. Urbana: University of Illinois Press, 1975.
Gatewood, Willard B. *"Smoked Yankees" and the Struggle for Empire: Letters from Negro Soldiers, 1898–1902.* Urbana: University of Illinois Press, 1971.
Gleijeses, Piero. *Conflicting Missions: Havana, Washington, and Africa, 1959–1976.* 1st ed. Chapel Hill: University of North Carolina Press, 2002.
Giovannetti-Torres, Jorge L. *Black British Migrants in Cuba: Race, Labor, and Empire in the Twentieth Century Caribbean, 1898–1948.* Cambridge Studies on the African Diaspora. Cambridge: Cambridge University Press, 2018.
Giovannetti-Torres, Jorge L. "The Elusive Organization of Identity: Race, Religion, and Empire among Caribbean Migrants in Cuba." *Small Axe* 19 (2006): 1–27.
Giusti-Cordero, Juan. "Beyond Sugar Revolutions: Rethinking the Spanish Caribbean in the Seventeenth and Eighteenth Centuries." In *Empirical Futures,* edited by George Baca, Aisha Khan, and Stephan Palmié, 58–83. Anthropologists and Historians Engage the Work of Sidney W. Mintz. Chapel Hill: University of North Carolina Press, 2009.
Gobat, Michel. *Confronting the American Dream: Nicaragua under U.S. Imperial Rule.* American Encounters/Global Interactions. Durham, NC: Duke University Press, 2005.
Gómez Navia, Raimundo. "Lo haitiano en lo cubano." In *De Dónde Son Los Cubanos,* edited by Graciela Chailloux Laffita, 5–51. Havana: Editorial de Ciencias Sociales, 2007.
González Martínez, Carmen, and Juan José Sánchez Baena. "El apoyo a la II République Española como referente de identidad antifascista en Cuba." In *Abarrotes: La construcción social de las identidades colectivas en América Latina,* edited by Lucía Provencio Garrigós, 375–414. Sevilla: Universidad de Murcia, Universidad Pable de Olavide, Agencia Española de Cooperación Internacional, 2005.
González, Reyes, and José Luis. "Los enclaves azucareros de la región nororiental de Cuba (1900–1930): El batey del Central Tacajó." *Tiempo y Espacio* 24, no. 61 (June 2014): 393–411.
Graham, Helen. *The Spanish Civil War: A Very Short Introduction.* Oxford: Oxford University Press, 2005.
Grandin, Greg. *The End of the Myth: From the Frontier to the Border Wall in the Mind of America.* New York: Metropolitan Books: Henry Holt and Company, 2019.
Grandin, Greg. "Forum: Your Americanism and Mine: Americanism and Anti-

Americanism in the Americas." *American Historical Review* 111, no. 4 (October 2006): 1042-66.

Greene, Julie. "The Wages of Empire: Capitalism, Expansionism, and Working-Class Formation." In *Making the Empire Work: Labor and United States Imperialism*, edited by Daniel E. Bender and Jana Lipman, 1-34. New York: New York University Press, 2015.

Grobart, Fabio. "The Cuban Working Class Movement from 1925-1933." *Science & Society* 39, no. 1 (Spring 1975): 73-103.

Grogan, Kevin. "Cuba's Dance of the Millions: Examining the Causes and Consequences of Violent Price Fluctuations in the Sugar Market Between 1919 and 1920." Master's thesis, University of Florida, 2004.

Gronbeck-Tedesco, John A. *Cuba, the United States, and Cultures of the Transnational Left, 1930-1975*. New York: Cambridge University Press, 2015.

Guerra, Lillian. *Heroes, Martyrs, and Political Messiahs in Revolutionary Cuba, 1946-1958*. New Haven, CT: Yale University Press, 2017.

Guerra, Lillian. *The Myth of José Martí*. Envisioning Cuba. Chapel Hill: University of North Carolina Press, 2005.

Guerra y Sánchez, Ramiro. *Azúcar y población en las Antillas*. Ciencias Politicas. Havana: Editorial de Ciencias Sociales, 1976.

Guridy, Frank Andre. "'Enemies of the White Race': The Machadista State and the UNIA in Cuba." *Caribbean Studies* 31, no. 1 (2003): 107-38.

Guridy, Frank Andre. *Forging Diaspora: Afro-Cubans and African Americans in a World of Empire and Jim Crow*. Envisioning Cuba. Chapel Hill: University of North Carolina Press, 2010.

Guridy, Frank Andre. "'War on the Negro': Race and the Revolution of 1933." *Cuban Studies* 40 (2009): 49-73.

Harold, Claudrena N. *The Rise and Fall of the Garvey Movement in the Urban South, 1918-1942*. Studies in African American History and Culture. New York: Routledge, 2007.

Harpelle, Ronald N. "Cross Currents in the Western Caribbean: Marcus Garvey and the UNIA in Central America." *Caribbean Studies* 31, no. 1 (June 2003): 35-73.

Harpelle, Ronald N. *The West Indians of Costa Rica: Race, Class, and the Integration of an Ethnic Minority*. McGill-Queen's Studies in Ethnic History. Montreal: McGill-Queen's University Press, 2001.

Hatzky, Christine. *Cubans in Angola: South-South Cooperation and Transfer of Knowledge, 1976-1991*. Madison: University of Wisconsin Press, 2015.

Hatzky, Christine. *Julio Antonio Mella (1903-1929): Una biografía*. Santiago de Cuba: Editorial Oriente, 2008.

Heatherton, Christina. *Arise!: Global Radicalism in the Era of the Mexican Revolution*. American Crossroads. Oakland: University of California Press, 2022.

Helg, Aline. *Our Rightful Share: The Afro-Cuban Struggle for Equality, 1886-1912*. Chapel Hill: University of North Carolina Press, 1995.

Henderson, Kaitlyn. "Race, Discrimination, and the Cuban Constitution of 1940." *The Hispanic American Historical Review* 100, no. 2 (2020): 257-84.

Hennessy, Alistair. "Cuba." In *The Spanish Civil War, 1936-1939: American Hemispheric Perspectives*, edited by Mark Falcoff and Frederick B. Pike, 101-58. Lincoln: University of Nebraska Press, 1982.

Hernández, José M. *Cuba and the United States: Intervention and Militarism, 1868–1933.* Austin: University of Texas Press, 2010.

Hernández, Kelly Lytle. *Bad Mexicans: Race, Empire, and Revolution in the Borderlands.* 1st ed. New York: W.W. Norton & Company, 2022.

Hill, Robert A. "Chronology." In *The Marcus Garvey and Universal Negro Improvement Association Papers,* 13: lxviii–lxxiii. Vol. 13 of *The Marcus Garvey and Universal Negro Improvement Association Papers.* Durham, NC: Duke University Press, 2016.

Hill, Robert A. "General Introduction." In *The Marcus Garvey and Universal Negro Improvement Association Papers 1826–1919,* 1: xxxv–xc. Vol. 1 of *The Marcus Garvey and Universal Negro Improvement Association Papers,* edited by Robert A. Hill. Berkeley: University of California Press, 1983.

Hill, Robert A. "General Introduction." In *The Marcus Garvey and Universal Negro Improvement Association Papers: The Caribbean Diaspora, 1910–1920,* XI: lix–xcviii. Vol. 11 of *The Marcus Garvey and Universal Negro Improvement Association Papers,* edited by Robert A. Hill. Durham, NC: Duke University Press, 2011.

Hill, Robert A. "Introduction." In *The Marcus Garvey and Universal Negro Improvement Association Papers: The Caribbean Diaspora, 1921–1922,* XIII: xxvii–xlv. Volume 13 of *The Marcus Garvey and Universal Negro Improvement Association Papers,* edited by Robert A. Hill. Durham, NC: Duke University Press, 2016.

Hill, Robert A. "Introduction." In *The Marcus Garvey and Universal Negro Improvement Association Papers: September 1920–August 1921,* III: xxxiii–xxxvii. Vol. 3 of *The Marcus Garvey and Universal Negro Improvement Association Papers.* Berkeley: University of California Press, 1984.

Hilty, Hiram H. "Zenas L. Martin, Quaker Pioneer in Cuba." *Quaker History* 59, no. 2 (1970): 81–97.

Hochschild, Adam. *Spain in Our Hearts: Americans in the Spanish Civil War, 1936–1939.* Reprint edition. Boston, MA: Mariner Books, 2017.

Hoernel, Robert B. "Sugar and Social Change in Oriente, Cuba, 1898–1946." *Journal of Latin American Studies* 8, no. 2 (November 1976): 215–49.

Horne, Gerald. *Race to Revolution: The United States and Cuba during Slavery and Jim Crow.* New York: Monthly Review Press, 2014.

Howard, Philip A. *Black Labor, White Sugar: Caribbean Braceros and Their Struggle for Power in the Cuban Sugar Industry.* Baton Rouge: Louisiana State University Press, 2015.

Howard, Philip A. *Changing History: Afro-Cuban Cabildos and Societies of Color in the Nineteenth Century.* Baton Rouge: Louisiana State University Press, 1998.

Howison, Jeffrey D. "'Let Us Guide Our Own Destiny': Rethinking the History of the Black Star Line." *Review (Fernand Braudel Center), The Black World and the World-System,* 28, no. 1 (2005): 29–49.

Hudson, Peter James. *Bankers and Empire: How Wall Street Colonized the Caribbean.* Chicago, IL: The University of Chicago Press, 2017.

Hulme, Peter. "Wilfred Domingo under Investigation: The 'Negro Menace' of 1919." In *Revolutionary Lives of the Red and Black Atlantic since 1917,* edited by David Featherstone, Christian Høgsbjerg, and Alan Rice, 55–71. Manchester: Manchester University Press, 2022.

Institut mezhdunarodnogo rabochego dvizheníià (Akademiíà nauk SSSR), and Sovetskii komitet veteranov voiny, *International Solidarity with the Spanish Republic, 1936–1939.* Moscow: Progress Publishers, 1974.

Instituto de Historia de Cuba. *Historia del movimiento obrero cubano, 1865–1958.* 3 vols. Havana: Editora Política, 1985.

Jackson, Michael W. *Fallen Sparrows: The International Brigades in the Spanish Civil War.* Philadelphia, PA: American Philosophical Society, 1994.

Jacobson, Matthew Frye. *Barbarian Virtues: The United States Encounters Foreign Peoples at Home and Abroad, 1876–1917.* New York: Hill and Wang, 2001.

James, Ariel. *Banes: Imperialismo y nación en una plantación azucarera.* Havana: Editorial de Ciencias Sociales, 1976.

James, Winston. "Culture, Labor, and Race in the Shadow of US Capital." In *The Caribbean: A History of the Region and Its Peoples,* edited by Stephan Palmié and Francisco A. Scarano, 445–58. Chicago, IL: The University of Chicago Press, 2011.

James, Winston. *Holding Aloft the Banner of Ethiopia: Caribbean Radicalism in Early Twentieth-Century America.* New York: Verso, 1998.

Joseph, G. M., Catherine LeGrand, and Ricardo Donato Salvatore. *Close Encounters of Empire: Writing the Cultural History of U.S.-Latin American Relations.* American Encounters/Global Interactions. Durham, NC: Duke University Press, 1998.

Kelley, Robin D. G. *Freedom Dreams: The Black Radical Imagination.* Boston, MA: Beacon Press, 2002.

Kirk, John M. *Healthcare Without Borders: Understanding Cuban Medical Internationalism.* Gainesville: University Press of Florida, 2015.

Knight, Franklin W. "Jamaican Migrants and the Cuban Sugar Industry, 1900–1934." In *Between Slavery and Free Labor: The Spanish-Speaking Caribbean in the Nineteenth Century,* edited by Manuel Moreno Fraginales, Frank Moya Pons, and Stanley L. Engerman, 84–114. Baltimore, MD: Johns Hopkins University Press, 1985.

Kohler, Peter C. "Chesapeake-Built and Caribbean-Bound: U.S.M.S. *Munamar.*" Wanted on Voyage: Ocean Liner Monographs, August 16, 2020. https://wantedonthevoyage.blogspot.com/2020/08/chesapeake-built-caribbean-bound-usms.html?lr=1

LaFeber, Walter. *The New Empire: An Interpretation of American Expansion, 1860–1898.* Ithaca, NY: Cornell University Press, 1998.

Lafita, María Luisa. *Dos héroes cubanos en el 5to regimiento.* Nuestra Historia. Havana: Editorial de Ciencias Sociales, 1980.

Lafita, María Luisa. *Rodolfo Ricardo Ramón de Armas y Soto (1912–1937), Héroe del internacionalismo proletario.* Havana: Concurso de Historia Primero de Enero, 1975.

Lambe, Ariel. *No Barrier Can Contain It: Cuban Antifascism and the Spanish Civil War.* Envisioning Cuba. Chapel Hill: University of North Carolina Press, 2019.

Landis, Arthur H. *The Abraham Lincoln Brigade.* New York: Citadel Press, 1968.

Langley, Lester D., and Thomas David Schoonover. *The Banana Men: American Mercenaries and Entrepreneurs in Central America, 1880–1930.* Lexington: University Press of Kentucky, 1995.

Laqua, Daniel. "Preface." In *Internationalism Reconfigured: Transnational Ideas and Movements Between the World Wars,* edited by Daniel Laqua, xi–xvii. London: I.B. Tauris & Co., 2011.

Lasso, Marixa. *Erased: The Untold Story of the Panama Canal.* Cambridge, MA: Harvard University Press, 2019.

LeGrand, Catherine. "Living in Macondo: Economy and Culture in a United Fruit Banana Enclave in Colombia." In *Close Encounters of Empire: Writing the Cultural History of U.S.-Latin American Relations,* edited by Gilbert M. Joseph, Catherine C. LeGrand, and Ricardo D. Salvatore, 333–68. Durham, NC: Duke University Press, 1998.

Leimdorfer, Karen. *Cultural Imperialism or Cultural Encounters: Foreign Influence through Protestant Missions in Cuba, 1898-1959: A Quaker Case Study.* Saarbrücken, Germany: VDM Verlag Dr. Müller Aktiengesellschaft & Co. KG, 2008.

Lemelle, Sidney J., and Robin D. G. Kelley. "Introduction—Imagining Home: Pan-Africanism Revisited." In *Imagining Home: Class, Culture, and Nationalism in the African Diaspora,* edited by Sidney J. Lemelle and Robin D. G. Kelley, 1–16. New York: Verso, 1994.

Levin, Jonathan V. *The Export Economies: Their Pattern of Development in Historical Perspective.* Cambridge, MA: Harvard University Press, 1960.

Lewis, Rupert. *Marcus Garvey: Anti-Colonial Champion.* 1st American ed. Trenton, NJ: Africa World Press, 1988.

Lindner, Thomas K. *A City Against Empire: Transnational Anti-Imperialism in Mexico City, 1920-30.* Liverpool Latin American Studies LUP. Oxford: Oxford University Press, 2023.

Lindner, Thomas K. "Standing with Sacco and Sandino: Anti-Imperialist Solidarity Campaigns in 1920s Mexico City." *Journal of Iberian and Latin American Studies* (March 2022), 131–151.

Linebaugh, Peter, and Marcus Buford Rediker. *The Many-Headed Hydra: Sailors, Slaves, Commoners, and the Hidden History of the Revolutionary Atlantic.* Boston: Beacon Press, 2000.

Maddox, Tyesha. *A Home Away from Home: Mutual Aid, Political Activism, and Caribbean American Identity.* Philadelphia: University of Pennsylvania Press, 2024.

Mahler, Anne Garland. "The Red and the Black in Latin America: Sandalio Junco and the 'Negro Question' from an Afro-Latin American Perspective." *American Communist History* 17, no. 1 (2018): 16–32.

Mahler, Anne Garland. "South–South Organizing in the Global Plantation Zone: Ramón Marrero Aristy, the Novela de La Caña, and the Caribbean Bureau." *Atlantic Studies* 16, no. 2 (April 3, 2019): 236–60.

Makalani, Minkah. *In the Cause of Freedom: Radical Black Internationalism from Harlem to London, 1917-1939.* Chapel Hill: University of North Carolina Press, 2011.

Martin, James W. *Banana Cowboys: The United Fruit Company and the Culture of Corporate Colonialism.* Albuquerque: University of New Mexico Press, 2018.

Martin, Tony. *Race First: The Ideological and Organizational Struggles of Marcus Garvey and the Universal Negro Improvement Association.* Contributions in Afro-American and African Studies. Westport, CT: Greenwood Press distributed by the Majority Press, 1976.

Martínez Heredia, Fernando. "El héroe romántico de la revolución proletaria." In *La revolución cubana del 30: Ensayos,* 196–212. Havana: Editorial de Ciencias Sociales, 2007.

McAvoy, Muriel. *Sugar Baron: Manuel Rionda and the Fortunes of Pre-Castro Cuba*. Gainesville: University Press of Florida, 2003.
Matory, James Lorand. *Black Atlantic Religion: Tradition, Transnationalism, and Matriarchy in the Afro-Brazilian Candomblé*. Princeton: Princeton University Press, 2005.
McDuffie, E. S. *Sojourning for Freedom: Black Women, American Communism, and the Making of Black Left Feminism*. Durham, NC: Duke University Press, 2011.
McGillivray, Gillian. *Blazing Cane: Sugar Communities, Class, and State Formation in Cuba, 1868–1959*. American Encounters/Global Interactions. Durham, NC: Duke University Press, 2009.
McGirr, Lisa. "The Passion of Sacco and Vanzetti: A Global History." *The Journal of American History* 94, no. 4 (2007): 1085–1115.
McLeod, Marc. "Cuba, Historical Commentaries." In Volume 11 of *The Marcus Garvey and Universal Negro Improvement Association Papers: The Caribbean Diaspora*, clxxxix–cxcv. Durham, NC: Duke University Press, 2011.
McLeod, Marc. "Garveyism in Cuba, 1920–1940." *Journal of Caribbean History* 30, no. 1 (1996): 132–68.
McLeod, Marc. "Los braceros antillanos y la crisis económica de 1921 en Santiago de Cuba: Movilización política, representación, diplomática y repatriación." *Santiago* 91 (2000): 129–56.
McLeod, Marc. "'Sin dejar ser cubanos': Cuban Blacks and the Challenge of Garveyism in Cuba." *Caribbean Studies* 31, no. 1 (2003): 75–106.
McLeod, Marc. "Undesirable Aliens: Race, Ethnicity, and Nationalism in the Comparison of Haitian and British West Indian Immigrant Workers in Cuba, 1912–1939." *Journal of Social History* 31, no. 3 (Spring 1998): 599–623.
McLeod, Marc. "'We Cubans Are Obligated Like Cats to Have a Clean Face': Malaria, Quarantine, and Race in Neocolonial Cuba, 1898–1940." *The Americas* 67, no. 1 (2010): 57–81.
McNamara, Sarah. *Ybor City: Crucible of the Latina South*. Chapel Hill: University of North Carolina Press, 2023.
McPherson, Alan L. *Anti-Americanism in Latin America and the Caribbean*. New York: Berghahn Books, 2008.
McPherson, Alan L. *The Invaded: How Latin Americans and Their Allies Fought and Ended U.S. Occupations*. Cambridge, MA: Harvard University Press, 2016.
McWilliams, Carey. *Factories in the Field: The Story of Migratory Farm Labor in California*. Boston, MA: Little, Brown and Company, 1939.
Melgar Bao, Ricardo. "Rearmando la memoria: El primer debate socialista acerca de nuestros afroamericanos." *Humania Del Sur* 2, no. 2 (June 2007): 145–56.
Meriño Fuentes, María de los Ángeles. *Una vuelta necesaria a mayo de 1912: El alzamiento de los Independientes de Color*. Pinos nuevos, ensayo. Havana: Editorial de Ciencias Sociales, 2006.
Mesa-Lago, Carmelo, and Jorge F. Pérez-López. *Cuba Under Raúl Castro: Assessing the Reforms*. Boulder, CO: Lynne Rienner Publishers, 2013.
Miller, James A., Susan D. Pennybacker, and Eve Rosenhaft. "Mother Ada Wright and the International Campaign to Free the Scottsboro Boys, 1931–1934." *American Historical Review* 106, no. 2 (April 2001): 387–430.

Mintz, Sidney W. "The Caribbean as a Socio-Cultural Area." *Journal of World History* X, no. 4 (1966): 912–37.

Mintz, Sidney W. "The Localization of Anthropological Practice: From Area Studies to Transnationalism." *Critique of Anthropology* 18, no. 2 (June 1, 1998): 117–33.

Moore, Robin. *Nationalizing Blackness: Afrocubanismo and Artistic Revolution in Havana, 1920–1940*. Pitt Latin American Series. Pittsburgh, PA: University of Pittsburgh Press, 1997.

Muñiz, Manuel María. "Julio Antonio Mella en las intersecciones del espacio político-cultural cubano y latinoamericano (1920–1925): Un estudio de historia intelectual." Universidad Nacional de General San Martín (UNSAM) Instituto de Altos Estudios Sociales (IDAES), 2014.

Naranjo Orovio, Consuelo. "Analisis historico de emigracion española a Cuba, 1900–1959." *Revista de Indias* XLIV, no. 174 (1984): 505–27.

Naranjo Orovio, Consuelo. *Cuba, otro escenario de lucha: La Guerra Civil y el exilio republicano español*. Madrid: Consejo Superior de Investigaciones Científicas, 1988.

Naranjo Orovio, Consuelo. *Cuba vista por el emigrante español a la Isla, 1900–1959: Un ensayo de historia oral*. Anexos de Revista de Indias; História de América. Madrid: Consejo Superior de Investigaciones Científicas, Centro de Estudios Históricos, 1987.

Neagle, Michael. *America's Forgotten Colony: Cuba's Isle of Pines*. New York: Cambridge University Press, 2016.

Neptune, Harvey. "At Sea: The Caribbean in Black Empire." *Small Axe* 10, no. 2 (2006): 269–75.

Nicolau González, Ramón, and Instituto de Historia de Cuba. *Cuba y la defensa de la República Española, 1936–1939*. Havana: Editora Política, 1981.

Núñez Machín, Ana. "Rafael de Hombre Mesa." In *Memoria amarga del azúcar*, 69–71. Historia de Cuba. Havana: Editorial de Ciencias Sociales, 1981.

Núñez Machín, Ana. *Rubén Martínez Villena*. 1st ed. Havana: Unión de Escritores y Artistas de Cuba, 1971.

Nwankwo, Ifeoma Kiddoe. *Black Cosmopolitanism: Racial Consciousness and Transnational Identity in the Nineteenth-Century Americas*. Rethinking the Americas. Philadelphia: University of Pennsylvania Press, 2005.

Pappademos, Melina. *Black Political Activism and the Cuban Republic*. Envisioning Cuba. Chapel Hill: University of North Carolina Press, 2011.

Patterson, Tiffany Ruby, and Robin D. G. Kelley. "Unfinished Migrations: Reflections on the African Diaspora and the Making of the Modern World." *African Studies Review* 43, no. 1 (2000): 11–45.

Pérez de la Riva, Juan. "Cuba y la migración antillana, 1900–1931." In *La república neocolonial. Anuario de estudios cubanos*, edited by Juan Pérez de la Riva et al., 2:1–75. Havana: Editorial de Ciencias Sociales, 1979.

Pérez de la Riva, Juan. "Los recursos humanos de Cuba al comenzar el siglo: Inmigración, economía y nacionalidad (1898–1906)." In *La república neocolonial: Anuario de estudios cubanos*, edited by Juan Pérez de la Riva et al. Vol. 1 of *Anuario de estudios Cubanos*. Havana: Editorial de Ciencias Sociales, 1973.

Pérez, Louis A. *Army Politics in Cuba, 1898–1958*. Pittsburgh, PA: University of Pittsburgh Press, 1976.

Pérez, Louis A. "Aspects of Hegemony: Labor, State, and Capital in Plattist Cuba." *Cuban Studies* 16 (1986): 49–69.
Pérez, Louis A. *Cuba Between Empires, 1878-1902*. 3rd ed. Pittsburgh: University of Pittsburgh Press, 1983.
Pérez, Louis A. *Cuba: Between Reform and Revolution*. Latin American Histories. New York: Oxford University Press, 2006.
Pérez, Louis A. *Cuba and the United States: Ties of Singular Intimacy*. 2nd ed. The United States and the Americas. Athens: University of Georgia Press, 1997.
Pérez, Louis A. *Cuba Under the Platt Amendment, 1902-1934*. Pittsburgh, PA: University of Pittsburgh Press, 1991.
Pérez, Louis A. "Insurrection, Intervention, and the Transformation of Land Tenure Systems in Cuba, 1895-1902." *The Hispanic American Historical Review* 65, no. 2 (1985): 229–54.
Pérez, Louis A. *Intervention, Revolution, and Politics in Cuba, 1913-1921*. Pitt Latin American Series. Pittsburgh, PA: University of Pittsburgh Press, 1978.
Pérez, Louis A. *On Becoming Cuban: Identity, Nationality, and Culture*. Chapel Hill: University of North Carolina Press, 1999.
Pérez, Louis A. "Politics, Peasants, and People of Color: The 1912 'Race War' in Cuba Reconsidered." *Hispanic American Historical Review* 66, no. 3 (1986): 509–39.
Pérez, Louis A. "Protestant Missionaries in Cuba: Archival Records, Manuscript Collections, and Research Projects." *Latin American Research Review* 27, no. 1 (1992): 105–20.
Pérez, Louis A. "The Pursuit of Pacification: Banditry and the United States' Occupation of Cuba, 1889-1902." *Journal of Latin American Studies* 18, no. 2 (November 1986): 313–32.
Pérez, Louis A. "Toward Dependency and Revolution: The Political Economy of Cuba between Wars, 1878-1895." *Latin American Research Review* 18, no. 1 (1983): 127–42.
Pérez Nakao, Yurisay. *Inmigración españoa, jamaicana, y árabe a Banes: Historia, cultura, y yradiciones*, Holguín: Ediciones Holguín, 2008.
Pérez Nakao, Yurisay. "Inmigración jamaicana a Banes: Historia, cultura y tradiciones." *Del Caribe* 50 (2007): 68–78.
Pérez Nakao, Yurisay. "The Jamaican Community in Banes: Its Institutions, the UNIA, and the Defense of its Cultural Identity." *76 King Street, The Journal of Liberty Hall: The Legacy of Marcus Garvey* 1 (2009): 145–56.
Petras, Elizabeth McLean. *Jamaican Labor Migration: White Capital and Black Labor, 1850-1930*. Boulder, CO: Westview Press, 1988.
Portuondo Moret, Octaviano. *El "soviet" de Tacajó*. Santiago de Cuba: Editorial Oriente, 1979.
Post, Ken. *Arise Ye Starvelings: The Jamaican Labour Rebellion of 1938 and Its Aftermath*. Vol. 3 of the Institute of Social Studies Series on the Development of Societies. The Hague: Nijhoff, 1978.
Preston, Paul. *Revolution and War in Spain, 1931-1939*. London: Methuen, 1984.
Pujals, Sandra. "A 'Soviet Caribbean': The Comintern, New York's Immigrant Community, and the Forging of Caribbean Visions, 1931-1936." *Russian History* 41, no. 2 (2014): 255–68.

Putnam, Lara. *The Company They Kept: Migrants and the Politics of Gender in Caribbean Costa Rica, 1870–1960*. Chapel Hill: University of North Carolina Press, 2002.

Putnam, Lara. "Eventually Alien: The Multigenerational Saga of British West Indians in Central America and Beyond, 1880–1940." In *Blacks and Blackness in Central America: Between Race and Place*, edited by Lowell Gudmundson and Justin Wolfe, 278–306. Durham, NC: Duke University Press, 2010.

Putnam, Lara. "Nothing Matters but Color: Transnational Circuits, the Interwar Caribbean, and the Black International." In *From Toussaint to Tupac: The Black International since the Age of Revolution*, edited by Michael O. West, William G. Martin, and Fanon Che Wilkins, 107–29. Chapel Hill: University of North Carolina Press, 2009.

Putnam, Lara. "Provincializing Harlem: The 'Negro Metropolis' as Northern Frontier of a Connected Caribbean." *Modernism/Modernity* 20, no. 3 (2013): 469–84.

Putnam, Lara. *Radical Moves: Caribbean Migrants and the Politics of Race in the Jazz Age*. Chapel Hill: University of North Carolina Press, 2013.

Putnam, Lara. "To Study the Fragments/Whole: Microhistory and the Atlantic World." *Journal of Social History* 39, no. 3 (2006): 615–30.

Putnam, Lara. "The Transnational and the Text-Searchable: Digitized Sources and the Shadows They Cast." *The American Historical Review*, vol. 121, no. 2 (April 2016): 377–402.

Putnam, Lara. "Unspoken Exclusions: Race, Nation, and Empire in the Immigration Restrictions of the 1920s in North America and the Greater Caribbean." In *Workers Across the Americas: The Transnational Turn in Labor History*, edited by Leon Fink, 267–294. New York: Oxford University Press, 2011.

Quirk, Robert E. *Fidel Castro*. New York: W. W. Norton & Company, 1995.

Randall, Margaret. *Exporting Revolution: Cuba's Global Solidarity*. Durham, NC: Duke University Press, 2017.

Reig Romero, Carlos. "Anexo III: Cronología de la vida y obra de Rubén Martínez Villena." In *El útil anhelo: Corespondencia de Rubén Martínez Villena*, 3:251–89. Havana: Homenages, Ediciones La Memoria, Centro Cultural Pablo de la Torriente Brau, 2015.

Requena Gallego, Manuel, and Rosa María Sepúlveda Losa. *Las Brigadas Internacionales: El context internacional, los medios de propaganda, literatura y memorias*. Vol. 1 of the *Colección La Luz de La Memoria*, 1a ed. Cuenca: Ediciones de la Universidad de Castilla-La Mancha, 2003.

Roa, Raúl. *Pablo de la Torriente Brau y la Revolución Española*. Havana: El Comité Pro-Homenaje a Pablo de la Torriente Brau, 1937.

Roa, Raúl. "Una semilla en un surco de fuego (Bosqujo biográfico por Raúl Roa)." In *La pupila insomne; con un bosquejo biográfico de Raúl Roa*, edited by Raúl Roa and Rubén Martínez Villena, 7–78. Tercer Festival del Libro Cubano. Havana: Editorial Lex. Amargura, n.d.

Rodríguez, Pedro Pablo "Marcus Garvey En Cuba." *Anales del Caribe* 7-8 (1987–1988): 279–301.

Rojas Blaquier, Angelina. *El primer Partido Comunista de Cuba, t1*. Vol. 1 of 3. Santiago de Cuba: Editorial Oriente, 2005.

Rojas, Ursinio. *Las luchas obreras en el central Tacajó*. Havana: Editora Política, 1979.

Rosell, Mirta. *Luchas obreras contra Machado*. Havana: Editorial de Ciencias Sociales, 1973.

Sánchez Cobos, Amparo. "Transcending Borders: ¡Tierra! And the Expansion of Anarchism in Cuba after Independence" in *State of Ambiguity: Civic Life and Culture in Cuba's First Republic,* edited by José Antonio Piqueras, Amparo Sánchez Cobos, and Steven Palmer, 181–207. Durham, NC: Duke University Press, 2014.

Santamaría García, Antonio. *Sin azucar no hay país: La industria azucarera y la economía cubana (1919–1939).* Historia y Geografía / Universidad de Sevilla 66. Madrid: Secretariado de Publicaciones de la Universidad de Sevilla: Diputación de Sevilla; Consejo Superior de Investigaciones Científicas, Escuela de Estudios Hispano-Americanos, 2001.

Santamarina, Juan C. "The Cuba Company and the Expansion of American Business in Cuba, 1898–1915." *The Business History Review* 74, no. 1 (Spring 2000): 41–83.

Saunders, Gail. *Race and Class in the Colonial Bahamas, 1880–1960.* Gainesville: University Press of Florida, 2016.

Scott, Julius S. *Common Wind: Afro-American Currents in the Age of the Haitian Evolution.* New York: Verso, 2018.

Scott, Rebecca J. *Degrees of Freedom: Louisiana and Cuba after Slavery.* Cambridge, MA: Belknap Press of Harvard University Press, 2005.

Shadle, Brett. "The Unity of Black People and the Redemption of Ethiopia: The Ethiopian World Federation and a New Black Nationalism, 1936–1940." *International Journal of African Historical Studies* 54, no. 2 (May 2021): 193–215.

Shaffer, Kirwin. *Anarchist Cuba: Countercultural Politics in the Early Twentieth Century.* Oakland, CA: PM Press, 2019.

Shaffer, Kirwin. *Anarchists of the Caribbean: Countercultural Politics and Transnational Networks in the Age of US Expansion.* Global and International History. Cambridge: Cambridge University Press, 2020.

Sluga, Glenda, and Patricia Clavin. "Rethinking the History of Internationalism." In *Internationalisms: A Twentieth-Century History,* edited by Glenda Sluga and Patricia Clavin, 3–14. Cambridge: Cambridge University Press, 2016.

Smith, Mark. "The Political Economy of Sugar Production and the Environment of Eastern Cuba, 1898–1923." *Environmental History Review* 19, no. 4 (Winter 1995): 31–48.

Smith, Wayne S. *The Russians Aren't Coming: New Soviet Policy in Latin America.* Boulder, CO: L. Rienner Publishers, 1992.

Soto, Lionel. *La revolución del 33.* 3 vols. Havana: Editorial de Ciencias Sociales, 1977.

Soto, Lionel. *La revolución precursora de 1933.* Havana: Editorial Si-Mar S. A., 1995.

Stevens, Margaret. *Red International and Black Caribbean: Communists in New York City, Mexico and the West Indies, 1919–1939.* London: Pluto Press, 2017.

Striffler, Steve. *In The Shadows of State and Capital: The United Fruit Company, Popular Struggle, and Agrarian Restructuring in Ecuador, 1900–1995.* American Encounters/Global Interactions. Durham, NC: Duke University Press, 2002.

Suárez Díaz, Ana. *Escape de Cuba: El exilio neoyorquino de Pable de la Trorriente Brau en Nuevo York, marzo 1935–agosto, 1936.* Havana: Editorial de Ciencias Sociales, 2008.

Sullivan, Frances Peace. "'For the Liberty of the Nine Boys in Scottsboro and against Yankee Imperialist Domination in Latin America': Cuba's Scottsboro Defense Campaign." *Canadian Journal of Latin American and Caribbean Studies* 38, no. 2 (2013): 282–92.

Sullivan, Frances Peace. "The Negro Question in Cuba during the Third Period." In *Transnational Communism across the Americas,* edited by Tony Wood et al., 55–78. Champaign: University of Illinois Press, 2023.

Sullivan, Frances Peace. "'No Surrender': Migration, the Garvey Movement, and Community Building in Cuba." In *Global Garveyism,* edited by Ronald J. Stephens and Adam Ewing, 59–88. Gainesville: University Press of Florida, 2019.

Thomas, Gordon, and Max Morgan-Witts. *Voyage of the Damned: A Shocking True Story of Hope, Betrayal, and Nazi Terror.* New York: Open Road Media, 2014.

Thomas, Hugh. *Cuba or the Pursuit of Freedom.* New York: Da Capo Press, 1998.

Thomas, Hugh. *The Spanish Civil War.* New York: The Modern Library, 2001.

Tolbert, Emory. "Outpost Garveyism and the UNIA Rank and File." *Journal of Black Studies* 5, no. 3 (1975): 233–53.

Tone, John Lawrence. *War and Genocide in Cuba, 1895–1898.* Envisioning Cuba. Chapel Hill: University of North Carolina Press, 2006.

Tremlett, Giles. *The International Brigades: Fascism, Freedom, and the Spanish Civil War.* London: Bloomsbury Publishing, 2021.

Trouillot, Michel-Rolph. "Theorizing a Global Perspective: A Conversation with Michel-Rolph Trouillot." *Cross Currents: Newsletter of the Institute for Global Studies in Culture, Power, and History* 4, no. 1 (1996).

Uralde Cancio, Marilú. "Orígenes de la Guardia Rural en Cuba." in *Nuevas voces/viejos asuntos: panorama de la reciente historiografía cubana, ensayos y articulos historico,* 196–216. Havana, Editorial Ciencias Sociales, 2005.

Urcelay-Maragnès, Denise. *La leyenda roja: Los voluntarios cubanos en la Guerra Civil Española.* León, Spain: Lobo Sapiens, S.L., 2011.

Vera Jiménez, Fernando. "Cubanos en la Guerra Civil Española: La presencia de voluntarios en las Brigadas Internacionales y en el Ejército Popular de la República." *Revista Complutense de Histora de América* 25 (1999): 295–321.

Vilaboy, Sergio Guerra. "La United Fruit Company en Cuba y la trata de braceros." *Études caribéennes,* no. 54 (April 15, 2023).

West, Michael O. "Decolonization, Desegregation, and Black Power: Garveyism in Another Era." In *Global Garveyism,* edited by Adam Ewing and Ronald J. Stephens, 265–85. Gainesville, FL: University Press of Florida, 2019.

Whitney, Robert. "Nation, State, and the Making of the Cuban Working Class, 1920–1940." In *State of Ambiguity: Civic Life and Culture in Cuba's First Republic,* edited by José Antonio Piqueras, Amparo Sánchez Cobos, and Steven Palmer, 292–321. Durham, NC: Duke University Press, 2014.

Whitney, Robert. *State and Revolution in Cuba: Mass Mobilization and Political Change, 1920–1940.* Envisioning Cuba. Chapel Hill: University of North Carolina Press, 2001.

Whitney, Robert, and Graciela Chailloux. *Subjects or Citizens: British Caribbean Workers in Cuba, 1900–1960.* Gainesville: University Press of Florida, 2013.

Wood, Tony. "Another Country: Cuban Communism and Black Self-Determination, 1932–1936." *Hispanic American Historical Review* 102, no. 4 (2022): 643–72.

Wood, Tony. "The Problem of the Nation in Latin America's Second Age of Revolution: Radical Transnational Debates on Sovereignty, Race, and Class, 1923–1941." PhD diss., New York University, 2020.

Worley, Matthew. "Courting Disaster?: The Communist International in the Third Period." In *In Search of Revolution: International Communist Parties in the Third Period*, edited by Matthew Worley, 1–17. London: I. B. Tauris, 2004.

Yaremko, Jason M. *U.S. Protestant Missions in Cuba: From Independence to Castro*. Gainesville: University Press of Florida, 2000.

Yelvington, Kevin A. "Dislocando la diáspora: La reacción al conflicto italo-etíope en el Caribe, 1935–1941." *Estudios migratorios latinoamericanos* 17, no. 52 (2003): 555–78.

Zanetti Lecuona, Oscar. *Los cautivos de la reciprocidad*. Historia neocolonial. Havana: Editorial de Ciencias Sociales, 2003.

Zanetti, Oscar, and Alejandro García. *Sugar and Railroads: A Cuban History, 1837–1959*. Translated by Franklin W. Knight and Mary Todd. Chapel Hill: University of North Carolina Press, 1998.

Zanetti, Oscar, and Alejandro García. *United Fruit Company: Un caso del domino imperialista en Cuba*. Havana: Editorial de Ciencias Sociales, 1976.

Zumoff, Jacob A. "The African Blood Brotherhood: From Caribbean Nationalism to Communism." *The Journal of Caribbean History* 41, no. 1/2 (2007): 200–X.

Zumoff, Jacob A. "Black Caribbean Labor Radicalism in Panama, 1914–1921." *Journal of Social History* 47, no. 2 (2013): 429–57.

Zumoff, Jacob A. "Black Caribbean Migrants and the Labor Movement and Communists in the Greater Caribbean in the 1920s and 1930s." In *Transnational Communism Across the Americas*, edited by Marc Becker et al. Champaign: University of Illinois Press, 2023.

INDEX

ABC Revolutionary Society, 119, 145
Abraham Lincoln Brigade, 170, 172, 230n106. *See also* Spanish Civil War
Abyssinia, 79
Adams, Frederick Upham, 14, 19, 34
Africa: Afro-Caribbeans and, 82; British lands in, 82; decolonization in, 183; enslaved persons from, 51; and Tricontinental Movement, 183; UNIA and, 47, 59, 75; United Kingdom and, 75, 82; United States and, 183
African Americans: and communism, 102, 142, 161; in Cuba, 40–41; and Cuban revolution of 1933, 144; disenfranchisement of, 40; lynching of, 144; and Scottsboro cases, 149, 155–56; and segregation, 40; at Segundo Congreso Internacional de Escritores para la Defensa de la Cultura, 164; and workers' struggles, 153
African/Black diaspora: British West Indians and, 49; building of, 50; civic organizing in, 55; and communism, 102; and community building, 78; global evolution of, 11–12; and Italian invasion of Ethiopia, 156; Jamaicans and, 49; Marcus Garvey on, 56; scholarship on, 191n36; UNIA and, 49, 53, 65, 81, 84
African Blood Brotherhood, 102
African Legions, 60, 73. *See also* UNIA
Afro-Caribbean/Antillano immigrants: and 1921 Cuban economic crisis, 67, 74–75, 76; and 1924–25 strikes, 94–95; in Banes, Cuba, 32, 49; banning of, from Cuba, 27; and British officials, 75, 76, 112, 209n181; in Camagüey Province, 35, 109; in Central America, 7, 15, 38, 45; CNOC and, 152; communities established by, 45; corporate employers and, 7, 27, 28, 29, 37, 83; cosmopolitan nature of, 37; in Costa Rica, 149; deportations of, 150; external and international networks of, 7–8, 15, 45, 83; forced repatriation of, 82; historical documentation on, 9; hostility toward, 45, 76, 93, 145; and labor nationalization, 151; and lack of financial resources, 80; lack of government protection for, 7; and movement between countries, 39, 45; nationalities of, 7, 15, 37–38; numbers of, 27, 28–29, 82; occupations of, 38, 62; and organized labor, 93, 94, 95; in Oriente Province, 35, 62, 109; in Panama, 7, 15, 37, 149; and PCC, 12, 104, 109, 111, 129, 134, 149–50, 151, 152; and Platt Amendment, 129; and revolution of 1933, 129–30, 131, 150; and SNOIA, 148; and social mobility, 38, 45; as sugar workers, 7, 12, 15, 27, 30, 53, 99, 104, 109, 131; terms for, 37, 190n22; treatment of, 28, 45, 53, 80, 94, 104, 114, 149, 210n208; and UNIA, 37, 53, 58, 67, 76; violence against, 53, 73, 74, 75, 84, 149; and wages and payments, 28, 38, 74. *See also* British West Indians; Haitians; Jamaicans
Afro-Cubans: and 1906 Liberal Party revolt, 52; and 1912 "race war"/PIC protest, 2, 70, 84; and Afro-Caribbean immigrants, 74; and anti-fascism, 157, 165; and anti-racism, 157, 165; and associations, 63; and communists and communism, 102, 104, 111; and Cuban independence movement, 2; and Cuban wars of independence, 51, 145; discrimination against, 52; English-speaking, 81–82; enslaved, 2; and farming, 25; freed, 2; and Italian invasion of Ethiopia, 156, 164; and labor nationalization, 146, 148–49, 150, 151; and land ownership, 25; as last hired, first fired, 145; motherland of, 63; and mutual aid societies, 51; and nationalization of labor, 145, 148, 150; Nicolás Guillén as, 165; and opposition to immigration, 146; and op-

pression, 164; and PCC, 148–49; population figures for, 108; and Gerardo Machado, 82–83; and racial organizing, 84; and revolution of 1933, 125, 142, 144; scholarship on, 63, 71; and Spanish Civil War, 157, 164, 165; and sugar workers' union, 110; threats to, 81; and UNIA, 63, 64–65, 70–71, 82, 84; as veterans, 2, 52; violence against, 53, 149; and voting, 71; and white Cubans, 144, 146; and white politicians, 71. *See also* Enslaved persons

Afro-Cuban societies, 146

Agricultura y Zootecnica, 194n52

Agriculture: Afro-Caribbean workers and, 7; and agribusiness, 26, 84, 191n6; banana cultivation, 3, 7, 15, 17, 22, 30, 37, 45, 84, 108, 113, 181, 230n106; in California, 26; coffee cultivation, 16, 17, 18, 20, 29, 35; communists and, 103; and Cuban wars of independence, 17, 18; fruit cultivation, 29, 35; mixed, 15, 16; pastureland cultivation, 17; pineapple cultivation, 21; provision farming, 16; rubber plant cultivation, 108; and soil quality, 21; sugar beet cultivation, 66; sugar cane cultivation, 66, 105, 108; tobacco cultivation, 18, 20, 35; in United States, 26, 105Albacete, Spain, 172

Alfonso Bello, Alberto, 230n104

Almeyda Montaña, Jorge, 166, 167

Alonso, Manuel, 178

Altagracia Sugar Company, 178

Alto Cedro, Cuba, 24, 31, 51

Álvarez Estévez, Rolando, 197n108

American Club, 38, 42, 121

American Communist Parties, 100, 132. *See also* CPUSA

American Federation of Labor (AFL), 93

American Friends Board of Foreign Missions, 35

Anglo-American Association, 42

Angola, 183, 184

Antigua, 30, 41, 47

Anti-Imperialist League, 112, 113, 222n142

Antilla, Cuba: abandonment of SS *Antonio Maceo* at, 80; associations and civic organizations in, 42, 43; DEU in, 121; dominance of sugar production in, 21; fictional depiction of, 114, 164; port at, 3, 14, 30, 179; and railroads and railroad laborers, 3, 31; and resistance, 115; revolution of 1933 in, 123; Spanish immigrant workers in, 3; sugar mills near, 31, 178; travel and shipping from, 39, 47, 50, 56; UNIA at, 55, 56, 58, 178; and United Fruit Company, 42

Antilla Sugar Company/Estates, 24, 55, 122, 123, 139

Antillean Union, Seventh-day Adventists, 36, 42

Antonio Guiteras sugar mill. *See* Delicias sugar mill

Antonio Maceo (ship), 80–81

Arbez, Jacobo, 194n58

Archivo Histórico Provincial Santiago de Cuba, 8, 185

Argelès Sur Mer, France, 177

Argentina, 86

Armour, Donald, 40

Arnaz, Desi (son), 217n9

Arnaz, Desiderio Alberto (father), 217n9

Arrendondo, Alberto, 146

Asia, 183

Asociación Amigos de América Latina, 170–71

Asociación de Auxilio al Niño del Pueblo Español (AANPE or Auxilio al Niño), 162–63, 166, 167, 185

Asociación de Mecánicos, Maquinistas, Herreros y sus Anexos, 91

Association of National Reconquest, 145

Associations: activities of, 51; Black, 63; British West Indian, 42; *cabildos de nación*, 51; and churches, 54; and education, 51; enslaved persons and, 51; external and international connections of, 42, 43; Haitian, 42; initiation fees and dues for, 42–43; Jamaican, 42; languages spoken at, 42, 43; locations of, 42; masonic temples and lodges, 41, 42, 54; membership numbers for, 43; mutual aid societies, 41, 51, 54; Oddfellows lodges, 43; publications of, 51; purposes of, 43, 51; *sociedades de color*, 51, 64, 70; sporting associations and clubs, 42; travel by members of, 201n205; and violence against Black persons, 52; youth clubs and leagues, 41, 42, 109, 112, 122, 150, 183. *See also* PCC (Partido Comunista de Cuba); UNIA

Astor, Vincent, 127

Atlanta, GA, 40

Atlantic Fruit and Sugar Company, 90, 126–27

Austria, 180

Auténticos, 160–61, 174

Ayala, César J., 23, 24
Ayuda, 163

Báguanos sugar mill: as Antilla Sugar Estates facility, 24, 122, 134; construction of, 24; cooperative formed at, 139; PCC at, 127, 134; revolution of 1933 at, 127, 130, 134, 139; union activities at, 96
Bahamas, 42
Bair, Barbara, 61
Baker, Lorenzo, 36
Baliño, Carlos, 98
Baltimore Afro-American, 144
Bandera Roja, 130, 134, 148, 149
Banes, Cuba: 1896 burning of, 18; Anita and Harold Collins in, 48–49, 102; area around, 14; Black community life in, 84; Black respectability in, 83; businesses and services in, 32, 39; class in, 32; cosmopolitan nature of, 46; diversity in, 39; education in, 25, 32, 36, 48, 120; employment and unemployment in, 25, 169; entertainment and recreation in, 25, 32; event venues in, 55–56, 61, 165; Fidel Castro and, 4; future revolutionaries in, 13; as heart of Cuban sugar economy, 4; as hometown of Fulgencio Batista, 4, 36, 120, 182; immigrants in, 37, 39, 47, 49, 182, 201n191; infrastructure in, 25, 32; and internationalism, 3, 13, 49; mayors of, 72, 123, 182; missionaries in, 36, 120; neighborhoods in, 31–32, 39, 49, 96, 125; occupations in, 62; opposition to PCC in, 129; as political crossroads, 4; present-day, 185; Pro-Santo Domingo campaign in, 43–44; race and ethnicity in, 32; Red Brigade at, 127; revolution of 1933 in, 13, 117, 123, 124, 125, 126, 134, 138; and Spanish Civil War, 165–66, 168–69, 179; as sugar town, 45; and transportation, 25, 31, 39; and United Fruit Company, 1, 4, 25, 31, 32, 40, 42, 44, 47, 48, 55, 83, 86, 88, 117, 165, 169, 181; wages in, 88; wealth in, 25; working conditions in, 32, 88
Banes, Cuba, associations and organizations in: Asociación de Auxilio al Niño del Pueblo Español (AANPE or Auxilio al Nino), 166; Baptist Church, 59; Black Cross Nurses, 60; Casa de Cultura, 166; Casa de la Cultura y Asistencia Social, 168; Círculo Republicano Español, 166, 168–69; CNOC, 105; DEU, 121; Haitian Club, 42; Jamaica Club, 42, 83; Jamaican Seventh-day Adventist group, 42; PCC, 106, 133, 134; SNOIA, 131; sporting associations, 42; Unión Haitiana, 42; Unión Obrera, 86, 96–97, 112; West Indian, 42; youth clubs, 42
Banes, Cuba, UNIA in: activities of, 48–49, 55–56, 59–60, 61, 62, 65, 67, 72, 76, 77, 78, 84, 166; African Legions of, 60; and Black Cross Nurses, 48, 49, 60; and Black Star Line, 79, 81; closing of, 73, 185; as early Cuban UNIA division, 54, 55; historical documentation on, 185; Ladies' Division of, 49, 61; leaders of, 47, 48–49, 58, 60–61, 62, 67, 77, 83, 182; as leading UNIA division in Cuba, 50, 55–56, 182; and local-global connections, 58, 78, 79, 182, 203n32; membership of, 55, 56, 62–63, 68, 81, 83; and UNIA officials, 51, 55, 56, 57–58, 59, 62, 65, 72, 79, 82
Banes, Cuba, visitors to: Arnolds S. Cummings, 47, 57, 58; communist organizers, 166; Cuban Spanish Civil War volunteers, 166; Eduardo Morales, 57, 65; George Alexander McGuire, 56, 59, 62, 79; Julio Antonio Mella, 4, 86, 87, 96–97, 106, 115, 123, 164; Leonardo Fernández Sánchez, 86, 96, 97, 115, 164, 173; Marcus Garvey, 4, 51, 56, 79; Mariblanca Sabas Alomá, 86, 96; R. A. Bennett, 59; Roberto Buzón Neira, 175; Rubén Martínez Villena, 4, 86, 96, 97, 106, 107; Spanish officials, 166
Banes Bay: area near, 14; and boundary of Oriente Province, Cuba, 4, 15; landholdings near, 17; sugar mills and towns near, 14, 22, 32; United Fruit Company facilities near, 1, 30
Banes Fruit Company, 17, 22
Banes-Nipe region, Cuba, 14
Banes Union Church, 42
Baracoa, Cuba, 171, 175
Barbados, 30, 82, 197n109
Barcelona, Spain, 158, 163, 170, 171, 176
Bartle colony, 36, 198n134
Basque Country, 155
Bateyes (term), 31
Batista, Fulgencio: 1952 coup of, 183; background of, 120; in Banes, Cuba, 4, 36, 182; and communists, 137, 151; comparison of, to Francisco Franco, 165; and Cuban army, 120, 136, 137, 138; Cuban exiles and, 182; as de-

facto leader of Cuba, 161, 182; education of, 36; exiles from dictatorship of, 161; and Grau administration, 136, 137, 151, 222n119; and immigrants, 137; killing by troops of, 137, 172; and labor movements, 139, 151; and Mendieta administration, 138; opposition to, 3, 157, 158, 170, 173, 179; in Oriente Province, 138; and Pablo de la Torriente Brau, 160; and PCC, 151, 162, 182; and revolution of 1933, 136, 137, 184; and Sergeants' Revolt, 120, 125; and Spanish Civil War, 161–62; as sugar worker, 120; and United Fruit Company, 36, 120, 125; and United States, 137

Bayamo, Cuba, 44, 106, 166

Bay of Banes, 97, 126

Bayton, TX, 39

Beals, Carleton, 104, 142, 144, 161, 220n88

Belguim, 43

Bennett, R. A., 59

Bennett, William, 72

Black Cross Nurses, 48, 49, 56, 60, 73. *See also* UNIA

Black Cubans. *See* Afro-Cubans

Black Star Line (BSL): advertising of, 80; as Black-owned and -crewed line, 80, 81; and Black redemption and prosperity, 79, 81; communists and, 102; and diaspora creation, 79–80; finances of, 69; George Alexander McGuire on, 59; in Havana, Cuba, 71; impact of, on UNIA memberships, 79–80, 81; investments and sales of stock in, 56, 58, 62, 79; places sailed to by, 79, 80, 81; scholarship on, 81; ships of, 64, 71, 79, 80–81; and spread of UNIA message, 79; as UNIA enterprise, 47, 54, 64, 69, 70; and United Fruit Company, 69. *See also* UNIA

Blake, Robert S. F., 60, 62, 77

Blaquier, Angelina Rojas, 136–37

Bohemia, 161

Boitel, William, 41

Bolivia, 146

Bolshevik Revolution/Russian Revolution: Communist International/Comintern and, 100; Cubans and, 8, 86, 88, 98; events of, 91; Mexican Revolution as predecessor of, 101; participants in, 118

Borno, Eustache Antoine François Joseph Louis, 79

Boston, MA, 39, 124

Boston Fruit Company, 22

Boston sugar mill: 1916 coal stokers strike at, 93; and 1921 Cuban economic crisis, 68; 1925 strike at, 97; establishment of, 22; facilities and services at, 33; hours of operation at, 32–33; labor at, 32, 123; location of, 3, 22, 32, 97, 117, 124, 221n100; nationalization and renaming of, 186; noise and odor from, 32; PCC at, 127; revolution of 1933 at, 98, 117, 123, 127; settlements around, 97; size of, 24; as United Fruit Company property, 14, 22, 32, 68, 97, 117; US observers on, 33

Braceros: and communism, 88; competition for, 30; definition of, 30; and housing, 33; immigrants as, 145; as itinerant workers, 39; nationalities of, 33; recruitment of, 197n109; and revolution of 1933, 129; and settlement in sugar enclaves, 39; and United Fruit Company, 33; violence against, 53. *See also* Occupations: field workers

Bradshaw, Beatrice, 60

Brazil, 146

Brecht, Bertolt, 164

Brice, Ernest P. V., 96

British Columbia, 35

British East Africa, 37

British West Indians: 1917 massacre of, 84, 91; and 1921 Cuban economic crisis, 66–67, 74–75, 95; and 1924–25 strikes, 94–95; and African diaspora, 49; and associations and organizations, 42, 55, 95; Black Cubans and, 74; and Black Star Line, 80; as British subjects, 9, 95–96, 147; in Central America, 7, 37–38; and class, 83; and corporate employers, 38; correspondence of, 9; in Costa Rica, 54, 55, 84; Cuban communist leaders and, 99; and Cuban legal system, 94; diversity among, 38; in Dominican Republic, 41, 146; and education, 38, 148; as English speakers, 38, 42, 55, 144; escape of, from deportation, 147; and Garveyism/UNIA, 11, 47, 51, 54–55, 57, 64, 71, 75, 77, 83, 95, 182; and intermarriage, 41; international networks of, 38; and labor recruitment, 30, 74; and mobility, 38; and mutual aid societies, 95; and news of violence against Afro-Caribbeans, 53; occupations of, 34, 38, 39, 66, 92, 148; and organized labor, 95; in Panama and Panama Canal Zone, 7, 37, 54, 55, 80, 84; and PCC, 150; protests and petitions by, 94–96; and publications, 55, 64; racial exploitation of, 84; and religion, 59, 95; and revolution of 1933, 118, 123, 130, 131, 150; scholarship on, 38; as sugar workers, 1, 7, 12, 15, 27, 31, 37, 66, 80; terms for, 37, 190n22; violence against, 57, 75; volume of immigration by, to Cuba, 28, 82; wages and payments for, 75

British West India Regiment, 81

British West Indies, 47, 55, 115, 198n125

Brooklyn, NY, 8, 23, 39

Brownstone, Jamaica, 49

Brunete, Spain, 173

Buchanan, Hugh Clifford, 115

Buchanan, Moses, 31

Buenos Aires, Argentina, 6, 101, 149

Burkett, Randall, 59

Buró Frented Unidos de los Centrales de la Costa Norte, 127

Buzón Neira, Roberto: and 1935 general strike, 175; and 1959 revolution, 231n126; as Afro-Cuban, 125, 154, 174, 177, 185; arrests of, 175; background of, 154, 174; characteristics of, 154; as labor organizer, 175, 177; organizations participated in, 175; and PCC, 125, 154, 175; and return to Cuba, 177, 180; and revolution of 1933, 125, 154, 158, 174–75, 177; and SNOIA, 125, 154; and Spanish Civil War, 125, 153, 154–55, 158, 175–77, 185, 231n126; as sugar worker, 154, 179

Cabildos de nación, 51. *See also* Associations

Cacos (Haiti), 140

Caffery, Jefferson, 138

Calderió, Francisco (Blas Roca), 135, 151, 152, 161, 183

Calderío, Remigio, 152

California, 26, 191n6, 192n22

Camagüey, Cuba (city), 92, 109, 113, 137, 154

Camagüey Province, Cuba: 1917 Liberal Revolt in, 91, 193n37; 1918 railroad workers strike in, 92; and border with Oriente Province, 4, 15, 23; as center of Cuban sugar economy, 24; deportation of sugar workers from, 110; displacement of peasants in, 91; economy of, before arrival of sugar companies, 16; immigrants in, 15, 35; labor organizing and activities in, 93–94; Marcus Garvey in, 56; Morón sugar town in, 82; *Negro World* reports from, 74; population of, 28–29; revolution of 1933 in, 137; and Spanish Civil War, 167, 173; sugar mills near, 127; and trade, 16; US Marines in, 91, 92; US settlers in, 20, 193n37; violence against Afro-Caribbeans in, 53

Canada, 35, 49

Canadian Pacific transcontinental project, 21–22

Canadian Regiment, 49

Caribbean: banana cultivation in, 17; British West Indians in, 49; class in, 83; communism and communists in, 108, 141; crime in, 40; emigration from, 28; immigrants in, 45; imperialism in, 114; National City Bank and, 23; scholarship on, 8; ship transportation throughout, 39; UNIA in, 102; United States and US companies and, 7, 15, 19, 27; unrest in, 108

Caribbean, Spanish, 37

Caribbean Bureau, Communist International: and class consciousness among Cuban workers, 135; as counterbalance to Eurocentrism, 108; establishment of, 101; historical documentation on, 9; and national oppression, 108; newspaper of, 108–9, 140; New York City location of, 101, 108, 109; and PCC, 108, 135–36; and race, 108; and revolution of 1933, 108, 140–41; Rubén Martínez Villena and, 109. *See also* Communist International/Comintern

Caribbean Sea, 7

Carnegie, Charles V., 81

Carpentier, Alejo, 164

Carr, Barry, 100, 130, 133

Casa de la Cultura y Asistencia Social, 163, 164, 166, 167, 168

Casa de la República Española, 166

CASC (Cuban American Sugar Company): and 1924 strike, 94; activities and businesses controlled by, 23, 194n53; administrators of, 32; business model of, 23; and colono system for sugar cultivation, 33; communists and, 116; and education, 36; and immigrant labor, 29, 30, 35, 38; infrastructure owned by, 23, 194n53; labor organizing at properties of, 94; and labor recruitment, 30, 37; lands owned by, 23, 194n52, 194n53; leasing of lands by, 23; Mario García Menocal and, 71, 91; and missionaries, 36, 37; nationalities employed

by, 37; and NSRC, 23; and private stores, 31; and Puerto Padre, 171; and revolution of 1933, 127–28; and Rural Guard, 30, 127–28; sugar mills owned by, 22–23; and transportation, 30, 31, 35, 127, 194, 194n53; and UNIA, 55, 74; in Victoria de las Tunas, 169; volume of sugar harvested by, 195n63. *See also* Chaparra sugar mill; Delicias sugar mill
Casey, Matt, 34, 38
Casino Nacional, 160
Castelao. *See* Rodríguez Castelao, Alfonso Daniel
Castellanos, Martín, 152
Castells Peig, Andreu, 226n9
Castro, Fidel: background of, 4; in Banes, Cuba, 4; and internationalism, 183–84; launch of guerrilla campaign by, 3; marriage and father-in-law of, 4, 123, 183; in Mexico, 185; and Orthodoxo Party, 183; popular enthusiasm for, 152; scholarship on, 183; and sugar production, 186; and Teté Casuso, 185; and Tricontinental Movement, 183; and United Fruit Company, 4
Castro, Raúl, 185
Casuso, Teté, 162, 185
Catalonia, Spain, 176
Catholics, 35, 42, 155, 158, 159
Cayo Duán, Cuba, 147
Cayo Mambí, Cuba, 55, 56, 59
Central America: banana industry in, 3, 7, 15, 22, 37, 45, 113, 230n106; class in, 83; communists in, 141; crime in, 40; and Cuban revolution of 1933, 140; immigrants in, 7, 15, 28, 37, 45, 49; Jewish refugees in, 180; labor recruitment in, 197n108; monocrop republics in, 113; railroads in, 22; United Fruit Company in, 68, 197n108; United States and US companies in, 7, 27
Central Boston. *See* Boston sugar mill
Central Committee, Communist Party, 150
Central España, 178, 179
Central Estrella, 74
Central Francisco, 90
Central Manatí. *See* Manatí sugar mill
Central Nazábal, 113
Central Palma, 154, 177–78
Central Preston. *See* Preston sugar mill
Central Punta Alegre, 110
Centro Asturiano, 160

Centro Catalán, 162
Centro Gallego, 160
Centuria Cubana Antonio Guiteras, 172, 173
Céspedes, Carlos Manuel de, 2, 120
Céspedes, Miguel Ángel, 63, 146
Céspedes sugar mill, 74
Champlain (ship), 172, 173
Chaparra, Cuba, 36, 37, 42, 44
Chaparra sugar mill: Casa de la Cultura y Asistencia Social at, 168; and CASC, 22–23, 25, 55, 71, 134, 194n53; construction of, 22; José Miguel Pérez on, 87; labor recruitment for, 74; Mario García Menocal and, 27, 44, 71, 91; nationalization and renaming of, 186; output of, 23; PBL at, 134; and railroads, 31; revolution of 1933 at, 127, 129, 134; size of, 24, 25; UNIA near, 55, 74
Chibás, Eduardo, 183
Chile and Chileans, 146, 164
China, 15, 37, 144, 164, 165, 183
Chinese, 15, 37, 90, 110, 130, 146
Chiong, Francisco, 37
Chiquita. *See* United Fruit Company
Chomsky, Aviva, 6, 146
Christian, G.R., 49–50, 74
Cienfuegos, Cuba, 91
Círculo Antonio Guiteras, 170
Círculo Español Socialista, 166, 169
Círculo Republicano Español, 8–9, 162, 163, 168–69
Círuclo Español Socialista, 163, 169–70
City Bank. *See* National City Bank
Clark, Charles, 65
Club Atenas, 63, 146
Club Cubano Julio Antonio Mella, 160, 172, 173
Club Moncada, 64
CNOC (Confederación Nacional de Obreros de Cuba): and 1930 general strike, 105; establishment of, 105; influence of, on Cuban labor movement, 120; and labor nationalization, 148, 152; legal recognition of, 132–33; and Machado administration, 120; members of, 105, 216n133; and PCC, 105, 133; and race, 148; and revolution of 1933, 120, 122, 130–31, 132, 133, 135; and Spanish Civil War, 170; and sugar workers, 109
Cold War, 183, 184, 186
Collins, Anita: 1921 welcome-home gala for,

48–49, 67; background of, 47, 49; as Banes, Cuba, resident, 49, 67, 102; and Black Cross Nurses, 48, 49, 56, 60; health lectures by, 62; in Jamaica, 49; in New York, NY, 49, 202n8; social status of, 48, 49; and UNIA, 47, 48–49, 102, 182

Collins, Ethel, 49, 61, 202n8

Collins, Frank, 49

Collins, Harold: background of, 49; as Banes, Cuba, resident, 47, 61, 102; and Black Star Line, 81; in New York, NY, 202n8; siblings of, 47, 61; and UNIA, 47, 48–49, 56, 62, 67, 81, 102, 182

Collins, Ivan, 49

Colombia, 45, 104, 108, 140

Colón, Panama, 80

Colonos: and 1921 Cuban economic crisis, 66, 68, 74; and communism, 88; and debt, 159; definition of, 18; and labor abuses, 30; laborers' protests against, 94–95; and labor recruitment, 30, 74; as peasants, 88; and political power, 25; and Spanish Civil War, 159; and sugar companies, 18, 23, 25, 33, 159; and wealth, 25; in western Cuba, 25

Comintern. *See* Communist International/ Comintern

Comité Antiimperialista de Revolucionarios Cubanos, 170

Comité de Ayuda al Frente Popular Español, 167

Comité Nacional de Ayuda Pueblo Español, 176

Comité Pro Ex-Combatientes y Presos de España, 177

Communist, The, 113, 217n136

Communist International, 131, 141

Communist International/Comintern: and American Communist Parties (CPs), 100; and anti-colonialism, 100–101; and Black workers, 101–2, 103, 116, 139; and capitalism, 100; Caribbean Bureau of, 9, 101, 108–9, 135, 140–41; and communication with Cuba, 100; congresses of, 100–101, 102, 139, 151; and Cuban revolution of 1933, 132, 139–41; Eurocentrism of, 100, 108; focuses of, 100; founding of, 100; and Garveyism, 111; historical documentation on, 9; and Latin America, 100, 103, 113, 139; leaders of, 228n59; membership campaign of, 103; and PCC, 88, 101, 102, 107, 108, 135; and Popular Front, 151, 162; purpose of, 100; and Spanish Civil War, 155, 178, 228n59; sugar workers and, 12; Third Period of, 100, 103, 107, 114, 116, 139, 140, 149, 150, 151, 162; and United States, 101

Communists and communism: and anti-imperialism, 98–99, 112; Black persons and, 144; and CNOC, 120; and Cuban nationalism, 98; and Cuban revolution of 1933, 132, 182; as form of internationalism, 10; Fulgencio Batista and, 137; international influences on, 99; and Italian invasion of Ethiopia, 156; leaders of, 98; and Old Left, 10; organizing campaign of, 89; in Oriente Province, Cuba, 8; outlawing of agitation by, 139; and Scottsboro Boys cases, 155–56; and seizure of foreign-owned property in Cuba, 135; and sugar workers, 1, 89; Trotskyist, 134, 144, 150; and UNIA, 67; and women, 112. *See also* PCC (Partido Comunista de Cuba)

Communist Youth League. *See* LJC (Liga Juvenil Comunista)/Communist Youth League

Confederación Nacional de Obreros de Cuba. *See* CNOC (Confederación Nacional de Obreros de Cuba)

Confederación Sindical Latinoamericana. *See* CSLA (Confederación Sindical Latinoamericana)

Congo, Kingdom of, 51, 65

Conquest of the Tropics (Adams), 14

Conservative Party, 104, 119

Cordero Nicot, Pelayo, 171, 230n95

Cordero Nicot, Sixto, 171

Corinealdi, Kaysha, 8, 41

Cornell University, 32

Costa Rica: Afro-Caribbean workers in, 149–50; banana plantations in, 84; Black publications in, 55; British West Indians in, 54, 84; communists in, 149–50; Cuban sugar workers and, 5; historical documentation in, 191n29; immigration restrictions in, 146; Marcus Garvey in, 54; racial exploitation in, 84; UNIA in, 57, 72; United Fruit Company in, 72, 197n108

CPUSA: African Americans and, 102; Cubans and, 173; and Cuban revolution of 1933, 135–36, 142–43; leaders of, 161; members of, 142, 173; and PCC, 103, 107, 135–36;

and Spanish Civil War, 172, 230n106; visits to Cuba by organizers of, 144
Crime of Cuba, The (Beals), 142, 144, 220n88
Cristo, Cuba, 166, 167
Crowder, Enoch, 93
CSLA (Confederación Sindical Latinoamericana): 1929 founding congress of, 103–4, 134, 142; in Montevideo, 103, 131; and recruitment of agricultural workers, 103; and revolution of 1933, 131, 143; sugar workers and, 110
Cuba: 19th-century, 15, 16–17; 1900 Constitutional Convention in, 20; 1902 founding of republic of, 145; and 1902 Reciprocity Treaty, 21; 1912 presidential election in, 71; 1940 Constitutional Convention and constitution of, 152, 176; since 1959 Revolution, 183–86; African Americans in, 40–41; and African decolonization, 183; archives in, 10; British government in, 82; civil organizations in, 41; class in, 21, 24; communism in, 5, 12, 88, 98, 101, 132; consumer goods in, 24–25; cost of travel in, 80; crime in, 40; and dictatorship, 104; education in, 24, 36, 45; employment in, 24; English speakers in, 82; field research in, 10; forced resettlement in, 18; during Fulencio Batista presidencies, 4; Garveyism in, 67; and immigrants and immigration, 6, 15, 20–21, 27–28, 29, 37–38, 147; intermarriage in, 41; and internationalism, 3, 5, 13, 15–16, 34, 42; and Isle of Pines, 97; and Jewish refugees, 180; and labor nationalization, 145, 150; labor struggle in, 88; lack of Black publications in, 55; land and landholding in, 6, 21, 159, 193n30; leisure in, 24; Marcus Garvey in, 56, 69; military of, 31, 120, 125, 136, 137, 138; missionaries in, 35–37, 41–42; nationalism and nativism in, 7, 145; nature of sugar towns in, 6; as new frontier, 19, 192n22; peasantry in, 75; and Platt Amendment, 20, 120; population of, 28–29, 35, 159; Pro-Santo Domingo campaign in, 43; provinces in, 189n1; quality of life in, 24; race in, 5, 41, 51–52, 53, 65, 145–46; radicalism and activism in, 3, 6; as republic, 24, 52, 159; scholarship on, 2, 6, 88; slave labor in, 16; soil quality in, 21; Spanish ambassador to, 167; and Spanish Civil War, 10, 161–63; as Spanish colony, 26, 157; Spanish embassy in, 163; sugar development in, 22; transportation in, 24; UNIA in, 47, 54, 55, 56, 57, 67, 81, 82–83; and United States, 19, 26, 132; urban centers in, 24; and US imperialism in, 6; US sugar companies and, 21; voting in, 120; women in, 61, 120; during World War I/Great War, 27

Cuba, economy of: and 1902 Reciprocity Treaty, 21; 1921 crisis in, 57, 66, 73, 82, 84, 105, 159; after 1959 Revolution, 186; before arrival of US sugar companies, 15; and capital, 19; and competition for Cuban sugar, 113–14; Cuban army and, 136; and Cuban corporate interests, 136; and debt, 19, 20, 159; and Great Depression, 43, 84, 105, 113, 159; and lack of antitrust restrictions, 21; landholders and, 159; and land prices, 21; and production quotas, 113; reduced diversification and local manufacturing in, 21; and revolution of 1933, 132; and Soviet Union, 186; after Spanish American war, 19; and sugar industry, 15, 24, 27, 28, 50, 66, 88, 92, 105, 107; and tariffs, 21; and unemployment, 50, 113; and United States and US companies, 15, 18, 19, 20, 21, 26, 107, 113, 159, 186; and wars of independence, 17–18, 19; during and after World War I/Great War, 66, 91

Cuba, heads of: Alfredo Zayas, 93; Carlos Manuel de Céspedes, 120; Carlos Mendieta, 137–38, 147, 151; Fidel Castro, 3, 4, 123, 152, 183–84, 185, 186; José Miguel Gómez, 27, 52, 53, 71, 91, 137, 211n14; Mario García Menocal, 23, 27, 32, 44, 71, 91, 92, 137; Raúl Castro, 185. *See also* Grau San Martín, Ramón; Machado, Gerardo

Cuba, uprisings and protests in: 1868–98 wars of independence, 2, 17–18, 19, 20–21, 23, 51, 71, 87, 98, 159, 167, 177, 184; 1879 Guerra Chiquita, 149; 1902 cigar workers' strike, 145; 1906 Liberal Party revolt, 52; 1912 "race war"/PIC protest, 2, 52–53, 63, 70, 71, 84, 111, 131, 146, 149, 203n27, 211n14; 1917 Liberal Revolt, 91, 131, 193n37; 1924–25 labor strikes, 88, 93–94; 1935 general strike, 156, 171, 175, 180; 1959 Revolution, 3, 13, 73, 133, 153, 183, 184; decrees governing, 139; after fall of Gerardo Machado, 149; post-1959 Cuban historiography of, 184–85;

protests against dictatorship, 101. *See also* Revolution of 1933
Cuba, US occupations of: and anti-imperialism, 157; arrival of US companies during, 11, 19; beginning of, 18, 22; and Cuban economy, 15, 19; and Cuban Liberation Army, 19; end of, 105; and immigration, 27, 35, 159; and land ownership, 15, 20, 24; and Rural Guard, 19–20; at turn of 20th century, 141; and US military action throughout Caribbean, 7; US perspective on, 19; US settlers during, 193n37
Cuba Cane Sugar Corporation. *See* Rionda group/Manatí Sugar Company/Cuba Cane Sugar Corporation
Cuba Company, 21, 22, 31, 198n134
Cuba Labor Ministry, 126
Cuban American Sugar Company. *See* CASC (Cuban American Sugar Company)
Cuban army, 31, 120, 125, 136, 137, 138
Cuban Communist Party. *See* PCC (Partido Comunista de Cuba)
Cuban Dominican Sugar Corporation, 23
Cuban House of Representatives, 183
Cuban interior ministry, 28, 147
Cuban labor ministry, 152
Cuban Liberation Army, 19, 20
Cuban Mining Company, 166
Cuban Revolution. *See* Cuba, uprisings and protests in: 1959 Revolution
Cubans: and 1921 Cuban economic crisis, 67; and 1924–25 labor strikes, 95; and African decolonization, 183–84; as dock workers, 3; and hostility toward immigrants, 61–62, 67, 145; and intermarriage, 41; and Italian invasion of Ethiopia, 156; and labor nationalization, 145, 147; and PCC, 99; as residents of Spain, 170; and revolution of 1933, 130, 131, 157; and Spanish Civil War, 111; and UNIA, 65, 68; and unions, 93
Cuban Secretary of Agriculture, 29
Cuba Railroad Company, 92
Cuba Review, The, 200n181
Cueria, Basilio, 173
Cueto, Cuba, 41, 51, 56, 65
Cummings, Arnold S., 47, 57–58, 62, 82, 182, 204n60
Curaçao, 30, 108

Curiel, Ivette, 176, 185
Czarnikow-Rionda house, 24, 72

Dailey, Ruben, 94
Davidson, Dave, 57, 63
Davis, Henrietta Vinton, 64, 68, 69, 72
De Armas y Soto, Rodolfo, 172, 173
Decree 51 (Cuba), 139
Decree 52 (Cuba), 139
Decree 2232 (Cuba), 147
Decree 2583 ("50 percent law"; Cuba), 147, 148, 150, 151
Decree Number 3 (Cuba), 139
Defensa, 149
Defensa Obrera Internacional. *See* DOI (Defensa Obrera Internacional)
De la Fuente, Alejandro, 25, 63
De Lara, Aurelio, 65
De la Torriente Brau, Pablo: and Club Cubano José Martí, 161; commemorations of, 163; death of, 160, 161; as journalist, 160, 161; as martyr, 157, 161, 185; and Spanish Civil War, 157, 160, 161, 172, 176, 185; widow of, 162
Delicias, Cuba, 36, 37, 40, 41, 42
Delicias sugar mill: and 1921 Cuban economic crisis, 68; as CASC property, 22, 23, 25, 55, 134, 194n53; construction of, 23; nationalization and renaming of, 186; revolution of 1933 at, 127, 129, 134; size of, 24, 25; UNIA near, 55, 68
De los Reyes Castillo Bueno, María "Reyita," 51, 65, 178
Demarcation and Division of Rural Properties/ US Military Civil Order no. 62, 20, 21, 25
Detroit, MI, 60
DEU (Directorio Estudiantil Universitario), 120–21
Dexter, Richard, 74
Díaz, Rodolfo "Chepe," 122
Díaz-Balart, Lincoln, 183
Díaz-Balart, Mario, 183
Díaz-Balart, Mirta, 183
Díaz-Balart, Rafael (father), 123, 126, 182
Díaz-Balart, Rafael, Jr. (son), 183
Dimitrov, Georgi, 228n59
DOI (Defensa Obrera Internacional): and anti-imperialism, 112; and Black workers, 112, 149; and Communist International/

Comintern, 103; members of, 216n133; and PCC, 106, 211n7; and political prisoners, 106; publications of, 211n7; and Red Aid International, 103; and revolution of 1933, 123; Roberto Buzón Neira and, 175; and Spanish Civil War, 170; sugar workers and, 112, 128, 153
Domingo, W.A., 68
Dominica, 30, 86–87
Dominican Republic: and immigration, 146; missionaries in, 36; US occupation of, 7, 43, 101, 140, 141
Dominicans, 37, 41, 86, 87
Dumois, Cuba, 31, 56
Dumois brothers, 17, 18, 22, 24, 192n13
Dumois Fruit Company, 17
Dumoulin, John, 92
Dutch Caribbean, 37

El Cobre, Cuba, 44, 171
El Machete, 161
"El problema de la raza negra y el movimiento proletario" (Junco), 104
El Salvador, 140, 146, 153
El Viudo (revolution of 1933 participant), 130, 139
Emancipation Day (UK), 61
Emiliano (communist), 122, 125, 130, 150
Enclaves, agricultural-export: anti-imperialists and, 44–45; class in, 31–32, 34; communism in, 89, 182; contemporary opinions on, 2, 14, 44; cosmopolitan nature of, 34–35, 131; creation of, 15; and displacement of previous residents, 15; diversity in, 89; heterogeneity in, 35; and immigrants, 27, 29–30, 35, 39; and imperialism, 2, 15; and internationalism, 2, 13, 15–16, 34, 45, 181; labor conditions in, 2, 6, 34; languages spoken in, 45; living conditions in, 6; local communities in, 16; locations of, 15; migration from, 39; occupations in, 39; race and ethnicity in, 11, 31, 34, 45; and resistance, 2; revolution of 1933 in, 118, 122–131, 133–135; scholarship on, 2, 6–7, 34, 45; as self-contained entities, 1, 15, 23, 26–27, 34; settlement in, 39; size of, 26; social and cultural networks in, 34; sugar companies and, 26, 30–31, 33–34, 44–45, 181; and transportation, 34; US observers on, 33
England. *See* United Kingdom

Enslaved persons, 2, 16, 28, 51, 191n34
EPR, 176, 229n92
España sugar mill, 178, 179
Estenoz, Evaristo, 52, 53
Estrella sugar mill, 74
Ethiopia, 156, 164
Ethiopian National Anthem, 61
Europe and Europeans: and Africa, 156; and beet-sugar production, 66, 82; and communism, 98, 99, 100, 108; and immigration, 27, 34, 37, 180; United States and, 183
Evans, Walker, 144
Ewing, Adam, 68

Facetas de la Actualidad Española, 166, 169
Falange Española, 155. *See also* Spanish Civil War
Federación Obrera de la Habana, 93, 134, 150
Federación Universitaria Hispanoamericana, 170, 171
Fernández Sánchez, Leonardo: in Banes, Cuba, 86, 96, 97, 115, 164, 173; and Club Cubano Julio Antonio Mella, 173; as Marxist, 115; at Segundo Congreso Internacional de Escritores para la Defensa de la Cultura, 164
Ferrer, Ada, 5
Ferrocarril Central railroad, 21, 24
Ferrocarril del Norte de Cuba, 93
Fifty percent law (Cuba), 147, 148, 150, 151
Figueras, Spain, 176
Figueredo, Miguel Ángel ("Zapata"): as communist, 117, 133–34, 150; as field organizer, 150; and revolution of 1933, 117, 118, 123, 124, 127, 130, 133; "Zapata" as alias of, 117, 118
Flore Magón, Enrique, 98
Flores-Villalobos, Joan, 6
Florida, Cuba, 73
Forbes, Elise M., 39
Ford, James, 102, 142, 161
Ford Company, 108
Ford-Smith, Honor, 61
Fort-Whiteman, Lovett, 102
France, 48, 108, 155, 172, 174, 177
Frances, Josia, 83
Francisco sugar mill, 90
Franco, Francisco: comparison of, to Vallariano Weyler, 177; Fulgencio Batista compared to, 165; and Spanish Civil War, 12, 153, 155, 156, 157, 158, 159, 160, 170, 171, 177

Franklyn, Morton, 40
Frederick Douglass (ship), 71, 79, 80
French, John, 10
French Caribbean, 37
French Communist Party, 175, 176
Frente Democrático Español, 162, 169, 163
Fuente, Luis Felipe, 106

García, Alejandro, 9, 22, 92, 192n13
García Agüero, Salvador, 176
García Lorca, Federico, 163
García Márquez, Gabriel, 108
García Menocal, Mario: and CASC, 44, 91; and Cuban army, 137; education of, 32; as president of Cuba, 23, 27, 32, 44, 71, 91, 137; protest against reelection of, 91; as sugar company administrator, 32, 71; and United States, 91; and work stoppages, 92
Garvey, Marcus: 1922 arrest of, 76; and African diaspora, 49, 50, 56, 102; and Arnold S. Cummings, 58; Back-to-Africa program of, 63; banning of, by Cuba, 83; and Black Cross Nurses of Banes, Cuba, 60; and Black Star Line (BSL), 79–80, 81; and colorism, 54; communists and, 102; in Costa Rica, 54; in Cuba, 4, 51, 56, 146, 203n27; denial of US re-entry visa to, 69; as fundraiser, 79; goals of, 81; in Harlem, NY, 54; impact of, 102; and Indian nationalism, 48; and Irish nationalism, 48; as Jamaican, 54; and labor unions, 69; and League of Nations, 48; in Panama, 54; scholarship on, 69, 203n27; support for, in Preston, Cuba, 74; travels of, 56, 58, 59, 64, 65, 67, 69, 72, 79; and UNIA, 1, 48, 54, 55, 57, 58, 67, 73; and United Fruit Company, 69, 72. *See also* UNIA
Garvey Day, 61
Garveyism: and 1921 Cuban economic crisis, 74, 95; and Africa and African diaspora, 5, 10, 51, 53, 54, 67; and Black respectability, 61; and Black unity, 51; and British authorities, 82; British West Indians and, 54–55, 95, 182; communists and, 67, 102–3, 104, 111; critics of, 67; in Cuba, 50–51; and Cuban officials, 76; global impact of, 102; height of, 50; historical documentation on, 10, 51; and immigrants, 131; and labor organization, 95; popularity of, 102; and race, 111; and religion, 59; scholarship on, 59, 68, 208n132;

strength of, in Cuba, 67; and violence against Black persons, 52. *See also* UNIA
Gates, John, 176, 178
Gavilleros, 140
Generación del'30s, 160
George V, king of England, 81–82, 95
Georgia, USA, 40
Germany: African colonies of, 48; Jewish refugees from, 180; Rubén Martínez Villena in, 113; and Spanish Civil War, 155, 157, 159, 165; sugar-beet farming in, 37; in Venezuela, 165; and World War I/Great War, 43, 91
Gibara, Cuba, 36, 44, 168
Giovannetti-Torres, Jorge: on 1921 Cuban economic crisis, 67, 76; on British West Indian immigrants, 9, 38, 147; on Garveyism in Cuba, 59; on hostility against Black immigrants, 76; on immigrants' global connections, 8, 38; on UNIA, 67
GOMA (Gremio de Obreros Metalúrgicos y Anexos), 93, 96
Gómez, José Miguel: and 1912 "race war"/PIC protest, 53, 71, 91, 211n14; and 1917 Liberal Party revolt, 53, 91, 211n14; and Liberal Party, 71, 91; as president of Cuba, 27, 52, 53, 71, 91, 211n14; and United States, 91
Gómez, Máximo, 87
Gómez Oliva, Ricardo, 173–74, 179, 230n104
Gonzáles, Valentín ("El Campesino"), 161
Gordón Ordás, Félix, 162, 167
Grand, Molvaina ("Miss Molly"), 65
Granma Province, Cuba, 189n1
Gran Teatro Nacional, 163
Grau San Martín, Ramón: anti-immigrant actions of, 145, 146, 147; communists and, 136–37; DEU support for, 120–21; and labor nationalization, 145, 147, 149; opposition to, 129; overthrow and exile of, 137, 138, 147, 151; and PBL, 134; and PCC, 133, 134, 150, 151; as president of Cuba, 117, 120, 121, 123, 126, 128, 129, 134, 136–37, 145, 146, 222n119; and racial tensions, 146; and reform, 120, 123, 136, 137, 145, 152–53; and revolution of 1933, 126, 129, 134, 136, 145; scholarship on, 136–37, 225n214; and sugar companies, 128; supporters of, 160; at University of Havana, 120
Great Britain. *See* United Kingdom
Great Depression, 43, 84, 105, 113, 147, 159

266 · Index

Great White Fleet, 39. *See also* United Fruit Company
Gremio de Obreros Ferroviaros, 93
Grenada, 30, 47
Grobart, Fabio, 161
Gronbeck-Tedesco, John A., 144, 153
Guadalajara, Mexico, 143
Guam, 18
Guanabacoa, Cuba, 87
Guantánamo, Cuba: 1924 strikes in, 94; Afro-Cubans in, 64; formation of Realengo 18 near, 2–3; Marcus Garvey in, 64; peasant resistance near, 2–3; promotion of Black Star Line in, 80; Pro-Santo Domingo campaign in, 44; and Spanish Civil War, 166; and UNIA, 56, 60, 64; US naval base near, 44
Guantánamo Province, Cuba, 189n1
Guantánamo Sugar Company, 23
Guaro, Cuba, 55
Guatemala, 7, 140, 194n58
Guatemala sugar mill. *See* Preston sugar mill
Guerra, Lillian, 183, 189n5
Guevara, Che, 186
Guggenheim, Harry F., 119, 132, 220n88
Guillén, Nicolás, 115, 157, 164–65, 175, 228n63
Guiteras, Antonio: as Cuban interior minister, 120, 128; death of, 172; and Grau administration, 120, 136, 137, 172, 222n119; as leftist, 120, 136; and reform, 120; and revolution of 1933, 128, 136
Guridy, Frank, 7, 63, 70
Gurs, France, 177
Gutiérrez (colono), 94

Hacienda Banes, 17
Haiti: anti-US resistance in, 79, 101, 140; and Dominica, 87; labor from, 7, 108; labor recruitment in, 197n108; missionaries in, 36, 42; revolution in, 17; sugar workers from, 1, 6, 27, 28, 37; US occupation of, 7, 48, 101, 140, 141
Haitian Club, 42
Haitian Communist Party, 115
Haiti and Santo Domingo Independence Society, 48
Haitians: and 1912 "race war"/PIC protest, 131; and 1917 labor mobilizations, 90; and 1917 Liberal Revolt, 131; and 1921 Cuban economic crisis, 66–67; Cuban communist leaders and, 99; deportation of, 147, 149, 156; in Dominican Republic, 146; and education, 38; fictional depiction of, 114; as field workers, 66, 148; and interaction with other national groups, 38; and labor exploitation, 104; as labor recruiters, 30; languages spoken by, 38, 130; and negotiation of labor conditions, 38; numbers of, 27; opposition to Haitian government by, 79; and organized labor, 95, 110; and PCC, 130, 150, 156; and railroad construction, 27; and religious communities, 38; and revolution of 1933, 118, 123, 129, 130, 131, 150; and Rural Guard, 147; at Segundo Congreso Internacional de Escritores para la Defensa de la Cultura, 164; and SNOIA, 148; terms for, 190n22; and UNIA, 57; and United Fruit Company, 131; violence against, 110, 137, 147. *See also* sugar workers, nationalities and ethnicities of: Haitian
Hamilton (ship), 127
"Hands Off Cuba" (Simons), 142
Harlem, NY: anti-imperialism in, 113; Black Cross Nurses in, 60; Club Cubano Julio Antonio Mella in, 160, 172; communists in, 136, 142; Cuban sugar workers' connections to, 5; Ethel Collins in, 49; and *negritude/afro-Cubanismo* movements, 228n63; Rubén Martínez Villena in, 113; UNIA headquarters in, 54, 57, 67, 81
Harlem Liberator, 142
Harmony UNIA division, 82
Havana, Cuba (city): and 1930 general strike, 105; 1933 transportation strike in, 119; 1934 communist labor congress in, 102; 1966 Tricontinental Conference in, 183; Afro-Caribbean associations in, 63; Afro-Cubans in, 64; British officials in, 95; bypassing of, by steamships, 39; Casa de la Cultura y Asistencia Social in, 168; Cecilia McPartland in, 87; Círculo Español Socialista in, 169; and communists and communism, 5, 100, 109, 136, 150, 182; Cuban army violence in, 137; disarmament of Spanish forces in, 40; and eastern Cuba, 16; as entry point for sugar workers, 30; Federación Obrera de la Habana in, 134; Franco supporters in, 160; Haitians in, 79; Instituto de Historia de Cuba in, 9; Julio

Antonio Mella's ashes in, 137; labor nationalization in, 150; Marcus Garvey in, 56; Mario García Menocal in, 71; Máximo Gómez in, 87; parks in, 163; and PCC, 98, 99, 106, 133; population of, 28; pro-Spanish Republic activities in, 163; publications in, 166; and radicalism, 116; Roberto Buzón Neira in, 175; Rubén Martínez Villena in, 119; sailings from, 154; social clubs in, 160; Spanish Civil War veterans in, 180; SS *Antonio Maceo* at, 80; SS *Orduña* at, 180; and support for strikers, 94; theaters in, 163; and transportation, 24, 39; UNIA in, 54, 64; Universidad Popular José Martí (UPJM) in, 86; US officials in, 132
Havana Province, Cuba, 16, 56
Hawaiian Sugar Planters' Association, 37
Hawley, Robert, 22
Hayden, Henry, 95
Hay-Quesada Treaty, 97, 98, 112
Haywood, Harry, 102
Helg, Aline, 63
Henderson, Kaitlyn, 152
Hennessy, Alistair, 158–59
Hermandad Asturania, 160
Hermandad Ferroviaria de Cuba, 93, 94
Hermandad Gallega, 160
Hernández, Jorge A., 122, 130
Hernández, Rafael, 106, 130, 165, 167, 168
Higgins, Leaman, 94
Hill, Robert, 10, 69, 204n60
Hill-Weed, Helena, 48
Hines, William, 94
Hispaniola, 16, 43
Hitler, Adolf, 128, 153, 155
Hogge, F.W.B., 49, 74
Holguín, Cuba, 36, 44, 166, 167, 175
Holguín Province, Cuba, 189n1
Holland, 108
Hombre Mesa, Rafael de, 127
Honduras, 7, 47, 140, 146
Horne, Gerald, 144
Howard, Philip, 93
Howard University, 144
Howison, Jeffrey, 81
Howley, Robert V., 49, 50, 74
Hoy, 160, 168
Hughes, Langston, 115, 164, 228n63
Huiswoud, Otto, 101–2
Hutchins, Grace, 141–42

ILD (International Labor Defense), 142
Immigrants: and 1921 Cuban economic crisis, 66–67, 75; and 1924–25 labor strikes, 94–95; African American, 40; Antiguan, 41, 47; Black, 29, 61; British, 35, 37; Canadian, 35; Canary Islander, 27, 35; Chinese, 15, 37, 90, 118, 146; Cuban allies of, 53; deportation of, 99, 110, 139, 145; Dominican, 37, 44, 86, 87, 146; European, 27, 34, 37, 99; fictional depiction of, 114–15; Finn, 35; Fulgencio Batista and, 137; and Great Depression, 43; Grenadian, 47; hostility to, 29, 54, 61–62, 75, 76, 145, 206n93; and intermarriage, 41; Jamaican, 27, 35, 38, 41, 67, 190n22, 197n108, 201n191; Jewish, 98, 99, 180; Lebanese, 15; North American, 20; Norwegian, 35; numbers of, 27–28; occupations of, 3, 7, 15, 27, 35; official concerns about, 196n98; and organized labor, 93, 94; and PCC, 119, 130, 156; as political issue, 6; Puerto Rican, 37, 41, 146, 160; and resistance, 114; restrictions on, 27, 146–47; and revolution of 1933, 129–30, 137; and Rural Guard, 67; scholarship on, 45; and self-rule, 96; and spread of sugar technology, 199n160; as strikebreakers, 130; Swedish, 35; terms for, 190n22; threats to, 81; transnational networks of, 15, 45; and unemployment, 50; and UNIA, 38, 53–54, 75; US, 20–21, 35, 40, 41, 45, 193n33; Venezuelan, 108; violence against, 53, 74; Virgin Islander, 37, 41; and wages, 28, 29; and working conditions, 110; and World War I/Great War, 49. *See also* Afro-Caribbean/Antillano immigrants; British West Indians; Haitians; Spanish immigrants; Sugar workers, nationalities and ethnicities of
Independence Day (Cuba), 61
India, 48, 100
Ingenio Rio Cueto, 178
Instituto de Historia de Cuba, 9
International Brigades: Abraham Lincoln Battalion of, 170, 172, 230n106; British Battalions in, 230n106; creation of, 155; Cubans in, 154, 172, 175, 176, 178, 182; French Battalions in, 230n106; historical documentation on, 9; number of volunteers in, 226n9; origins of, 228n59; retreat of, 177; specific divisions of, 230n106. *See also* Spanish Civil War
Internationalism (term), 10, 191n33

268 · Index

Ireland, 48, 101
Isaroon, Amanda, 41
Isle of Pines, 97, 193n33
Italy, 155, 156, 157, 159, 164, 165
ITUCNW (International Trade Union Committee of Negro Workers), 102, 104
Ivonet, Pedro, 53
Izquierda Republicana Española, 162

Jackson, William L., 132
Jacobson, Matthew Frye, 36
Jamaica: 1938 labor revolt in, 115; Antonio Maceo in, 73; banana cultivation in, 30; communism in, 115; immigration from, 38; labor imported from, 108; labor recruitment in, 37, 74; as Marcus Garvey's birthplace, 56; missionaries in, 36, 42; size of, 57, 204n52; and trade, 16; UNIA and UNIA officials in, 49, 54, 58, 61, 78, 82; United Fruit Company in, 36; women in, 61
Jamaica Club, 42, 83
Jamaicans: and 1917 labor mobilizations, 90; and 1921 Cuban economic crisis, 67; and communism, 102; and education, 38, 39; as English speakers, 130; hostility toward, 62; and immigration costs, 38; and labor organization, 95; and marriage, 201n191; numbers of, 148; occupations of, 3, 38; and PCC, 130; as potential British officials, 96; protests by, 95; and revolution of 1933, 130, 131; and SNOIA, 148; as strikebreakers, 130; and UNIA, 47, 49, 65; and United Fruit Company, 131; violence against, 53, 137. *See also* British West Indians; sugar workers, nationalities and ethnicities of: British West Indian; sugar workers, nationalities and ethnicities of: Jamaican
Jamaican Workers and Tradesmen Union (JWTU), 115
James, Ariel, 17, 192n13
James, John A., 62
James Connolly Column, 172
Japan and Japanese, 79, 149, 165
Jarama, Spain, 173
Jaronú sugar mill, 137
Jatibonico sugar mill, 22, 90, 113
Jefferson, Thomas, 19
Jenks, Leland Hamilton, 20, 35
Jesús González, Juan de, 41

Jesús Menéndez sugar mill. *See* Chaparra sugar mill
Jews, 79, 98, 99, 142, 180
Jiménez, Antonio, 166
Jobabo sugar mill: construction of, 22; as Cuba Company facility, 22; UNIA at, 57, 63; violence against Afro-Caribbeans at, 53, 57, 75, 91, 203n27
Johnson-Reed Act (US), 146
Joven Cuba, 160–61, 174
Juan Claro port, 127–28
Julián Alonso (ship), 147
Junco, Sandalio, 67, 104, 116, 134, 143, 150
JWTU (Jamaican Workers and Tradesmen Union), 115

Kanawha (ship), 80
Kane Lodge, 42–43
Kanter, Oscar, 143
Keith, Minor Cooper, 22
Kelley, Robin D. G., 78
Kelso, Jemima, 60–61, 72, 76
Kingston, Jamaica, 39, 78, 80
Kingston Gleaner, 67
KKK Kubano, 145

Labor Defender, 142
Labor organization and activities: 1917 strikes, 91–92; 1918 railroad strike, 92; 1924–25 strikes, 93–94; 1930 general strike, 105–6; and anarcho-syndicalism, 94, 96, 105; communists and, 103; and Cuban sovereignty, 97–98; and elitism, 93; fictional depiction of, 115; and freemasonry, 94; and gender, 95; and immigrants, 93, 94–95; and nationality and ethnicity, 93, 94, 95; numbers of strikes, 91; and occupations, 92, 93, 94, 96, 105; and race, 93, 104, 115; and radicalism, 93; scholarship on, 92; and Spanish anarchism, 96; and sporadic nature of unionization, 12; and workers' demands, 92, 94, 95, 96, 97
Lafarga Fernández, Benjamín, 171, 230n95
Lafita de Juan, María Luisa, 171, 172
La Gloria settlement, 35, 79
La Güira neighborhood, Banes, Cuba, 32, 39, 49
Lake, James, 83
Lambe, Ariel Mae, 156–57, 162, 180, 184–85
La Pallice, France, 175
La Rochelle, France, 154

"Las contradicciones internas del imperialismo yanqui en: Cuba y el alza del movimiento revolucionario" (Martínez Villena), 217n136
Las Tunas, Cuba, 169
Las Tunas Province, Cuba, 189n1
Las Villas, Cuba, 173
Las Villas Province, Cuba, 82, 83, 113
Latin America: anti-colonialism and anti-imperialism in, 101; Catholic Church in, 159; civic organizing in, 41; communism in, 89, 100, 103; Franklin D. Roosevelt and, 141; and Grau administration, 137; labor strikes in, 101; militaries in, 137; nationalism in, 7, 44; and pan-Americanism, 44; and Spanish Civil War, 157; Sullivan and Cromwell legal firm in, 194n58; and Tricontinental Movement, 183; United States and, 7, 12, 132, 137, 141, 143; university-reform movements in, 101
Laurell Olivera, Carlos Manuel Alejandro, 178–79
League of Nations, 48, 79
Leftist radicalism. *See* Radicalism
Legislation: anti-imperialist (US), 19; antitrust (US), 21; banning Spanish immigrants from heading labor unions (Cuba), 159; Decree 2583/50 percent law (Cuba), 147, 148, 150, 151; on designation of state lands (Cuba), 97–98; Johnson-Reed Act (US), 146; Morúa law (Cuba), 52, 64, 70, 83, 163; Nationalization of Labor Law (Cuba), 147; Verdeja Act (Cuba), 105
LeGrand, Catherine, 6, 34, 45
Lemelle, Sidney J., 78
Lenin, Vladimir, 101
Leslie, Abraham, 75
Liberal Party: and 1906 revolt, 52; and 1912 Cuban presidential election, 53; and 1917 revolt, 53, 91, 131, 193n37; Carlos Mendieta and, 138; José Miguel Gómez and, 71, 91; and Machado administration, 104, 119
Liberia, 54
Liberian Construction Loan program, 47, 58
Liga Antiimperialista de las Américas, 86, 106
Liga Comunista de Cuba, 174
Limón, Panama, 60, 83
Lindner, Thomas, 6, 215n93
Linebaugh, Peter, 191n34
LJC (Liga Juvenil Comunista)/Communist Youth League: founding of, 106; membership of, 123; and PCC, 106, 109, 112, 150; and revolution of 1933, 122, 150; Roberto Buzón Neira and, 175
Logan, Rayford, 144
London, England, 6
López, Alfredo, 93
López Estévez, Ángel, 154, 177–78, 179
Lora, Alfredo, 69–71, 72, 75, 76, 80
Louisiana, 54, 194n53
Louisiana Planter and Sugar Manufacturer, The, 19, 23, 92
Lovsky, Witold ("Juan"), 129, 130
Luis, José, 130, 139
Luz Unida Oddfellows lodge, 43

Mabay sugar mill, 106, 121, 133
Macabí, Cuba: Boston sugar mill in, 32, 117, 124, 221n100; docks at, 3; labor unrest in, 117; location of, 32; PCC in, 221n100; revolution of 1933 in, 125, 126
Macabí cay, 97–98, 112
Maceo (ship), 80–81
Maceo, Antonio ("Bronze Titan"), 51, 64, 73, 80
Machado, Gerardo: and Black persons, 82–83; and Cuban army, 137; departure of, from Cuba, 120, 121, 122, 123, 133, 143, 145; fall of, 125, 131, 141, 149, 150, 175; and murder of Julio Antonio Mella, 104; opposition to, 113, 117, 119, 120, 121, 157, 158, 160, 172, 173, 179; and political repression and violence, 82–83, 99, 104, 105, 106, 119, 120; as president of Cuba, 113, 117, 120, 125, 137; and prevention of US intervention in Cuba, 99; security apparatus of, 110; and UNIA, 82–83
Madrid, Spain, 5, 155, 157, 158, 161, 170–71
Majadahonda, Spain, 161
Manatí, Cuba, 59, 72–73
Manatí Sugar Company. *See* Rionda group/Manatí Sugar Company/Cuba Cane Sugar Corporation
Manatí sugar mill, 23, 24, 55, 90, 127
Manhattan, NY, 17
Manuel Arnús (ship), 161–62, 167
Manzanillo, Cuba: and 1930 general strike, 105; and calls for Cuban independence, 2; communism in, 133; emancipation of enslaved persons near, 2; PCC in, 99, 135;

revolution of 1933 in, 113, 121, 133; shoemakers' union in, 151
Marcané, Cuba, 71–72, 77, 78
Marcané sugar mill, 127
Marcantonio, Vito Anthony, 142
Marcus Garvey and Universal Negro Improvement Association Papers (ed. Hill), 10
Marinello, Juan, 115, 161, 164, 231n127
Martí, José, 7, 51–52, 98, 177, 231n127
Martin, James W., 37
Martin, Zenas, 36
Martínez Villena, Rubén: and 1933 return to Cuba, 113, 119; background of, 106; in Banes, Cuba, 4, 86, 96, 97, 106, 107; and Club Cubana Julio Antonio Mella, 161; and Communist International/Comintern, 107, 109, 113; and CPUSA, 107; on Cuba and US imperialism, 114, 141; death of, 151; in Europe, 113; health of, 97, 106, 113, 119, 135; and Juan Marinello, 115; and Julio Antonio Mella, 86, 106; last public appearance of, 137; and PCC, 106, 107, 135, 143, 161; publications of, 217n136; at reburying of Julio Antonio Mella's ashes, 137; and revolution of 1933, 135; in Soviet Union, 106, 113; and sugar towns and facilities, 116; and sugar workers, 107–8; in United States, 106, 113
Martinique, 108
Marxism and Marxists, 54, 87, 88. *See also* Communists and communism
Masons and masonic temples and lodges, 8, 41, 42, 54
Masters of the Dew (Roumain), 114–15, 164
Matanzas, Cuba, 178
Matanzas Province, Cuba, 16
Mayarí, Cuba, 42, 44, 121, 154, 174, 175
Mayarí River, 33
McGillivray, Gillian, 25, 72, 94, 128
McGuire, George Alexander: as Antiguan, 47; and Arnold S. Cummings, 58; on Banes, Cuba, UNIA division, 55; on Black Star Line investors, 79; on event spaces for UNIA, 61; as fundraiser, 47, 67–68, 79; as membership recruiter, 47; as speaker, 56, 59; travels of, 47, 56, 58, 59, 62, 63, 67–68; as UNIA leader, 47, 67
McKay, Claude, 102

McKenzie, Charles S., 74, 77
McLeod, Marc, 60, 63, 208n132, 208n154
McNamara, Sarah, 6
McPartland, Cecilia, 86, 87
McPartland, Nicanor. *See* Mella, Julio Antonio
McWilliams, Carey, 191n6
Mediodía, 176
Mella, Julio Antonio: and anti-imperialism, 86, 98; background of, 86–87; in Banes, Cuba, 86, 87, 115, 123, 164; on commerce in sugar bateyes, 98; as communist leader, 4, 87, 98; and Cuban sovereignty over Isle of Pines, 97; and exile in Mexico, 104; legacy of, 97; murder of, 104, 106, 171; and PCC, 87, 98, 157; reburial of ashes of, 137; and Rubén Martínez Villena, 106; scholarship on, 87; as student leader, 86, 98; and sugar industry, 87, 116; and Tina Modotti, 104, 171; travels of, 4, 86, 96–97; and Universidad Popular José Martí (UPJM), 86, 88, 106; and university-reform movement, 98
Mella y Brea, Nicanor, 86–87, 211n2
Mendieta, Carlos, 137–38, 147, 151
Menelik II, emperor of Ethiopia, 156
Menéndez, Jesús, 152
Mercade Pupo, Delfín E., 97
Mesa-Lago, Carmelo, 185
Mexican Revolution, 101
Mexico: communists in, 140, 141, 161; Fidel Castro in, 185; Julio Antonio Mella in, 86, 137, 171; labor restrictions in, 146; missionaries from, 42; Octavio Paz in, 164; Ramón Grau San Martín in, 137; revolution in, 86; Seventh-day Adventist Group meeting in, 8; Spanish ambassador to Cuba and, 167; and Spanish Civil War, 161; US invasion of, 7; violence in, 140
Mexico City, Mexico, 6, 104, 116, 153, 215n93
Military Order 155, 27
Mintz, Sidney, 8, 50, 211n8
Miranda, Cuba, 56
Miranda, L., 108
Mississippi (US battleship), 142
Modotti, Tina, 104, 171
Monserrat, 30
Montego Bay, Jamaica, 78
Montevideo, Uruguay: communists in, 89, 140,

182; CSLA in, 103, 134, 142, 143; and Cuban revolution of 1933, 153
Moors, 48
Morales, Eduardo: and 1920 Panama Canal Zone labor strike, 68; and 1921 economic crisis, 66; background of, 57; and Black respectability, 62; and Cuban officials, 69, 70, 71, 72; on Oriente Province, Cuba, 57; as Spanish speaker, 65; travels of, 56, 57, 61, 62, 65, 69; and UNIA, 55, 56, 65, 66, 69, 70, 71, 72, 76; and United Brotherhood, 69
Morocco, 48, 155
Morón, Cuba, 56, 82, 93, 173
Morúa Delgado, Martín, 52
Morúa law (Cuba), 52, 64, 70, 83, 163
Moscow, Russia/USSR: and American Communist Parties, 100; Bolshevik schools in, 102; and communications with Cuba, 132; Communist International/Comintern in, 12, 88, 101; Cuban communists in, 111, 174; and Cuban revolution of 1933, 153; and Cuban sugar workers, 5, 89, 182; and global communism, 100
Motor Corps, 60
Munamar (ship), 47, 49, 50, 202n8
Mundo Obrero: contents of, 108–9; contributors to, 109, 113, 142; creation of, 108; on revolution of 1933, 130, 131–32, 134–35, 140–41, 143
Munson steamships, 39, 200n181, 202n12
Mussolini, Benito, 155

Nassau, Bahamas, 120
National City Bank, 23, 66
National Conference of Sugar Industry Workers, 132
National Geographic, 33
National Sugar Refining Company (NSRC), 23, 39
National White League, 145
Nazábal sugar mill, 113
Negro Worker, The, 102
Negro World: on 1921 Cuban economic crisis, 74, 77; anti-British articles in, 82; banning of, in UK colonies, 75; and community and diaspora building, 78, 79; contents of, 79; contributors to, 57, 60, 61, 62–63, 74, 77, 82, 84, 182, 203n32; on Cubans at UNIA meetings, 64–65; as historical resource, 10; immigrants and, 54; importance of, in Cuba, 55; on male UNIA members leaving in search of work, 63; as means of international connection, 49, 79; merchant mariners and, 54; "News and Views of UNIA Divisions" section of, 78–79; on Oriente Province governor's attendance at UNIA meeting, 69–70, 72; and radicalism, 68; sharing of, 78; on shutting down of UNIA at Preston sugar mill, 49; on Spanish-language UNIA meetings, 64–65; Spanish section in, 64; on speech by George Alexander McGuire, 59, 204n60; thanks to sugar company administrators in, 72; on UNIA fundraising, 67; as UNIA publication, 47, 49; on violence against Afro-Caribbean immigrants, 74; W.A. Domingo as editor of, 68; on working conditions in Camagüey, 77
Neptune, Harvey, 5
Neruda, Pablo, 115, 164
Neuvitas, Cuba, 35
"New Creed for a New Negro, A" (McGuire), 59
New Deal, 120
New England, 28
New Jersey, 21, 22, 50
New Masses, The, 161
New Negro Movement, 49, 50, 101
New Niquero Sugar Company, 23
New Orleans, LA, 39, 60, 87
Newton, MA, 49
New York, NY: Abraham Lincoln Brigade from, 170, 174; and African diaspora, 50; anti-Batista movement in, 173; anti-Machado movement in, 173; Black cultural and political renaissance in, 50; Caribbean Bureau of Communist International in, 101, 108, 109; Club Cubano Julio Antonio Mella in, 172; communism and communists in, 5, 89, 102, 140, 172, 173; Cuban consulate in, 141; Cuban opposition leaders in, 160; and Cuban revolution of 1933, 153; Cubans in, 179; Cuban Spanish Civil War combatants from, 170, 171–72; and Cuban sugar workers, 182; East River at, 47; and exile networks, 158, 173; fashion trade in, 87; George Alexander McGuire in, 63; Hipólito Dumois in, 17; immigrants in, 39, 50; international connections in, 50; legal firms in, 24; Máximo Gómez in,

87; McPartland family in, 86; newspapers in, 50; nursing education in, 39; Pablo de la Torriente Brau in, 160, 161; piers in, 47, 50; and radicalism, 6, 116, 173; Rubén Martínez Villena in, 106, 109, 113, 119; ships sailing from, 172; Sloan YMCA in, 172; and Spanish Civil War, 161; stores in, 48, 172; sugar brokerage firms in, 24; travel and shipping from, 39, 47, 50, 81; tropical-fruit trading district in, 17; UNIA in, 47, 49, 56, 78

New York Times, 121

Nicaragua, 7, 101, 108, 140

Nicaragua sugar mill. *See* Boston sugar mill

Nicolau González, Ramón: on Afro-Cubans, 111, 129, 174, 216n126; and Castro's Revolutionary Armed Forces, 185; on Club Cubano Julio Antonio Mella, 230n104; as communist, 111; in Moscow, 111, 129; and PCC, 111, 174; on Ricardo Gómez Oliva, 230n104; and Spanish Civil War, 174, 185; on treatment of banana workers, 230n106; as white person, 174

Nipe Bay: area near, 14; Christopher Columbus in, 181; DEU tour of, 121; dominance of sugar production near, 21; intermarriage near, 41; landholdings near, 17; and Oriente Province, Cuba, boundary, 4, 15; sugar mills and towns near, 14, 22, 24, 33, 71; United Fruit Company at, 1, 30

Nipe Bay Company, 27, 195n76. *See also* United Fruit Company

Niquero, Cuba, 3

Norman, Harry, 143

North Carolina, 82

Nosotros, 164

Noticias de Hoy, 162

Nuevitas, Cuba, 56

Nuñez, Antonio, 138–39

Occupations: accountants, 35; administrators, 37; agricultural workers, 103; architects, 34; artisans, 62; bakers, 34, 105, 119, 125; banana workers, 140; barbers, 119; Black women and, 38; bookbinders, 39; bookkeepers, 35; booksellers, 62; bricklayers, 39, 62, 105; businessmen, 159–60; butchers, 39; cane cutters, 109, 110; cane haulers, 110; carpenters, 35, 39, 47, 62, 92, 105; cattle ranchers, 16, 25; chauffeurs, 38; chefs, 34; chemists, 24, 34, 37, 178; cigar workers, 145, 175; cleaning railroad engines, 40; clergymen, 35; clerks, 35; coachmen, 92; coal stokers, 39, 62, 90, 93; cobblers, 34, 39; coffee growers, 16; construction workers, 35, 154; cooks, 34, 37, 38, 125, 131; day laborers, 83, 93; dockworkers, 124; doctors, 34; domestic servants, 3, 15, 34, 38, 45, 62, 63, 95, 131; drivers, 62, 92, 125, 131; editors, 35; engineers, 3, 24, 34, 37, 63, 93, 199n160; entrepreneurs, 35; factory workers, 88; farmers, 16, 19, 21, 24, 25, 35, 94; field workers, 34, 35, 38, 63, 83, 88, 92, 93, 94, 123, 131, 148; gardeners, 38; household staff, 38; housekeepers, 34, 38; industrial workers, 96; laborers, 3, 45, 50; laundresses 34, 38, 125, 131; lawyers, 35; leisure facility employees, 38; maids, 131; manual laborers, 63; masons, 92; mechanics, 35, 39, 62, 63; medical professionals, 63; men and, 38; merchant mariners, 4, 54, 143, 173; merchants, 3, 15, 31, 35, 94, 159, 160, 174; metallurgical workers, 34, 90, 93; miners, 167; missionaries, 3, 15, 34, 35–36, 41–42, 45; nannies, 34, 38, 125; nurses, 3, 34, 39; and organized labor, 92–93, 94, 96; painters, 105; pharmacists, 34, 47, 62; physicians, 35; planters, 16, 17–18, 23; plumbers, 39; printers, 119; private security, 31; professionals, 15, 62; and racial discrimination, 52; railroad engineers, 35; railroad laborers, 3, 35; railroad workers, 90, 93, 94, 96, 119; repair shop workers, 106; sailors, 81, 191n34; shoemakers, 125, 151; shopkeepers, 35, 39, 119; skilled workers, 62, 83, 91, 92, 148; soldiers, 52; Spanish and, 92; stevedores, 3, 90, 93, 94; stokers, 93; street sweepers, 105; and strikes, 119; sugar company managers, 63; tailors, 34, 39, 62, 86; taxi drivers, 119; teachers, 3, 34, 35, 39, 52, 62; technicians, 45; telegraphists, 93; tinsmiths, 39; tobacco rollers, 125; tobacco workers, 105; tradespeople, 3, 15, 34, 45, 62, 63, 83; train conductors, 39, 62; transportation workers, 88, 105, 106, 120, 124; truck drivers, 119; vendors, 45; waiters, 119; watchmakers, 34, 39, 62; West Indians and, 92; workshop workers, 106; and work stoppages, 92. *See also* Sugar workers

Oddfellows lodges, 43

One Hundred Years of Solitude (García Márquez), 108
ORCA (Organización Revolucionaria Cubana Antiimperialista), 160
Ordoqui, Joaquín, 173
Orduña (ship), 177, 180
Orientación, 177
Oriente Province, Cuba: during 19th century, 25; 1868–78 Ten Years' War in, 17; 1912 "race war"/PIC protest in, 52–53, 63, 131; 1917 Liberal Revolt in, 91, 193n37; and 1921 economic crisis, 67, 68, 74; and 1924–25 labor strikes, 95; activism in, 49; agricultural-export enclaves in, 26; agriculture in, 15; Alfredo Lora as governor of, 69, 75, 80; alleged labor scarcity in, 29; antifascism in, 5, 8; anti-immigrant nationalism in, 11; anti-imperialism in, 1; Bartle colony in, 36; Black nationalism in, 8; Black population of, 53, 109, 111, 144; boundaries of, 4, 15, 23; Carlos Manuel de Céspedes in, 2; as center of Cuban sugar economy, 24; and class, 3, 25; communism in, 5, 8, 112; corporate imperialism in, 4; cosmopolitan nature of, 5, 10–11; as cradle of Cuban revolutionary tradition, 182; Cuban army in, 125, 138; Cuban frontier zone of, 23; Cuban independence movement in, 2–3; Cubans in, 46, 144; deportations from, 147, 149; displacement of residents of, 14, 15, 28, 52, 91; economic dependence in, 5, 15; economy of, before sugar companies arrived, 16; education in, 36; fictional depiction of, 115, 164; Fidel Castro in, 3, 183; foreign capital in, 46; Frederick Upham Adams in, 14; Fulgencio Batista in, 120; and Garveyism, 5, 50, 54; immigrants in, 15, 27, 35, 44, 46, 53, 109, 147, 149; impact of sugar economy in, 5, 11; imperialism in, 1, 5; Irene A. Wright in, 14, 35; labor exploitation in, 1, 2, 181; labor migration in, 49; land in, 16, 25; local societies in, 3; location of, 4; Marcus Garvey in, 56; migration within, 25; missionaries in, 35–36, 41–42; networks built by residents of, 8; New Negro Movement in, 49; NSRC in, 23; overlooking of local communities in, 14–15; PCC in, 106, 112, 148; peasantry in, 15, 25; political power in, 25; population of, 1, 16–17, 28–29, 181; populism in, 13; Pro-Santo Domingo campaign in, 44; race and ethnicity in, 46; and radicalism, 116; revolution of 1933 in, 113, 118, 121, 125, 126, 127, 131, 133, 138; Rionda group in, 23; Santiago de Cuba as capital of, 69; scholarship on, 2; size of, 57, 204n52; solidarity movements in, 184; and Spanish Civil War, 2, 5, 168, 171, 180; sugar company towns in, 74; and trade, 16; transnationalism in, 1, 2, 3, 4, 5–6, 8, 13, 15–16, 42, 46, 181–82; travel and shipping from, 50; UNIA in, 50, 53–54, 55, 56, 57, 58–59, 60, 62, 64, 67–68, 70, 79, 84, 182; US companies in, 1, 2, 15, 21, 24, 25–26, 138; US economic expansion and imperialism in, 4, 22, 45; US Marines in, 91; US perspectives on, 14, 21; US settlers in, 21, 193n37; violence against Black persons in, 52, 63; volume of sugar production in, 22; wealth in, 25
Oropesa (ship), 154, 175, 177
Orthodoxo Party, 183
Ortiz, Fernando, 106, 163
Ortíz Drigg, Mario, 168
Our Cuban Colony (Jenks), 20–21

Palestine, 79
Palma Soriano, Cuba, 44, 166, 174
Panama and Panama Canal Zone: 1920 labor strike in, 68, 69; Black publications in, 55; British government in, 82; communists in, 140, 149–50; construction of Panama Canal in, 3, 7, 15, 28, 197n108; Cuban sugar workers and, 5; English-speaking Afro-Caribbeans in, 82; immigrants in, 37, 54, 80, 84, 146, 149–50, 210n208; Jewish refugees and, 180; labor recruitment in, 197n108; labor restrictions in, 146; racial exploitation in, 84; UNIA in, 54, 57, 68, 69; UNIA opponents in, 67; United Brotherhood in, 69; United Fruit Company in, 104, 210n208; US residents in, 45
Pan-American Club, 42
Pappademos, Melina, 63, 71
Paris, A. E., 37
Paris, France, 6, 87, 116, 158, 175, 228n59
Paris Peace Conference, 43
Parris, J.T., 59

Partido Comunista de Cuba. *See* PCC (Partido Comunista de Cuba)
Partido Independiente de Color. *See* PIC (Partido Independiente de Color)
Partido Revolucionario Cubana, 98
Paz, Octavio, 164
PBL (Partido Bolchevique-Leninista), 134
PCC (Partido Comunista de Cuba): and 1930 general strike, 105–6; 1935 plenum of, 178; and 1940 Cuban constitution, 152, 176; and anti-imperialism, 105; and Batista-Mendieta administration, 151; and Black workers, 12, 102, 109, 119, 123, 125, 129, 145, 148–50, 151, 152; and CNOC, 105, 106, 133, 216n133; and collaboration with other leftist groups, 152; and Communist International/Comintern, 88, 101, 102, 103, 107, 108, 135–36, 162; and CPUSA, 103, 135–36; and Cuban labor movement, 105–6; and DOI, 211n7; early years of, 98, 99–100; expansion of, 127; finances of, 99, 100, 107, 108; founding of, 87, 88, 98, 99, 105, 112, 157; and Fulgencio Batista, 136, 162; geographic distribution of cells of, 112; global left and, 142; and Grau administration, 136, 150, 151, 160–61; historical documentation on, 9; and immigrants, 99, 109, 130, 150–51; increased support for, 104; influence of, 106–7; international influences on, 98; issues addressed by, 105; and labor nationalization/immigrant deportations, 145, 148, 149–50, 151–52, 156; and labor unions, 103; legal recognition of, 120, 132–33, 162, 182; and Machado administration, 99, 100, 104, 119; membership campaigns of, 89, 100, 103, 109, 111, 143; and membership demographics, 99, 108; membership numbers for, 99, 106, 112, 150; and occupations, 106; and other regional communist parties, 98; outlawing of, 104; and PBL, 134; and peasants, 103; persecution of, 109; and Popular Front, 162; popularity and expansion of, 104–5, 106–7; at Preston sugar mill, 125; and race, 99, 108, 111; and relationship with Moscow, 100; and revolution of 1933, 12, 113, 117, 118, 120, 122, 123, 130, 131, 132, 139, 150, 152, 178, 179, 182, 183; scholarship on, 100, 136–37, 152, 157; and Scottsboro Boys cases, 156; and seizure of foreign-owned properties, 135; and shift toward moderation, 151; and Spanish Civil War, 157, 164, 170, 174, 177, 178, 228n59; and sugar crop restrictions, 105; and sugar workers, 88, 89, 98, 99, 100, 103, 104, 109–10, 127, 152, 182; and Trotskyists, 144; and unemployed, 103, 105; women and, 170. *See also* Communists and communism

PCC (Partido Comunista de Cuba), leaders of: Blas Roca (Francisco Calderió), 117, 135, 151, 152, 161, 183; Carlos Baliño, 98; Fabio Grobart, 161; imprisonment and deportation of, 99; Jesús Menéndez, 152; José Miguel Pérez, 87, 99, 157; Juan Marinello, 115, 161, 164, 231n127; Lazaro Peña, 152; Lovett Fort-Whiteman, 102; Martín Castellanos, 152; Remigio Calderío, 152; Sandalio Junco, 67, 104, 116, 134, 143, 150. *See also* Figueredo, Miguel Ángel ("Zapata"); Martínez Villena, Rubén; Mella, Julio Antonio

PCE (Partido Comunista de España), 170, 171, 178, 229n90, 229n92
Peña, Lazaro, 152
People's Republican Army, 174
Pérez, José Miguel, 87, 99, 157
Pérez, Louis, Jr., 32, 192n22
Pérez-López, Jorge, 185
Pérez Nakao, Yurisay, 8, 201n191
Perschonok, Mary, 144
Peru, 37, 86, 101, 146
Philadelphia, PA, 39
Philippines, 18, 140, 141
PIC (Partido Independiente de Color), 2, 52–53, 111, 145, 211n14
Pina Cardoso, Víctor, 174
Pinar del Rio, Cuba, 173
Pinares de Mayarí, 14
Pita Rodríguez, Félix, 164, 175, 176
Pittsburgh Courier, 144
Platano (ship), 119
Plato Unico, 160
Platt, Orville H., 20
Platt Amendment, 20, 45, 120, 129, 193n29
Poland, 180
Polk, James K., 19
Pont-Bou, France, 177
Ponupo, Cuba, 166
Popular Front, 151, 154, 156, 169, 176. *See also* Spanish Civil War
Portbou, Spain, 176

Porter, Llewellyn, 95
Portuondo Moret, Octaviano, 121
Pravda, 143
Preston, Andrew, 22, 186
Preston, Cuba: British West Indians in, 42; masonic lodge at, 42, 43; revolution of 1933 in, 126; SNOIA in, 175; and travel to Antilla, 39; UNIA in, 49–50, 55, 56, 59; and United Fruit Company, 55
Preston sugar mill: and 1921 Cuban economic crisis, 68; Cuban army at, 138; DEU at, 121; establishment of, 22; evictions from, 138, 139; housing at, 33, 39; immigrants at, 37; labor association at, 123; location of, 14, 22, 33, 174; management at, 37, 49; nationalization and renaming of, 186; occupations at, 39; PCC at, 127, 175; population at, 33; race and ethnicity at, 33; railroad at, 33; revolution of 1933 at, 123, 125, 126, 127, 138, 175; size of, 24, 33; and Spanish Civil War, 171; UNIA at, 49–50, 73–74; and United Fruit Company, 14, 22, 33, 47, 49, 73–74, 121, 138, 154, 171, 174; US visitors on, 14, 33, 37; violence at, 138
Previsión, 52
Prince Edward's Island, 35
Pro-80% Committee, 145
Procope, Gordon, 74
Pro-Santo Domingo campaign, 43–44
Protestants, 35
Puerco Gordo colony, 95
Puerto Padre, Cuba: associations and civic organizations in, 42; and CASC, 22, 23, 30, 31, 42, 44, 55, 65, 171; Cubans in, 65; missionaries in, 36; PBL in, 134; PCC in, 134; Pro-Santo Domingo campaign in, 44; during revolution of 1933, 128; and Spanish Civil War, 171; and transportation, 31, 39; Trotskyists in, 134; UNIA in, 55, 65, 68
Puerto Principe. *See* Camagüey Province, Cuba
Puerto Rico: immigration to Cuba from, 146; labor recruitment in, 37; missionaries in, 42; Pablo de la Torriente Brau in, 160; Spain and, 18; United States and, 18, 140; US occupation of, 7, 141
Pujals, Sandra, 108
Punta Alegre sugar mill, 128
Putnam, Lara: on associational life in the Americas, 41; on British West Indians and UNIA, 77; on enclaves, 34; on field research, 10; on immigrants' global connections, 8; on nativism and border control, 146–47; on travel by association members, 201n205; on workers, 6
Pyrenees, 175, 176

Quakers, 35–36, 41–42, 120
Quintana, Manuel López, 122
Quirigua (ship), 143

Radicalism: geography of, 182; global networks of, 116; organized labor and, 93; origins of, 5, 186–87; scholarship on, 6; UNIA and, 68
Radway, Samuel P., 57, 63, 74–75
RAI (Red Aid International), 101, 154, 171. *See also* DOI ((Defensa Obrera Internacional)
Railroads: and 1918 strike, 92; and 1924 strikes, 93–94, 99; and 1925 strikes, 94; Canadian Pacific transcontinental, 21; company-owned, 89; construction of, 193n26; and Cuban sugar industry, 92; Ferrocarril Central, 21–22, 24; and labor organizing, 93, 94; private, 93, 99; public, 93; Santiago-Santa Clara rail line, 31
Reciprocity Treaty, 21
Rediker, Marcus Buford, 191n34
Red International of Labor Unions (Profitern), 101, 102, 129
Red Militias, 121, 124, 127
Relief Association, Banes Union Church, 42
Remedios, Cuba, 64
Revolutionary Armed Forces, 185
Revolution of 1933: Batista-Mendieta administration and, 138, 139; Black persons and, 125, 129–30, 144, 148; at CASC properties, 127–28; causes of, 133; as challenge to imperialism, 145; CNOC and, 131, 135, 148; communists and, 118, 132–33, 135, 140–43; concerns about US intervention in, 129, 133, 138, 140, 141, 144, 153; cosmopolitan sensibility of, 118; CSLA and, 131; Cuban army and, 125, 137, 138; end of, 136, 137, 138, 139, 153; as example to emulate in Latin America, 140; failure of, to achieve Cuban political unity, 157; Fulgencio Batista and, 136; and general strike, 119–20; and global aspect of, 128–29; global left and, 118–19, 140–45, 153; groups formed after, 174; impact of,

170; international coverage of, 10; and labor nationalization, 148; legacy of, 152–53, 182, 184; participants in, as Spanish Civil War volunteers, 178; PCC and, 131, 134, 135, 150, 152, 178, 179, 182, 183; scholarship on, 133, 144, 152; scope of, 117; and seizure of foreign-owned properties, 135; SNOIA and, 131, 148; Spanish immigrants during, 159, 171; sugar workers and, 2, 12, 117, 118, 121–31, 132, 135, 136, 137, 138, 140, 143, 144–45, 148, 153, 155, 182, 183; transportation workers and, 119, 124; Trotskyists and, 134; United Fruit Company and, 123–26, 143; and US warships, 137; violence during, 120, 138–39; women and, 121, 123, 124, 125

Reynolds, Philip K., 26

Richards, Catherine, 56

Richards, Irene, 77, 78

Richards, Samuel Augustus, 81

Río Banes, 32

Rio Cauto, Cuba, 125

Río Cauto sugar mill, 65

Rionda, Manuel, 23–24, 72

Rionda, Salvador, 127

Rionda group/Manatí Sugar Company/Cuba Cane Sugar Corporation: and Céspedes sugar mill, 74; communists and, 116; and Manatí sugar mill, 23, 24, 55, 90; and transportation, 31; and UNIA, 73; and unionization attempt, 90

"Rise of the Revolutionary Movement in Cuba, The" (Martínez Villena), 113–14

Rivera, Diego, 104

Rivera, Julio Rivera, 41

Roa, Raúl, 163

Roberts, Fred, 40, 41, 45

Roca, Blas. *See* Calderió, Francisco (Blas Roca)

Rockefeller, Percy, 127

Rodríguez, Edilberto, 197n109

Rodríguez Castelao, Alfonso Daniel, 168

Roig de Leuchsenring, Emilio, 163

Rojas, Ursinio, 122, 123, 150

Roosevelt, Franklin D., 119, 132, 141, 142, 149

Roumain, Jacques, 114, 115, 116, 164, 228n63

Rubiales Martínez, Luis, 171

Rural Guard: and 1912 "race war"/PIC protest, 52–53; at CASC properties, 127–28; and communist organizing, 99; creation of, 19–20; duties of, 20, 30–31; and immigrants, 67, 73, 147; and labor organizing and unrest, 20, 30, 90, 93, 94; and race, 20, 53; and revolution of 1933, 113, 126, 127–28, 138, 139; and sugar companies, 20, 25, 30; and sugar workers, 30–31, 99, 110, 116; violence by, 31, 53, 110; and visits by UNIA leaders, 57; and worker intimidation, 20, 30, 90

Russia and Soviet Union: Aggeo Suárez Pérez in, 129; Bolshevik Revolution in, 91; and collapse of Soviet Union, 186; and Cuba, 186; focus of, on interracial, international proletarian unity, 1; Ramón Nicolau in, 129; Rubén Martínez Villena in, 106, 109; and Spanish Civil War, 155, 184; and state control of production, 92; United States and, 183. *See also* Bolshevik Revolution/Russian Revolution

Russian State Archive of Socio-Political History (RGASPI), 9

Sabas Alomá, Mariblanca, 86, 87, 96, 97

Sacco, Nicola, 128, 155

Sagua de Tánamo, Cuba, 121, 175

Sagua la Grande, Cuba, 82–83, 206n93

Saint Domingue, 17

Samá Fruit Company, 17, 22

Sánchez, Hipólito, 95

Sandiford, Charles, 94

Sandino, Augusto César, 7, 101, 108, 140

San Germán sugar mill, 24, 55

San Gerónimo, Cuba, 56

Santa Clara, Cuba, 21, 64, 92, 110

Santa Clara Province, Cuba, 106

Santa Lucía, Cuba, 125

Santa Lucía sugar mill: location of, 168; repression at, 127; revolution of 1933 at, 127, 129, 130, 133, 168; and Spanish Civil War, 168; violence against Jamaicans at, 53; working conditions at, 127

Santiago de Cuba, Cuba: and 1918 railroad strike, 92; and 1921 Cuban economic crisis, 75, 76; and 1924 labor strikes, 94; antimachadista violence in, 217n9; British officials in, 75, 84, 96; as capital of Oriente Province, 16, 69; Casa de la Cultura y Asistencia Social in, 168; Casa de la República Española in, 166; Círculo Español Socialista in, 166; and Cuban wars of independence, 18; Desiderio Alberto Arnaz as mayor of, 217n9; Domini-

can Consul in, 43; as entry point for sugar workers, 30; immigrants in, 75, 76, 94–95; iron mines near, 166–67; labor organizing in, 95; Marcus Garvey in, 56; migrant quarantine near, 30, 95–96; murder of Haitians near, 110; Pro-Santo Domingo campaign in, 44; race in, 144; and railroads, 21, 94; Rubén Martínez Villena in, 119; and Spanish Civil War, 166, 174; Spanish consul in, 166; SS *Antonio Maceo* at, 80; and UNIA, 54, 56, 58, 64, 69–70, 71–72, 75, 76, 84; US consul in, 70; visit of Oriente Province governor to, 69–70
Santiago de Cuba Province, Cuba, 189n1. *See also* Oriente Province, Cuba
Santiago-Santa Clara rail line, 31
Santo Domingo: Haitian occupation of, 211n2; as independent state, 211n2; labor from, 108; Nicanor Mella y Brea in, 86–87; resistance in, 140; Seventh-day Adventists in, 42; as Spanish colony, 211n2; UNIA in, 77; US occupation of, 48; War of Restoration in, 211n2
Scarlet, Bonita, 59
Scottsboro Boys, 149, 155–56
Segundo Congreso Internacional de Escritores para la Defensa de la Cultura, 164–65
Senado sugar mill, 110, 137
Sergeants' Revolt, 120, 121
Seventh-day Adventists, 8, 36, 42
Shackleton, Henry, 95, 96
Ships: barges, 194n53; conditions on, 80; crews of, 40; itineraries of, 39; nationalities of, 39; owners of, 39, 119; schooners, 39, 80, 81; steamships, 39, 81; steam tugs, 194n53
Showalter, William Joseph, 33
Sierra Maestra, 3
Simón, Nicolás, 110
Simons, William, 142
Sims, B. B., 73
Sindicato Nacional de Obreros de la Industria Azucarera. *See* SNOIA (Sindicato Nacional de Obreros de la Industria Azucarera)
Sindicato Provincial de Trabajadores de Camagüey (SPTC), 93–94, 110
Sitges, Spain, 163
Skelly, Jack, 37
Sloan YMCA, 172
Sluga, Glenda, 191n33
SNOIA (Sindicato Nacional de Obreros de la Industria Azucarera): activities of, 110–11, 112; and Antillanos, 150; and CSLA, 110; founding of, 110; and internationalism, 110; issues addressed by, 110–11; and labor nationalization, 148; leaders of, 175; membership of, 110, 112, 123, 125; and race, nationality, and ethnicity, 110, 112, 123, 129, 148; and revolution of 1933, 123, 126, 127, 128, 129, 131, 133, 150; Roberto Buzón Neira and, 175; and United Fruit Company, 126
Sociedades de color, 51. *See also* Associations
Sociedades Hispanas Confederadas de Ayuda a España, 172
Soto, Lionel, 6, 137
South Africa, 79, 149
South America, 7, 140, 180
Spain: Catholics in, 155, 158; and colonialism, 48; Cuban organizations in, 170–71; Cubans in, 170, 179; and Cuban wars of independence, 17–18; and Dominica, 87; immigrants from, 15, 28; Langston Hughes in, 228n63; and migration, 15; Ministry of Public Instruction and Fine Arts in, 164; in Morocco, 48; Nicolás Guillén in, 228n63; and PCC, 99; Popular Front in, 176; Second Spanish Republic in, 155, 156, 158, 164, 177; and United States, 18, 40. *See also* Spanish Civil War; Spanish immigrants
Spanish-American War, 18, 40
Spanish Caribbean, 37
Spanish Civil War: Afro-Cubans and, 125, 157, 164; and anti-fascism, 156; background and events of, 155, 156, 161; Catholics and, 155, 158; Communist International/Comintern and, 155, 228n59; communists and, 125, 154, 157; CPUSA and, 172; Cuban combatants in, 170–79, 185, 226n16, 229n90; Cuban government and, 161–62; Cuban organizations and, 162, 163–64, 166, 167, 168–70; Cubans and, 5, 111, 154, 156–57, 158–61, 162, 165–70; death of José Miguel Pérez during, 99; exile networks and, 158, 182; France and, 155; Fulgencio Batista and, 161–62; Germany and, 155, 157, 165; international groups and, 157–58; Italy and, 155, 157, 165; numbers of international participants in, 156; Pablo de la Torriente Brau and, 161; PCC and, 164, 170, 174, 177, 178, 228n59; post-1959 Cuban historiography of, 184–85; revolution of 1933 participants and, 125, 178, 182; scholarship

on, 157, 158–59; Soviet Union and, 155, 184; Spanish immigrants and, 157, 159, 162; Spanish landholders and, 158; sugar workers and, 2, 5, 12–13, 154, 158, 167–68, 173, 174, 177–80; United Kingdom and, 155; United States and, 155, 161, 172; women and, 166, 167, 168, 170, 171, 179

Spanish Honduras, 47

Spanish immigrants: and 1935 general strike, 171; businesses owned by, 150; as businessmen, 159–60; children of, in Spain, 170; and Círculo Español Socialista, 169; and Cuban labor movement, 159; employers' preference for hiring, 52, 145, 150; and government encouragement to immigrate, 35; and imperial expansion, 15; and intermarriage, 41; and labor nationalization, 150; and labor organizing, 93; as merchants, 159, 160, 174; as metalworkers, 93; and PCC, 99; as proportion of Cuban population, 35, 159; as proportion of immigrants, 28; as railroad workers, 3; regional origins of, 27, 35; and revolution of 1933, 118, 138–39, 171; sending for nephews by, 159; and social clubs, 160; and Spanish Civil War, 157, 159–60, 162, 168, 169, 174; as sugar barons, 23–24; as sugar workers, 37, 118; and wealth, 160

Spanish Republic. *See* Spain: Second Spanish Republic in; Spanish Civil War

SPTC (Sindicato Provincial de Trabajadores de Camagüey), 93–94, 110

Standard Oil, 45

St. Andrew, Jamaica, UNIA division, 82

Steamships. *See under* Ships

Sterling, Ernesto Fonts y, 32

Stevens, Margaret, 108, 151

Stimson, Henry L., 132

St. John's College, 17

St. Kitts, 30

St. Louis (ship), 180

St. Martin, 30

Stockdale, Frank, 198n125

Stoute, William Preston, 69

Strait of Gibraltar, 155

St. Thomas, 30

St. Vincent, 30

Suárez Pérez, Aggeo, 111, 129, 216n126

Sugar companies: and 1921 Cuban economic crisis, 66, 68; acreage for, 1, 15, 22, 23, 24, 26; arrival of, in Cuba, 15; characteristics of, 15; and class, 37; and collaboration with local authorities, 11; and compartmentalization, 90; and control over workers and life in properties of, 1, 3, 6, 15, 25, 26–27, 28, 31, 90, 138; and Cuban army, 31; and Cuban government, 29, 30; Cuban planters and, 17–18; and Cuban wars of independence, 17–18; and education, 36; elites and, 24–25; employees of, 37; fictional depictions of, 114–15, 116; goals of, 15; and immigrant labor, 11, 15, 27, 29, 37; and imperialism, 88; and industrialization, 88, 211n8; and internationalism, 3, 15; and labor nationalization, 150; and labor organizing, 91; lands owned by, 1, 22, 23, 24, 26; and missionaries and missions, 36; post-1959, 186; and private security guards, 11, 31; and race, 88; and revolution of 1933, 117, 138; and Rural Guard, 20, 30–31, 138; scholarship on, 6, 72, 211n8; and social inequity, 88; and soil quality, 21; and sugar prices, 27; and trade, 15; transfer of, from Cuban to US owners, 68; and transnationalism, 181; and transportation, 15, 30, 31, 92; and unemployment, 88; and UNIA, 68; and US capital, 18; and violence against sugar workers, 31; and wages, 29; and worker debt, 11, 80; and work stoppages, 91–95; and World War I/Great War, 27, 91. *See also* Antilla Sugar Company/Estates; CASC (Cuban American Sugar Company); United Fruit Company

Sugar company towns: and African diaspora, 49; anti-imperialism in, 44; associations and civic organizations in, 41, 42–43; and class, 31–32; and communism, 89; cosmopolitan nature of, 11, 46; and global commodities trade, 9, 11, 16; immigrants in, 45; imperialism in, 49; international activism in, 49; and international connections, 11, 16, 41, 42, 44; and migration, 9, 11, 16; occupations in, 45; Pro-Santo Domingo campaign in, 44; racial subordination in, 49–50; residents of, 62; scholarship on, 9; single-crop economic dependency in, 49; sizes of, 74; and solidarity movements, 181–82; and Spanish Civil War, 158, 180; transnational nature of, 181. *See*

also Banes, Cuba; Enclaves, agricultural-export; Puerto Padre, Cuba
Sugar Estates of Oriente, 23
Sugar workers: and 1921 Cuban economic crisis, 66–67, 68, 74–75; and abuse and exploitation, 2, 28, 30, 88; and anti-imperialism, 2, 12, 112; clashes between different nationalities of, 90; and communists and communism, 1, 12, 88, 89, 99, 100, 103, 104, 107–8, 109, 112, 114, 117, 153, 182; company control over, 6, 30, 31, 89, 90; cosmopolitan and multinational nature of, 116, 153; and Cuban sovereignty, 12, 88, 182; dispersion of, after harvest, 90; geographic distribution of, 89–90; and geographic mobility, 38; and global economic system, 88; historical documentation on, 9–10; immigrants as, 11, 15, 28, 45, 110; international character of, 1, 4, 6, 12; and labor organizing, 1, 12, 88, 89, 90, 93, 178, 182; and labor resistance, 88, 89–91, 92, 93, 94, 95, 97, 99, 110–11, 114, 116; and land loss, 2; living conditions of, 6, 33, 110; migrants as, 29–30; multilingual character of, 116; and political issues, 11; and poverty, 6, 50; as proletariat, 88, 89; and race and nationality, 1–2, 11–12, 90; recruitment of, 30, 38; and Sacco and Vanzetti executions, 155; scholarship on, 6–7, 45, 153; and seasonal employment, 77; and Spanish Civil War, 2, 5, 12–13, 154, 158, 167–68, 173, 174, 177–80; tasks of, 7, 12, 27, 29, 90, 116; and transnationalism, 5, 11; and unemployment, 50, 88; and UNIA, 1; violence against, 31, 110; wages and payments for, 28, 38, 66, 68, 75, 88, 90, 92, 93, 97, 110, 111; and working conditions, 88, 90, 92, 110–11. *See also* Braceros; Revolution of 1933: sugar workers and
Sugar workers, nationalities and ethnicities of: Afro-Antillean, 99, 119; Afro-Caribbean, 7, 12, 15, 32, 45, 109, 131; Afro-Cuban, 99; Afro-descended, 11; Antiguan, 30; Antillano, 27, 29, 38, 55, 104, 131; Barbadian, 30; British West Indian, 1, 12, 15, 27, 31, 37, 66, 80, 118; Canary Islander, 27; Chinese, 110, 118; Cuban, 12, 28, 32, 33, 36, 90; Curaçaoan, 30; Dominican, 30, 108; Dutch Caribbean, 37; French Caribbean, 37; Grenadian, 30; Haitian, 1, 6, 12, 15, 27, 28, 30, 33, 36, 37, 38, 66, 90, 104, 108, 110, 118, 130, 131; Jamaican, 6, 27, 28, 30, 33, 36, 90, 104, 108, 110, 115, 130, 131; Kittitian, 30; Martiniquais, 108; Montserratian, 30; Spanish, 12, 118; St. Martiner, 30; St. Thomian, 30; US Virgin Islander, 37; Vincentian, 30; West Indian, 29
Sullivan and Cromwell legal firm, 24, 194n58
Suriname, 101

Tacajó sugar mill: and Antilla Sugar Estates, 55, 122, 139; Black workers at, 123; construction of, 24, 121; and DOI, 128; evictions from, 139; location of, 24, 31, 122; Miguel Ángel Figueredo ("Zapata") at, 127; PCC at, 106, 127, 133, 134, 139; revolution of 1933 at, 121–22, 127, 129, 130, 134, 138–39; Rural Guard at, 31, 139; UNIA at, 55; union activities at, 96
Taite, George, 47, 49
Tamano sugar mill, 126–27
Tampa, FL, 6, 40
Tarazona, Spain, 176
Tarea Álvaro Reynoso plan, 186
"Theses on the National and Colonial Question" (Communist International), 101
Third country labor system (term), 190n23
Thomas, Theodora, 60
Thompson, H., 59
Thorpe, J. A., 74
Tierra!, 93
Tisa, John, 172
Todd, Joseph A., 82
Torres, Armando, 154, 178
Transnational (term), 10
Tricontinental Movement, 183
Trigo (communist organizer), 166, 170
Trinidad Workingmen's Association, 68
Trotskyists, 134, 144, 150
Trouillot, Michel-Rolph, 8
Turner, Frederick Jackson, 192n22

UK National Archives, 9
UNIA: and 1921 Cuban economic crisis, 67, 68, 73, 74–76, 84; and Africa, 47, 48, 57, 59; and African diaspora, 53, 65, 76, 78, 81, 82, 84; and African redemption, 54, 63, 70, 75, 76, 203n32; alternative names for, 64; and anti-colonialism, 47–48; and anti-immigrant

280 · Index

hostility, 76; and anti-imperialism, 47–48, 49; Black Cross Nurses of, 48, 49, 56, 60, 73; Black Cubans and, 11, 51, 63, 64–65, 70–71; and Black respectability, 62, 84; and Black rights, 82; and Black solidarity and uplift, 48, 49, 50, 54, 57, 58, 64, 65–66, 70, 71, 75, 76, 84; and British officials, 75, 76; British West Indians and, 11, 47, 51, 54–55, 82; Bureau of Passports of, 48; characteristics of membership of, 62–64, 71, 83; and class, 54, 83; and communists, 67, 102; and community building and community life, 54, 58–60, 61–62, 65, 77–78, 84; connections between divisions of, 78; and cooperation between linguistic, cultural, and national groups, 51, 54, 57, 63, 64; in Cuba, 1, 47; and Cuban authorities, 69–71, 73, 75, 82–83, 84; and Cuban patriotism, 64, 73; dangers to, 53; and defense fund for Marcus Garvey, 76; doctrine of, 48; dues for, 42–43; and economic dependency and insecurity, 76, 84; and education, 47, 48; expansion of, 53; field organizers for, 57; founding of, 54; and freedom of the press, 47; and fundraising, 67; geographic reach of, 47, 54; growth of, 54, 57, 76, 82; headquarters of, 54, 57–58; immigrants and, 38, 54–55, 75; impact of 1912 "race war"/PIC protest on, 63, 84; infrastructure and organization of, 77, 78; inspiration for joining, 56, 57; international conventions of, 47–48, 49, 50, 54, 56, 57, 58, 74, 81, 82, 102; international nature and reach of, 8, 49, 50, 58; and labor radicalism, 68; Ladies' Division of, 49, 61; languages used in, 64–65, 72, 73; as largest Black organization in history, 182; and Liberia, 47, 54, 58; locations of divisions of, 42; and lynching, 47; members' travel between divisions of, 48, 77, 78; messages of, 38, 54; mission of, 70, 71, 72, 75, 79; name change of, 163; numbers of members of, 56, 82; official song of, 61; and political interference, 65; popularity of, 5, 11, 54, 68, 76; publications of, 47, 49, 54; and racial organization, 63–64; recruitment for, 58, 64, 65, 178; and religion, 58, 59–60, 62, 65, 71, 75; scholarship on, 59, 60, 61, 63, 67, 72, 82; and segregation, 84; and social capital, 55; and *sociedades de color,* 51; as source of international news, 49, 58; and sugar company officials, 72–74, 76; symbols of, 60, 78; and transnational networks, 84; and United Fruit Company, 49–50, 54, 55, 68–69, 72; in United States, 47; women and, 48, 49, 60–61, 63, 77–78. *See also* Black Star Line (BSL)

UNIA, activities and services of: aid, relief, and protection, 60, 75, 76, 84, 208n154; auto maintenance and driving lessons, 60; bands and choirs, 60; boy scouts, 60; burials and death benefits, 58, 60; ceremonies and parades, 60, 61, 62, 73, 77, 78; dances and parties, 61, 65; day schools, 60; fundraising fairs, 65; grocery stores, 60, 76; health care and public health education, 47, 48–49, 60, 62, 76; juvenile savings program, 60; Liberian Construction Loan program, 47, 58; libraries, 58; maintaining order, 60; practicing military skills and discipline, 60; providing meeting places, 59, 61; providing social support, 58; religious meetings and support, 59, 77, 78; sending reports to *Negro World,* 60, 61, 62–63, 64, 72, 74–75, 77, 78–79, 82, 84; shipping line, 76; sickness support, 58; strengthening local communities, 77; Sunday schools, 60, 62, 76; visiting isolated members, 58; visiting unemployed members, 58

UNIA, leaders of: Anita Collins, 47, 48–49, 56, 60, 62, 67, 102, 182; Arnold S. Cummings, 47, 57–58, 62, 82, 182, 204n60; B. B. Sims, 73; Charles Clark, 65; Clarice Walters, 69; Clarise Walters, 70, 71; Dave Davidson, 57; education of, 206n86; Ernest Peterson, 64; Ethel Collins, 49, 61, 202n8; Gordon Procope, 74; G.R. Christian, 49–50, 74; Harold Collins, 47, 48–49, 56, 61, 62, 102, 182; Henrietta Vinton Davis, 64, 68, 69, 72; James Lake, 83; Jemima Kelso, 60–61; John A. James, 62; Josia Frances, 83; Molvaina ("Miss Molly") Grand, 65; occupations of, 83; R. A. Bennett, 59; Robert S. F. Blake, 60, 62, 77; Samuel P. Radway, 57, 63, 74–75; William Bennett, 72. *See also* Garvey, Marcus; McGuire, George Alexander; Morales, Eduardo

Unión de Morón, 93, 94

Unión de Obreros Antillanos (UOA), 95, 104, 112

Unión de Trabajadores de la Industria Azucarera de Puerto Padre, 94

Unión Haitiana, 42
Unión Nacionalista, 119
Unión Obrera de Banes, 86, 96, 97–98, 112, 123, 124
Unions, 88
United Fruit Company: 1933 protest against, 117; Black employees of, 40; Boston, MA, headquarters of, 124; cane fields of, 55; in Central America, 68, 197n108; and class, 32; in Colombia, 104; communists and, 103–4, 108, 116, 126, 171; and control over commerce, 31, 97–98, 104; in Costa Rica, 72, 197n108; Cuban headquarters of, 1, 4; depiction of Cuba by, 181; dominance by, 181; and economic imperialism, 181; entry of, into Cuba, 17; Fidel Castro and, 4; Fulgencio Batista and, 36, 120, 125; in Haiti, 197n108; historical documentation on, 9, 191n29; and immigrant labor, 27, 30, 32, 37, 83, 131, 197n108; incorporation of, 22; infrastructure and industries owned by, 26–27, 30; in Jamaica, 30, 197n108; and labor actions and disputes, 93, 97, 104, 117; and labor nationalization, 220n82; and labor recruitment, 197n108; and labor subjugation, 181; and labor unions, 69, 93, 96, 97–98; land and territory of, 1, 22, 26, 31, 35, 50, 51, 97–98, 114, 123; leaders of, 132; and local residents, 14–15; managerial staff of, 32, 74; occupations in, 62; Pablo Neruda poem condemning, 164; in Panama, 104, 210n208; prominence of, 22; publicity for, 33; Rafael Díaz-Balart and, 182; as representation of US imperialism, 4; and revolution of 1933, 123–26, 130, 138, 143; and Rural Guard, 30; on Spain's administration of Cuba, 26; Spanish Civil War volunteers and, 173; subsidiaries of, 27, 195n76; sugar mills owned by, 3, 14, 22, 32; and Sullivan and Cromwell legal firm, 194n58; towns associated with, 42; and transportation, 31, 39, 69, 72, 119, 143, 210n208; and UNIA, 49–50, 54, 55, 68–69, 72; US employees of, 40; US visitors' perspectives on, 14–15, 33; volume of sugar harvested by, 195n63; wages and payments by, 93; and worker housing, 33; working conditions on properties of, 103–4. *See also* Banes, Cuba: and United Fruit Company; Boston sugar mill; Preston sugar mill

"United Fruit Company" (Neruda), 164
United Kingdom: and Africa, 48, 82; and British subjects in Cuba, 75, 82, 209n181; communism in, 108; officials of, in Cuba, 112; and Panama, 82; and Spanish Civil War, 155; and sugar tariffs, 66; and Venezuela, 165
United States: and 1902 Reciprocity Treaty, 21; and 1912 "race war"/PIC protest in Cuba, 52–53; and 1924 strikes in Cuba, 93–94; and 1933 dispatch of warships to Cuba, 120; and Africa, 183; African Americans in, 144; agriculture in, 26; ambassadors to Cuba from, 93, 119, 132, 133, 137, 138; anti-imperialist legislation in, 19; arrest of Marcus Garvey in, 76; banana consumption in, 17; Black migration to, 49; and China, 183; and Cold War, 186; and communists and communism, 12, 101, 102, 108, 132, 140, 141–42, 144, 161; and Cuba, 18, 19, 91, 137, 138; and Cuban revolution of 1933, 132, 137, 140, 141–42, 144, 153; Cubans in, 173; and Dominican Republic, 43; Dumois brothers in, 18; and early 19th-century Cuba, 19; eugenics in, 146; and Europe, 183; and expansion into Caribbean, 19; Fulgencio Batista and, 136; growth of influence of, 7; and Haiti, 48, 79; immigration restrictions in, 146; and Isle of Pines, 97; Jewish refugees in, 180; and Latin America, 132, 137, 140, 141; lynching in, 47, 144, 149; military intervention by, 7; missionaries from, 42; and race, 40, 68, 149; and Santo Domingo, 48; and Soviet Union, 183; and Spain, 18; and Spanish Civil War, 155, 161, 172; and sugar industry, 88; and sugar tariffs, 66, 105; and third country labor system, 190n23; and UNIA, 47, 58, 60, 65, 75, 82, 102, 206n86; warships of, 137, 141, 142, 144; western frontier of, 19; and World War I/Great War, 27, 91. *See also* Cuba, US occupations of
Universidad Popular José Martí (UPJM), 86, 106
University of Havana, 106, 160
Urcelay-Maragnès, Denise, 157, 228n59, 230n104
Uruguay, 146
US-Caribbean world, 7–8
US Congress, 19, 97, 98, 183
US Marines: in Cuba, 52, 91, 92, 112, 141; in Dominican Republic, 101, 140, 141; in Haiti,

140, 141; and labor organizing and strikes, 90, 91, 93; in Nicaragua, 7, 140, 141; violence by, 101
US Military Civil Order no. 62/Demarcation and Division of Rural Properties, 20, 21, 25
US Navy, 128
USSR. *See* Moscow, USSR; Russia and Soviet Union
US State Department, 69, 132

Van Horne, William, 21–22, 27, 193n26, 198n134
Vanzetti, Bartolomeo, 128, 155
Varona, Enrique, 93, 94, 99, 110
Venezuela and Venezuelans: communists in, 140; dictatorship in, 101; and immigration restrictions, 146; and petroleum industry, 45, 153, 165; and seizure of Dutch arsenal in Curaçao, 108
Veragua (ship), 143
"Verdades sobre la Guerra de España" (Círculo Español Socialista), 169
Verdeja Act (Cuba), 105
Veterans and Patriot's movement, 106
Victoria de las Tunas, Cuba, 44, 169
Vidal Zaldívar, Ramón, 168
Villa Clara, Cuba, 113
Villanueva de la Jara, Spain, 172
Virgin Islands, 37, 41

Walters, Clarise, 69, 70, 71
Walters, William, 75
Webley, Theo, 71
Welles, Sumner, 119, 120, 132, 137
West Africa, 47
West Indies Mission, 36, 37
Weyler, Valleriano, 18, 177
White Cubans, 146
Whitney, Robert, 222n119
Wilmington, DE, 39
Winette, Sonia, 144
Winston-Salem, NC, 58
Women: and communism, 112, 170; and revolution of 1933, 121, 123, 124, 125; and Spanish Civil War, 166, 167, 168, 170, 171, 179; and UNIA, 48, 49, 60–61, 63, 77–78
Wood, Leonard, 19, 27, 193n26
Wood, Tony, 111, 152, 216n126, 225n214
Workers Collection, Instituto de Historia de Cuba, 9
World War I/Great War: Canada and, 49; Cuba and, 27; and German occupation of Belgium, 43; Jamaicans and, 49; as point of demarcation, 21, 23, 43, 89; and sugar prices, 193n37; United States and, 27, 91, 193n37
Wright, Irene A., 14, 35, 37
Wright, Simon, 94

Yarmouth (ship), 79, 81
Ybor City neighborhood, Tampa, FL, 6

Zanetti, Oscar, 9, 22, 92, 192n13
Zapata. *See* Figueredo, Miguel Ángel ("Zapata")
Zumoff, Jacob, 149

Frances Peace Sullivan is associate professor of history at Berklee College of Music in Boston.

Caribbean Crossroads: Race, Identity, and Freedom Struggles

Edited by Lillian Guerra, Devyn Spence Benson, April Mayes, and Solsiree del Moral

More than any other region of the Americas, the Caribbean has been continuously defined by the push and pull between global white supremacy and Black liberation, colonial and anticolonial impulses, and the struggle for freedom against externally imposed economies and political systems. This series focuses on these varied and contradictory histories of the region with a particular focus on Cuba, Puerto Rico, Haiti, the Dominican Republic, and their transnational ties. Importantly, books explore the Caribbean as a racialized space and are not afraid to name the ways whiteness and Blackness work in the region.

Black Freedom and Education in Nineteenth-Century Cuba,
by Raquel Alicia Otheguy (2025)

Cuba's Cosmopolitan Enclaves: Imperialism and Internationalism in Eastern Sugar Towns,
by Frances Peace Sullivan (2025)

www.ingramcontent.com/pod-product-compliance
Lightning Source LLC
Chambersburg PA
CBHW030821230426
43667CB00008B/1318